BILLY JOEL

THE BIOGRAPHY

MARK
BEGO

THUNDER'S MOUTH PRESS
NEW YORK

Billy Joel:
The Biography

Published by
Thunder's Mouth Press
An Imprint of Avalon Publishing Group, Inc.
245 West 17th Street · 11th Floor
New York, NY 10011

AVALON
publishing group incorporated

First Printing June 2007

Library of Congress Cataloging-in-Publication Data is available.

ISBN-10: 1–56025–989–2
ISBN-13: 978–1-56025–989–3

Book design by Pauline Neuwirth, Neuwirth & Associates Inc.

Printed in the United States of America
Distributed by Publishers Group West

To Derek Storm

It's great to have a friend in my life who not only looks out for me personally, but who also happens to be a longtime Billy Joel expert. You took it upon yourself to make sure that my fiftieth book has become my best one yet. It would not have been as focused or insightful without you being involved, and the two years that it took to write this book would not have been as much fun without you being part of the adventure.

CONTENTS

ACKNOWLEDGMENTS

Richard Aaron
Bobby Bank
Hank Bordowitz
Bob & Mary Bego
Dana Bove
LaLa Brooks
Bob Buchman
Richie Cannata
Lou Christie
Rita Coolidge
Tom Cuddy
Ken Dashow
Brad DeMeulenaere
Kara DeMeulenaere
Liberty DeVitto
Anita Diggs
Micky Dolenz
Heather Donnelly
Steve Ericson
Bobby Funaro
Jerry George
David Gest
Deborah Gibson
Susan Gilbert

Christopher Gilman and the staff
    of the Palm in New York City
    (250 West Fiftieth Street)
Jimmy Greenspoon
Todd Gretton
Isiah James
Russell Javors
Randy Jones
Sindi Kaplan
Cheryl Khaner
Mark Kostabi
Dr. Judy Kuriansky
Marcy MacDonald
Kevin McCarthy
Scott Mendel
May Pang
Jay Pomerantz
Martha Reeves
Andy Rosen
Ian Russo
Jed Ryan
David Salidor
Joe Salvatto
Peter and Melanie Schekeryk

Lynn Shaw
Andy Skurow
Alan Sneeth
Phoebe Snow
Mark Sokoloff
Derek Storm (Great job as
    this book's photo editor!)
Race Taylor
Steve Van Zandt
Steve Walter and the staff
    of the Cutting Room in New York
    City (19 West Twenty-fourth Street)
Harry Weinger
Mary Wilson

In memory of two dear friends: Laura
Gabriel and Mitch Ducksworth

PROLOGUE

IT IS 8:23 P.M., January 23, 2006, and I am seated about thirty feet from stage right at Madison Square Garden. It is opening night for the first solo New York City concert by Billy Joel since he has successfully completed rehabilitation for substance abuse. His drinking is now in check, and he is back in a big way. The famed singer is out to prove that he is feeling, singing, and playing better than ever. To further flex his box office muscle, this is to be the first of a record-breaking series of twelve sold-out concerts at the Garden.

The house lights go down, and Billy and his grand piano rise up from the center of the stage. Even before the spotlights are turned on, the cheering crowd has already risen to its feet. When the introductory notes of "Angry Young Man" starts, Manhattan-style rock & roll bedlam breaks out. The sound of the music is nearly eclipsed by the screaming, cheering, and clapping of eighteen thousand fans who have waited eagerly for this very moment.

The show has theatrical special effects aplenty. Smoke pours out from the back of the large, rounded stage. Colored lights flash. And, at center stage, the singer at the piano looks more relaxed and confident than he has in ages. He wears a black sport jacket over a black T-shirt, and a comfortable pair of blue jeans. However he is no longer the fresh-faced young man millions of fans remember from the cover of *The Stranger* album. His physique is a bit more soft and round in the middle nowadays. He is currently bald on top, and the hair that he does have on his head is gray at the temples and is cropped very close on the sides. It matches his graying goatee and mustache.

As the first song comes to an end he receives a thunderous standing ovation and flashes a broad and genuine smile. After singing "Everybody Loves You Now," he says to the crowd, "Thank you for coming. I hope you didn't get your tickets from scalpers." This is a long-running tradition of his. He has a history of setting the printed "face value" of his concert tickets at prices far below what he could command at the box office. He has also waged a careerlong battle against ticket scalpers. For this entire tour, none of the "face value" prices of the tickets exceeds $100.

When he begins to play "The Ballad of Billy the Kid" his grand piano revolves from facing stage right to facing stage left. When he comes to the line about Oyster Bay, Long Island, a swell of cheers erupts. Billy Joel is still a Long Island/New York local hero and this is his biggest homecoming celebration yet.

In addition to being something of a triumphant comeback for Billy, it marks the beginning of his planned 2006–2007 world tour. As the familiar first notes of "New York State of Mind" are played, the crowd eagerly anticipates Billy Joel's trademark ode to the Empire State, and an instantly bonding sense of camaraderie spreads over this New York City audience, to whom Billy sings the song with passion, as though it is an anthem.

Dressed in a sharp black velvet jacket, Richie Cannata moves downstage to join Billy and blows his now-famous saxophone solo, giving the song a solid blast of inspired jazz. It sounds hauntingly familiar, in a note-to-note fashion, and it ought to, since it is being performed by the man who conceived of it and played it on the original recording. This is Richie's first gig with Billy in years, and his first tour with him since the early 1980s. Standing close to the edge of the stage, Richie blasts the sax solo in a way that becomes the heart of the song. It is the professional reunion of two lifelong friends. The crowd erupts into a loud round of applause, and Billy announces midsong, "On the saxophone, from Brooklyn, New York: Richie Cannata."

When the familiar sound of helicopter blades signal the beginning of "Goodnight Saigon," another longtime friend, Billy Zampino, plays the upstage snare drum solo. Next, "Movin' Out" again features Richie, along

with two other favorite musicians from Billy Joel tours past: Crystal Taliefero and Mark Rivera, and the trio performs a three-part sax segment downstage. The one conspicuously missing member of the troupe is his longtime drummer, Liberty DeVitto, whose presence is sincerely missed by the fans.

Billy's headline-grabbing life has made him the subject of lots of tabloid coverage through the recent years. His jokes about his bad business deals and his newfound sobriety don't need any setup for the crowd to understand. Introducing "The Great Wall of China" he announces, "I would like to dedicate this to my ex-manager." With that, Billy makes the Italian "up yours" gesture with his raised fist to the man whom he sued for embezzling millions of dollars from him.

While singing "Scenes from an Italian Restaurant," when he comes to the familiar line about choosing a wine, Billy amusingly changes the lyric to: "A bottle of white. A bottle of red, perhaps a glass of ginger ale instead."

He also gamely makes jokes amid his performance. In the jazz song "Zanzibar," from his *52nd Street* album, he retools the lyric line about baseball great Pete Rose being a credit to the game, to make a 2006 reference, "But he knows he'll never make the Hall of Fame."

Tonight the Garden is packed to the rafters, and seats are sold out all the way around—even to the back of the stage. During all of the show Billy is always going to have his back toward some segment of the crowd. To compensate for this, the platform that his downstage grand piano sits upon continues to turn electronically to face different directions for different songs. At upstage stage left and upstage stage right, Billy has positioned swiveling electric keyboards so that periodically he can go to a totally different level of the stage and turn to face every corner of the auditorium as he plays and sings. Likewise, for "Keepin' the Faith" the trio of sax players moves upstage to give the people seated in the back of the stage an up-close show.

As at any rock concert of this magnitude, it is fascinating to see what kind of a crowd a performer draws. Tonight's audience has come from a wide circumference of Long Island, Connecticut, New Jersey, and New York. There are families of parents and their teenagers, and younger kids. There are couples on a date, and die-hard Billy Joel fans of all ages. On my left side is one of my closest friends, photographer Derek Storm, who is very intent on watching the show. On my right side is a skinny woman who is dressed in black leather pants, has a tiny waist, and fervently screams out the lyrics to all of the songs. As she does, Derek glances at me and rolls his eyes in a look of disapproval. In between lyrics she shouts "I love you, Billy" at the top of her lungs and whips her shoulder-length hair around like a go-go dancer. That is indicative of the audience tonight. Half the crowd is sitting and listening attentively, and half is on its feet hollering out song titles, shouting the lyrics, and cheering their musical idol.

Meanwhile, onstage, Billy effortlessly changes moods midshow. I note, during the ballad "She's Always a Woman to Me," how the whole show runs like a well-oiled precision machine. The tone of the evening has the loose feeling of sheer rock & roll excitement, yet every moment is calculated and choreographed. Every light cue and every movement by Billy and his band are carefully planned.

As the mood changes again for the rhythmic excitement of "River of Dreams," special-effect smoke billows out from the back of the stage. Everyone in the orchestra seats is standing up and dancing their way through an infectious clap-along. Billy enthusiastically pounds on the keys of his grand piano while he bounces on the bench joyously getting into the groove of the music. He has truly hit his stride, and he looks like he is enjoying himself immensely.

To my right, Ms. Overzealous Fan is now in full frenzy mode. She is whipping her hair through the air and swinging her arms as if she is mimicking Tina Turner. Thankfully, in the middle of the show she suddenly feels the need to move away from me and proceeds to run up and down the aisles, screaming out Billy's name. Hey, rock & roll moves us all in different ways.

On the evening's twentieth song, the rapid-fire rocking history lesson "We Didn't Start the Fire," Billy's grand piano sinks into the stage, and he moves downstage with a guitar hanging from a strap around his neck. "If I mess up the words to this next song, sing along or it becomes a train wreck," he announces with a laugh. The Madison Square Garden audience is now ablaze with the bright flashes of digital cameras. They flicker throughout the audience like fireflies on a summer night.

Billy picks up a wireless microphone stand, which he proceeds to poke from the stage toward the crowd as if he is Sir Lancelot jabbing at a jousting opponent. In "Big Shot" Billy moves about the stage, gamely playing the audience. He dances with a sort of Gene Kelly kinetic ease during the sax and guitar solo spots. He is clearly singing and playing better than he has in recent years. And, judging by the look on his face, he is still obviously having a ball.

The concert also has several unique moments. "We lost one of the great voices of rock & roll: Wilson Pickett," Billy announces midshow. "I wanted to do something to honor him." With that, he and the band launch into "Wicked" Pickett's hit "The Midnight Hour." Afterward he spontaneously goes downstage to accept a bouquet of roses from a fan. During "It's Still Rock & Roll to Me" he starts by dancing an impromptu jig to the intro music.

His grand piano rises back up from the stage floor in time for him to play it to the rocking beat of "You May Be Right." After the song ends, he goes down to the very edge of the stage to touch, grasp, clap, and shake the hands of his faithful fans who are there to reach up to shake hands with their musical hero.

At 10:27 P.M. Billy Joel exits the stage and the lights begin to dim. As the lights go down on Madison Square Garden, and the audience anticipates an encore, Derek turns to me and says, "Look, it's the new lighter."

As I visually scan the crowd, I see the interior of the Garden illuminated with the blue glow of people's cell phones turned on, flipped open, and waved overhead. They have replaced Bic lighters as the Woodstock-like candlelight glow to show approval and musical solidarity at a rock concert.

After two minutes of cheering, the jeans-clad Billy Joel is back at the grand piano, singing the Catholic girls' ode, "Only the Good Die Young." The crowd sings along with the lyrics with enthusiasm and gusto. The omnidirectional stage lights flash in a multicolored blast like the old days at Studio 54, the club that was all the rage when this song was originally released.

"Thank you, New York," Billy shouts, taking a bow at 10:41 P.M. As the band exits the stage he looks around as though he has been prematurely deserted. They then return to join him on the stage, and he launches into the familiar harmonica intro of "Piano Man." For this song he places around his neck a metal harmonica holder so that he can play the piano at the same time. Again, with the waving of open cell phones, the audience shows their luminescent approval. He is bathed in a white spotlight, and basking in the sense of victory that has come from his first completely clean and sober tour.

For "Piano Man," the interior of Madison Square Garden is aglow in blue and purple light as he sings the cocktail lounge song that began the whole Billy Joel phenomenon some thirty-four years ago. The crowd goes berserk with cheering, and then they join in, singing the lyrics along with Billy.

As Billy finishes "Piano Man," he announces, "Thank you, New York! Don't take any shit from anybody." It is his standard concert-ending statement. The time is 10:49 P.M. The audience has had two hours and twenty-six minutes of music from Billy Joel, during which he has had in return the unabated adulation of his eighteen thousand gathered fans. He has sung twenty-three of his most popular songs, and proven conclusively that he still has the chops to command a long, exciting, and hit-filled show with ease.

His fictional song characters, Brenda and Eddie, might be light-years from their high school glory days, but tonight they are alive and well in Madison Square Garden. Some things have definitely changed. Ginger ale has replaced booze for Billy. Digital cameras have replaced Kodak Instamatics. And, the blue glow of open cell phones have replaced the flickering flames of Bic lighters. But some things remain solidly the same. Billy Joel's music is still as in demand as ever. His talent, his slightly cocky street attitude, and his incomparable musicianship remain indelibly intact.

It has been over thirty years since Billy Joel released his first hit song, "Piano Man." There has been a lot of water under the bridge of his personal river of dreams. In recent years things haven't always been great for Billy. Many of his critics predicted that his glory days are behind him. However, tonight, in front of a sold-out crowd in Manhattan, Billy Joel has proven once again, that he still has "it."

INTRODUCTION

BILLY JOEL IS universally acknowledged as being one of the rock & roll world's most talented singer-songwriters. His songs have provided the soundtrack for a generation of music fans, and his versatility has crossed over many genres of music. He has sold over 100 million records internationally, and he has won dozens of accolades, including six Grammy Awards, a Tony Award, an American Music Award, and the Johnny Mercer Award from the Songwriter's Hall of Fame, to name a few. He has established for himself a revered place in musical history. In his five decades of being an entertainer he has also been something of a stylistic chameleon. He has been known as a rebellious rock star, a lounge singer, a doo-wop crooner, a classical composer, a sensitive balladeer, a Broadway composer, and—most of all—the world's ultimate piano man.

However, he is also something of a dichotomy. He has been beloved by his fans, admonished by his critics, honored by his peers, and in many ways he still remains something of a mystery. His personal life has been a rocky one, and he has often made headlines for all the wrong reasons. In the twenty-first century, Billy Joel has continued to remain a beloved and controversial figure in the rock & roll music realm. He has been plagued with substance abuse troubles, very public divorces, business deals gone sour, and a series of irritating lawsuits. Never quite recovering from his heartbreaking divorce from Christie Brinkley, he subsequently developed a serious drinking problem. In recent years his problems escalated to the point where he was involved in a string of unfortunate single-vehicle automobile mishaps. On one occasion, while driving, he sideswiped a building near his Long Island home, and another time he lost control of his car and crashed it into a tree.

In 2004, at the age of fifty-five, he married a twenty-two-year-old girl, hoping that at last he had found happiness. The press wondered if it was true love, or if he was in reality, desperately chasing his fleeting youth. Only months after the ceremony, he checked himself into a clinic, publicly admitting that his recent woes drove him to alcohol abuse. *Entertainment Weekly* magazine went so far as to refer to him as "a falling down drunk."[1] In 2006 Billy's fans were ecstatic that the singer made a dramatic "come-back" with a triumphant concert tour. He emerged like a conquering hero. Playing several of the same rock & roll venues in which many of his past glories took place, he was heralded as a returning warrior.

Billy has had an exciting and event-filled career that has many dimensions. One of the most fascinating aspects of Billy Joel's life is the story of his core 1970s rock band, a quartet that included saxophonist Richie Cannata, drummer Liberty DeVitto, and bass player Doug Stegmeyer. It forms a central story worthy of its own episode of VH1's rock band exposé show, *Behind the Music*. The foursome started out as a solid Long Island band of best friends. Together they all contributed to the most memorable rock music of Billy's career. For years they were inseparable. When they weren't in the recording studio, they were traveling the globe together on years of worldwide concert tours. The camaraderie among the foursome was undeniable.

However, as the years went on, money, pressure, drugs, and fame eroded Billy's friendships. Richie Cannata was the first to go. He left the band in the early 1980s "by mutual consent." He took the money he had made with Billy, invested it, and today owns a very successful recording studio. Doug Stegmeyer was later unceremoniously fired from the band. He was so despondent about his "fall from grace" that he fell into a deep depression and he took his own life. Longtime friend and drummer Liberty DeVitto stuck around the longest—until 2003—and was always confident that his job with Billy was secure.

Liberty went to him for help in 2004. "I told him I was getting divorced, my ex-wife was getting everything, could he help me out? I helped him create hits, but I wasn't getting any royalties. The next day, he had the tour manager tell me, 'No way!'" says DeVitto. "I wrote him a letter, confronting him about his drinking and certain management issues. People said I discredited him. But he went into rehab and proved me right."[2]

When Billy announced his 2006 concert tour, it was the first one he didn't invite Liberty to join in over thirty years. The drummer defiantly complains of his banishment from the Joel camp: "Billy expects you to disappear off the face of the Earth when you leave 'Billy World,' but that's not the case. There is life after Billy Joel!"[3]

Meanwhile, Billy's career has continued to flourish, including the 2006 concert tour that Richie Cannata returned for, the one that Liberty DeVitto was specifically not asked to participate in. In fact, the 2006 touring band was required to sign a nondisclosure agreement specifically stating that they were not to speak to the exiled drummer while in Billy's employment. What happened to this union of four friends who were once so tight with each other? This, too, is a large and important part of the Joel saga.

There are also other important relationships with his subsequent band members, such as Russell Javors and Mark Rivera, and his controversial relationships with his staff members, including his first wife, who ran his career, and his former manager and brother-in-law Frank Weber.

Billy's musical history is also a fascinating one. Having found his greatest success in the pop and rock music realm, his talent has never been disputed. Although he is, on the one hand, the product of the Long Island cover-band scene, it is not surprising to know that he is also a classically trained pianist.

As an artist, Billy has always been serious about his musical compositions. Often he proclaimed that it was his sincere goal to write and record music that defined a musical point in time, and yet he wanted to write it in a way that endures. He has been able to succeed in every arena that he has chosen to enter.

From 1976 to 1993, there were only three years that didn't find at least one new Billy Joel hit on the top 40 record charts. Thirteen of his thirty-three hits climbed to the top 10, and three of them—"It's Still Rock & Roll to Me" (1980), "Tell Her About It," (1983) and "We Didn't Start the Fire" (1989)—were number 1 smashes on the American charts. Along the way he also garnered devoted fans in Australia, Japan, England, France, Germany, Spain, Australia, and Italy.

It is also revealing to find that his musical influences are as diverse as the music he has created. His first musical hero was none other than Ludwig van Beethoven, and from there he added jazz master Dave Brubeck, standards composer George Gershwin, R&B's Ray Charles, 1950s rocker Fats Domino, "Wall of Sound" purveyor Phil Spector, and ultimately the most versatile rock group of all—the Beatles.

He took the inspiration of each of his musical idols and built upon it. "New York State of Mind" has the same jazzy universality that Dave Brubeck's legendary *Take Five* album possesses. "Just the Way You Are" has become a pop standard that has been recorded and interpreted with the same passion that ballad singers cover Gershwin tunes. Long in awe of Ray Charles, he didn't just talk Charles into singing one of his songs, he recorded a hit single—"Baby Grand"—with him. His song "It's Still Rock & Roll to Me" has the same 1960s rock passion of Fats Domino's classic hits. His "Say Goodbye to Hollywood" pays brilliant homage to producer Spector. And as for the Beatles, they were the main inspiration for his *Nylon Curtain* album. Billy's record-selling popularity puts him right behind the Beatles in a tally for the most million-selling albums sold in the United States.

In 2001, when his classically composed album, *Fantasies and Delusions*, was released, he hit number 1 on *Billboard* magazine's Classical Albums chart. It was a move that would have made his idol Beethoven proud.

Is it any wonder that he has always confounded his critics? They have routinely tried to pigeonhole him into a narrow category, and write him off as something less than a musical genius. No mere chameleon, Billy Joel grasps a musical style or influence and takes it to the next level.

The history of Billy's grandparents is such a fascinating tale that it has been the subject of a 2001 famous documentary called *The Joel Files* [*Die Akte Joel*]. It was made by acclaimed German filmmaker Beate Thalberg, with the participation of Billy himself. When the Nazis declared it illegal for anyone Jewish to own a German company, Billy's grandfather was forced to sell his lucrative Berlin-based manufacturing operation for a fraction of its worth in 1938. Billy's father, Howard Joel, escaped from Nazi Germany with his parents and immigrated to the United States via Cuba. When he made it to New York City, Howard met and fell in love with a young girl named Rosalind. They married and produced Billy and his sister Judy.

Howard was a classically trained pianist, and he instilled his love of music in Billy at a young age. In fact, young Billy began taking piano lessons from the age of four and continued for eight years. After moving the family to Levittown, Long Island, Howard Joel left and returned to Europe to live. Rosalind was forced to seek a series of different jobs to support Billy and his sister.

In the 1960s Billy had garnered a reputation for being something of a tough street kid yet, underneath the leather-jacketed exterior, he was in reality a complex and sensitive musician. Lured into the world of rock & roll, in 1967 he joined a local Long Island group called the Hassles. Their sound was defined as a combination of white-boy soul, mixed with late sixties psychedelia. Then he was part of a short-lived duo by the name of Attila. His tenure with both the Hassles and Attila gave him his first tastes of life as a legitimate recording artist.

One of the worst experiences of Billy's life came as a novice singer-songwriter, when he signed a contract that he would regret for years to come. His debut solo album, 1971's *Cold Spring Harbor*, was somehow recorded at the wrong speed, giving him a bitter taste of how unfair and unforgiving the New York music scene can be.

Disgusted with the business, he moved to Los Angeles, and temporarily gave himself a new stage name to maintain his anonymity. To support himself, he took a job in the San Fernando Valley as a piano singer in a lounge. His experiences led him to write his first smash recording, his signature hit "Piano Man."

Sought after by the head of Columbia Records, Clive Davis, Billy returned to New York City, ready to record his first top 10 album. One of the biggest reasons for its success was that the songs he included on it were culled from his own deeply personalized experiences. As he took a bus from the airport, he found himself so happy to be back in his native state that he penned one of his most famous songs, "New York State of Mind."

On his albums *Streetlife Serenade* (1974) and *Turnstiles* (1976), he turned his own emotions into signature songs. "The Entertainer" became his scalding criticism of the harshness of the record business. "Say Goodbye to Hollywood" was his kiss-off ode to the West Coast. Yet—in spite of a lot of FM radio airplay—his lukewarm degree of sales success branded him as a "cult" artist at best.

His big breakthrough album was the 1977 classic: *The Stranger*. It became such a hit-yielding LP that at the time of its release it overtook

Simon and Garfunkel's *Bridge over Troubled Water* as the biggest-selling album in the history of Columbia Records. *The Stranger* had such life and such fire that it made Billy a bona fide rock star. Again, his versatility gleamed through the grooves. From the sensitive "Just the Way You Are" to the rebelliously rocking "Movin' Out (Anthony's Song)" to the controversial "Only the Good Die Young," he not only hit his stride as a songwriter and a performer but it instantly turned him into rock royalty.

Billy managed to amass hits as though he were racking up a triangle full of billiard balls on a pool table. "Big Shot," "It's Still Rock & Roll to Me," "She's Got a Way," and "Allentown"—all added to his status as a hit-making legend. As he continued to record and grow and change, his own personal life evolved as well. He divorced his wife, Elizabeth, who had also served as his manager, handing over the reins of his career to his former brother-in-law, Frank, which turned into a huge nightmare.

Then, one of his greatest inspirations crossed his path. She was supermodel Christie Brinkley. She is acknowledged as the love of his life. Christie inspired Billy to write several of his biggest hits including "Uptown Girl." Released at the crest of the advent of MTV video television, Billy Joel was greatly assisted in his quest for fame by the video of the same name—a video that featured his supermodel girlfriend, which helped keep it in the regular rotation of MTV for months on end.

Billy's success continued to grow on his albums like *The Bridge* (1986). Wanting to do something historically significant, he went on a headline grabbing tour of the Soviet Union in 1987, yielding a massively successful live album, a video presentation, and a television special. Continuing to mine twentieth-century culture, Billy turned a history lesson into a smash rock song, "We Didn't Start the Fire," on the 1989 album *Storm Front*. Both the album and the single hit number 1, cementing Billy Joel's position as one of the most enduring superstar rockers in musical history.

In 1993, Billy released what has turned out to be his final rock & roll studio album: *River of Dreams*. It entered *Billboard* magazine's album chart at number 1. The last track on the *River of Dreams* album was titled "Famous Last Words." It became the final new studio-recorded rock or pop song he would release. The majority of the 1990s saw Billy continuing his reign as one of the most successful touring acts on the planet. He finished off the century with a wild gala Millennium Eve concert at New York's Madison Square Garden, which became the "live" album *2000 Years: The Millennium Concert*.

Billy's 2001 emergence as a classical composer was one of his proudest moments. One of his most recent career accomplishments found him successfully teamed with Elton John for a series of highly attended concert tours. For a number of global legs, the concert series was a smashing success. Then, as time went on, Billy became unreliable, canceling several of the concerts at the last minute, pleading "exhaustion."

Throughout all of this, he has had something of a stormy existence within the confines of the media (Some years he is the media's "darling"; other years the press rakes him over the coals unmercifully).

Creative endeavors aside, in addition to all of his obvious successes, Billy is known as a headline-grabbing enigma. Some people find him to be a compassionate and sincerely generous man who often rallies behind causes that are dear to his heart. Yet, at the same time, others report that he is "unfriendly," "difficult," "sour," and a "pain in the ass" to deal with.

Even some of his friends and co-workers paint portraits of him as being miserly with money, and self-absorbed. Longtime band members would suddenly be fired without any notice. Says Russell Javors, "I always thought our band had a great chemistry with Billy. Kind of like the E-Street Band has with Bruce [Springsteen]. I would have been disappointed, but would have understood if Billy wanted to play with different guys. As an artist he has that right. But, after playing with Billy for more than twelve years, I was riding in my car one day and heard on the radio that Billy had a new album and a restructured band. I had no idea. I didn't even get the courtesy of a phone call. I later read that Billy said that all Doug and I cared about was money. I can only speak for myself, but to say that I was only in it for the money is a joke. I certainly didn't get rich playing for Billy."[4]

This book contains the story of the fascinating and often controversial life and career of a man who will forever be known as "The Piano Man." From his early struggles, to his finding mainstream success, through his failed first marriage to his love affair with Christie Brinkley, his story includes a rocky road to the top. With his divorce from Brinkley, to his drinking problems, this book will also follow the downside of this brilliant singer-songwriter's fame, including his several car accidents.

With regard to his record behind the wheel, one Columbia Records insider claims, "I had always heard that he was a lousy driver, from friends who live in the Hamptons. It was a running joke out there."[5] Although there were no formal substance abuse charges filed, there remains little doubt for many as to whether or not he was under the influence of anything while driving these vehicles.

Says one longtime friend, "On the one hand he is a very bright and funny guy but he has a dark side. I've always thought that he was deeply hurt as a young boy when his father left his family." Claims this source, "I believe he has an emotional void inside him that he's been trying to fill with alcohol for all these years. It's quite sad that he would need this after all of the wealth he has amassed."[6]

It is impossible not to know and recognize the brilliant hit songs. Yet, on the other side of the music, who is the real Billy Joel? Is he the charming but misunderstood musical genius that some claim he is, or an unhappy man who has often watched his personal life unravel before his very eyes?

Although everyone seems to have a fond awareness of Billy's music in general, and his latest news-making mishaps, few people realize what a complex and serious musician he truly is. And, through it all, there are so many unanswered career questions. What made him sign away the rights to his songwriting, early in his career? What was the inspiration for his greatest songs, including "Scenes from an Italian Restaurant," "The Entertainer," "Just the Way You Are," "Leningrad," and "River of Dreams?" What made him turn his back on rock? Does he now consider himself a classical artist? How instrumental was producer Phil Ramone in Billy's success?

So is he "Billy the Kid" or just an "Angry Young Man" who is still dealing with his personal problems during middle age? Billy Joel's career thus far has spanned over forty years of sex, drugs and rock & roll. And, it has certainly taken its toll on the life of this extraordinary musician. But behind every great musician is a great band. This is certainly true in Billy Joel's case. If Bruce Springsteen fired Clarence Clemmons, Steven Van Zandt, or Max Weinberg, there would be an uproar heard round the world. If "the Boss" detached himself from his world-famous band that helped write and produce his hits, would the world know? Would the fans care? Would the music suffer? Absolutely.

Richie Cannata, Russell Javors, Doug Stegmeyer, and Liberty DeVitto made up Billy Joel's version of the E Street Band. An inseparable group of close friends who grew up together, played together, traveled together, wrote music together, and—on tour buses and planes—lived together. They were—in different configurations—the sound and the force behind the music that spanned Billy Joel's Rock & Roll Hall of Fame–inducted career from *The Stranger* in 1977 to *River of Dreams* in 1993. That was when time gave way to greed, and now this band of brothers is separated and barely speaking to one another.

What happened to these once-inseparable friends from the Long Island suburbs? Now, Russell Javors is in Hong Kong working for a toy manufacturer and completely removed from the music business. Doug Stegmeyer is dead, a victim of suicide. Richie Cannata, who even though he was the first to leave the band in 1980, sporadically works and tours with Billy part-time. And, Liberty DeVitto, Billy's well-respected drummer and best friend through four decades, is now working freelance jobs in the music business. His thirty-five-year career with Billy Joel left him vivid memories and little else to show for it.

And then there is Billy's roller-coaster-like personal life. What made his father leave his mother, and what impact did that have on young Billy? Is there any truth to the rumors of Billy's trouble with the law? Did he really steal his first wife away from his best friend? Has he ever recovered from his breakup with Christie Brinkley, and are they close friends or professional rivals? Where does his current bout of depression come from? Has this caused his drinking woes? What are the circumstances that surround his crashing his cars into trees and buildings? Is his third wife, Katie Lee Joel, the person behind his recent trip into rehab?

The following book not only spans Billy Joel's musical career but also explains the force behind the music, with in depth interviews with the three surviving longtime band members and best friends: Cannata, DeVitto, and Javors. These three incredible musicians come together for the first time to tell their stories in this aftermath of how they became casualties in this war of fame.

We'll delve into Billy's family history, from the dramatic story of his grandfather in Nazi Germany, to his parents' divorce, to the career contributions of his half brother in Austria. You'll find a lot of his family in his lyrics of "Rosalinda's Eyes" and "Vienna," to "Christie Lee," and "Lullaby," and see his thought process behind some of the biggest and most recognizable songs in music history. Was every beat, every riff, and every note actually written by Billy Joel, as credited on his twenty-three albums? What does the band have to say about that? What was life like on the road with Elton John? What was Billy's relationship with all the women in his life? What charitable contributions has he made to his Long Island home? From Billy's first band, the Hassles, and performing in bars on Long Island in the sixties, to his record-breaking sold-out shows at New York City's Madison Square Garden forty years later in 2006; we'll span the entire life of this music legend.

The story of Billy Joel is at times a river of dreams, however, at other times it is a sea of disappointment. Ultimately it is a tale of accomplishment, determination, and creative attainment. It is one that is as fascinating as it is thought provoking. To find out all of the answers to these questions, one has to go all the way back to Nazi Germany, and progress forward to the Bronx, Levittown, Hollywood, Manhattan, and beyond.

BILLY JOEL

THE JOEL FAMILY OF GERMANY

BILLY JOEL IS the grandson of a once-wealthy German-Jewish garment manufacturer who was a very clever businessman. This fascinating
story shines a light on the motivation for some of the decisions that Billy's
father made in his life. Billy's father, Helmuth [a.k.a. Howard] Julius Joel
was born on June 12, 1923. He was the only child of Karl Joel and his wife,
Meta Fleischmann. They lived in the city of Nuremberg, in Bavaria, which
is located in the southeast area of Germany. When Karl discovered that
mail-order clothing companies were successful in America and other
countries, he decided to launch his own similar operation.

The Joel Company was started in 1928 in Nuremberg. It was a mail-
order catalog company, and their specialty was ready-to-wear clothing.
According to Rudolf Weber, an accountant and boyhood friend of Helmuth
Joel's, "They started a very modest business in their apartment. They had
to carry the stuff to the post office with a hand cart. It was a difficult beginning."[7] At this point in time, the German economy was strained at best, so
this was a very risky venture.

A year later, in 1929, the company was already successful and growing.
Weber recalls, "After that the business went very well. They increased their
production and product range, but the main focus remained textiles."[7] For

several years the Joel Company continued to expand and flourish in Nuremberg.

Things seemed to be going very well for this family-owned business. However, after the last fully democratic elections, held on March 5, 1933, Hitler came to power and began pinpointing Jews in Germany as the root of the country's concurrent economic woes. In what is known as the Blood Purge of June 1934, German field marshal and president Paul von Hindenburg died, leaving the country unquestioningly in Adolf Hitler's hands. Seizing power of the country, Hitler instantly set himself as a dictator. He then appointed Heinrich Himmler, Hermann Göring, and Joseph Goebbels as his like-minded hatred-mongering underlings. After that, Hitler became obsessed with populating Germany with a white, blond-haired, blue-eyed Aryan "master race."

Although the Jews were viewed as enemies in Germany and elsewhere in Europe, they were not the only ones who were persecuted by the Nazis. As a part of their "ethnic cleansing" the Nazis also demoted Gypsies, gays, and the mentally retarded to noncitizen status. When concentration camps later came into existence, anyone who opposed the Nazi doctrines, regardless of religious background, mysteriously disappeared forever. And so began the bloodiest reign of terror in recent history.

After Hitler came into power, Jewish-owned shops and companies in the country were often looted and had their windows smashed routinely. Some Jewish citizens who saw the dark clouds of what was coming for Germany sold all of their belongings and businesses and fled the country altogether. Others, especially those who fought on the German side of the First World War, felt that the Nazis would never touch them, as they were decorated war heroes who considered themselves loyal Germans.

For Karl Joel, the matter came to a head in Nuremberg when a fanatical pro-Nazi paper called *Der Strümer* began running scandalous articles about him and his business practices. These charges were unfounded, and in reality his only crime was that he was both Jewish and successful. The editor of the newspaper, Julius Streicher, made it his personal mission to ruin Joel's company and drive him out of town. In the pages of the publication, Streicher accused him of fraud and labeled him "a mortal enemy of the German people."[8]

Helmuth Joel remembers, "My father came home one day and said, 'I'm in *Der Strümer*, so now I'm famous.' One is afraid though because it affects

BILLY JOEL

you. You try to avoid the whole business. You cross the street, you move to another neighborhood, hide behind corners."[7]

To further persecute and harass Karl Joel, the authorities in Nuremberg began arresting him in the most public of places. Since he was considered a noncitizen, he could be arrested at any time without probable cause; even though he was always released, it began to emotionally wear upon him and his family. Finally it looked as if there was no recourse but to close up shop and leave Nuremberg. However, Joel's planned move took him out of the frying pan and directly into the fire. His relocation spot? The Nazi regime's capitol city of Berlin. Big mistake.

According to Helmuth Joel, his father must have rationalized that the rabidly hateful Julius Streicher was his enemy, and not the government of Germany. Ultimately, it would be another serious miscalculation.

Determined to salvage his career, Karl Joel packed up the contents of his entire factory, loaded it onto 160 railroad freight cars, and relocated both the firm and his home in Berlin. As a Jew in Nazi Germany, Joel now had to have an Aryan representative involved in his business operation, to legally negotiate leases and other deals for him. The person he aligned himself with was a man by the name of Fritz Tillmann, who was the economic town counselor for Berlin. This, too, was a mistake, as it would be Tillmann who later oversaw the systematic expulsion of Jews all over Germany.

However, between 1934 and 1937 Karl Joel's plan of reestablishing his once-flourishing mail-order garment business in bustling Berlin was a financial success. Tillmann assisted him in renting four floors of a factory. Joel purchased a new villa for his family to live in and set about furnishing it. He then invested his money in sewing machines and other necessary equipment.

Even while the Joel family company was doing well in their new city, Aryan anti-Jewish activities were escalating, too. In Berlin, Nazi rallies regularly took place not far from Joel's villa. The political climate in all of Germany was becoming more and more ominous for its Jewish citizens. At the Joel home, the shutters on every window were now kept shut and locked at all times. The family felt like prisoners in their own home.

Says Helmuth, who was twelve years old in 1935, "The Hitler Youth, the SA, and the SS trained on weekends in a forest right next to our villa. My mother was terrified. She trembled all over. What is a child supposed to do about that? What is a grown-up to do about such things? Withdrawing was the only option."[7] In addition, even the schools were becoming segregated. The public schools in Germany were suddenly reserved for Aryan children only.

Billy Joel's father recalls, "One felt excluded, excluded from everything. It was impossible to go to a normal school. You were simply not accepted."[7]

At one point young Helmuth and his boyhood friend Rudolf Weber were taunted and threatened by a group of young boys around their own age at a local garden. Weber recounts, "A group of five or six boys came along and said, 'You're Jewish, aren't you?' And Helmuth answered, 'Us? We're not Jews!' Then they all pointed at me and said, 'But you must be a Jew!' Helmuth said, 'Hey, that's my friend.' They tried to drag me by the arm, but we simply left. It was a scary experience."[7]

After that, discrimination against Jewish citizens became more and more blatant. Not only were Jewish-owned shops defaced, but even public park benches were routinely marked with the words "Nur für Arier" ["For Aryans Only"]. To keep him safe, around this same time, Helmuth's parents sent him away to school in Switzerland.

An annual Nazi party rally that was held in Nuremberg in 1935 introduced several new laws and edicts, which were to define the most racist and hate-based policies of the entire Nazi ideology. These laws were meant to strip German Jews of any remaining rights. They also went so far as to specifically prohibit all Jews from marrying—or having sex with—people of Aryan German blood. Similar laws also removed all Jewish political and voting rights. These were known as "The Nuremberg Laws."

Yet, everything continued to go well for the flourishing Joel Company in Berlin. In 1937, the profits for the company were a million reichsmarks per month, in spite of what was happening in Nazi Germany at that time. But time was running out.

Meanwhile, also in the 1930s, in Würzburg, Germany, a young man was about to see his life and business entwine with the fortunes of Karl Joel. He was Josef Neckermann and he was the well-to-do son of a coal salesman. Recalled Neckermann's secretary, Gerda Singer, "They were a strictly Catholic and conservative family, upper middle class."[7] By 1933, Josef Neckermann was already working for the family business, and he had a fiancée. He was personally driven to make his fortune in the changing climate of Germany.

According to Singer, "Mr. Neckermann once took part in an event organized by the Reiter SA. That might have been the beginning. [Ernst] Röhm, who was later shot by Hitler, organized a parade with horseback riders in Würzburg. Neckermann was asked to participate. He was put into

an SA uniform and took part in the parade. He was interested in all that, and thought it was great."[7]

For Aryan Germans in this era, there are several plausible reasons why one would align oneself with the Nazi party. The first would be, if one truly were a Nazi and believed in all of the party's fanatical laws. Or, another scenario might simply be rooted in one's knowing that the Nazis controlled the money that ran Germany. If one wanted to play ball with them, one wanted them to think one was on their side. The latter is the rationale that Josef Neckerman claimed best fit him.

In October 1933, Neckermann became a fully documented member of the Reiter SA, and he officially joined the Nazi party. Says his son Johannes, "My father was never a Nazi by heart and by conviction. He always declined that. He never wore the emblem. He did not like the regime at all."[7]

Clearly the tide was turning. Aryan or non-Jewish families or businesses now actively took advantage of what was going on, able to purchase Jewish companies for a fraction of their real value. When Josef Neckermann married his fiancée, his new father-in-law told him that he would be on the lookout for a Jewish-owned company that came up on the market. Although such a practice was morally deplorable and out-and-out theft, these takeovers were within the rights of prevailing Nazi German laws.

One such company that fell to prey to this was a prominent department store by the name of Ruschkewitz, which was literally put out of business by the Nazi supporters. Josef Neckermann jumped at the opportunity to purchase, for very little money, this once-successful Jewish-owned store, and suddenly he was in the garment business.

Neckermann was later to state in his memoirs, "Had I realized exactly what I was entering into on the twenty-fifth of October 1935, I might have cancelled the appointment at the Dresdner Bank at the very last minute. But I didn't. I just carefully stirred my cup of coffee and thus became an Aryanator."[7]

In 1938, an estimated 280,000 Jewish families were forced to leave their homes and move out of Berlin. At the same time, approximately the same number of Aryan Germans flooded into the city, anxious to take advantage of the shifting number of opportunities associated with living in the capital of the Reich.

According to Ignatz Bubis (1927–1999), the president of the Central Council of Jews in Germany, "In 1938 there were hardly any Jewish businesses operated by Jews, even if they were technically still the owners."[7]

Aryan businessmen arrived, all seeking opportunities to take advantage of the recent German laws that demoted Jews to noncitizenship. One newcomer who gravitated to the changing Berlin that year to seek his fortune was the twenty-year-old Josef Neckerman.

That same year, Karl Joel was forty-nine years old. He lived in a fashionable part of Berlin, on Uhlandstrasse, with his wife, Meta, and his fifteen-year-old son, Helmuth. Joel was then at the height of his career. Says Helmuth, "My father's business was the second-largest textile mail-order house in Germany. The largest was Witt, in Weiden."[7]

April 1938 brought a governmental resolution calling for the "Aryanization" of all Jewish-owned companies. All were now to be either owned by Aryans or forced out of business. Still, many proud German Jews felt that this was a phase that the government was going through. They felt certain that soon the pendulum of the balance of power would again shift in the opposite direction. However, things were going to get a hell of a lot worse first.

By now, all German passports that were held by Jewish citizens not only bore the ominous Nazi swastika but were also stamped with a bright red J to denote that their carrier was Jewish. In 1938, all parcels that were sent out of Karl Joel's mail-order clothing factory to their 850,000 regular customers now had to carry a bright red letter J on them as well. Then Joel was suddenly banned from advertising his goods and his company in the local newspaper. The end was clearly near. When Aryan cloth suppliers suddenly refused to fulfill textile shipments to the factory, another omen of disaster fell into place. Finally, when the Aryan manager whom Joel had hired boycotted the company from within, Joel had no recourse but to close up shop. The company's once bustling beehive of activity came to a grinding halt in the summer of 1938.

What could Karl Joel do but sell the company immediately, for whatever price he could obtain? Word of the company's forced closing very quickly reached representatives of the Dresdner Bank. They, in turn, immediately notified several of their key investment customers with textile connections. Enter Josef Neckermann.

Neckermann had always wanted to get involved in the mail-order clothing business, and here was the perfect chance. On July 11, 1938, contracts were signed by both Neckermann and Joel, agreeing to make the former the new and sole owner of the once-flourishing Joel Company. And even then, by German law, as a Jew Joel could not, himself, negotiate the business deal that effectively put him out of business. It was his supposed ally,

Fritz Tillmann, who handled all of the talking for him in the meeting that took place on July 11. Neckermann was accompanied at the meeting by his own lawyer, and his father-in-law.

Although the Joel Company was estimated to be valued at 12 million reichsmarks at that time, Neckermann was able to purchase it for a fraction of its value: two and a half million reichsmarks.

Helmuth Joel's friend Rudolf Weber recalls, "I was an apprentice at the time when we were told that Neckermann was taking over the company. We weren't told what had happened to the Joels. I heard later that it had happened like this: Mr. Joel and his wife were in a hotel waiting for a meeting with Mr. Neckermann. The Gestapo found out about it and was going to arrest them. Mr. Joel somehow got wind of this, and they ran out the backdoor and disappeared."[7]

Helmuth Joel explains, "The situation got worse day by day. They could arrest [my father] anytime and send him to the Moabit prison and never let him out again. So he had to save his life."[7]

With the use of counterfeit passports, Karl and Meta Joel boarded a train at the Bahnhof Zoo station in the middle of downtown Berlin and fled for their safety. They traveled through the night toward Zurich, Switzerland.

Somehow they made it across the border into Switzerland without their true identities being discovered. When they arrived in Zurich, they knew that they had safely escaped. They instantly phoned nearby Saint Gall, to reach the Institut auf dem Rosenberg, where their son Helmuth was enrolled. He had no clue what had been going on with his family in Germany. He remembers, "My mother called me. She said, 'We're in Switzerland and we're never going back.' Being a child, I just said, 'Yes.' I mean, what else could I say? And then she said, 'Do you understand? We will never go back. We *can never* go back again.' And I said, 'Yes.'"[7]

The family took up residence in a boarding house in Zurich. While they were living there, a letter arrived from Josef Neckermann. Apparently there was some sort of discrepancy in the money that was due to Karl Joel. It implored him to return to Berlin to straighten things out. The salutation on the letter was, "Heil Hitler!" complete with the exclamation mark. It was possibly a trap. Karl Joel was clever enough to realize that if he set foot back in Germany, it could mean certain doom for him. Yet his entire life's earnings were at stake. So he left his wife and son and returned to Germany, under the cloak of secrecy, to straighten the matter out.

In a secret meeting in a café in Berlin, Karl Joel met with Fritz Tillmann. In this coffeehouse rendezvous, Tillmann said that he would help Joel get the monies that were due to him. However, Tillman also announced that he would need Joel to pay him a fee of 100,000 reichsmarks for his services. Joel wrote Tillman a check. Tillmann then informed him that all German Jews had legally been dispossessed of their funds and their bank accounts. In reality, no more monies would be coming to him, and the very check he had just written was worthless.

Looking back on this whole chain of events, it is easy to surmise that Tillmann knew exactly what he was doing when he agreed to assist Karl Joel in setting up shop in Berlin. He basically helped Joel get the business off and running, armed with the knowledge that the confiscation of all Jewish holdings in Germany was right around the corner. In fact, Tillmann had lied to Joel at the café—he had no problem cashing Joel's check and pocketing the 100,000 reichsmarks.

Helmuth Joel was later to explain his father's situation, "He never really got all the money from the sale. . . . He was detained in Berlin for a week or so, then he joined my mother and me in Switzerland."[10]

It was that same year that the infamous Kristallnacht took place, and then it was undeniable that German Jews were officially no longer welcome in their own country. As part of a national movement, Jewish-owned stores and homes all over Germany were legally looted. The term "Kristallnacht" literally means "crystal night," reflecting the sound of breaking glass that was heard throughout the country amidst that hateful event.

Karl, Meta, and Helmuth Joel emigrated from Switzerland to England. It was there that they boarded a holiday cruise vessel bound for the Caribbean. That was to be their escape route from Europe. Meanwhile, in Berlin, Josef Neckermann was now, not only the owner of Joel's mail-order clothing company, he and his family resided in the villa that Joel had purchased, where he possessed all of Joel's furnishings. He even employed the Joel's personal driver. It was as though he had totally taken over Karl Joel's life.

When the ship that the Joel family was aboard arrived in Havana, Cuba, they were permitted to disembark. According to Helmuth Joel, the Cuban visas that they purchased for approximately $500 each permitted their remaining safely on Cuban soil. Not everyone was so lucky: Karl Joel had also obtained passage to Cuba for his brother, and the brother's wife and son; however, when their ship—the St. Louis—arrived in Havana, they were denied the right to disembark, and they were taken back to Europe, to certain doom.

On September 1, 1939, German troops marched into Poland, and World War II was officially underway. There were strict quota numbers in place for immigration into the United States, and the Joel family patiently waited in Cuba for their numbers to come up with the immigration board. Finally, in the early 1940s, they were allowed to enter the United States from Cuba. The family moved to New York City, where they resided in a tiny apartment in the borough of the Bronx.

In 1942 Helmuth was granted a work permit, and he took his first job in New York City. At the age of nineteen, he became the primary bread-winner of his family. He recalls this as having been a scary time, when often the family had no idea where the next dollar was going to come from. It was quite a contrast from the wealthy lifestyle that they had once lived in prewar Germany.

Karl Joel returned to the only business he knew: clothing and apparel. Although the first business he got into was modest, he reestablished his identity in the marketplace by manufacturing headbands and other accessories. The important thing was that he and his immediate family had escaped Germany with their lives.

In the 1940s, Helmuth Joel was drafted into the U.S. Army. In 1945 much of Germany was aflame as Allied bombs were dropped from overhead. Among the buildings that burned was the headquarters of the Neckermann factory, formerly known as the Joel Company.

Helmuth Joel, who had recently changed his name to Howard, returned to his homeland as an American soldier. He recalls, "I went to Nuremberg by jeep and I tried to locate some old friends, but I only found Schrodel, our former driver. Before that, I had gone to my father's old factory. I don't know what it had been previously. He had his name painted on the chimney. There were no buildings left, only rubble, and right in the middle stood that chimney with the name painted on it: Joel."[7]

What he witnessed was a nation reduced to rubble. There, Howard saw firsthand some of the worst horrors of the twentieth century.

Although it has been erroneously published that Howard Joel was a prisoner in the concentration camp in Dachau, that is not true. He was in fact one of the American military soldiers sent to free its captives. To clarify things, he explains, "It's true, in a way, that I was in Dachau. But I was not imprisoned there. I was with the army outfit that liberated Dachau, near Munich, in the end of April 1945. We . . . went . . . there and looked around. And took pictures of the heaps . . . of the dead people. And then we moved

on, because we were a combat troop and never stayed anywhere. . . . I had relatives that were in concentration camps—although Dachau—and some of them were put to death. But at Dachau . . . it was terrible. We were too late to help."[10]

Said Billy Joel, "He fought in Italy and then went with Patton's third army and watched them blow away his hometown."[11]

Billy was later to state that what his father witnessed, when he returned to Germany in the military, left an indelible impression on him. "All his cynicism and sourness came from his experiences in the war," says Billy.[10]

After the Second World War, Josef Neckermann was legally sued from three different fronts. He was sued by the descendants of the owner of the Ruschkewitz department store for illegally obtaining ownership of it. He was sued by the German government for having started up a business too closely to the end of the war. And he was sued by Karl Joel, for never paying for the company he took possession of from him. The Joel suit was filed in New York City on June 8, 1949.

According to Howard Joel, "Of course [my father] had been waiting for years. It was a matter of money. He wanted the money that was due to him, but he didn't know whether there was any left. After all, the company had been restructured and reopened. So he wasn't sure if he had any legal claims."[7]

The case went to the court in Nuremberg, where the proceedings would drag out for eight years. Since Neckermann was found guilty of the charge of illegally restarting up his business right after peace came to Germany, he faced up to four years in prison. However, it was decided by the court that if he settled his debt with Karl Joel, a deal could be worked out. Ultimately, he ended up agreeing to pay Joel the sum of 2 million deutsche marks. By doing so, Neckermann had his prison sentence dismissed.

However, before the case was closed, a letter was discovered, which was dated September 15, 1938. It stated that Josef Neckermann had deposited 2 million reichsmarks into an account marked "Joel." Somehow the discovery of this document nullified Karl Joel's claim to the 2 million deutsche marks. Since the records had been destroyed during the war, there was no evidence to the contrary. It was one man's word against another: in other words, it was a legal stalemate. And so the case was closed.

Says Billy's half brother Alexander Joel, "In the end, my grandfather, I'm sure he got very tired. He had been fighting. He had the whole immigration behind him; his time, too, in New York; and relative poverty. And I think he just maybe gave up a little bit at the end. Not gave up, but gave in. I think for him, the case was resolved. He put the thing behind him."[7]

Ultimately, the profits for the Neckermann company were eaten up in rising inflationary costs, and, in 1976, Josef Neckermann was forced to sell all of his business holdings to his department-store-owning competitor, Rudolf Karstadt. And so ended the company that Karl Joel had started.

In the early 1960s, Karl and Meta Joel made the decision to return to Nuremberg, Germany. They lived out their remaining days in a rented apartment there. Meta died in 1971, at age seventy-eight, and Karl passed away in 1982 when he was ninety-two. Josef Neckermann died in 1992 at the age of seventy-nine.

Although this neatly ties up the story of Karl and Meta Joel's survival of the Nazis, another huge and very important story unfolded in their lives during the last midcentury. Only a month prior to the filing of the *Joel Neckermann* lawsuit in 1949, Karl and Meta celebrated the birth of their first grandson. He was destined to grow up into the man the world would come to know as musical legend Billy Joel.

2
HIS
CHILDHOOD

AS A CHILD in Germany and Switzerland, Helmuth Joel had studied music formally. From an early age he had displayed a natural aptitude for music, and he soon became especially proficient at playing the classics on the piano. Beethoven, Chopin, and Bartók were among his favorite composers. Was there ever an option of pursuing a career as a classical pianist? He says, "The possibility was there, but my father wanted me to do something serious. I became an engineer because that's what he wanted. In those days, you did what the old man told you to do."[10]

After moving to America, and before being drafted into the military, his fascination with music continued. He found a new creative outlet when he joined one of the theater troupes at the City College of New York (CCNY). Although he was aiming for a career in engineering as his father wanted him to do, Howard found himself in a group of students that performed stage musicals. And, that's how young Joel met the woman he was destined to marry.

It was Rosalind Hyman, daughter of Phillip Hyman and his wife Rebecca. In addition to being beautiful and outgoing, Rosalind was also musically talented. Billy Joel explains, "My mother sang. She was in a Gilbert & Sullivan company at CCNY. That's how they met."[12] As part of the troupe, Howard and Rosalind performed together in *The Pirates of Penzance* and *The Mikado*. And, the fact of the matter is that Gilbert and Sullivan had also played a similar matchmaking role in the lives of Rosalind's parents. They had originally met at a presentation of Gilbert and Sullivan music at the Royal Albert Hall in London, England.

After they married, Phillip and Rebecca Hyman moved across the Atlantic and settled in Flatbush, Brooklyn. As Rosalind later described her upbringing, "My family didn't have a pot to pee in, but we were cultured English Jews with a lot of pride."[13]

When Howard Joel returned from the war in 1946, he came back to the girl with whom he had fallen in love. Although Rosalind and Howard loved each other, it was not always a storybook romance. Reportedly, the Hyman family and the Joels didn't exactly get along all that well together. However, they managed to agree that they wanted their children to be happy. And so, Howard and Rosalind were wed. Together they moved to a small apartment on Strong Street. A year after they were married, in 1947, Rosalind gave birth to their first child, Judith (Judy). Then on May 9, 1949, their son, William Martin Joel, was born to them.

The year that Billy was born, the world was still getting adjusted to its new postwar circumstances. The music that was on the charts that year reflected the kind of escapist entertainment people were looking for: love songs and odes with a western theme to them. Among the biggest hits that year were "Some Enchanted Evening," sung by Perry Como; "A Little Bird Told Me," by Evelyn Knight; "She Wore A Yellow Ribbon," by Eddie "Piano" Miller; "You're Breaking My Heart," by Vic Damone; "Forever and Ever," by Russ Morgan; "(Ghost) Riders in the Sky," by Vaughn Monroe; and "That Lucky Old Sun" and "Mule Train," both by Frankie Laine.

Billy recalls of his young life in the Bronx: "My father's parents didn't get along with my mother or my mother's family. There was a big division, as a matter of fact; as long as I can remember, there never was any big family thing going on. My mother's parents lived in Flatbush in Brooklyn, and it was a narrow, dark, typical tenement-style apartment. My father's parents had this big, open, sunken living room and with very nice furniture and Oriental rugs; but I was very young, and don't remember them very well."[10]

At the time, Howard Joel had a job working for General Electric. It wasn't long after their son, Billy, became part of the household that plans started to formulate for the family to leave New York City, and move out to Long Island. The boroughs of Queens and Brooklyn are both located on

Long Island, and to the east border on Nassau County. Most of the way out to the eastern border of Nassau County, a unique and innovative community of prefab structures sprang up after the Second World War. It was called Levittown.

The real estate upon which Levittown was built was formerly prime acreage of Long Island farmland. Knowing that thousands of GIs would be returning from the war, property developer William Levitt purchased four thousand acres of potato fields in 1946 and proceeded to place 17,400 nearly identical tract homes on tiny plots of land. They were especially appealing to soldiers returning from the war, as the houses could easily and cheaply be purchased using "GI loans" from the government. It was a clever speculative strategy by Levitt. It wasn't long before every house was sold.

Describing his life in Levittown, Billy Joel was later to explain, "It's a suburb, but not like most—it's just an extension of New York City. We were blue-collar poor people, which is different from *poor* poor people. You don't go to welfare when you're blue-collar poor. You somehow work. Kind of [like] Archie Bunker: You never ask for a handout. You would die first. Your kids would starve to death first. This guy named Levitt founded the town. He brought up a lot of land and people from the Army could get a house with a GI loan for $40 down. It was supposed to be a house in the country. So all these people fleeing from Staten Island and New York City moved out to Long Island but ended up living next door to people they just moved away from. It was the inner city all over again. There weren't even any playgrounds in Levittown, so we played stickball in the streets. Everybody had the same house, so they'd try to make theirs different by fancying up the driveway or painting the trim different. All the kids on the block would look at the houses and laugh, because we all knew they were the same houses and it didn't make any difference what you did."[12]

On one hand, Howard Joel was just another of the returning GIs who came back from the war and settled in Levittown. However, he wasn't like all of the native-born New Yorkers he found himself surrounded by in suburbia. His sensibilities were still very strongly in the fashion of what he learned in Europe. Billy says of his father, "I recall him being different than a lot of other people's fathers, because he was German and he had a European sense of humor, which was very cynical, very sarcastic, very dark. He would talk to me as if he was talking to someone his own age; he wouldn't talk in a very condescending way, as parents do with young children. I didn't always understand what he was talking about, but I thought I was being treated in a special way. And I remember him saying once that 'life is a cesspool,' which is a heavy thing to say to a young kid."[10]

Billy indeed came from a unique household. His grandparents have been described in the press as having been active Socialists. Although he admits that fact, he is quick to explain that his parents had their own political beliefs. "No, their parents were [Socialists]," he has said of Howard and Rosalind. "I don't think they [his grandparents] were in the party, but that was their philosophy. My [maternal] grandfather fought in the Abraham Lincoln Brigade in the Spanish Civil War. My mom and dad were registered as Democrats, but they were never less than liberal in their politics."[14]

Although Billy is the first to admit that he is Jewish by heritage, the Joel family was not observant as regards their faith. As he explains it, "My parents were both from Jewish families. I was not brought up Jewish in any religious way. My circumcision was as Jewish as they got," he admits with a laugh.[16]

Billy grew up deeply admiring his mother's father, Phillip Hyman. He recalls of his Grandpa Hyman, "I don't remember a steady gig the old man ever had, but he was the happiest person I ever knew. He was a total education freak who read everything—algebra books, books about paleontology. He turned me into a reader. I think I got a lot of my romantic notions reading Fitzgerald and Hemingway and Twain. He'd also take us to the Brooklyn Academy of Music to see [Rudolf] Nureyev or the Prague Chamber Orchestra. He never had enough money for tickets, so he'd bribe the ushers with a pack of cigarettes."[15] This broad knowledge of the arts was to add to Billy's well-rounded appreciation of cultural endeavors.

Billy and his sister Judy remember growing up in a house full of music, mainly classical and jazz. "Well, my father was an accomplished pianist. I remember him playing the piano when I was very young," Billy explains. "My mom played a lot of Gilbert & Sullivan, and classical records. There was music all around, and it just seeped in, I suppose."[12]

However, not *all* music was played in the Joel household. "My father was completely disparaging of pop music," says Billy. "He thought it was crap. Popular music for him stopped when he got to the Big Band era. He respected the jazz guys like Errol Garner, who he thought was the tops, and he had kind words for Nat King Cole, but nobody after that."[10]

What Billy did get out of his dad's taste in music was a deep and devoted love of the classics: "My father was my idol as a pianist as a kid, because he was classically trained and could read music. He would come home from work at General Electric, and take Chopin and Bartok pieces and work through them laboriously; this was his entertainment. He could interpret them and make them sound as good as anything that was being played on WQXR radio or the records, but he thought he was never good enough; he never gave himself any slack. He said, 'I'm a hack, I can't play, I'm just doing it for me.'"[10]

Howard had been outspoken about his strong negative feelings for the country he had moved to, particularly its being a throwaway culture. Howard was similarly disparaging about his career: "He'd say, 'This is how I make my living in America: I work for G.E., and everything is plastic, American plastic.'"[10]

Billy admired his father's musical talent. "He was a very good pianist," he explains. "We had this crappy old upright [piano], painted 50,000 times and rusty and everything. But he would make it sound pretty good. I loved to hear him play. He'd play nocturnes and Bartok."[17]

Howard Joel's love of music almost instantly rubbed off on Billy, who showed musical aptitude at a very early age. Billy's mother recalls, "By the age of three, Billy was on the piano bench picking out Mozart, and a year later I made him put on his coat on a cold day in the fall and took him to get his first lesson from a Mrs. Francis down the block in Hicksville."[10] Both of his parents were very supportive of their son's obvious musical talent.

Although young Billy didn't necessarily like the structure that studying classical music had, he still loved the music. He learned to play very quickly, and he also became very clever at improvising if he hadn't studied: "If I had a new Beethoven piece to learn and I was too lazy to read the music, I'd make something up in the style of Beethoven. I had to do a convincing job because my mother had good ears. She'd say, 'You're learning that one pretty quick.' The next day I'd forget what I'd made up and play something else. She'd ask, 'What's that?' and I'd go, 'Oh, that's the Second Movement.'"[15]

However, his father wasn't quite as easy to fool. "The only time I ever got beat up," recalls Billy, "I had a Beethoven piece, one of the sonatas, and I started boogie-woogieing to it. And my old man came downstairs and smacked the hell outta me. It was the only time I ever remember getting beat up as a kid."[18]

Although Billy occasionally complained about his piano lessons, his displeasure had nothing to do with the music, it had to do with the way it was taught. He would often retreat into his own little world when he played the instrument. As his mother recalls, "I think the piano has been a friend to Billy all his life."[15] Indeed it has been.

By the time Billy started school, he was just a typical suburban baby boomer. That term of course refers to the generation of children born in the fifteen years after the Second World War. Growing up in the 1950s and '60s gave Billy a unique perspective on the world. The advent of television in the fifties, like radio before it, brought many new ideas and sounds to Americans. It ushered in a tidal wave of new and exciting images, and broadcast them right into everyone's living room simultaneously. It was also the dawn of a new and ever-changing phenomenon: pop culture.

While the Second World War was just something that young baby boomers read about in history class or heard discussed on the media, other serious threats to world security were looming. It was the cold war era, and often the news on television was full of images about what the Communists, particularly the Soviets, were up to, and the speculation that at any minute they were going to drop a nuclear bomb on Americans' heads. There was even one winter when U.S. children were all warned not to eat any of the snow that had fallen, as it had nuclear particles in it from an atomic bomb blast. Schoolchildren were routinely instructed in the pro-tocols of safety in the instance of a nuclear war. Everyone was taught to curl up in a ball under their respective school desk in case a bomb was dropped and the ceiling overhead collapsed. Ironically, if it really happened, sur-vivors might find the ashy remains of hundreds of children curled up in balls, like the ones archaeologists discovered in the ruins on Pompeii, after it was buried in the lava of Mount Vesuvius in ancient Italy.

As Billy later amusingly explained this uniquely bizarre era, "I was born in 1949; I was a Cold War kid all my life. I thought we were going to get blown to hell any day."[19] The residual effects of growing up with this kind of knowledge, certainly fueled baby boomers' characteristic lust to "live for today" throughout their entire lives. It was to be a philosophy that Billy Joel obviously held dear throughout his entire life.

In other ways, for much of his young life Billy had a childhood just like any other suburban baby boomer. He was later to jokingly say, "Oh yes, I grew up in Hicksville, Long Island, a town famed for producing musical geniuses and distinguishable from other Long Island towns by its Ronzoni spaghetti factory."[20] Yes, indeed, Hicksville and Levittown were about to become famous, not only for producing pasta, but for yielding the world-famous "Piano Man" as well.

While he was going to school and studying the piano, Billy was already so imaginative and creative as to start seriously composing music. Recalls his mother, "By six, he was writing full songs with stories in them, just like the tales and literature he always heard recited by my storytelling father."[10]

Although he was studying classical piano, according to Billy, he never considered the idea of growing up to be a classical performer. "It never looked to be a very much fun life to be a concert pianist. I never wanted to be Vladimir Horowitz. I never really enjoyed playing the classics, although I'm glad I did it. As a matter of fact, when I was taking lessons, the teacher would give me a piece to read, and I'd go out and buy the record. So I developed an ear early on," he claims.[18]

It wasn't long before young Billy Joel started to have his own very strong opinions about what he wanted to play, and what he didn't. "I grew up playing classical piano, so I have tension and release philosophy from that training," he says. "I hate boogie for the sake of boogie; it's got to be tension and release. I hate to beat an idea to death."[18] Well, that certainly ruled out big band pianist for an occupational choice for Billy. He would eventually find his own path.

From playing the piano alone for hours at a time, his knowledge of music made him develop a greater sense of independence that all creative people know and embrace. Rosalind Joel remembers, "By the time he was seven, Billy was a bookworm, and if I went to the library I had to bring home 20 books: picture books, storybooks, history books. He was self-sufficient; you could give him a kitchen chair and he'd spent hours pretending it was a choo-choo train. It didn't take much to make him happy."[10]

Billy has many fond memories of his father from his early childhood. "I also remember him working in the garden," he says. "You know, everybody had his quarter acre. Man, he worked so hard at getting that lawn just right. It was like his little piece of the rock. I remember him standing there with that roller thing that fertilized, and he had a little potbelly that hung over."[17]

When Billy was in grade school, Howard Joel's job for General Electric suddenly started to take him out of the country for long periods. He was often sent to Central and South America, where these foreign countries were actively wiring themselves with electricity for the first time. Of those years, Billy recalls, "I didn't see much of him, because he was always away on business trips, overseas or in South America."[17]

He also remembers his parents reaching a point where they didn't get along at all well. When he was eight years old, Billy's mom and dad suddenly announced that they were going to get a divorce. "I remember they used to fight, and when they split it was sort of a relief. I had a loving upbringing. I didn't have that fear of male authority a lot of people grow up with," he would later explain.[21]

For whatever reason, Howard Joel was finished with his marriage, and finished with America. "I guess it was a real bitter split, because he went back to Europe. He went back to Switzerland, and I guess he had a hard time. It's got to be hard splitting up. I mean, I know that it's hard. With kids and everything, it's got to be even harder. I know they felt guilty about splitting up because of us kids, but me and my sister were actually relieved, knowing there wasn't going to be all that turmoil and arguing in the house. Like, *'Whew!* O.K.'"[17]

Rosalind was later to confide that the Howard Joel who returned from the Second World War was significantly different than the one who left to fight in it. "Tragically, he was never the same when he came back," she claimed.[10] Apparently, seeing the horrors of Dachau, where he had witnessed such extreme evidence of man's inhumanity to man, was more than he could bear.

As Billy remembered it, "I didn't see him [again] until I was grown up. My mother raised us—me and my sister—by herself."[12] Rosalind was reportedly deeply heartbroken about the split. Says Billy, "My mom, I would see her standing by the window, looking out the kitchen window, and she knew that my dad, he wouldn't be coming home that day, but she was maybe hoping he would pull up [out] front. I'd say, 'Mom, what are you doing?' and sometimes she would say, 'Just looking out the window. Maybe your father's coming home.'"[10] It was quite a sad sight for young Billy to behold. It left an indelible impression on him. Sometimes love turns to heartbreak, and sometimes heartbreak is channeled creatively to become unforgettably sensitive music.

Billy is quite defensive about his father's having left the family. "My father never abandoned us," he insists. "He sent a check every month. We went hungry a lot. Sometimes it was scary not eating. We were in the suburbs . . . but we were the antithesis of the suburban situation. Do you know what it's like to be the poor people on the poor people's block?!"[14]

"Things got different after he left. This was Levittown, the prototypical family housing development. All of a sudden, here was a family on the block without a father and with a single mother. This was still an era of *Donna Reed* values. My mother got *divorced,* as if there was some shame in that. She was perceived by the other wives to be some kind of threat; she was a good-looking woman. And she couldn't get a decent job because this was before the days of the women's movement. She could only get menial jobs and our situation changed; we had less money, we never had a TV."[10]

He recalls, "She was an intelligent, skilled woman, but all she could get was bookkeeping or secretarial work. So we couldn't fix up the house, couldn't get a new car—all the things suburbanites are supposed to do."[11] Billy was very much aware that their situation was a bit different than that of his neighborhood friends. "We weren't dirt-poor. We were just never able to get ahead of the game."[15]

According to Billy, his father's sudden absence from his life gave him a slightly different perspective on life: "I knew a lot of kids when I was growing up who were afraid of their fathers; their fathers beat them up, were bastards, creeps," he says. "I happen to have had a nice upbringing. The worst my mother did was grab hangers off the rack and whip me over the shoulders. Your mother, your father, it doesn't matter—that hanger hurts. But I never grew up in fear of men."[14] He claims that being "fatherless" gave him a more sensitive outlook and temperament: "I think I was less angry and resentful than my friends who had dictator fathers."[15]

Liberty DeVitto insightfully points out that adult Billy Joel keeps himself at arm's length when it comes to his relationships with people. "Maybe he feels like he was wronged by his dad—when he left the family—and that's why he feels justified in keeping himself emotionally isolated to this day," he surmises.[3] It seems to be a logical psychological outcome of his father's sudden absence from his life.

Another big difference was that they were the only Jewish family on their street. "We were the gypsy family; the only family where there had been a divorce, the only one that wasn't Catholic, the only one without a driveway."[22]

According to Billy, most of his playmates were Italian Catholics. At the time, he never really perceived any difference. This later made for a bit of religious confusion, but it also made him more of a broad-minded thinker. He became open to other ideas and other ideologies. "I used to go to Roman Catholic church with my friends, and, when I was 11, I got baptized in a Church of Christ in Hicksville. I'm a cultural Jew. I like the Lower East Side humor, the food. I think the Yiddish language is terrifically expressive. Does that make me a complete Jew or a partial Jew? I'm not really sure."[16]

In addition to taking piano lessons, Billy's mother made certain that her son and daughter attended social and cultural events. This would include family outings, or concerts at nearby Westbury Music Fair. There were also excursions into Manhattan to take advantage of all of the music and art that was there, and inexpensively accessible.

"I really loved it," Billy declares. "We didn't have a TV, and I'm glad, in a way, because I didn't get hung up on the TV syndrome. We'd see the opera, ballet, Philharmonic, everything. A lot of people thought classical music was boring and staid, but I saw the exciting parts, like Tchaikovsky, Rachmaninoff, Chopin. I mean, that's really passionate music. You know, when you're a kid, *Peter and the Wolf*—wow!"[17]

Indeed, Rosalind made certain that both her daughter, Judy, and her son were exposed to as much art and music as she could afford. "I got a lot of culture because Mom enjoyed it and wanted to pass it along. Plus, she saw I had a talent for it, so she was going to kick my ass," says Billy.[17]

She wanted Billy to become a well-mannered and cultured young man, and not some sort of street hoodlum with a cocky attitude. At least that was her plan. But along the way, young Billy was destined to become someone who was a little bit of both.

BILLY JOEL

3
LIVING HERE IN LEVITTOWN

ALTHOUGH BILLY CLAIMS that his family rarely had a working TV set in the household, he was still bombarded with cultural images and ideas. He would watch television at his friends' homes, he would go to the movies, and he was exposed to pop and rock music on the radio. Many of the film, TV, and musical images that he was exposed to while growing up in the 1950s and '60s showed up in his music, his singing, his songwriting, and the way he dressed and carried himself.

When he was a young teenager, he and his friends mimicked the *West Side Story*–style gangs they saw in such juvenile delinquent films as *The Blackboard Jungle* and *Rebel without a Cause* (both released in 1955). When the Beatles came along in 1964, Billy became part of a Beatles-style rock band. When the late 1960s ushered in the hippie era, and Jimi Hendrix and Jimmy Page were his musical heroes, he formed a Led Zeppelin–like duo. In fact he went through several incarnations before he clearly defined his own rock & roll identity.

Musically, the early 1950s was an era dominated by such pop singers as Rosemary Clooney, Patti Paige, Frank Sinatra, Peggy Lee, and Frankie Laine. However, in the middle of the decade, suddenly these singers were all pushed to the sidelines by the musical avalanche known as rock & roll.

From 1956 to '59, the incredibly dynamic presence of Elvis Presley almost single-handedly brought a whole new generation of record buyers—1950s teenagers—to the stores. Starting with "Heartbreak Hotel" (1956) and proceeding through "Don't Be Cruel" (1956), "Hound Dog" (1956), "Love Me Tender" (1956), "All Shook Up" (1957), "(Let Me Be Your) Teddy Bear" (1957), "Jailhouse Rock" (1957), "Don't" (1958), "Hard-Headed Woman" (1958), and "A Big Hunk o' Love" (1959), Elvis Presley seemed to dominate consistently the number 1 spot on the charts.

In between Elvis hits, such performers as Johnny Mathis ("Chances Are"), Pat Boone ("Don't Forbid Me"), Debbie Reynolds ("Tammy"), Paul Anka ("Diana"), Buddy Holly and the Crickets ("That'll Be the Day"), the Teddy Bears—featuring Phil Spector ("To Know Him, Is to Love Him"), and the Everly Brothers ("All I Have to Do Is Dream") also managed to hit the top of the chart during these formative years of rock & roll. It was a musical era of Connie Francis, the Platters, Brenda Lee, Ricky Nelson, and Sam Cooke. Because of the miracle of television, which offered such series as *The Ed Sullivan Show* and *American Bandstand*, these performers were the teen idols of the day. This was the kind of popular music that Billy was exposed to as he was growing up on suburban Long Island.

Actually, Billy Joel's first public performance was an homage to the King of rock & roll. "Elvis was a little before me," he recalls, "but I do remember doing an Elvis Presley impression when I was in the fourth grade. It was the first thing I ever did in front of people. I sang 'Hound Dog' and I was jiggling my hips like Elvis. I remember this because the fifth-grade girls started screaming. I really dug the fifth-grade girls. I thought, 'Hey this is pretty neat.' When the girls started screaming, the teacher pulled me off the stage. She said it was because I was wiggling my hips. Now, in fourth grade, you don't have hips."[12]

A suggestive hip-gyrating Elvis impersonation is not exactly the image of what the school was trying to promote for its students. However, Billy remembers that breaking the rules was part of the fun. "That was where it began. When I got pulled off the stage for singing like Elvis in the fourth grade, it was kind of like I beat the system. I got away with something before they could stop me," he recalls.[12] This was to become a recurring theme in his life.

Billy confesses that he was something of a juvenile delinquent himself during his school years: "When I was a kid in school, I always saw how stupid rules were. I would do something that didn't hurt anybody, but it broke the rules and I would get in trouble for it. My life has been a constant rebellion against that. 'This is my life! Leave me alone!'"[12] For him, that attitude has been a constant thread throughout the years.

Billy began hanging out with the local gang of "wannabe" juvenile delinquents, whom he referred to as "the guys with the pompadours." According to him, "It just seemed really romantic at the time. You know, the Knights of the Round Table. They wore poncho shirts. I was just starting to get interested in girls, and they seemed to like a little flash at that age. We were always daring each other. We'd run across the overpasses that go over the parkway, and they were only like eight-inches-wide. If you fell, man, you'd hit the parkway thirty-feet-below and get run over. We used to see how fast we could run back and forth, wearing these [pointed shoes with] Cuban heels. We were crazy. We hung out and tried to look tough, but we weren't as tough as we thought we were."[17]

He and his gang may not have actually been "hoods," but they sure had the "look" down. "We used to sneak off to find Italian-style clothes, tight black shirts and stuff. Some guys had the really pointy shoes, casino pants," says Billy. "Me? I was one of those crewcut guys with white sneakers. That was before punks, before greasers. 'Punk' was an insult. 'Whaddya mean, I'm a punk? I'm a hitter.' We didn't really know what to call ourselves. We thought we were just cool."[23]

What was the purpose of this teenage rebellion? According to Billy, "There's an identity crisis. You're a nothing, you're a zero in the suburbs. You're mundane, you're common. You have 2.4 children, you have a quarter acre plot of land, you have a Ford Wagoneer. Who gives a damn about you?"[18]

This wasn't just a New York phenomenon. "We used to do the same thing in the L.A. suburbs," says Micky Dolenz of the Monkees. "We thought we were such big hoodlums. The biggest crime we committed was opening the unlocked glove compartments of parked cars. How many maps of Los Angeles did we really need?" he asks rhetorically and laughs.[24]

You could take the city kids to suburbia, but it seemed that one couldn't take the street out of some of the kids. Billy remembers that there were several cliques that one could get into in his school at the time. "You got into junior high, you could go one of three ways. You could be a collegiate, a hitter or a brownie—the kid who wears brown shoes with white socks, carries a schoolbag and always gets the monitor jobs."[26]

"There were all these cliques—the collegiates, the brownies, the greasers. We were the hoods. Actually our older brothers were the hoods; we were 'dittyboppers.' We dressed like hoods but we didn't have fights."[15]

"We were hitters. I mean I had a gang and that's what we did. They called us punks—we didn't call ourselves punks—we thought we were hoods."[26]

However, he is quick to explain that it was mainly innocent antics he was involved in. "We'd just play handball all day, kick over garbage cans, sniff glue, and use phony draft cards to buy beer. Every evening I'd say good-night to my mom, go up to my room, crawl out on the roof, and sneak away. I'd run over to the green to . . . drink Tango wine and screw around with the gang."[15]

One evening during his hoodlum phase, his street tough looks alone got him into trouble with the law. He was sitting on the steps of a house in Hicksville in the darkness, when a patrol car pulled up and the cops questioned Billy on suspicion of robbery. The next thing he knew, he was nabbed and thrown into the back of the car, and hauled off to jail. Unbeknownst to him, the house he was sitting in front of had been robbed earlier that evening. Although he spent the night behind bars, his charge was dismissed the next day.

For a while Billy continued to embrace a "hood" mentality. He once proclaimed self-defensively, "They say beating someone up doesn't prove anything. But at the time, it did prove something: 'You can't push me around.' I suppose I was looking for my own masculinity."[21]

However, acting like an intimidating juvenile delinquent could only go so far when you stand five feet six inches tall, as Billy does. It wasn't long before the teenager had transitioned out of the "punk" phase, and into his latest "tough boy" venture. If one has frustrations one can't work out, what better way to vent than to beat the hell out of a punching bag? With that in mind, Billy took up boxing at a local Boy's Club gym in a shopping center in Hicksville on Long Island.

This was one of those phases of his life that he looks back on with mystery: "Well, I probably got away with murder. I was brought up by women, my mother and my sister. So it was a very gentle upbringing, very loving. I'm not afraid to be affectionate or any of that stuff. But on the other hand, there was an identity crisis. So I had to go out and find my manhood and prove myself by boxing. So I proved I wasn't a sissy and moved on from there. [12]

"I think about it now and I just have been out of my mind, because boxing is very violent, brutal. It's dangerous—and, yes, crazy. But I really enjoyed it while I was doing it. [I] got my whole male identity crisis out of the way in those three years of boxing. Now . . . my manhood is a matter of gender and not of physical force."[12]

According to Billy, this bit of acting out his macho feelings in the boxing ring lasted from the ages of sixteen to nineteen. "I was pretty good, too," he recalls. "I had 26 fights—two decisions, two losses by knockout, and 22 wins. I lost my first fight and I lost my last fight. The last one was enough to convince me to stop. This guy's arms were the size of my entire body. I was dancing around this guy like a fly buzzing around. I couldn't hurt him. I thought, 'If this guy don't know I'm a better boxer than he is, I can't convince him.' He got me with a left hook. Boom! I went right down. I could have gotten up, but I decided to hell with it, who needs this?"[12]

During one particular bout, he took a significant blow right in the nose. When he examined his face in the mirror, he was horrified at the image that stared back at him. His nose was not only bleeding, it was smashed to one side of his face.

Just then one of his boxing buddies came up to him and said in a nonchalant fashion, "It's only cartilage; it'll be okay."[12] In an effort to help Billy, he reached up and pushed the damaged proboscis somewhat back into position.

"I won that fight," Billy claims. But the victory was bittersweet, as his nose would never be the same. "I thought it was [just] swollen. The doctor took it and moved it back and just put a bandage on it. It was broken, though, and never healed right. I've got two different-sized nostrils. Hey, I used to have a pug nose. I used to be *cute,* believe it or not."[12] A bit of surgical tape and some gauze later, the future singer was left with the slightly squashed-looking nose he now has.

According to him, "My nose was never the same after that. I've got one nostril smaller than the other. See, my nose is kind of bent. I thought about having an operation, but I wondered if it would change my voice. Now I kinda like it. I don't know if I'd want to look like I did when I was a kid. As my mother would say, 'It gives you character.'"[14]

Like most people, the Billy Joel of his high school days is a bit different from the man he grew up to become. He defensively explains, "The tough-guy image has been blown out of proportion. I never thought of myself like that. I was just like everybody else, trying to look cool, like *West Side Story,* but never really that cool."[12]

Boxing and looking like a punk might not have been good for his nose, but his tough-guy persona was certainly good for attracting girls. "Well, if you were from the more industrial, blue-collar part of Long Island, you wanted to go out with the girls from the North Shore—Oyster Bay, Cold Spring Harbor, and Syosset—because they had a lot of class," he says.

"Those girls weren't supposed to go out with us, because we were on the other side of the tracks—and that made the girls *want* to, of course. There were a lot of great local girls, too. We'd go to somebody's house whose parents weren't home and try to get beer and blast rock & roll music and everybody would sit around and make out. Nobody went all the way, but everybody *said* they did. We spent a lot of time trying to convince girls they should."[12] This era was obviously the inspiration for one of Billy's most memorable songs of teenage rebellion: "Only the Good Die Young." Actually, the Catholic girl whom he later sang about amid the lyrics of that song was someone he went to school with, by the name of Virginia Callahan. He had a really mad crush on her, but she had no idea that he was even alive.

He also claims to have been something of a bookworm during this era of time: "I was gonna be a history teacher. See, I didn't have a TV when I grew up. We had a TV, the set went on the fritz, we didn't have the money to get it fixed. So, what do I do? I started to read. I read. I read everything. I used to read history books like they were novels—anything I could get my hands on. A lot of my romanticism comes from novelists: F. Scott Fitzgerald, Ernest Hemingway, Mark Twain, Sartre, Kafka, Hesse."[18]

Throughout his childhood in suburban Levittown, Billy had several kids his own age to play and hang out with. Some of these kids have grown to become lifelong friends. Together they shared an interest in music, girls, rebellion, and eventually rock & roll.

One of these longtime friends is Billy Zampino. He started out as a childhood buddy of Billy's. He played drums in the musical group the Lost Souls along with Billy, he worked as engineer and production coordinator of several of Billy's albums, and he even had a featured drum spot in the 2006 concert tour.

According to Zampino, throughout the years Billy had a consistent interest in music, and it even encompassed the classic musicals. Zampino says, "As kids, Billy and I used to watch *Yankee Doodle Dandy* on *Million Dollar Movie* on TV. Even then, I could see Billy's wheels turning, him thinking, 'I could do that.' And at Hicksville Junior High he did, singing a George M. Cohan medley of 'Over There,' 'You're a Grand Old Flag,' and 'Yankee Doodle' that brought down the house. As teenagers, we went together to see *My Fair Lady* on Broadway, sat through the film version of *West Side Story* at least 12 times, and listened to *Oklahoma, South Pacific,* or the music of Aaron Copland over at my house, and he'd always say, 'Maybe I could do something like that,' and he would."[10]

Simultaneous with this whole teenage *Rebel without a Cause* phase of his life was a totally different plane of consciousness. It was Billy the sensitive musician. Who would have suspected that the same rough-edged teenager who already had a police arrest on his record also loved classical music and was fascinated by Broadway musicals?

During this period, pop and rock music were slowly working their way into young Billy's consciousness, too. Having his older sister, Judy, in the household gave him access to her music. It was her collection of 45 rpm vinyl singles that gave him his first exposure to the world of pop, rock, and R&B music. "I liked some rock & roll before that, but it was my sister's rock & roll: Elvis Presley, Smokey Robinson. I like that stuff, but she always had the 45s in the little carry pack with the girl with the ponytail on it. You know, it had 'I Love Boys' written on it, and those little musical notes," Billy recalls.[17]

Billy would listen to Judy's 45s and acquaint himself with the latest top 40 pop hits. "My sister and her friends were into Fabian and Elvis stuff. Pop music didn't hit me until The Righteous Brothers and Ronettes—the Phil Spector [produced] records—and Sam & Dave, Wilson Pickett, and Otis Redding. That's the first music I felt. There was passion in it, intensity."[12]

He confesses that he mainly gravitated to R&B records, especially the ones with a big, dramatic, sweeping sound: "'You've Lost That Lovin' Feelin' by The Righteous Brothers. And almost every record The Ronettes did—their sound was bigger than the radio. To me, [producer] Phil Spector was like composer Richard Wagner. Any song Otis Redding, Sam & Dave, Wilson Pickett—early Motown."[14] Indeed, it was the first golden era of Motown Records: Mary Wells ("You Beat Me to the Punch," 1962), Smokey Robinson and the Miracles ("You Really Got a Hold on Me," 1962), the Marvelettes ("Playboy," 1962), Martha Reeves and the Vandellas ("Heat Wave," 1963), and Marvin Gaye ("Pride and Joy," 1963) all became stars during this era. Billy loved what he heard on that little record player, and the radio.

When Billy Joel was fourteen years old, it was a very strange and volatile time in America. The cold war was raging, the Cuban missile crisis was a dramatically looming threat. And then on November 21, 1963, President Kennedy was assassinated in Dallas. The entire country seemed to suddenly go into a winterlong season of mourning. It was the end of a certain age of innocence for an entire generation of Americans. By the beginning of the following year, the whole country needed to be snapped out of their somber mood. Well, it came in an explosively big way on February 9,

1964. That was the day that the Beatles first appeared on *The Ed Sullivan Show* on American TV. The perfect antidote for the postassassination blues was the music, the energy, the look, the style, and the excitement of the phenomenon known as "Beatlemania."

Suddenly, Billy Joel knew what he wanted to do with his life: "I didn't start going out and buying records until The Beatles in '64. I saw them on *The Ed Sullivan Show* and that just knocked me out. I thought, 'These guys don't look like Fabian. They don't look like they were manufactured in Hollywood. They look just like me and my friends.' I could see this look in John Lennon's eye that told me something: They were irreverent, they were making fun of the whole thing. It was this smirk on his face. They were a bunch of wise guys like me and my friends! That's when it all took shape. I said, 'That's what I want to do!'"[12]

What really caught Billy's eye was their look. Although they were dressed in collarless matching gray suits, their hair was decidedly "mop top," and radically different than any style that had existed previously in the twentieth century. They didn't have the DA-coiffed, fifties-style look, they were new and unique. That immediately appealed to him: "I heard The Beatles, and they were mine," he claimed. "Man, I could do that. I could *try* to do that, anyway."[17] It wasn't long before Billy grew his hair to a Beatle-inspired length.

And then there was the music of the Beatles. At this phase it was stripped-down drums and guitars, and incredibly sung harmonies. According to Billy, "When they came along, I was ripe for the plucking. Basically I'm a melody freak and they were the masters. You went out and bought a Beatles album, listed from cut one to the end and liked them all. I started writing real *Beatley*-sounding songs of my own, with words like 'Close to me . . . you should be.'"[15]

Although he was also amidst his teenage boxing phase, slowly it was the idea of being a rock musician that began to take his imagination. "I knew from the time I was fourteen, when I started being a professional musician, making money as a musician, that I was not going to live an ordinary life," he recalls.[18]

When the Beatles kicked the door open, that same year they brought along with them Gerry and the Pacemakers ("Don't Let the Sun Catch You Crying") Herman's Hermits ("I'm into Something Good"), Petula Clark ("Downtown"), Peter and Gordon ("A World without Love"), and Dusty Springfield ("Wishin' and Hopin'"). "The British invasion" of the American musical charts was officially underway, and Billy was right in the middle of it. As he explains, "[In] 1964: I discovered rock & roll via The Beatles and begin jamming with my friends: [the] Kinks, [the] Zombies, [the Rolling] Stones, English rock stuff."[20] Teenaged Billy had found his cause.

It seemed as if everyone had an opinion about the Beatles. The "Fab Four" suddenly commandeered the radio airwaves, TV shows, and magazine covers; they were an unavoidable phenomenon in America. Heck, even his mother, Rosalind Joel, liked John, Paul, George, and Ringo. Recalls Billy, "She thought The Beatles were great. She liked the harmony. I don't see how anybody who had an appreciation for music could avoid liking The Beatles."[12]

Indeed, the Beatles did to the 1960s record charts what Elvis Presley had done in the 1950s. They virtually dominated it.

John Lennon, Paul McCartney, George Harrison, and Ringo Starr were overnight stars whose every movement made front-page news for the majority of the decade. From 1964 to 1966 their record-breaking string of number 1 hits—on both sides of the Atlantic—included "I Want to Hold Your Hand," "Can't Buy Me Love," "A Hard Day's Night," "I Feel Fine," "Eight Days a Week," "Ticket to Ride," "Help!" "Yesterday," "Day Tripper," "We Can Work It Out," "Paperback Writer," "Yellow Submarine," and "Eleanor Rigby."

The Beatles' closest rival in the race to have more number 1 hits that decade was the Supremes. During this same time span, the Supremes hit the top of the charts with "Where Did Our Love Go," "Baby Love," and "You Keep Me Hanging On." It was also an era in which the Beach Boys ("Help Me, Rhonda"), the Four Tops ("I Can't Help Myself"), the Byrds ("Mr. Tambourine Man"), the Rolling Stones ("Get Off of My Cloud"), Simon and Garfunkel ("The Sounds of Silence"), the Mamas and the Papas ("Monday, Monday"), Sonny and Cher ("I Got You, Babe"), the Dave Clark Five ("Over and Over"), and Lou Christie ("Lightnin' Strikes") also scored huge number 1 smashes as well.

Lou Christie recalls, "It was such an exciting time of my life to be part of the early years of rock & roll. One of the highlights of my career was traveling around America with the *Dick Clark Caravan of Stars*. A dozen other recording artists and I jumped on a bus and traveled around the country doing shows for fans who are still out there. Diana Ross, Mary Wilson, Florence Ballad—the Supremes—and Gene Pitney, the Ronettes, Chubby Checker, Fabian, Frankie Avalon, Johnny Tillotson, Brian Hyland, Paul and Paula, Dick and Dee Dee, Jan and Dean, the Beach Boys . . . it doesn't get any better than that! What's nice is that most of us are still friends and are part of a special family that spread music and fun throughout the world. Billy Joel obviously felt the message and sat down to write and record some of the most poignant songs of our time. He has taken rock to the next level!"[28]

In addition to the Beatles, Billy especially loved the music of the Stones: "I liked The Rolling Stones a lot. Their music was dirty and ragged and there were mistakes all over the place. My friends would go, 'Wow, did you hear that note the drummer played?' They claimed they were doing that stuff on purpose, but I knew they were mistakes. I liked every song on every Beatles album. In school, I was always in chorus, even though I thought chorus was faggy. I did it because it was one of the easier classes to do and I did like to sing. So there was that kind of music."[12] Although taking a chorus class was considered "square" at the time, his knowledge of vocal harmonies clearly benefited from these classes, when he began to record and sing his own music.

It wasn't long before Billy was inspired to join his first rock band. He immediately found it much more interesting than concentrating on his schoolwork. His teachers even noticed a change in him, in his appearance and his manner. He explains, "I started playing with my friends at night and stopped showing up for classes. Soon after The Beatles came out, there must have been 20,000 garage bands. I was in one of those, not so much playing the piano, but singing. School never got in the way. That's one thing I always kind of liked to do: to see how far I could push the system."[12]

It wasn't long before his fascination with music had totally eclipsed his schoolwork. "I liked school at first," he says, giving an overview of his academic career. "I did good without doing any studying or anything. I used to read history books like they were novels to pass the time, since we didn't have a TV. But in junior high school, I started hanging out with a wild crowd. I started in my first band when I was 14 or so and I would come into school missing three classes. My eyes were red. Teachers thought I was a drug addict: 'You look stoned.' 'That's just the way I look naturally.' I would show up and get a B on the tests, but the teachers wouldn't pass me, because I wasn't in school enough. I would say, 'Well, I passed the test. I know the stuff I'm supposed to know. What's wrong with you?' It's the same thing—the running battle I have with bureaucracy."[12]

Almost instantly, Billy set about learning all of the popular new songs. He formed a band with his friends that very year. A schoolmate by the name of Jim Bosse had formed his own band, which he called the Echoes. It was 1964 and they were mainly playing at local events with this guitar and drums ensemble. According to Bosse, "We decided it would be nice to add a keyboard to the group. Someone told us there was a real good piano player named Billy Joel at our school so we invited him to one of our rehearsals to try him out. We were all immediately impressed with his already well developed skill on the piano. We were all still struggling with the basics of our instruments. Billy fit in instantly and quickly became the main attraction of our band, The Echoes."[29]

Billy recalls learning all of the latest tunes by groups including Sam the Sham and the Pharaohs, and the Safaris: "I was playing all these golden oldies: 'Wooly Bully,' 'Wipe Out'—and I got paid! It was only five dollars or something, but I said, 'Man, you get paid for this too?' And that was it. I really didn't have any choice after that."[17] Now he was really hooked!

Like all high school/teenage bands, the Echoes became a revolving door for all sorts of members to come and go, like passengers on a subway car. Bosse remembers, "Billy Zampino also performed as our drummer for a while. By then we were performing somewhat regularly at parties, school dances, and 'Teen Center' dances on Friday nights at various locations, commonly at Holy Family Church close to where Billy, Billy and Howie [Blauvelt] lived. Billy Zampino was a close friend of Billy Joel's—and remains so to this day—and he was likely the best drummer our band had."[29]

One thing led to another, and soon young Billy was playing in Long Island recording sessions with producer Shadow Morton. The significant rock and pop artists Morton worked with in his career include the Shangri-Las, Janis Ian, and Vanilla Fudge. When he was producing the Shangri-Las' two biggest hits, "Remember (Walking in the Sand)" and "Leader of the Pack," fourteen-year-old Billy was brought in by a local manager to play the piano tracks to the songs. However, to this day he has no idea whether it was ultimately his version of those recordings that appear on the singles that were released. That was immaterial. More important was that it was his first taste of what life was like in the recording studio. The recording facility, Dynamic Studios, belonged to songwriter Ellie Greenwich and was located in the basement of her Long Island house. Not exactly the kind of place one would put a whole studio orchestra but, hey, it was a recording studio nonetheless.

Although it seems odd that someone as young as Billy would work in a recording studio, he wasn't the only fourteen-year-old to end up on a record. LaLa Brooks recorded "Da Doo Ron Ron" in 1963 with the Crystals at the same age. And, that song was produced by Billy's idol, Phil Spector. Both Billy and LaLa leapt at the chance to be in a recording studio.

Did LaLa feel that she was in any way exploited? "When I was turning fourteen," she says, "I was already singing with the Crystals at the Brooklyn Academy of Music. For me—with Phil Spector in the studio—I never experienced any negative feelings from him. In my mind, it was pleasant because it was recorded in California, and I am from New York; I stayed in one of these beautiful hotels and I was picked up in a car driven by Sonny Bono. He would bring me to the studio for the recording date. At that age—fourteen—I can't even begin to imagine how much damage could have come to a child! But it was all so innocent back then. I never was aware of any sort of exploitation. Being so young, what I remember as the most impressive part of the business was being on stage, singing, touring, having fun. The other Crystals and I were like sisters. I wouldn't have missed that experience for anything."[30] This parallels Billy Joel's feelings at the time. Having a recording date in a real studio was a fascinating learning experience for a young teenager.

Meanwhile, Billy's band's name also went through several changes along the way. When they discovered in 1965 that there had been a fifties through sixties group called the Echoes ("Baby Blue" 1960), they tried out several other monikers, including Billy Joel and the Hydros. Ultimately they renamed themselves the Lost Souls, and then the Hassles.

Since the band was comprised of teenage school friends, the personnel of the band kept changing. Recalls Bosse, "[Billy] Zampino, however, had strict parents who insisted family obligations were a priority over band practices. When he had to go away on a family camping trip leaving us with no drummer for a gig, the decision was made to get a new drummer. We performed mostly cover songs. Top 20 material from that time, but we started playing some of Billy's originals and always included them at our performances. We had a manager named Bob Parish who worked with us for a while, to try to secure a record deal for us. We were now getting pretty well-known in our area playing frequently for school dances, fraternity parties and larger private parties. We entered a statewide band competition, winning our regional at the Long Island Fair and playing for the final round at the World's Fair in New York in October of 1965. We took second place behind The Rockin' Angels from North Woodmere. We had some other big gigs that year; Ray Heatherton's radio show in August of 1965 and some performances at Macy's [department store] in New York City; they had sponsored the 'Battle of the Bands.' Later in 1965 we hired a new manager, Dick Ryan, who had a connection with Mercury Records. He lined up an audition for us and they signed us. We recorded about half an album with them—all of Billy's original songs. The players on that album were Billy [Joel], Jim Bosse, Kenny Recher, Howie Blauvelt, and Dave Boglioli. For some reason they lost interest in us halfway through the recording sessions and we never heard from them again."[29]

In addition to the Rockin' Angels, the other groups the Hassles competed with at the Tent of Tomorrow Pavilion at the World's Fair were the Enchanters from White Plains, and the Road Runners who came from Scarsdale. [Note: Although Bosse recalls that the event took place in October 1965, a World's Fair press release sets the date of the competition as having occurred the month before: on Wednesday, September 15.] Each group was allotted thirty minutes to play its individual sets.

Since the band was now including Billy's own compositions in their set, it ws a huge creative leap for him. Another important part of his musical development clicked into place when he attended his first concert. As a teenager, the first rock & roll/R&B show that he ever saw was James Brown at the world famous Apollo Theater in Harlem. Recalls Billy, "It just blew me away—the footwork, the beat, the screaming. It was the most exciting thing I'd ever seen."[15]

Staying out late at night playing rock & roll music became Billy's latest obsession to channel his teenage angst and adolescent frustrations into. As he explained it, "I was 16, very hormonal, very angry, needing to release a great deal of pent-up hostility: anger at my mother's situation, not liking school, sexual frustration."[11]

Another of Billy's "firsts" from this era was the discovery of his first favorite jazz album. After all of his classical training, he suddenly had a deep appreciation of jazz. In this case it was Dave Brubeck's classic album *Time Out*. Recorded by pianist Brubeck, it included drummer Joe Morello, bassist Gene Wright, and alto sax player Paul Desmond. Billy was to directly mimic this same type of instrumental quartet lineup in the mid-1970s, to find his greatest creative success.

One of the major distinctions of the *Time Out* album is the inclusion of two of the most famous jazz tunes ever recorded: "Blue Rondo à la Turk" and "Take Five." The album was originally recorded in 1959, and it is still heralded as a jazz classic. It also has the distinction of being the first instrumental jazz album to have sold over a million copies. Billy loved the *Time Out* album so much that master pianist Brubeck became one of his true idols in the business.

It is no wonder that Billy gravitated toward that famed instrumental album. In fact, it was always the music—not the lyrics—that appealed to him first in rock and pop music. As he explains it, "That's how I hear popular music. I remember my first exposure to popular music was probably at a beach listening to a portable radio or at a party listening to somebody's little dinky record player where they played the 45s where a speaker was about two or three inches big and you really couldn't hear lyrics. What you heard was a melody, some chords, a rhythm. The drums were always prevalent in rock & roll, and pop music. You heard the sound of the singer's voice and you heard the production of the recording. One of the last things you ever heard was what the hell they were saying. Maybe you could catch something, and as a matter of fact, a lot of songs that were popular, teenagers, especially in my era, made up dirty lyrics for them anyway, which we always liked better than the originals," he says with a laugh.[31]

Since Billy has written some of the most memorable music in the late twentieth century, it is fascinating to note that for him the lyrics were always secondary. It ended up influencing him throughout his entire career. According to him, he used to buy the 45s to listen to again and again until he memorized the lyrics and the music. "They didn't have sheet music for rock & roll back in the late '50s, early '60s—only maybe a Number One hit by a white group," he says. "But in black music, which we liked, they didn't have lyric sheets. You had to listen to the 45 and you had to stop the record or lift the needle off to get the words. If you take a group like The Rolling Stones and you try to figure out what they're saying: Mick Jagger was trying to sing like a black guy and he was an English guy. So, to a white kid from Levittown, this was like double jeopardy. What is he saying? We never really knew. Does anybody know the lyrics to 'Louie, Louie?' I don't think even The Kingsmen know the lyrics. So my exposure to popular rock & roll was that lyrics were one of the last things you ever got to. So, I write music first. Actually, I wrote music when I was a little kid. I made up my own operas, made up my own compositions. I didn't need words. Then I got into a band and we started to write songs and they looked to me to be a lyricist. And I said, 'What're you looking at me for?' 'Well, you read a lot, you read a lot of books.' 'So what? That doesn't make me Robert Browning. It doesn't make me Bob Dylan.' 'Well,' they said, 'give it a shot.' So I ended up with the task of writing words for these songs. But I did it backwards."[31]

It was a true era of "first times" for Billy Joel. This was not only true in his musical education but in his personal life as well. Now that he was in a rock band, he was suddenly looked upon as being quite the "catch" by women in the audience. He wasn't just that bug-eyed awkward high school kid, he was now a local "rock star."

Billy and his band would take every gig they could get, from high school dances to house parties to church sponsored functions. "I had a gas," he recalls. "Girls were looking at me for the first time, who'd never looked at me twice. At the end of the gig, we got $5 from the priest each—that was it, I was in, I was hooked. It was one of the highlights of my life: 'You get paid for this?'"[32]

And then there was—naturally—his first sexual experience. In Billy's case, it was an older woman. "It had nothing to do with romance," he remembers. "She seduced me. I learned just enough to know that I really wanted more and couldn't get it! I was never a matinee idol. I was kind of a schnooky guy with buggy eyes that always looked tired because at night I was playing underage in clubs with a phony draft card."[11]

One of the few examples of the music and the sound of the Lost Souls is a roughly mixed recording of a song that Billy wrote called "My Journey's End." It features Billy on keyboards and vocals, Howard Blauvelt on bass, Jim Bosse on lead guitar, Ken Recher on rhythm guitar, and Bill Zampino on drums. Recorded in 1965, it appears in Billy's 2005 boxed set, *My Lives*. It was their attempt at being the Long Island garage band version of the "British invasion" artists they heard on the radio, and saw performing on such TV programs as *Hullabaloo* and *Shindig*.

Jim Bosse explains, "We were old enough now to get phony ID's and played regularly at bars and nightclubs. Through 1966 and part of 1967 we played regularly at a bar several nights a week. I think it was The 305 Club? We played a few times at a huge nightclub that was an old airplane hanger at Roosevelt Air Field and frequently at a nightclub owned by Danner [sic] Mazur called My House."[29]

Billy took his love of music, and his desire to have a career in rock & roll, very seriously: "I was always the one calling everyone up going, 'Come on, let's rehearse.' I was a real ball buster," he says of his dedication to his music.[11] Not all of his band mates had that same passion.

On January 11, 1966, Hicksville High School student Billy Joel was given a paper to fill out titled "Idea Associations." He was asked to finish ideas that were prompted by one- to four-word statements. From records made public in the 1990s this two-page document contains Billy's answers in his own printed-letter handwriting. At times his responses are deeply insightful; at others, they demonstrate a sharp and slightly sarcastic sense of humor. The provided ideas (uppercase letters) and the associations that he came up with (upper- and lowercase) were as follows:

1. I LIKE: good music, New York City, pretty girls, Chinese food
2. THE HAPPIEST TIME: Recording a record in Mercury Studios
3. I HATE: loud-voiced people, phoney people, prejudiced people
4. WHAT ANNOYS ME: uncleanness, cold weather, getting up early
5. I AM BEST WHEN: I have slept well and eaten well
6. SOMETIMES: I wish I was older
7. WHEN I WAS YOUNGER: I was a perfect student
8. THE BEST: swinger of popular music was Nat King Cole
9. I AM VERY: aware of how people think about me
10. I SUFFER: from a lack of taking things seriously

1. I WANT TO KNOW: why Negroes are persecuted
2. AT HOME: I read a lot and listen to records
3. AT BEDTIME: I read and eat something
4. A MOTHER: is indispensable
5. I CAN'T: be what I am not
6. I NEED: a good shot of confidence
7. A BROTHER: never had one
8. WHEN I AM ALONE: I eat or read
9. MY FATHER: left when I was younger
10. WHEN I GROW UP: I want to be successful

1. I AM SORRY: that I got in with the wrong crowd
2. THE ONLY TROUBLE IS: what's done is done
3. PEOPLE: make you or break you
4. I FEEL: uncomfortable in this chair
5. I AM MOST AFRAID OF: ruining someone's life
6. OTHER KIDS: have their own lives
7. MY NERVES: are pretty good
8. I WISH: I had a million dollars
9. I SECRETLY: want to do something no one has ever done
10. MY GREATEST WORRY IS: what my family thinks of me

1. BOYS: today are in sad physical shape
2. I CAN'T: stand a loud voiced person
3. IN THE LOWER GRADES: I was an especially good student
4. SPORTS: I love boxing and swimming
5. I SUFFER: when my family is angry with me

6. I FAILED: to enter the Golden Glove finals because of my wrist
7. READING: is one of my favorite pastimes
8. MY MIND: is slowly falling asleep
9. AT SCHOOL: I try to listen to what is being taught
10. DANCING: today is for the birds
11. MOST GIRLS: can't stand being spoiled[33]

However, his interest in high school was seriously waning. "I'd stayed through the 12th Grade, just for my mother," he claims.[21]

His mother was getting increasingly more concerned about Billy's lack of concentration on his schoolwork. With just these sentiments in mind, Rosalind Joel wrote a letter to Leon Green, PhD, the school psychologist, dated June 15, 1966. In the letter she expressed her concern over her son's obvious lack of interest in school. "This letter is being written because there are signs of regression in Billy," she wrote. "I know, it's perfectly normal at this time, but if he goes through withdrawal, you may never find out what he's got in him, and in the short time you have to work with him, (vacation coming up) a little clue may be of help."[34]

According to her, Billy's ambivalence toward his formal education took many forms. She wrote, "The regression part consists of him being late again, asking not to go to school, etc. You know the pattern." However her greatest concern was a fear that he might abandon his music. "He is not touching the piano," she reported to Dr. Green, with deep concern.[34]

The letter also has its amusing touches. At one point she added, "Yes, that's right—I'm a Jewish mother sticking her nose in."[34]

After saying that, she went on to warmly salute her son's undeniable talent. "Did you know that Billy has extraordinary talent for playing classical music?" she wrote. "This is not my opinion alone. Morton Estrin, one of Long Island's foremost concert pianists, saw in Billy (he was his teacher) at the age of six (6) an unusual talent, not only in performing but in composing. He begged me to continue the lessons. The separation of myself and husband prevented me paying for it. (He was expensive—but worth it—but at the time we were lucky if we had enough to eat.) He had various teachers since then. His next to last one (Paul Rudoff) recommended that he take lessons from the student connected with Duke Ellington (the student was a talented Juilliard scholarship graduate). Billy resented taking lessons from 1) a woman. 2) I had to drive him to Queens (ugh! sitting that long in a car with a Mother!) 3) He refused to practice." After having spent several paragraphs explaining her frustration, the letter was signed "Sincerely yours, Rosalind Joel."[34]

Billy had narrowly managed to slide by with all of his studies up to this point, and he figured that he would just graduate and get on with his life as the piano player in a rock band. Then, one day, it all sort of fell apart. "I went all the way to the 12th grade, and then I was called down to the office, and they said, 'We're not going to graduate you, because you haven't showed up for classes enough.' I felt bad, because my mother wanted me to graduate, but I told them, 'Well, the hell with it. If I'm not going to Columbia University, I'm going to Columbia Records and you don't need a high school diploma over there.' I just split. I suppose I broke my mother's heart. But I told her, 'Don't worry, Mom, I'm, I'm going to make it up to you. Someday I'll buy you a house.' . . . One way or another, I was going to make it up to her for that. All the little troubles I had growing up, I never brought it home. I never shamed my family. It was a big thing in our neighborhood: Don't bring trouble back to the house. It's hard enough to get by without problems from your kids."[12]

Looking back on it, Billy was to explain of his status as a high school dropout, "I didn't show up enough. I passed all the tests, but I was always absent because I was playing in bands. Who's gonna make an 8:00 homeroom when you've been gigging 'til 3:30 in the morning?"[35]

While all of this was going on, there was also a bigger issue at hand: the war in Vietnam. If one wasn't going to college and wasn't physically impaired, there was always the looming threat of being drafted. By the time that Billy turned eighteen, in 1967, the country was becoming more and more divided about its support of the war. Was it senseless for America to have gotten involved in this war? In the long view, the answer is yes. In the short view, Billy had figured that out and he wasn't about to have any part of it.

"I lied to get out," he explains his escaping the draft. "The richer kids could get psychologists to write letters and attorneys that had pull and all that stuff. Kids who didn't have money went. I didn't have any money, but I said, 'To hell with this, I'm not going.' I would have gone to Canada. But I told them, 'I'm my mother's sole support. My 'X' amount of dollars a year as a musician is supporting the family.' They went, 'Oh, O.K.' I got a temporary deferment. Then, when I was 20, they instituted the lottery. My number was 197 and the draft went to 195. I swear. And that's how I got out of the draft. I'm no less guilty than the guys who went off to Sweden and Canada and went underground as draft dodgers. When amnesty was declared, I felt a pang of relief myself. I'm not particularly proud of it, because I didn't dodge the draft for these political reasons. I just had nothing against the Vietnamese."[12] And, the prospect of being shot at in a rice paddy in Asia really didn't sound all that appealing to him.

Another thing that Billy wanted to get out of at this point, was his mother's house. As he put it philosophically, "Our parents moved out of Manhattan because they hated it, but we wanted to go into the city because that was 'Disneyland.' A lot of people subscribed to 'The American Dream'—they wanted a big house, more money. There weren't a lot of alternatives. Maybe if you won the lottery or made a killing in Vegas. Or if you worked in the factory 'X' amount of the time, you'd get to be foreman. They weren't grandiose dreams at all. The first thing to do was get out, get away."[17]

His freedom from high school, the draft, and parental direction became very important to him at this point. "I've always had this thing about independence," he admits. "It's a theme I always go back to. Breaking away, starting your own independence, moving away from home, standing on your own two feet: 'Movin' Out,' 'My Life,' 'Captain Jack.'"[18] Now, if he could just figure out where he was going, Billy, too, would be *moving out* soon.

4
WITH
THE HASSLES

IT WAS THROUGH having played at the New York State Tent of Tomorrow at the World's Fair in 1965 that the Lost Souls first became acquainted with Irwin Mazur, the manager of a group called the Hassles. Apparently Mazur was scouting for new acts to manage.

It just so happened that Mazur's family owned a rock club called My House. It was located in the Long Island town of Plainview, off Old Country Road, and situated in the Plainview Shopping Center. Not exactly the most chic or likely of locales for the launch of a major rock star, but that club was to become a pivotal location in Billy Joel's career.

When Mazur, who had been studying dentistry by day, assisted the Lost Souls in their becoming one of the regular house bands at My House, they were better able to continue to hone their craft. Several top pop acts would headline the club, such as Motown stars the Four Tops, and local Long Island hit makers the Young Rascals. These established acts appearing on the same stage gave them something to aspire toward achieving. And predictably, another band that often played at My House was the Hassles.

At the time the Hassles' lineup included vocalist John Dizek, drummer Jon Small, and the latter's brother-in-law Harry Weber. Harry was quite a talented keyboard player within the group. But unfortunately he also had a slight substance abuse problem: he liked to sniff glue.

Dizek recalls, "He was sniffing a lot. One time, on stage, I was singing my part and waiting for Harry to come in. I looked back to see where his harmony was. . . . Harry was playing the organ with one hand and had his head in a bag sniffing! Harry was crazy . . . as he became more into the glue, the scenes got uglier and uglier."[36]

Jim Bosse, the lead guitar player of the Lost Souls [a.k.a. the Commandos] remembers of this period, "We became kind of a house band at My House nightclub along with another band named The Hassles. Danny Mazur [My House club owner] came up with the idea of combining the two into a mega band with two drummers, two bass players, three guitars, two lead singers, and keyboard. After a few rehearsals it was chaos and would not work. So, in 1967 the better performers from the two bands were selected to stay in the new Hassles, and The Lost Souls ended. I didn't make the cut; Billy and Howie were the only ones from our band who did, although eventually only Bill stayed with The Hassles and Howie ended up with Ram Jam."[29]

Another one of the casualties of this new arrangement was glue-sniffing keyboard player Harry Weber, who was crushed by his discovery that he was going to be replaced in the Hassles by Billy Joel. His substance-induced mood swings and depression led him down a dark, downward spiral of despair. Unable to imagine life outside the band, Weber decided on suicide. He went to the nearest set of railroad tracks, reclined on the tracks, and was killed by an oncoming train. It seems to be a bizarre and dramatic way to take one's life. "Yes, he literally laid down on the train tracks," confirms Liberty DeVitto. "What an awful way to go!"[37]

One of the key members of the Hassles was the drummer Jon Small. As he remembers it, "I needed a replacement keyboard player after having a knock down, hair pulling fight. . . . I was now on a mission: find the next keyboard player who could kick Stevie Winwood's ass, playin' and singin.' . . . Enter Billy Joel. He was little, about 5′ 6″, his look was not of a rock star, but I didn't care. He could sing. I mean sing. What a voice! And bonus, he played the keys amazingly, in fact he played better than I could have ever wished for. But he was not interested in leaving his band. I pushed—actually bullshitted—him that The Hassles were the best. My efforts were lost; he was not leaving his band. I had to have him and he had too much integrity and love for the other guys in the band. What was I to do? No problem, I would just bribe him. I offered him a Hammond B-3 organ. . . . It was a $5,000 organ, not in Billy's reach—at least not yet. So you guessed it: Billy was now a Hassle."[29]

Irwin Mazur was convinced that his newly reformed lineup of the Hassles was going to be a hit for him, but the key to true success was to obtain a record deal for the band. Since Mazur didn't have the business contacts to do that, he decided that the best route toward accomplishing this task was to place himself in a record company job, and then sign the band he managed to the label. It wasn't long at all before he gave up on going to dental school, and landed a staff position working for Morris Levy, the head of Roulette Records.

Levy is quite a legendary guy in the music business. He had his fingers in just about every imaginable piece of pie—from publishing to recording to live venues to his own retail outlets. If there was ever a monopoly in action, it was Morris Levy.

Morris had also been in business with legendary deejay Alan Freed in the early 1960s. Freed was famous not only for his pop music promotional skills but also for his notorious payola scandal. (The term *payola* refers to bribing a radio station to play an artist's records on the air.) Freed's story was to serve as the inspiration for the film *American Hot Wax* (1978).

Roulette Records had been around for quite some time, and in fact their original hit act came when they signed Frankie Lyman and the Teenagers (of "I'm Not a Juvenile Delinquent" and "Why Do Fools Fall in Love" fame) to the brand-new label in 1960. However, it was in the mid-to-late sixties that the label made its greatest fortune on the group Tommy James and the Shondells. That group's string of a dozen smashes included "I Think We're Alone Now," "Mony Mony," and the number 1 hit "Hanky Panky." It is also part of rock & roll legend that Morris Levy made a fortune off Tommy James and the Shondells, and paid the band next to nothing—they became big stars, yet ended up financially broke. This illustrates the circle of music businessmen with whom the Hassles and seventeen-year-old Billy Joel were suddenly involved. In other words, it isn't exactly legitimate or legal when one person is the artist's manager, the record company president, *and* owns a piece of the record store as well.

The year 1967 was one that witnessed all sorts of musical changes, as well as being the time of the famed "Summer of Love." Tipped off by the release of the Beatles' incomparably revolutionary album *Sgt. Pepper's Lonely Hearts Club Band,* from that point forward, the rest of the decade would be heralded as the hippie era in America. It was time for music to go psychedelic, and on the charts that was exactly what happened. Such songs as "Incense and Peppermints" by the Strawberry Alarm Clock, "Green Tambourine" by the Lemon Pipers, "Hello, I Love You" by the Doors, and "Crimson and Clover" by Tommy James and the Shondells were changing the sound of popular rock music. Also, in the soul vein, artists such as Aretha Franklin ("Respect"), Otis Redding ("Dock of the Bay"), Sam & Dave ("Soul Man,"), and Marvin Gaye ("I Heard It through the Grapevine") were the hot voices of R&B.

Billy's musical heroes, the Beatles, still led the pack, with the group's continued string of number 1 hits, including "Penny Lane" (1967), "All You Need Is Love" (1967), "Hello, Goodbye" (1967), "Lady Madonna" (1968), "Hey Jude" (1968), "Get Back" (1969), and "Come Together" (1969). They continued to be his main songwriting and performing influences during this formative time in his musical development. Their creativity and their long-running reign on the charts was something that Billy longed to emulate.

In 1967 the Hassles were signed to United Artists Records, which was at the time the parent company of Roulette Records. Among the songs in the group's debut album was their first single, "You've Got Me Hummin,'" which was written by Isaac Hayes and David Porter. The song actually did make the charts and was a minor hit for the group. However, it never broke into "The Hot 100"singles chart in *Billboard* magazine. Instead it peaked at number 112 in that publication. The album tracks on their debut LP, *The Hassles,* also included the first recorded version of the song "Coloured Rain," which was later made famous by the group Traffic.

Originally the song "You've Got Me Hummin'" was a song that had been a minor hit for the soul duo Sam & Dave. It was Billy's attempt at being a "blue-eyed soul" singer. "This was typical of the kind of thing a lot of bands were doing then, covering the more obscure R&B artists. Of course, ours doesn't compare to the Sam & Dave recording," he admitted with a laugh.[1]

In 1968 the group went back in the studio to record their second album for United Artists: *Hour of the Wolf* (1969). This time around, instead of recording songs by other songwriters, Billy Joel's compositions dominated the disc. It became the first major showcase for his songwriting.

Describing the music found on that album, Billy explains, "It was an attempt at being psychedelic without ever having taken acid. It was a stab at that kind of imagery, but it really wasn't my kind of thing. The early songs were either about love and girls or pretty abstract stuff. When you're a teenager, you go through very heavy heartbreaks. You think your love is the only love in the world. I wrote a couple of those songs and then said, 'Well,

I've said that. Now I have to say something abstract and surreal.' So, I'd go on about the cosmic rings of Saturn. I couldn't relate to the San Francisco music like Grateful Dead and Jefferson Airplane. It was all a little too profound for me. I couldn't get into the heavy drug message of 'One pill makes you larger and one pill makes you small.' I thought Grace Slick was talking about aspirin. I didn't find out about drugs until later in life. I liked the folk stuff, but I couldn't relate to a lot of it because it was all acoustic guitar. It didn't transfer very well to the piano. 'Blowin' in the Wind' sounds pretty horrible on piano unless you do a sort of Gospel version."[12]

It was during this period that Billy moved out of his mother's house in Levittown, and rented his own apartment. According to him, it gave him a great sense of independence. "I was in a band—I think it was The Hassles—and we were making pretty good money, gigging steadily. Somehow I was making ends meet, and that was a big moment. I was a professional musician. So I moved out and got this little apartment. *My own place.*"[17]

The height of the Hassles' fame came when they were the opening act for Jose Feliciano in a 1969 concert as part of the Schaefer Music Festival in Central Park in New York City. Right afterward, the band split up. Summing up the Hassles' career, Billy says, "The group I was in, The Hassles, continued to appear in clubs and we put out an album. Our second album came out and when nothing happened, we just broke up."[12]

Jon Small explains the demise of the Hassles this way: "Two United Artists albums later we hated the other members of The Hassles. Billy and I had a bond. It's hard to say what the attraction was, but I can honestly say we were best friends. We did everything together. And I mean everything. What's it called? 'Sex, drugs and R&R?' We were rock stars. At least in our heads we were."[29]

The year 1969 was the height of the new hippie counterculture. It was a time to tie-dye everything one owned, load a bong, drop a tab of acid, and trek up to Woodstock for the most famous rock concert of all. And twenty-year-old Billy Joel was right in the middle of it.

However, Woodstock didn't exactly turn out to be the hippie utopia that Billy had hoped for. As he recalls, "I went to Woodstock, but I hated it. It was rain and mud and acid. I didn't like any of that. I stayed for one day. . . . I couldn't find any place to sleep but the mud. If you wanted to go to the bathroom, you had to wait in these long lines for these smelly Port-O-Sans. After a day, I thought, 'Well, I guess you have to be stoned.' I had nothing against it, just that I didn't do it. I hitchhiked home."[12]

His favorite performer from the whole Woodstock event was guitar god Jimi Hendrix. "I'm a Jimi Hendrix freak," proclaims Billy. "To me, he was a genius. And I don't throw 'genius' around. To me there's only a few of 'em. Jimi Hendrix was a genius like Mozart was a genius, George Gershwin, Aaron Copland, Bach."[18]

In the late 1960s, Billy and his buddy Jon Small once talked their way into a Jimi Hendrix concert that was being held at a venue called the Singer Bowl, which was located in the borough of Queens. The show was sold out, but that made the challenge even more exciting. Says Billy, "I did a pretty good English accent, and we bullshitted the people who worked for the promoter, like: 'Jimi's waiting for us, we've got to set up the amps.'" Well, the little charade actually succeeded. "We were told to sit on the stage and make sure the amps didn't fall over. Jon and I were on this revolving stage and I was waving to friends in the audience: 'Yeah,—it's me!'"[1]

Although he tried to fit in, Billy didn't feel entirely at home with the hippie movement. As he recalls, "We had long hair and we looked like drug addicts, but I hadn't even smoked pot yet. People assumed we were on drugs, but I missed it somehow. Later, I tried being a hippie for about two years. I was an absolute failure as a hippie. I didn't make it. I didn't turn on, I wasn't into 'flower power.' I'd give the peace sign like everybody else, but I just didn't feel it. The counterculture movement was a system all its own. Everybody had to wear beads and smoke pot and not wash his hair."[12]

Even the Beatles were in their hippie and pot-smoking phase, as witnessed on their latest and most drug-influenced album, *Abbey Road*. That was the album that supposedly revealed hidden messages when played backwards. One couldn't get more psychedelic than that. It was a time of "love-ins" and "be-ins." Trying to "go with the flow" after the demise of the Hassles, Billy and Jon Small formed their own psychedelic keyboard and drums duo, which they christened Attila.

Jon Small describes the band's evolution: "We started playing together every night and before we knew it we had a new sound. That's how Attila was born. A two man group—me on drums and Billy on his Hammond B-3. We played through 10 Marshall AMPs. We were heavy metal. If either of us had any sense we would have aborted it. But we signed with Epic Records, got a $50,000 advance and went on tour. We sucked. To be a rock star was easy. All you needed were English clothes, boots from your Granny Take[s] A Trip [a hip 1969-era clothing store] from the East Village, grow long hair and get a bad R&R attitude. We had it all. We were both overwhelmed by any English band: Traffic, [Jethro] Tull, and of course The Zep [Led Zeppelin]. We lived for English bands."[29]

As Billy explained it, "Jon and I decided to form a two-man group, really heavy Led Zeppelin, heavy-metal stuff. I figured out a way to wire the Hammond organ to amplifiers and make it sound like a guitar and also to play the bass on the keyboards. I played the organ, the guitar sound, my left hand was playing the bass and I played the harmonica and was screaming at the top of my lungs. Jon played the drums."[12]

Through Irwin Mazur's connections they got signed to Epic Records and released a self-titled album in 1970. Says Billy, "This was about the time Hendrix was out. His music really got to me, and The Hassles drummer and I decided we were gonna do a power duo. It was the loudest thing you ever heard. We made one album for Epic, called *Attila*. It had this weird cover. The art director has us in a meat locker, with carcasses hanging around us, and we were dressed up as Huns. I got talked into it."[14]

He later laughed about that whole experience, "Oh, God. I hated doing that photo session. Hated it! We were in the meat locker. I knew the record sucked. I thought, 'Maybe the album cover will help.' Ha!"[16]

With regard to the music, Billy explains, "Attila—destroyed the world with amplification. I had ten huge amplifiers. People would come just to see the setup. We released one album and played five or six gigs."[12]

One of the best tracks on the album was an instrumental Attila song called "Amplifier Fire," which is included in the *My Lives* boxed set. Says Billy, "This particular track was more of a jazz thing than a heavy metal thing. A lot of Attila was us trying to be Led Zeppelin with two instrumentals. This shows a different side of things. One of my big heroes was jazz organist Jimmy Smith."[1]

There were very few live performances by Attila; in fact, less than two dozen are reported. Entertainment investor Roger DiMaio remembers catching one of Attila's few concerts, in Connecticut. "Even then you could tell that Billy Joel was incredibly talented. I remember really liking the music that they played and their showmanship. I also recall that there was a lot of marijuana smoke in the air that night. You didn't even have to smoke anything, you just had to inhale, and you got high!"[38]

On the other side of the coin, Jimmy Greenspoon, the keyboard player for Three Dog Night, recalls, "I did own a copy of the *Attila* record, and I gotta say, buy them all up and destroy them," he laughs. "It's kinda like Michael Bolton in the leather phase, when he did *The Hunger*."[39] In other words, some people loved Attila, and some people totally hated it.

Either way, the group was short lived. Billy describes the duo's career by laughingly stating, "An album and my two-man group called 'Attila' receives rave reviews from two people—both of them our road managers. Exit: Atilla."[20]

Billy seriously felt that his life was on "hold" as the decade of the 1970s dawned. After releasing three albums with two groups, he was still not a rock star. Discouraged and broke, he began taking a series of odd jobs to make ends meet. In Locust Valley he painted the walls of the Piping Rock Country Club, and for a while he worked in a factory.

During this same period he also played piano on a track for rock legend Chubby Checker ("The Twist.") His work with Checker came as the opportunity to be the studio band behind the famed singer for a TV commercial for Bachman brand "twisted" pretzels. As Billy later explained it, "Between screwings by assorted sundry overnight managers, I got some studio work backing remarkable talents such as The Shangri-Las and Chubby Checker."[20] Still, this wasn't the kind of rock & roll stardom that he had been seeking.

After that, several more odd jobs followed in an attempt to make quick money. At one point he tried his hand at freelance writing. He started doing concert reviews for a couple of locally based publications: *Go* and *Changes* magazines: "Twenty-five bucks a pop: pretty good!" However when he found himself giving bad reviews to musicians he admired, he "didn't have the stomach for it." After writing a lousy review about an Al Kooper show he attended, he pulled the plug on his occupation as a critic. "To this day, I want to apologize [to Kooper]," he claims.[1] Billy found this a daunting assignment. Why should he be the one to dash the hopes of other musician's aspirations by writing critical reviews about their music? Obviously he was not cut out to be a rock critic. Instead, he was destined to be judged by them.

In the middle of 1970, with both the Hassles and Attila behind him, and no money in the bank, Billy felt that he was about to hit rock bottom. "My life was very scary. I didn't have a high school diploma. Nothing was working out for me musically. My big, heavy romance had broken up. I had no money, no place to live. I was sleeping in a laundromat. . . . I couldn't pay the rent. I was sneaking into empty houses, sleeping wherever I could. In the wintertime in New York, when it gets really cold, the only places that were warm on Long Island were the all night laundromats."[12]

What about returning to his mother's house? According to him, that was an option that was not very favorable to him at the time. "I did once or twice," he says, "but I felt like such a bum. I couldn't do it. Some way or another, I was going to stick it out, but I started thinking, 'What's the use?' You take yourself so seriously at that age. I'm sure everybody goes through it. I was feeling suicidal. . . . I thought my problems were the worst in the world. . . . I had been going with this girl and we split up. I felt really sorry for myself."[12]

At the height of his despair he decided that suicide was the only answer. In a fit of depression Billy Joel chose his highly unconventional "poison"— a bottle of Pledge furniture polish. It was not quite as toxic as Drano chemical sink declogger, nor as innocuous as Joy dishwashing detergent, but he literally and figuratively attempted to "polish" himself off.

As he explains it in retrospect, "I was 21 and I had no prospects: no high school diploma, my band had broken up, the girl I was with had split up with me. It was a period of intense self-pity. I thought, 'This is the easy way out.' I looked in the closet, and there was chlorine bleach, with that skull & crossbones warning. And then there was some kind of furniture polish, with a smaller skull & crossbones. So it really came down to a matter of flavor. I drank the furniture polish. I'll never forget: I was sitting on a chair, waiting to die. All of a sudden, my stomach starts to process this stuff. I ended up farting furniture oil. It came out in little dabs."[16]

As he sat there burping and farting furniture polish, he had an epiphany. It was time to seek professional help: "That's when I said, 'This is really sick,' and I checked myself into the observation ward at Meadowbrook Hospital. It was really the best thing I've ever done, because I saw people who really had problems. Guys kicking 'junk,' homicidal maniacs, schizophrenics. These people had no way out."[17]

Checking himself into the psychiatric ward of a hospital was a true wakeup call for Billy. "It was a version of [the film] *One Flew Over the Cuckoo's Nest.* I went to Meadowbrook Hospital in East Meadow, Long Island, and said, 'Listen, I'm going to do myself in. You'd better look me over.' Once you check in, you have to stay for three weeks. You have to take your clothes off. They give you a smock to wear with your ass hanging out, and they give you Thorazine all the time . . . and you sleep in a big room with all these other guys. They keep you sedated all the time while they observe you.[12]

"It was just a real shock to be in a ward where there were bars on the window and electric sliding doors. You were given a robe—no clothing, no laces, no belts. You weren't allowed to carry matches or razor. And you couldn't leave. You're in the snake pit. And I would go to the nurse's station and knock on the window, just like in *One Flew Over the Cuckoo's Nest*, and say, 'Hey, look, I'm O.K. These people are crazy, but I'm really O.K. Let me out of here.' They'd say, 'Sure Mr. Joel. Here's your Thorazine.' . . . They were giving everybody Thorazine. I didn't take them. I put them under my tongue and then spit them out. I met with these shrinks at the end of a couple of days, and they said, 'How do you feel?' I said, 'Get me out of here!' I said, 'I checked in because I was feeling suicidal. I no longer feel suicidal. I made a big mistake.' I suppose it was a healthy answer—you're supposed to want to get out. I was led out, the door was slid behind me, and I ran, and I never looked back. I said, 'Wow, that's the end of that chapter. . . . It scared the hell out of me."[40]

Finally he realized that he had come out the other end of the dark tunnel of despair in which he had been drowning. Looking back on this whole event, Billy was able to say that the whole suicide misadventure was quite therapeutic to have gone through. "It was like shock therapy in life and in what the priorities are: 'You're O.K. These people are not O.K.' When I got out, I had a different outlook. I said, 'I can make music, and I can fall in love again.' See, I never really said that my ambition was to be a rock star. I had been in groups for years and had gotten that out of my system. I wanted to be a songwriter. And everything else just followed after that."[17]

He felt that his senses had actually been sharpened. He also emerged from the hospital with a readjusted attitude as to what was or wasn't important in his life. He claims that he felt his emotions could then safely run the gamut from happy to sad, without remorse: "I feel things very deeply. I can get very angry, I can get sad. I don't get into self-pity—I was cured of that by going to this observation ward and seeing people who really had deep-seated problems. I'll only give myself about thirty seconds of good self-pity, and then this button switches on and goes, 'Get off it!'"[40]

Reflecting upon this rocky patch, he was later able to state with confidence, "[In] 1970 I went through some incredible mental changes. After seven years of trying to make it as a rock star, I decided to do what I always wanted to do: write about my own experiences and chuck the commercial influences. My friends encouraged me to go out as a single [act]: Oh well, what the hell, here I go!"[20]

Now, when he speaks of that traumatic "transitional time between adolescence and adulthood," he is able to make jokes about it. "That was a dark time, a time of great self-examination and self-obsession. I was examining my own navel so much that my head actually went up my butt," he laughs.[1]

With his three albums of music as part of a group, Billy had been able to showcase his piano- and organ-playing prowess. He had his own compositions recorded and released both by the Hassles and Attila. Now it was finally time for him to define his identity as a solo performer.

BILLY JOEL

5
COLD SPRING HARBOR

AFTER HIS BRIEF mental health interlude at Meadowbrook, for a while Billy lived in the home of Jon Small and his wife, the former Elizabeth Weber. The suburban Long Island house was constructed of large stones and concrete, in an Early American stone farmhouse fashion. Billy and his circle of pals dubbed the residence "the Rock House." He was among friends, and it sure was a far cry better than sleeping in an all-night laundromat to keep warm.

Jon and Elizabeth had a young son together, Sean, and for several months the couple, their son, and Billy lived there in a copacetic fashion. The house became what might be called during that era a "crash pad." In other words, it was a place where Jon's musical friends could crash for the night, or even take up residence when they needed a place to stay. Among the other musicians to stay there from time to time were their local buddies Bruce Gentile and Tom Davis.

With his misadventure from drinking Pledge furniture polish and his sojourn in the mental facility behind him, Billy was feeling more centered, more upbeat about his life. He was living with friends, he had a roof over his head, and Jon even had a white baby grand piano in the house for him to play.

The Rock House had a steeply pitched roof and a nice fireplace and was built very solidly on a strong foundation. What wasn't so strongly constructed was Elizabeth and Jon's marriage. According to several sources, Jon was something of a flirt, and his union with his wife was already on the wane. And there was her husband's former music partner and current buddy—lonely, cute, twenty-one-year-old Billy Joel—right in the house. Well, one thing led to another, and it wasn't long before Billy and Elizabeth were carrying on an affair in the Rock House, right under Jon's nose.

It was the dawn of what was known as the "me" decade of the 1970s. It was a time of swinging, wife swapping, and free love. If Jon Small realized or was upset that his former Attila partner was sleeping with his wife, apparently he didn't show it. Their marriage was about to dissolve anyway; if he did suspect anything, he didn't make an issue of it.

This was a time of partying and hanging out, and often Billy and his musician buddies would go out together to the local clubs. According to rock industry publicist David Salidor, "I saw Billy Joel several times in 1970 and 1971 at a club in Roslyn, Long Island, called My Father's Place. Everybody started there, Bruce Springsteen, Joan Jet, Dave Mason, everybody. WLIR-FM would even do live rock & roll broadcasts from My Father's Place. If you were on Long Island and you were looking to make it and make contacts, you had to go to My Father's Place. It was the Long Island version of Manhattan's Bottom Line in the Village. The funny thing about My Father's Place was that it was located right under a section of the Northern State Parkway, so they could make as much noise as they wanted. It was such an important club. In reality it was an unassuming dump of a club, but it was the place to go if you were an aspiring musician. Billy played there, hung out there, and got drunk there. That was like being at the Fillmore East of Long Island."[41]

The year 1970 marked the end of an era for Billy and millions of Beatles fans around the world. After a seven-year run as the most popular rock group in the history of record music, all four members of the band went off on their own. The group's final number 1 hits, "Let It Be" and "The Long and Winding Road" topped the charts that year. George Harrison was the first Beatle to score a number 1 solo hit with "My Sweet Lord" that December.

Billy was very unhappy about the breakup of the Beatles. For years they were his greatest musical idols. He longed to make music that was of the caliber that the Beatles' past decade of creativity had yielded. Bill Zampino recalls, "He loved The Beatles so much that after they broke up, he'd say,

'It's a shame you can't hear more songs from The Beatles. Maybe I'll write myself one to cheer me up,' and then he would."[10]

Throughout that year a whole new musical style had begun to emerge with the Jackson 5 ("I Want You Back"), Three Dog Night ("Mama Told Me [Not to Come]"), the Carpenters ("[They Long to Be] Close to You"), the Guess Who ("American Woman"), Sly and the Family Stone ("Thank You [Falettinme Be Mice Elf Agin]"), the Supremes ("Stoned Love"), and Bread ("Make It with You") all topping the charts.

This was a frustrating era for Billy, because his career seemed to have stalled already. Late one night, Irwin Mazur received an out-of-the-blue phone call from him. Billy was desperate to meet with Mazur immediately on Long Island. He sounded concerned and troubled, so Mazur met with him at an all-night diner. Billy poured out his whole story to the manager— from his post-Attila musical disappointment, to his suicide attempt, to his angst over his affair with Elizabeth.

Aside from using Mazur as his "shrink," Billy also made other confessions to him. He told him that he was totally broke, and depressed, and he didn't know what he was going to do with his life. According to Mazur, he told Billy Joel, "Listen, you've got to be a solo artist. This Attila bullshit is not going to happen. You've got to write me some great hit songs, and we're going to make you a star."[36]

Billy recalls, "I started writing songs on my own, taking odd jobs in New York in the meantime. I thought, 'Okay, I'm gonna be a songwriter and write for other people.' I had gotten the whole rock & roll thing out of my system, or so I thought. But everybody in the business told me, 'If you want other artists to hear your material, why don't you make a record?'"[14] With that, Irwin Mazur set about getting Billy signed to his own record deal.

During this time, Peter Schekeryk was a record company owner, and his label was called Neighborhood Records. He signed famed folk singer Melanie to his label, became the producer of all of her hit albums, and eventually married her. In 1970 he had an office on the eleventh floor of what was at the time the Gulf and Western Building. It was also the floor on which Paramount Records had their offices, and a man by the name of Artie Ripp was the head of that company. Schekeryk provides the details: "Billy Joel's manager at the time was Irwin Mazur. Irwin came to me and asked if I would pay for Billy's first solo singer-songwriter demo. Once I heard Billy sing, I agreed that he had a bright future in the business, and I agreed to finance the demo recording. I paid for the session, and told Mazur to come back to me when it was finished. By the time

Billy had recorded the demo, I had changed offices, and I was now located on the twelfth floor of the same building. Well, Irwin came up to the eleventh floor of the Gulf and Western Building to bring me the demo tape, so I could listen to it. Unfortunately, instead of going back down to the lobby to find out that I had since moved upstairs to the twelfth floor of the same building, Irwin got to the eleventh floor, couldn't find me, and knocked on the door of Paramount Records instead. There he ran into Artie Ripp. Irwin was so desperate for money at the time that, the minute that Artie Ripp offered him a cent for Billy's contract, he accepted the deal, and instantly signed Billy Joel to the worst possible deal that he could take."[42]

Claims Schekeryk, "If he had only gone upstairs one floor to find me, I would have gladly signed Billy Joel to Neighborhood Records, like I intended on doing in the first place. Billy would have had a much better deal than the one that Artie saddled him with. Not only did Artie Ripp end up making an eventual fortune by signing Billy Joel to Paramount Records, but Irwin Mazur never paid me the money that he owed me for financing the demo. I could have saved Billy millions of dollars by signing him to a fair and equitable deal with my label, Neighborhood Records. To this day I feel that Irwin Mazur not only defaulted on paying me for the demo recordings that got Joel his first record deal, but I never received credit for being the first record company president to recognize Billy's true talent. I feel like I was the one who was the first to discover and appreciate Billy's true talent, but it was Artie Ripp who ended up with all of the credit and a ton of money."[42]

Unfortunately, the deal he made for Billy's solo recording career painfully exposed Mazur's naïveté in the business. Since they had been turned down by every other label in town, he grabbed a horrifyingly slanted deal that called for Billy to sign a management contract with Family Productions, a company held by Ripp, a man with a long history in the record business.

Here was Billy Joel, straight out of the mental institution, and back into the music biz. Well, that is at least somewhat better than it going in the opposite direction! According to him, "The music business back then was run by 'looney tunes' and outlaws from the *schmatte* [Yiddish for "rag," i.e., garment] business. Did they care that I'd been in the hospital? No. Those were freewheeling days when anything was possible."[1]

The deal that he signed with Mazur and Paramount Records also signed away a huge piece of Billy's rights to his songwriting royalties, his publishing, and his copyrights. From a certain perspective, it seemed like the thing to do at the time. Financially speaking, he felt he was between a rock and a hard place. They presented the contract, he picked up a pen and signed it, and he received a check. At the time, it was the only check that anyone was offering.

Looking back on this deal, which was to financially cripple him for years, Billy explains, "I was only 20, and it's so easy to take advantage of musicians. I didn't know what was going on. . . . I didn't know anything about publishing or monies that were owed to me."[43] In other words, this was one of the most shortsighted deals ever conceived. It spelled out quick cash, and a potential lifetime of financial disaster.

However, at the time, all he could think of was the fact that he was going to be getting a monthly paycheck, and that he actually had a solo record deal. According to Billy, "As you sign a record contract, you go through this change, because as soon as you put your name on the paper, you're an 'artist.' The record contract says, 'Billy Joel, herein referred to as 'The Artist,' and automatically you become an artist just by signing."[43]

Seated in his photo-lined Long Island recording studio office, Richie Cannata, Billy's longtime saxophone player, speaks of the crooked publishing deal Billy had signed with Artie Ripp. "You would have to get the real story from Billy, but as the story goes, is that Billy was down and out, and he had—it could have been ten songs, it could have been thirty songs, I am not sure how many. See the gold records on the wall? Well, see that little insignia? Well that's the Artie Ripp symbol on it," he says, gesturing to the Family Productions insignia that uses the famed image of the mother wolf nursing Romulus and Remus, of pre-Roman Italy. "As the story goes, Billy sold a great deal of his publishing; gave it up to Artie for a very small price. I heard a number, and I was shocked. But when you are starving, a couple thousand dollars sounds great: 'I can get a car, and I can eat!' And, that's what happened. Artie Ripp had the publishing. It was a poor situation for Billy at that time. Then again, if you talked to Artie Ripp about this deal, I am sure he would say, 'Hey, he was broke at the time, and I offered him the money. I didn't push him. I didn't twist his arm.' And, who knew that those were going to be hit songs? Who knew? I mean, my God, it might have been twenty or thirty songs."[44]

This was all new territory for Billy Joel. All he knew was that he had a record deal, and he was about to record his first solo album. As far as he was concerned, he had "hit the big time." It wasn't until this deal went sour that clarity came to the young singer-songwriter.

Looking back on it, he concedes, "It was a real screw job. I didn't know what I was signing. But I probably would have signed anything to get a deal. I got an advance so I could buy a piano and pay the rent."[12]

Billy complained that he was sick of the way he was being treated by the New York music business, and he wanted a change of scenery. When Irwin Mazur made the arrangements for Billy to record in L.A., he leapt at the opportunity. It was in California that Billy recorded the majority of his first solo album for Paramount Records, at the Record Plant in West Hollywood in July 1971. This was his initial taste of the California sun, and he genuinely liked what he saw out there. After that, he returned to New York. Two additional songs, "Why Judy Why" and "You Look So Good to Me," were recorded at Ultrasonic Recording Studios in Hempstead, New York. Says Billy offhandedly, "So, we made a record, and I'm not gonna go into what a trauma *that* was."[18]

Billy wrote all of the songs on the album and recorded every one of them live on the piano in the studio. There was no time to overdub any of the tracks. This was his big chance to become a recording star, and he tried to get everything to turn out just the way he wanted it. For instance, Billy hated the press bio that Paramount Records had prepared to send out about him, so he took matters into his own hands. He wrote his own letter to the press, and let that speak for him. In part it read:

Dear Whomever:

After reading the biography the record company has written about me, I have decided that unless I write this myself, you're going to get a lot of jive superlatives and dull 'hep-cat' talk . . . I record an album with some incredible people: Larry Knechtel, Rhys Clark, Denny Siewell, [*sic*] Sneaky Pete. I call it *Cold Spring Harbor* because—well you figure it out . . .

Right now I'm living in a beautiful little hamlet called Oyster Bay on the North Shore of Long Island. We do a lot of fishing there. And an unhealthy amount of drinking. But then, that's my idea of the good life.

The record company gave me a piano so I'm writing a lot of new things. As you know, they'd like to present me as a dynamic electric personality. Well, on-stage I get it on pretty well, but otherwise, I'm about as sparkling as warm beer.

I hope you like the album, but if you're not crazy about it, it makes a great Frisbee.

Love,
Billy Joel[20]

Unfortunately, everything went haywire when it came for Billy's debut album *Cold Spring Harbor* to be released. The most disastrous thing to take place was the fact that the entire album was literally mastered and pressed at the wrong speed. And, the worst thing about it was that no one even discovered the problem until it was too late to fix.

According to Artie Ripp, "The strangest thing happened. The sixteen-track machine ran slow, and when we mixed the final master, Billy sounded like a chipmunk. I said, 'Billy, it doesn't matter if it's fast or slow. We'll remix it sometime later in our lives.'"[14]

What kind of crap is that to tell an artist? Here Billy had poured his heart and soul into these songs, and the record company completely screwed up the album by mastering it at the wrong speed. How could Billy not be pissed off and disgusted?

Although the technical difficulties with the vinyl version of the *Cold Spring Harbor* album marred its initial release, in 1984 it was purchased, remixed, and rereleased by Columbia Records in a speed-corrected version. The CD incarnation of the album that is available today reveals that it is in reality a simply produced, well-crafted, finely written collection of sensitive songs. The album contains ten Billy original compositions, and it remains the purest example of his raw talent as a young songwriter and singer, as well as an accomplished pianist. His keyboard work is very clearly up front in the mix, and his voice sounds young and fresh.

The other musicians on this album were comprised of several studio pros, including "Sneaky" Pete Kleinow (who—along with Graham Parsons and Chris Hillman—was one of the founding members of the Flying Burrito Brothers). Pete also played on Joni Mitchell's highly acclaimed *Blue* LP, John Lennon's *Mind Games,* and Jackson Browne's self-titled debut album, so he was very well respected in the business. *Cold Spring Harbor* also included on its tracks bass player Larry Knechtel, who also found fame as part of the group Bread during this era.

The album opens with the beautiful love ballad "She's Got a Way," in which Billy sings of a love who has mesmerized him. It represents one of his most serious and adult compositions. Still one of his finest pieces, "She's Got a Way" instantly labeled him as a masterfully sensitive balladeer in the Cat Stevens/James Taylor mode.

"You Can Make Me Free" finds Billy singing to his complex, and lightly classical, piano work. It starts out slowly and then effectively builds and soars midsong, to become something of a soulful rock number.

"Everybody Loves You Now" shows off his true keyboard dexterity. This rapidly paced rocker is about someone who becomes famous, and then changes his or her personality along the way. "Everybody Loves You Now" perfectly confronts the ironic duality of a life in show business. There is also some great drum work on this album—Rhys Clark and Denny Seiwell— which in this song is a brilliant precursor to some of the excitingly drum-heavy rock music that Billy would later make on record.

"Why Judy Why," which finds Billy singing to an acoustic guitar solo, is a charmingly lamenting ballad of love lost. Here Billy sings to his older sister. In the lyrics he asks Judy why his latest love affair has ended poorly, with the object of his affection hanging up the telephone on him. "Falling of the Rain" features Billy's beautiful piano playing, which intricately mimics the downpour of a rainstorm. Although he would later claim that song lyrics aren't as important to him as a melody is, here he captures the mood of a rainy afternoon in this simple but effective tune. It foreshadows the sensitivity of his later work.

With "Turn Around" Billy made the first of many forays into country music. In this song, which features the Nashville-tinged steel guitar work of Sneaky Pete, Billy sings of a girl named Eliza whom he can't get off his mind. Does he turn around and come back? One never finds out in this haunting ode to a love lost.

"You Look So Good to Me" is a clear attempt for Billy to write a light and radio-friendly pop ballad. Complete with his own Dylan-like harmonica playing, he was clearly out to hit all of the bases. "Tomorrow Is Today" is more of a serious and introspective song. In the lyrics, Billy ponders the concept of time, as night becomes day. He questions waiting for good things to come "tomorrow" and then laments that tomorrow—in reality—never comes. This is a beautiful showcase for Billy and his lone piano. The result is simple and it is one of his most effective performances on this under-stated album.

"Nocturne" is the album's lone instrumental piece. A solo piano piece by Billy, it would be his first recorded foray in composing and playing his own form of classical music. It was a preview of coming attractions for him, as he would resume his fascination with penning classical music in the late 1990s.

The *Cold Spring Harbor* album ends with "Got to Begin Again," which finds Billy again accompanying himself on the piano. In this beautiful and soul-searching song, Billy ponders going to sleep and rising out of the ashes of his former self in the morning, like the mythical Phoenix bird of Greek lore. In reality, that was exactly what he was attempting to do with this album.

Technical problems or not, he still had a record out there in the marketplace, and now he had to do all he could to sell it. As he explained of his situation at that time, "So now that you made a record, the only way people are gonna hear the record is if you go on the road and promote it. I didn't mind doing it, it just seemed an awful weird way to be a songwriter. What the hell did I know? I was 21, which is old enough to be legal and sign things away, but still young enough to be stupid. So I did that, and went on the road . . . with this album that was never gonna go anywhere anyway."[18]

One of the most unfortunate things that happened was that the music included on Billy's debut solo album received virtually no radio airplay. Record producer Peter Schekeryk recalls a conversation with one of the most respected disc jockeys in the business: Alison Steele. Possessing a rich and distinctive "whiskey" voice, Steele went by the on-air moniker "the Nightbird." She was an influential legend in the radio world. "I remember talking to Alison," says Peter, "and we spoke about Billy Joel and his first album on Paramount Records—which I should have been the producer of. She said to me, 'Billy is great as a songwriter, but I just hate his voice. It is horrible for radio. He will never make it in this business. I can't play his songs on my show.'"[42]

By virtue of having an album out in the marketplace, Billy Joel now had a reason to go out on the road to perform in front of live audiences. From the very beginning, Billy was known for being lively and animated onstage. Since Joe Cocker and his *Mad Dogs and Englishmen* tour and album were huge hits at the time, Billy would regularly do his own impersonation of Cocker as part of his act. It was a short-lived routine, however. "In the early days, I did it, but we couldn't hinge everything on that. We had to give a good show. I stopped doing the impersonation because everybody went, 'He's the guy who does a great Cocker impersonation,' which was not what I wanted to be known for," Billy recalls.[12] On occasion he was also known to impersonate Ray Charles, Stevie Wonder, and Paul McCartney amid his act.

The *Cold Spring Harbor* tour not only took him all over the United States but was his first introduction to foreign locales. One of these stops was being billed as the Caribbean version of Woodstock. It was being held in Puerto Rico, and it was an outdoor musical event called Mar y Sol.

BILLY JOEL

Among the eclectic group of acts on the bill for this festival was Billy's jazz idol, Dave Brubeck. That alone was a huge thrill for Billy. Also appearing at Mar y Sol were Alice Cooper, Herbie Mann, the Mahavishnu Orchestra, and Emerson, Lake and Palmer.

However, Mother Nature didn't quite cooperate with this supposed festival in the sun, as it poured the day of the concert. Attendance was sparse and spirits were dampened, but Billy and his band were to end up being one of the prime hits of the event. To get the crowd's attention he had to make a dramatic move. Mazur takes credit for having suggested that Billy open up his act with his version of the Joe Cocker rendition of the Box Tops' hit "The Letter." So, he took Mazur's advice and launched into the song, and—much to his surprise—the crowd went wild.

A writer for the *New York Times*, Don Heckman, covered the event and reported, "The first real excitement was generated by Billy Joel's gospel-tinged rock band. Building up a charge that was reminiscent of the work of the old Leon Russell–Joe Cocker combine, the Billy Joel group brought some life to what had been a generally dispirited environment."[45] Unbeknownst to Billy, among the people who were there huddled in the rain observing him were representatives from Columbia Records. He couldn't have known at the time how important a fact that would be for him in the future.

Another of his performances on the *Cold Spring Harbor* tour was a gig in Philadelphia's Sigma Studios. It was part of a specially broadcast live concert for contest winners, sponsored by radio station WMMR. As part of the show, Billy performed a song that he had yet to record, a song about a drug dealer, "Captain Jack." The show was recorded, and WMMR started playing the song regularly. It became such a big hit that it wasn't long before New York City stations got a hold of the copy, too. Due to this sudden FM radio exposure, on a certain level, Billy Joel was becoming something of a "cult" artist. Columbia Records heard him via that track being played constantly on the airwaves. Already he was starting to make some noise in the industry.

Yet, in his eyes, the *Cold Spring Harbor* album and subsequent tour was something of a disaster. First, there was the disappointing sound quality of the album itself. Then there was the seemingly futile concert tour. "We toured for six months," Billy recalls. "Nobody got paid. We ate peanut butter sandwiches. I never saw the record in a store anywhere. I never heard it on the radio," he adds with disgust. "After six months, I said, 'Something's not right here.' That's when I realized I'd blown it. When I got home, I was supposed to get a rent check from the record company. It didn't come. I hate being in debt. I hate owing money."[12]

Meanwhile, there was a lot going on in Billy's personal life as well, particularly his relationship with Elizabeth Small. According to Billy, "We had been friends since The Hassles. While I was making *Cold Spring Harbor,* she had divorced Jon [Small]. When I came back to Oyster Bay, we started seeing each other more and more and finally got a house together in Hampton Bays [New York]—the working section of the Hamptons, not South Hampton or East Hampton. We got a little house right on the water and lived there in the off season 'cause we wanted to be alone. She was going to Adelphi [College]. She came out on tour with me then, and we've been together since."[12] They were both ready for a change, and the idea of moving to California seemed like the perfect antidote for everything that was going wrong in their lives.

They packed their bags one day, and away they went. "We put everything in Elizabeth's station wagon and drove across the States," explains Billy. "I was going to get out of a bad business deal and get myself a lawyer and different management. I knew I'd got screwed. The people who did it were in L.A. I figured that was a good base of operation for me to try to get out of the deal. And, that they weren't going to look for me right under their noses."[12]

The music business wasn't the only thing they were running away from. According to Liberty DeVitto, "Jon came home one day, and they were gone. At the time Jon had custody of their son, Sean. Billy and Elizabeth took Sean, and they ran off to California together. Jon had no idea where they were."[3]

Artie Ripp was having financial problems of his own at the time. It seemed that the deal he made between his company, Family Productions, and Paramount Records, was going sour. Says Billy, "I went to the West Coast. I just disappeared. I really didn't want to leave, but I had to get out of these contracts [with Paramount, and with Artie Ripp] and I didn't want these people to know what I was doing."[14] He wanted out of his record contract, no matter what the cost!

At first, Billy, Elizabeth, and Sean lived in a small place located just off of one of the Los Angeles freeways. Although they were residing in the West Coast paradise of Southern California, their existence was anything but glamorous. Then they fell into a deal that was much more to their liking. The director of publicity for Artie Ripp's Family Productions was a woman by the name of Sandy Gibson. At the time she owned a house in the Malibu Hills. When Gibson suddenly moved to New York City, Billy assumed her mortgage payments of $219 a month. For the rest of their time in L.A., he, Elizabeth, and Sean lived in Sandy and her husband John's vacated A-frame house.

To completely separate himself from the "Billy Joel" who released the album that was mastered at the wrong speed, he decided to bill himself as "Bill Martin." He virtually reinvented himself, and in his new persona he became a piano bar/lounge singer.

Why "Bill Martin?" According to William Martin Joel, "That's my name. So I thought I was going to live in L.A. temporarily, just long enough to get my contract renegotiated, but because it was nice and an easy place to live, we stayed—for three years. I got an agent to book me and I worked first at a place called Corky's."[12]

Then, he ended up taking a job as the lounge singer at the Executive Lounge, in "the Valley": "I used the name Bill Martin, and I got a gig working in a piano bar for about six months. It was all right. I got free drinks and union scale, which was the first steady money I'd made in a long time. I took on this whole alter-identity, totally make-believe; I was like Buddy Greco, collar turned up and shirt unbuttoned halfway down. The characters that Steve Martin and Bill Murray do as a goof [on TV's *Saturday Night Live*, circa 1980], I was doing it too, only people didn't know I was kidding. They thought, 'Wow, this guy is really hip!'"[14]

While in the L.A. sunshine, he also indulged in all of the key countercultural activities of the day. "I smoked pot when I lived in California. For some reason or another, it made sense. It was just part of what they call 'the mellow life.' Everything was laid back. We got into natural foods: the whole thing," he says. "I tripped on acid when I was in California. I saw rocks move. It scared the hell out of me: 'I don't know if I'm ready for that stuff!'"[12]

It was while he was performing as Bill Martin that a vision of his new identity and his surroundings came to him, which became his signature song, "Piano Man." Obviously the piano man in the song is Billy himself. "John was the bartender," he explains. "There was this guy, Davy, who *was* in the Navy. Paul *was* a real-estate broker, but he wanted to be a novelist. Elizabeth was working there as a cocktail waitress. She wore this hot little cocktail outfit and tried to go fishing for tips. We never let people know we were living together."[12]

Meanwhile, the record charts from 1971 to '72 continued to grow and evolve. Singer-songwriters were consistently hitting number 1 in America during this era, including Carole King ("It's Too Late"), Melanie ("Brand New Key"), Don McLean ("American Pie"), Neil Young ("Heart of Gold"), Neil Diamond ("Song Sung Blue"), and Harry Nilsson ("Without You"). Other chart-topping acts included Isaac Hayes ("Theme from *Shaft*"), Cher ("Gypsys, Tramps and Thieves"), America ("A Horse with No Name"), and Three Dog Night ("Black and White").

Another significant event that happened during this time was Billy's reunion with his father, Howard Joel. It was the first time he had seen his dad in over a decade. "In 1972, I did a European tour and I was trying to track him down. All I knew was there was a Howard Joel who worked for General Electric. Just as I was leaving to go back to the States from Milan, I got a telegram: 'urgent: we've reached your father.' My heart's pounding. I flew back to the United States and it was like a movie, really dramatic. The strings would have come in then."[12]

Billy was surprised to find that his father was not living in Germany at all, as he had thought. Instead, Howard Joel resided in Vienna, Austria. The real bombshell came when he found that in the interim, since Billy had last laid eyes upon him, Howard Joel had remarried a woman by the name of Audrey, and together they had a son, Billy's half brother Alexander. Billy had previously known nothing of this.

"We had moved to California and he was coming in to LAX," Billy recalls. "He got off the plane. I knew immediately it was him. For all he knew, I had been killed in Vietnam or I was a drug addict. We've got the same eyes. . . . Anyway, it was awkward for a while. We just kind of sat. We didn't know what to talk about. So he came to my house. This was around the time of 'Piano Man.' I wasn't making a lot of money, but I was doing all right. So, basically, it turned out that this guy who I was fantasizing about all my life was a nice man. It's been fine since then."[12] Although his reunion with his father went well, there has never been a real warm closeness that has ever taken place between the two of them. There is still reportedly an uncomfortable feeling between them, caused by Billy's unresolved feelings of abandonment.

Billy was fascinated to focus his gaze on the man he might grow up to resemble. It was as though his own father was a mythical character come to life. "He's got the same bug eyes," says the singer with amazement. "It's very strange. I mean, we look a lot alike in a way, and he's looking at me like, 'Is that what I *used* to look like?' and I'm looking at him like, 'Is that what I'm *gonna* look like?' He's a great piano player in the classic sense. Trained by a Prussian."[14]

Finally, after several months in California, Billy was released from his contract with Paramount Records: "Eventually, the people who had me under contract—and couldn't find me—realized that they were either going to have to renegotiate and compromise or they weren't going to get anything out of me. It was 1972. I was about twenty-three. I still had no idea what a mess this whole business is."[14]

Meanwhile, Irwin Mazur shopped Billy and his newly written music around. After a couple of serious offers from different record labels, Billy ended up accepting a new contract at Columbia Records. It seemed that the head of the label, Clive Davis, took a genuine interest in him, and offered him a lucrative contract.

As the *New York Daily News* later reported, "Columbia Records head Clive Davis, who had seen Joel play a festival date in Puerto Rico, came by the Executive Lounge and offered him a handsome deal."[21]

Billy confirms, "They renegotiated my deal and I got signed to Columbia. I was finally on a good label. Clive Davis was the president and had seen me play before. When word leaked out that Billy Martin at the Executive Room was actually Billy Joel, he came down and heard me there. So we were offered a deal."[12]

Clive's tenure at Columbia Records had been a long and very fruitful one. It was Davis who in the past had signed such diverse talents as Janis Joplin, Bruce Springsteen, and Sly and the Family Stone. He was known as being something of a Svengali in the music business. Recognizing Billy's talent and signing him to Columbia were to be two of Clive's most insightful moves. Obviously Billy's move to California did much more than just offer him a change of scenery. It really straightened things out. Billy Joel ended up making a whole new start with a new record deal and a sizable paycheck. Fortunately for him, the best was still yet to come.

6
PIANO
MAN

BY 1972 A whole new movement was sweeping the music business. It was officially the era of the singer-songwriter as recording star. It all started when Carole King's historic *Tapestry* album hit number 1 the previous year, and proceeded to sit on top of the charts for a record-breaking fifteen weeks. In March 1972 Carole virtually conquered the Grammy Awards, picking up several honors including Record of the Year, Song of the Year, and Album of the Year. The onetime best-selling album of all time, *Tapestry* is still ranked as the biggest-selling solo album by a female artist. With the success of Carole, suddenly every record label in the business was scrambling to discover and sign their own singing songwriters and turn them into recording stars.

The new wave of singing and songwriting solo recording artists who emerged in the spotlight during this time included Cat Stevens, Paul Williams, Roberta Flack, Carly Simon, Jonathan Edwards, Laura Nyro, Melanie, Nickolas Ashford and Valerie Simpson, Jim Croce, and Harry Chapin. Without a doubt, this was the perfect juncture for Billy Joel to be signed to a new solo recording contract.

According to Melanie, "It was an incredibly exciting time to be in the music business, especially if you could play your own guitar or your own piano, and you also wrote your own songs. After 'Brand New Key' hit number 1 I was able to immediately produce three more top 40 hits right afterward. We were all scrambling to come up with innovative and deeply personal songs. It was no wonder Billy Joel was sought out and signed by Columbia Records during this era. He had the voice, he had the insightful writing skills, and he could play the piano brilliantly."[46]

With his new recording deal at Columbia, everything was in place for Billy Joel to become one of the hot new singer-songwriters on the scene. It was the ideal time for him to emerge as an important voice in popular music. Although he originally thought of himself as a Burt Bacharach or Kris Kristofferson type of songwriter, the kind better known for his compositions, he was clearly destined for a life in the spotlight.

Although he had been on two albums by the Hassles, one Attila album, and his own *Cold Spring Harbor*, Billy didn't feel like a full-fledged headliner until the *Piano Man* album. Looking back on this period, he describes how others' careers affected the path he took: "James Taylor, Joni Mitchell, Paul Simon, Judy Collins, Jackson Browne, Jimmy Webb; all these singer/songwriters were coming into the forefront. So I said, 'Okay.'"[31]

While he was living in Malibu, Billy Joel wrote the majority of the songs that were to appear on his first Columbia Records album, *Piano Man*. He used the time that it took to iron out his legal and contractual problems to pen several new tunes: "In the meantime, I had written all the songs for our album. I was just trying to be a better songwriter."[12]

Billy went into the recording studio with producer Michael Stewart, sound engineers Michael Omartian and Jimmie Haskell, and a group of top-notch session musicians. All of the songs on the album weren't freshly written compositions, "Some of the things on *Piano Man* are old. 'Captain Jack,' 'Billy the Kid,' and 'Travelin' Prayer' are two years old. The rest of it comes from about six months ago. . . . I'm not sure what I'm aiming at with this album. I guess they're just songs."[47] Regardless of what he was or wasn't aiming for, what he ultimately ended up with was something of a career-defining LP.

In the show business realm, the project that you initially become famous for is the one that you will forever be associated with. "The way you enter the game in this business is usually the way you stay," says Joni Mitchell with regard to the record world. "It takes a lot to break typecasting and the way you come into the game is crucial, which was something I didn't realize at the time. In retrospect, I didn't realize the importance of it."[48] This was about to happen to Billy Joel when he released this new album. From this point forward he would constantly be referred to as "the Piano Man."

From his very first solo album, Billy also set a lifelong pattern for touching on several different musical styles on each disc. "I really don't know when I start an album, where it's gonna end up," he explains. "The process usually works like this. I always try to come up with some kind of concept so I'm motivated to sit down and begin this huge process. I'll say, 'Here's the concept for the album,' and it never goes the way I plan it to go, never. I try to organize things, I try to direct where it's going to go. I can't control the muse. I write one song and then because my musical instinct is to write some kind of variation away from that type of music, I'll write something in reaction to the song I just wrote. If I wrote a slow song, I'll write something fast. If I wrote something really loud and hard, I'll write something soft. If I wrote something in one key, I'll write something in a completely different key, an unrelated key. Purely for variation. I love variation. I can't stand tedium. I can't stand monotony. It drives me nuts."[31] This was to become a career-long pattern for him.

The *Piano Man* album opens with one of Billy's quirkiest compositions, the country-flavored "Travelin' Prayer." It sounds like more of a skiffle tune than a rock ballad but plays right into the whole country rock movement that was taking place at the time. Linda Ronstadt was delving into country songs at Capitol Records at the time, and the Nitty Gritty Dirt Band brought their guitar and banjo style of country rock to the top 10, with the recent hit "Mr. Bojangles." The fact that country singer-songwriter Kris Kristofferson had given blues rocker Janis Joplin her biggest hit—1971's posthumously released "Me and Bobby McGee"—only further blurred the border lines between rock and country.

The folksy, country-sounding "Travelin' Prayer," although an odd song in the extensive catalog of Billy Joel recordings, actually set the tone for this to be more of a friendly and accessible album. In "Travelin' Prayer," Billy sings of wanting his lover to get home safely from her travels. The banjo solo by Eric Weissberg, of "Dueling Banjos" fame—in the middle of the number—conjures a mental picture of travel by train. In a way, this song sounds a bit like Billy-does-Woody-Guthrie, but somehow he makes it work.

Says celebrity photographer Derek Storm, "'Travelin' Prayer'—banjos and mouth harps from a *piano rock guy?* I'd say this song alone shows Billy can truly write a song. Dolly Parton did a cover of this, too."[49]

Obviously, the one song on this album that Billy will forever be identified with is the infectious and intricately crafted title track, "Piano Man."

BILLY JOEL

In this piano- and harmonica-based song, he weaves an involved story around a simple but beautiful melody. He sings of the misfits who hang out in dark cocktail lounges, drinking away their problems. He tells of cocktail waitresses, and sad men whose lives are passing them by, and how they all converge here, in this piano bar in Anytown, USA.

According to him, the song is not a spoof or a takeoff, it is an homage. He refers to it as "an appreciation for the fact that I don't have to do that gig anymore. I've never, in all my tribulations in the music business with lawsuits and ripoffs and endless tours and whatever turmoil goes on in myself, I've never given myself more than two seconds of self-pity ever since I realized that the piano bar gig is something a lot of people have to do for years and maybe for their entire lives. And they're happy to have the work. I didn't like doing that job, but it was the only job I was qualified to do, so I have an appreciation of that. Also, an understanding of how other musicians are sometimes forced to make a living. It was a street experience and I think you turn that into a source of material. I also learned that when I don't know a song, and when I was asked to play a standard and I didn't know it, if you play enough major sevenths in a row, people think you're actually playing the song they requested!" he says with a laugh.[31]

When this album was released he was constantly asked in the press if he was mimicking Dylan when he added the harmonica to the song "Piano Man." According to Billy, "Of course I was. I remember I saw Bob Dylan when he played in the Village in the early '60s. He was wearing that harmonica holder. The first thought was, 'Oh, this guy's been in a car accident'—I thought it was some kind of neck brace. I always loved Dylan's style of harmonica playing: he breathes in, he breathes out. And if his lips happen to hit the right notes, great."[16]

"Ain't No Crime," with its gospel chorus backing, is something of a song of forgiveness. In it, Billy Joel sings about all of the questionable behavior that he can tolerate, about binge drinking and passing out on the floor, and how it isn't a crime to get out of hand every once in a while. Billy also proclaims in these lyrics how he is not at all judgmental about someone who floats in and out of another relationship. Yet this woman comes to see that person sometimes on lonely nights. It logical to assume that part of the inspiration for this song was Elizabeth's relationship with Jon Small and Billy. This is a rock & roll composition that is very indicative of the changing sexual mores of the '70s decade.

Each of the songs included on the *Piano Man* album seem to derive its inspiration from very different and very real aspects of Billy's life. As for any good balladeer, love is a recurring theme in his writing. Love, the pursuit of it, the attainment of it, the frustration for lack of it, and the loss of it, is a subject that has always been present in his music. During this phase of his life, the person whom he clearly composed his love songs for was Elizabeth.

Another beautiful medium-paced ballad with a country touch is "You're My Home." Throughout the years Billy found that "You're My Home" has grown to become one of his best-loved songs about love and devotion. Here he addresses his life on the road, and how lonely it gets out there when Elizabeth is not with him.

He recalls, "I wrote 'You're My Home' for her. It's corny but true. I didn't have any money to give her a present, so I said, 'This is for you,' and she said, 'Does that mean I get the publishing rights?' That's when I started thinking about her getting involved in management."[21] Again, "You're My Home" relies on Sneaky Pete's distinctive steel guitar cries in the background. Also, the reverberating guitar work by Larry Knechtel definitely sounds like some of the effects he was also contributing to several of the classic Bread songs he recorded during this period.

As this was the height of Billy Joel's big West Coast phase, what could be more American West than a song about one of the most legendary of the Wild, Wild West's outlaws? In "The Ballad of Billy the Kid," he took his shot at singing about a life of bank robberies and horseback riding escapes. The song sums up the historic outlaw's life of crime, up to and including his capture, and ultimate hanging. Musically, there is a whole sweeping orchestral background that makes it sound like the music from a western epic film such as the grandiose *How the West Was Won*.

In "Worse Comes to Worst" Billy again relies on his cocktail lounge job for inspiration. Here he summarizes his life situation in California circa 1972. He again sings of making his living in a piano bar, yet he instinctively predicts that somehow he will get ahead. He keeps claiming in the chorus of this song that he knows a woman in New Mexico. Who is this woman? Georgia O'Keefe? An ex-lover? Who knows? All Billy knows here, in this slightly calypso-sounding number, is that if worse comes to worst, somehow he will end up landing on his feet.

"Stop in Nevada" is another foray into country rock territory. Here he sings of a woman who is running away in her automobile. Like some sort of solo *Thelma and Louise* trip, she is escaping from her life. In this instance, she is running from the East Coast to the western haven of California. Along the way she stops off in Nevada. For a Reno divorce? So it seems.

Again the whining steel guitar conveys the distinct feeling there is gonna be a heartache tonight for someone.

"If I Only Had the Words (To Tell You)" is a somber piano-based ballad about trying to talk a lover into stopping what she is doing, and coming back to him. Here Billy laments the fact that the words that might make her stay are somehow escaping him. Anyone who has loved and lost knows the desperate chords that Billy Joel hits on this sincerely sung song of heartbreak.

"Somewhere Along the Line" is a medium-paced ballad that finds him singing about sitting in Paris with his stomach full of gourmet French food and wine. He takes a drag off of his cigarette and sings of how tobacco will "get me," too, "somewhere along the line." The entire song is a lament over the fact that no matter what one does, there is always some sort of painful payback. Although these aren't Billy's most profound lyrics, it is a very evocative and introspective song that lets one know in a witty fashion that behind every silver lining is a cloud.

Then, for something totally different, the album ends with Billy's ode to drugs and masturbation, "Captain Jack." In the song, Billy narrates the tale of a sad lad whose biggest joys are getting high on a Saturday night and having a "wank." The "Captain Jack" in the lyrics is a suburban drug dealer. According to him, "That's what I call one of those 'look out the window songs.' I was living in an apartment across the street from a housing project and watching these suburban kids pull up, and they were scoring drugs from a guy who lived in the project, and that was Captain Jack. I was sitting in my apartment thinking, 'What am I going to write about? Well, I guess I'll write about that.' There it was right in front of me. But I didn't get it. What's so horrible about an affluent young white teenager's life that he's got to shoot heroin? It's really a song about what I consider to be a pathetic loser kind of lifestyle. I've been accused of, 'Oh, this song promotes drug use and masturbation.' No, no, no. Listen to the song. The guy is a loser."[50]

Well, it was the early 1970s, and by that time period the vast majority of the under-thirty population had been exposed to marijuana or some sort of mind-altering drug. Recalls Billy Joel, "I wrote it when drugs were in full flower. A lot of useless, wasted deaths. Friends of mine were killed. Drugs can be fun, but they can kill, too. Some guys who lived near me in Oyster Bay used to score smack from a guy called Captain Jack, although I didn't write it to necessarily mean heroin. I meant any kind of drug you have to take over and over again."[12]

BILLY JOEL

The song "Captain Jack" is a perfect vignette piece about New York City in the early 1970s. When he sings about going to Greenwich Village in jeans, and staring at the openly gay guys and the closet queens, one cannot have lived through that post-Stonewall-riots era of Manhattan without feeling that Billy Joel captured that whole countercultural atmosphere.

"Captain Jack" is successful for the same reasons that make "Piano Man" a classic. In both of these songs, Billy Joel is the observer and the narrator. He captures a mood, a scenario, and all of the characters he encounters. Like Joni Mitchell's song "For Free," about a sad street musician, and James Taylor's "Fire and Rain," these two songs by Billy find the songwriter cast in the role as the careful eyewitness to the lives of the people around him. In each instance, the singer tells a story as a spectator and yet in an involving and deeply touching way.

Piano Man made its debut in record stores in November 1973. Not long after it was released, Billy set out on an extended concert tour to support it and promote it. On February 20, 1974, he played at the legendary Andy Warhol hangout, Max's Kansas City. Located on Park Avenue South and Eighteenth Street in New York City, Max's was a no-frills rock nightclub that was right around the corner from Warhol's art- and history-creating loft, the Factory, on nearby Union Square. It is a place that was famous as a breeding ground for several of the period's most eclectic rock groups, including the Velvet Underground, Bruce Springsteen, Bob Marley, the Troggs, and Warhol protégé Nico. For some bands, such as Ducktail and dozens of other wannabe stars, playing Max's was the height of their fame. When he appeared there, it was still unclear upon which side of the fence Billy Joel's career would land. When Billy and his first touring band played Max's Kansas City, there were also several people from Columbia Records in attendance to see what he and his music were all about.

Music critic John Rockwell of the *New York Times* wrote a review of Billy's show at Max's Kansas City. According to him, "Billy Joel is a singer and song writer from Long Island who has begun to make it over the last few months. . . . Mr. Joel . . . is fast developing into an important artist. Mr. Joel plays the piano, rather than the more customary guitar, and he plays it both versatilely and virtuosically. His backup quartet is similarly proficient: tight and subtle. But what is important is Mr. Joel's songs and the way he sings them. There is an overt theatricality in his work. . . . The tunes and arrangements court the bombastic. . . . Words are inflected; even his voice—an orotund high baritone—has a melodramatic, throbbing vibrato."[51]

And, at an even more glamorous Manhattan evening, on May 20, 1974, Billy was on a double bill with Jesse Colin Young at Carnegie Hall. This was one exciting evening for the twenty-five-year-old Billy. He may not have received his high school diploma—but here he was—a headliner at prestigious Carnegie Hall! That night Billy felt that he had officially made it to a high water mark in his career just by performing there.

According to a review in the *Village Voice*, "Billy Joel and Jesse Colin Young shared the stage at Carnegie Hall a week ago Monday. . . . Joel and his songs are a dynamic combination and a tough act to follow, especially for such a relaxed performer as Young." The article ultimately praised the craft of the singer. "Joel himself was indeed in top form, playing from among the best songs on his two albums, singing of suburbia with a deep perception of the mundane and the vital."[52]

A lot of new fans of Billy's who bought his first hit album were in for a pleasant surprise. Rock & roll author May Pang recalls, "When I heard that *Piano Man* album I was thrilled to find out that he was the same Billy Joel who I loved on the Hassles' album! I was happy to see that he was still singing! I had a Hassles album, and I was really a big fan of their music."[53]

The single version of the song "Piano Man" was released in late 1973, but it languished on radio playlists. Finally, six months after its release, in April 1974, "Piano Man" entered the Hot 100 in *Billboard* magazine singles chart.

Eventually, the single peaked at number 25 in the United States. It became the first Billy Joel single, in a succession of thirty-three top 40 hits for the singer. "It took a while," he admits. "'Piano Man' was pretty uninteresting melodically. The lyrics are probably stronger than the melody. It surprised me that it was a hit. It made some noise. The album eventually went 'Gold.' Since 'Piano Man' was the single, I got pegged right away. A lot of people confused it with 'Taxi,' the Harry Chapin song. They thought I was another Chapin, a storyteller. But the album had a lot of other things, like 'Worse Comes to Worst' and 'Captain Jack,' which were very different."[12]

Although the "Piano Man" single never reached the top 10 on the mainstream pop charts, it did hit number 4 on *Billboard* magazine's Adult Contemporary list. For his first single release on Columbia Records, Billy was off to a great start.

Two more 45 rpm singles were released from the album: "Travelin' Prayer" hit number 77 and "Worse Comes to Worst" crested at number 80. The *Piano Man* album peaked on the *Billboard* charts in America at number

27. It gave him a strong feeling of self-worth in the music business: "I never had a lack of confidence. I have a good, healthy ego, and I don't think it's bad. I don't think 'ego' is a bad word."[18]

In his first major record review in *Rolling Stone* magazine, writer Jack Breschar set the slightly smug tone for what was to be what seemed like a career-long vendetta between the publication and the singer-songwriter. According to the magazine's critical examination of the *Piano Man* album, "Billy Joel's music has suffered in comparison to better established acts. His group Hassles were a Vanilla Fudge/Rascals spinoff, his work with Attila was bettered by Lee Michaels, and his only semi-hit was a bit of pop schlock. Recent gigs at a piano bar on the seamy side of L.A. have given him a new perspective and his *Piano Man* reflects a new seriousness and musical flexibility. . . . His ten new tunes also introduce a more mature, less frantic musician . . . Joel's facility at portraying others, he seems unable to come to terms with himself. The title tune tries to reflect the piano man through his patrons, but Joel fails to illuminate his own character. . . . [Producer Michael] Stewart sometimes builds his walls of sound too quickly, making anti-climatic what might have been powerfully dramatic, but Billy Joel's enthusiasm and musical straightforwardness keep everything together and moving briskly along."[54] Eventually, Billy was going to find that critical reviews and album and concert ticket sales often have nothing to do with one another.

For people from the metropolitan New York area, the song "Captain Jack" instantly spoke to them. Recalls rock writer Susan Mittelkauf, "I really related to that song because it captured what 1950s and 1960s suburbia was all about. I used to hang out on Eighth Street and in Washington Square Park. I would come in to meet friends and go to events like the Schaefer Music Festival. At that time the city was fabulous. It was the beginning of the seventies—the tail end of the hippie era. WNEW constantly played 'Captain Jack' during that era, and Billy Joel was looked upon as the New York/New Jersey/Connecticut 'hometown boy.'"[55]

Even before "Piano Man" peaked on the charts, the awards and accolades had begun to appear. As 1973 came to a close, music industry magazine *Cash Box* crowned him "Best New Male Artist" of the year. Prestigious *Stereo Review* magazine named *Piano Man* their "Album of the Year." And, record trade magazine *Music Retailer* heralded him as their "Male Artist of the Year." Billy Joel had officially arrived. It took two years of steady sales, but finally the *Piano Man* album was certified gold for over five hundred thousand copies sold in the United States.

Columbia Records seemed like the perfect place for him to be at the time. After all, it was also the label that Bob Dylan was signed to, and Dylan was looked to as something of a folk rock singer-songwriter god. Billy's big supporter at the time of his signing was label head, Clive Davis, who had also brought Earth, Wind and Fire to the label during this same period. It could have been a dicey situation for Billy at the time, when Davis was suddenly fired from his job in a controversial corporate "bloodbath" at the company in 1973. According to legend, when Clive tried to charge his son's $30,000 bar mitzvah to his expense account, he was let go. To this day Davis strongly denies this allegation. However, the end result remained the same. A very clever man in the business, Davis simply reinvented himself by purchasing the former Bell Records, renaming it, and establishing the empire known as Arista Records. The two singer-songwriters he inherited from Bell were Melissa Manchester, and Barry Manilow. With Clive gone from Columbia, Walter Yetnikoff took his place.

This might have spelled sheer disaster for Billy. Fortunately, thanks to Manhattan gigs at Max's Kansas City, Carnegie Hall, and a performance at a Columbia Records Company convention, the label executives who saw him and heard him during this crucial period of time were impressed. They could see the yet-to-be-polished potential that was there in his performances and in his songwriting.

With the success of "Piano Man" and his FM radio hit "Captain Jack," Billy started to find his own audience. "Slowly we built up sort of a cult," he says. "Well, maybe there's a better word—when I think of a cult, I think of people with black capes and incense out killing babies or something. But we built up an audience around the country. People came to hear us because of word of mouth. It wasn't necessarily that they heard a song on the radio and then wanted to hear us. First it was small, small clubs. Then we started doing some better clubs, and then I was opening for The Beach Boys, or Doobie Brothers, or Eagles, or Linda Ronstadt—just about everybody. Half the time we didn't even get billing. We were just 'special guests.' I would start 'Piano Man' or something and they'd go, 'Boo, we want to hear The Beach Boys.' So we had to get good pretty quick."[12]

Several people have noted that Billy Joel, even at this early stage of his career, was often difficult to deal with at times. Apparently he had something of an obstinate streak and from time to time he displayed a bit of a chip-on-his-shoulder attitude. One such person to observe this was TV show host-producer Don Kirshner. In the 1960s Kirshner had made a name—and a fortune—for himself as the musical director behind the first two albums by the Monkees, a singing group created specially to star in their series of the same name. He is the one who selected all of the songs for their albums *The Monkees* (1966) and *More of the Monkees* (1967), and, in doing so, Kirshner assured them number 1 hits. The songs came from his roster of songwriters at the famous Brill Building in New York City and included Carole King, Tommy Boyce and Bobby Hart, Carole Bayer Sager, and Neil Diamond.

By the 1970s, he had his own late-night TV series called *Don Kirshner's Rock Concert*. Around the time of "Piano Man," Don presented Billy Joel on his show. According to Kirshner, "I gave him his first national exposure. I knew he was going to be a big star, *and* so did he. At that early stage of his career, he was cocky even then."[56]

Billy's wife, Elizabeth, also commented to the press that Billy would get moody from time to time. There were days when he was depressed and incommunicative. She was once to comment, "When he didn't have anyone to talk to, he'd go to the piano."[15] Fortunately, he had the ability to turn his frustrations into some of the most memorable music to grace radio airwaves.

Billy was experiencing his first wave of financial success at that moment, and he didn't want to lose the momentum that he had built up in his career. Between touring, and the money that he made on the *Piano Man* album, he and Elizabeth finally arrived at a certain comfort level in their lives.

At the height of the success of the *Piano Man* album, Billy realized that as a manager, Irwin Mazur could do little or no more good for his career. He could already see that there were bigger things in his future, and Mazur was clearly ill-prepared to direct him into these new pathways. He must have finally figured out that if Mazur was going to steer him into a deal with Artie Ripp—a move that lost him a huge chunk of his musical copyrights—that firing him would best be described as "damage control."

Even though Billy was safely signed to Columbia and Mazur was now out of the mix, Artie Ripp still loomed in the picture for years to come. Even Clive Davis and the executives at Columbia Records had tried to separate Billy from the whole Ripp deal, but the contract he had signed with Artie was ironclad, and totally legal. Ripp was later to reveal, "My deal with Columbia was ten original Billy Joel albums, plus the 'best of.' Anything that came from those albums was part of my deal, and my deal wasn't based on years. My deal was based on ten original studio albums. You're not going to give me back the half million dollars I have in, you'll pay me this royalty, you'll pay Billy his royalty, you'll pay him, his producers, and Michael

Lang his override from my company. I'm the bad guy who has the contract that couldn't be broken. I get 25 cents a record, okay, Billy didn't have to pay it to me. The record company pays it to me. And that only happened if Billy sold records."[36] Yes, Billy Joel did not have to pay Ripp directly, but with Ripp getting his cut, that was still twenty-five cents less per album sold that Billy didn't make. Over the next couple of years, this lingering payment to Artie Ripp was to become a true thorn in Billy Joel's side.

Elizabeth already had her eye clearly focused on becoming the manager of her husband's career. She was one sharp cookie, and she had been taking classes in business at the UCLA School of Management; however, she was not quite prepared to take the baton yet in his financial relay race. Her trial-by-fire as a manager was still somewhere down the line.

Billy Joel's career clearly needed an effective management team behind it. Everyone who had seen him perform or who had heard his song "Piano Man," knew that he was obviously very talented. He was potentially on the highway to major-league fame, but he was on that route without a map or someone to navigate for him.

That's where a strong manager comes into the picture. A professional manager makes decisions regarding the monies paid to his clients, and directs them toward predefined goals. In an effort to get a better handle on his semishapeless career, Billy signed a management deal with a company called Caribou. It was an organization that was run by James William Guercio and Larry Fitzgerald. Among the major artists they were also managing at the time was the highly successful group Chicago.

They also owned Caribou Recording Studios in Colorado. More important, they had concurrent deals going with Elton John, who was then making Caribou Studio famous for recording several of his hit albums there: *Caribou* (1974), *Captain Fantastic and the Brown Dirt Cowboy* (1975), and *Rock of the Westies* (1975).

For Billy Joel, signing with Caribou seemed like a natural move for him. If there was a career that Billy admired, or wanted to emulate at this point, it was Elton John's. Elton, too, had started out his career as a popular songwriter, whose subsequent albums had turned him into a star on the record charts. The whole Caribou connection could end up very good for Billy.

Ironically, Elton was not an instant hit on the charts, either. American record buyers' first taste of Elton's music had come about when a popular rock group "covered" one of his compositions. The group was Three Dog Night, and "Lady Samantha" was the song. It was included on their hit album *Suitable for Framing* (1969). According to Jimmy Greenspoon, the keyboard player of Three Dog Night, "We were the first recording artists to record and release an Elton John–Bernie Taupin song to the American public. I knew he had a hell of a career ahead of him the first time I heard his recordings and his compositions. Being a keyboard player, I had a special appreciation of his talent from the very beginning, just like I felt about Billy the first time I heard 'Piano Man.'"[39]

In addition to both being virtuoso keyboard men, throughout the years, Billy and Elton's careers ran some very close parallels. This was not a matter of "six degrees of separation," it was more like "half of a degree" at most! One of the first ones was when Elton scored the soundtrack for a film called *Friends* in 1971. It was released by Paramount Records, which was owned by the same parent company that released Billy's debut album, *Cold Spring Harbor*. Now the parallels were getting even stronger between them, with Caribou in the picture.

According to Billy, signing with Caribou Management seemed like the right thing to do at the time. "I couldn't identify with the Hollywood factory," he says. "I had a lawyer, and Columbia was urging me to make a change. And Caribou at the time was the heavy management. What'd I know from management? So I went with them. I got along very well with Larry Fitzgerald; he's a great guy. Jimmy [Guercio]; I never knew too well."[18]

Upon Caribou's insistence, Billy Joel went into the recording studio with an outside producer, whom the managers had chosen. The producer they selected was again Michael Stewart, who had so successfully produced the *Piano Man* album. However, according to Billy, they started to have conflicts in the studio. Interestingly, it was not Caribou Studios where he recorded *Streetlife Serenade,* but Devonshire Sound Studios in North Hollywood. Stewart would hear things one way, and Billy would want them to sound another way. Says the singer, "I was writing songs on the piano, but I wrote sometimes, 'This is a guitar song.' But the producer had in his head, 'O.K., Billy Joel plays piano, so we bring out the piano. Never mind the rock & roll part of it. We've gotta feature Billy Joel.' It was like pullin' teeth in the studio."[18]

According to Billy it was his new managers who were responsible for making certain that he was positioned in the marketplace in the same fashion in which Elton John was being presented. "I got along good with Michael Stewart. I got a lot of empathy for Michael Stewart. He was under a lot of pressure."[18] Listening to this album, it is easy to see that there was a bit of stylistic tug-of-war going on between the producer and the star.

BILLY JOEL

The resulting album, 1974's *Streetlife Serenade* is a mixed bag of musical styles, with two of the ten tracks being instrumental numbers. Again, during the recording process for this album, studio musicians were brought in as the session players. They included Larry Knechtel, Emory Gordy, Wilton Felder, William Smith, and Tom Whitehorse. Even producer Michael Stewart was one of the session guitar players as well. Billy played the piano and the Moog synthesizer, which was the hot new electronic keyboard instrument that was all the rage in rock music at this point in time. Stevie Wonder's latest Grammy-winning albums, *Innervisions* (1973) and *Fulfillingness's First Finale* (1974), were virtual showpieces for what could be done musically with a Moog.

At this time, Billy wanted to stretch out a bit stylistically. He tried to pay attention to what other innovative musicians were creating. "I listened to everything," he claims. "I loved Traffic later on. Steve Winwood is a hero. Paul McCartney."[12]

He was influenced by the grand musical suites that other synthesizer rock bands were doing at the time. *Close to the Edge* (1972) and *Fragile* (1972) by Yes and the *Emerson, Lake & Palmer* (1970) debut album (featuring "Lucky Man") were brilliant examples of how the synthesizers could be used to simulate whole orchestras. This really intrigued Billy greatly. "I liked some of the music Yes was doing. Emerson, Lake and Palmer was kind of a bloated pseudo-classical sound. That whole album, *Streetlife Serenade*—I had just gotten a Moog synthesizer so I kind of drizzled synthesizer oil all over the album. I probably overdid it, and I haven't listened to that album since," he was to claim in the year 2000.[16]

Billy admits he knew that he was courting his most grandiose musical intentions in *Streetlife Serenade*. "I was gonna be Debussy. And all of a sudden, *de boom* lowered," he laughs sarcastically.[17]

With reference to his albums being a patchwork quilt of different musical styles, Billy Joel explains, "I like to be as eclectic as possible. I don't like to stick in one bag, because then you become, 'Oh, he's the guy who does this. . . . ' I like different kinds of music, whatever's good. I don't want to limit myself to writing in one vein."[43] *Streetlife Serenade* reflects this musical recipe.

The *Streetlife Serenade* album was released in October 1974, less than a year after *Piano Man* hit the record bins in stores. Viewed from the perspective of his entire recording career, *Streetlife Serenade* remains one of his least dynamic albums.

"Streetlife Serenader" is an ode to a street singer. It is sung with emotional conviction and heavily highlights Billy's piano work in the mix. He starts off singing in a mournful vibrato of a voice, then the song progresses with a sweeping and building arrangement, and sets the tone for a more intently focused album. Making his succinct observations of the City of Angels in "Los Angelenos," he rocks out with more intensity than he had exposed since his days with the Hassles. Los Angeles is a sprawling metropolis similar in its diversity to New York City, yet it is uniquely a concoction all its own. This song celebrates that very fact and essays his life in the West Coast beautifully, with a critical eye.

In "The Great Suburban Showdown," Billy sings of flying home to the East Coast, for a visit home to see "the folks." With steel guitar crying in the background, he again courts country music shadings. He sings in an idealistic fashion of his dad tending the yard and the outdoor barbecue, on this charming ode to suburban America. Apparently, this is the type of life that he wished he had, if his father had not left the family.

The instrumental number "Root Beer Rag" is exactly what the name implies, with Billy Joel doing his best Scott Joplin impersonation. During the past year, the huge success of the film *The Sting* (1973) had single-handedly brought ragtime music back into the forefront for the first time since the 1920s. This was apparently Billy's homage to the piano-led music form. Here his piano work is predictably stellar. This was his one recorded ragtime number, and he milks it for all its worth with his lightning-fast keyboard work.

The ballad "Roberta" finds Billy lyrically trying to seduce a girl of that name. Another piano-based song, its narrative lyrics find him serenading the object of his affections, and trying to woo her with his keyboard crooning. Again, his piano playing here reveals his years of classical training.

In "The Entertainer," Billy gives his own cynical take on what the record business is all about. In this fast-paced jig of a song, he claims to be the entertainer who delights fans with his music, and who measures success in hit records and chart figures. In a way, it is "Piano Man" revisited. According to Billy, "My songs are usually a combination of being autobiographical and imaginary: 'Piano Man' was me, 'The Entertainer' wasn't. The things I write have a seed of personal experience, but my life isn't interesting enough to have every song be about me."[57] However, this composition pretty accurately captures Billy to an autobiographical T. He sings about his make-it-or-break-it lifestyle in his attempt at being the new musical flavor-of-the-month.

"Last of the Big Time Spenders" is a solo-piano lament about how its narrator never seems to have any money. Although Billy claims in his lyrics that he can't spend a great deal of money on the girl of his dreams, what he does have to invest in her is his time. Again the steel guitar casts a shadow of Nashville to the musical proceedings here.

"Weekend Song" is kind of an "it's Friday night and I just got paid" sort of a number, where Billy casts himself in the role of a nine-to-five worker who lives for the weekend. And, in "Souvenir" he sadly laments that ticket stubs and theater programs are often all that is left of the past. While poignant in its lyric content, this song lasts a scant two minutes. This was sort of a preview of coming attractions, as Billy Joel would more fully develop this same sentimental mood on his subsequent albums.

His second instrumental number closes this album: "The Mexican Connection." It is oddly named, as it is more of a light jazz number than a south-of-the-border-sounding song. A beautiful melody, but "The Mexican Connection" sounds more like a song that Quincy Jones or Burt Bacharach would have done at the time, and nothing like the later rock music that Billy would create.

Again *Rolling Stone* magazine proceeded to blast him, giving him his worst review yet. Wrote Stephen Holden, "Billy Joel's pop schmaltz occupies a stylistic no man's land where musical and lyric truisms borrowed from disparate sources are forced together. A talented keyboardist, Joel's piano style creditably imitates early Elton John, while Joel's melodic and vocal attacks owe something to Harry Chapin. . . . 'Piano Man' and 'Captain Jack,' the centerpieces of Joel's last album, compelled attention for their despairing portraits of urban fringe life, despite their underlying shallowness. By contrast, *Streetlife Serenade* is desiccated of ideas. . . . 'Streetlife Serenader,' fails to develop a melody or lyrical theme. . . . In 'The Entertainer,' a spinoff from Chapin's 'WOLD,' Joel screams homilies about the callousness of the music business. Joel's keyboard abilities notwithstanding, he has nothing to say as a writer at present. Two instrumental trifles, 'Root Beer Rag' and 'The Mexican Connection,' provide nothing more than filler."[58]

Yet, in other publications Billy's third solo album did well in the press. In their 1974 year-end issue, industry magazine *Cash Box* named Billy Joel their "Best New Male Vocalist." Likewise, *Music Retailer* christened him 1974's "Male Artist of the Year," and *Stereo Review* named *Streetlife Serenade* their "Album of the Year." His critical reception was obviously highly mixed. Some people loved this album, some hated it.

On the record charts, the album *Streetlife Serenade* made it to number 35, and its lone hit single, "The Entertainer," peaked at number 34. Neither became huge blockbuster hits, but at least Billy was consistently hitting the top 40.

The year 1974 saw another mixed bag at the top of the American music charts. Three of the solo Beatles hit number 1 with hits: Ringo Starr ("You're Sixteen"), Paul McCartney and Wings ("Band on the Run"), and John Lennon and the Plastic Ono Band ("Whatever Gets You through the Night"). That was the year that the Steve Miller Band produced "The Joker," Elton John sang about "Bennie and the Jets," Bachman Turner Overdrive promised "You Ain't Seen Nothing Yet," Roberta Flack claimed that she'd suddenly "Feel Like Making Love," and one-time Beatles keyboard player Billy Preston did the math and found out that "Nothing From Nothing" doesn't add up well—unless it's a funky chart-topping record like this.

And, to top it all off, the week of July 6, 1974, the disco era was officially underway as the first major dance song of the era hit number 1 on the pop charts: "Rock the Boat" by the Hues Corporation. It was replaced the following week at number 1 by another disco favorite, "Rock Your Baby" by George McCrae. In September 1974 disco-flavored crooner Barry White hit number 1 with "Can't Get Enough of Your Love." The whole disco movement would grow to become a musical entity that Billy would be forced to compete with on the charts for the rest of the decade.

Billy didn't always endear himself to everyone back in those days. He was very outspoken in concert, and he was quick to let his displeasure be known publicly. He was known to get onstage and do a mocking imitation of Bruce Springsteen. His reputation for saying surly things about his fellow performers didn't exactly charm his peers in the music business. He also got into it with Australian-born ballad singer Helen ("I Am Woman") Reddy. Looking back on this period, Billy admitted, "This was after [Springsteen's LP] Born to Run, in '75. I didn't think they were sarcastic; I thought they were homage. The only time I was sarcastic was when Helen Reddy covered one of my songs, 'You're My Home.' I used to introduce it by saying, 'This is a song that Helen Reddy cut to shreds.' Then I got a letter saying, 'Helen Reddy heard about you saying this; she's going to stop doing your song.' And I said, 'Is that a threat or a promise?' I was a little smart-ass in those days. But any impersonation I did [of Bruce] was not sarcastic."[16]

For a while, the Southern California lifestyle seemed alluring to Billy Joel. Then there was a sudden sense of discontent in paradise. "The weather was nice, the rent was low, everybody was easy to get along with. Then I woke up one day and screamed, 'What the hell am I doing here? I'm from New York!' L.A. is very seductive: 'Like wow man!' Views of the Pacific, palm trees, sports cars, everybody's beautiful. The whole fuckin' town is full of gorgeous people. Everybody who thinks they're pretty moves out to L.A. to become a movie star. But after a while it's like, 'Where's the crap? You know?' I need some variation. There's no winter. No contrast. It's too hypnotic. I'm not putting down California. Native Californians are good people, very welcoming," he claimed.[59]

For Billy it was time for a new era to start, and it was time for him to move back to the East Coast. "I lived in California for three years," he was later to explain, "I still like California, the West Coast in general. The weather is nice, the native California people are nice, the rent was cheap. When I needed it, it was there. I didn't go out there with the intention of staying. I just went there to try to get my business affairs straightened out."[18] He managed to get his life back on track, and now he was about to move a huge step closer toward defining his own hit making formula. He knew what he needed the most was a massive change of scenery and his own band. He was about to say good-bye to Hollywood, and say hello—in a big way—to New York City.

7
SAYING GOODBYE TO HOLLYWOOD

THE YEAR 1976 was quite a pivotal one in the United States. It was partially a time of celebration, partially a time of reflection, and the perfect time for people to make a new start in their lives. First of all, it was America's big bicentennial year, and the whole country was in a bit of a stir because of it. One couldn't miss the fact that the nation was in the midst of wishing itself "Happy 200th Birthday" the entire year. Everything was coming up fireworks and celebrations, and many cultural changes were underway.

Interestingly enough, while the United States was in party mode, America was still smarting from its first big gasoline crisis. For a country that thrived on "more" and "bigger" and "better," it was a rude awakening to suddenly find that there might not be any "more." Additionally, 1976 was the year that the flagship city of the whole country—New York City—was teetering on the edge of bankruptcy. Its mayor was forced to ask the federal government for assistance in the form of massive loans. What would President Gerald Ford do? The answer from the White House became one of the most famous headlines in the *New York Daily News*. It was the 1976 cover story that read: "Ford to New York: Drop Dead."

Billy Joel distinctly recalls, "When the New York financial crisis [early 1970s] started happening, there was a lot of anti-New York sentiment in L.A. from former New Yorkers and I got pissed off. I woke up one day and just said, 'I'm going back.'"[18] Billy was to turn this sentiment into a couple of his most insightful songs.

By 1976, the Vietnam War was finally over and done with, and the taboos associated with centuries old sexual mores were beginning to fly out the window as suburbia was embracing bisexuality, wife swapping, swinging, and gay discotheques. The "me" decade was officially underway.

This was the year that Sony first introduced the Betamax machine to the marketplace. Betamax was the first home videocassette recorder, and television would never be the same after that. And, speaking of revolutionary devices, it was on April 1, 1976, that the Apple computer first hit the marketplace. That was the first home computer ever available to the American public. That would have a huge impact on the last quarter of the twentieth century.

On the musical charts in 1976 was a true mixed bag of different and divergent styles. Bouncy pop songs and cheery TV show themes were hitting the top of the charts, including "Saturday Night" by the Bay City Rollers, "Afternoon Delight" by the Starland Vocal Band, "Silly Love Songs" by Paul McCartney and Wings, and "Welcome Back [Kotter]" by John Sebastian. The Rolling Stones were singing "Fool to Cry," and Rod Stewart was claiming "Tonight's the Night (Gonna Be Alright)." Disco music continued to sweep the country. Donna Summer was scoring smashes like "Could It Be Magic" and "Spring Affair," while Dr. Buzzard's Original Savannah Band ("Cherchez la Femme") was blending big band and disco rhythms on dance floors. Even truckers and CB (citizen's band) radios were all the rage that year, as evidenced when the song "Convoy" by C. W. McCall hit number 1 in *Billboard*. This was the completely eclectic musical atmosphere that Billy Joel would be competing in that particular year with his *Turnstiles* album.

Fortunately for him, ever since Billy had made the decision to leave California, the year before and move back to his home state, the creative juices had really started flowing. There is an old proverb that says, "Change your location, change your luck." This seemed to apply in the case of Billy Joel.

Again, he turned his life's experiences into music. When he made the decision to exit from L.A., how did that make him feel? It made him feel like writing the song "Say Goodbye to Hollywood."

Says Billy, "That was a celebration song. I was moving back to New York, and I was really happy to be getting out of L.A. I didn't like living in Los Angeles. The first year I was there, I was kind of seduced by the nice weather, the palm trees, and the views from the Hollywood Hills, the Pacific Coast Highway, and all that stuff. That wore off after about a year. Then I realized there were a lot of phony people there. I didn't make many friends. The sense that I got was that people wanted to get to know you because of what you could do for them. I wanted to get back to New York. It wasn't meant to be a taunting song. It was just a celebration, like, 'Okay, thank you, Hollywood.' I did it in a Phil Spector style. I was thinking of Ronnie Spector and The Ronettes when I did it."[50]

Elizabeth moved back to New York ahead of Billy. She scouted out a house for the two of them and her son Sean to live in, while he was still out on the road promoting the *Streetlife Serenade* album. Finally, the time came for Billy to join her in the house she found in upstate New York.

Another famed song came from Billy's arrival back to the state of his birth. As he explains it, "I woke up one day and said, 'What am I still doing here in California? I'm a New Yorker.' Elizabeth found us a house in Highland Falls. I got off the Greyhound bus and walked into the new house and sat down at the piano and wrote 'New York State of Mind.' That's how I was feeling: glad to be home in New York."[12]

When he arrived at the house he had the song flowing through his head, and he couldn't rest until he got it down on paper. "It took me about a half an hour to write," he recalls. "I got back to New York, I moved into the house, literally had my suitcase with me. I got off a bus that I took up the Hudson [River] and dropped my bags. There was a piano in this house, and I went right over to it and played 'New York State of Mind.' I love it when it happens like that. Thank you!"[50] This was one of the easiest songs for him to write as the inspiration for this song is one of grateful joy.

Other changes were underway as well as he moved out of California hippie mode. Billy claimed that some of the things he stopped doing when he moved back to the East Coast was dropping acid and smoking pot. "When I got back to New York, I stopped," he says. "It just didn't make sense anymore, and I was eating too many chocolate-chip cookies. I smoked a joint and walked on stage *once*. It was the worst. I got real paranoid. I wanted to hide under the piano. I started going into this cosmic rap and all the guys in the band were going, 'Oh, shit, we're in big trouble tonight.' Somebody's got to be in control up there. That was the last time I did that. When you're up there and there are thousands of people going, 'Yeah,' that's intoxicating on its own."[12]

There was a bit of pressure on Billy at the time. He had made a name for himself with "Piano Man" and, when "The Entertainer" broke the top 40, he had demonstrated that he had consistent hit making capability. What he really needed was a top 10 hit single, as that was the key to everything in the music business. *Streetlife Serenade* didn't exactly set the charts on fire, so it was back to the drawing board. Billy had to come up with a hit record, one way or another. As he explains, "It was the formula way of doing business. Which is, you have a hit record—great. If you don't have a hit record, you gotta come up with a hit record. Everything is based around a hit record, hit song, hit single, hit image, hit schtick, gimmick, bullshit, whatever it is. Just like the movie business was—the star thing."[18] Unfortunately, that is the way the music business works. He had to chase that elusive smash hit if he was going to keep his deal with Columbia Records.

Meanwhile, he was slowly building a cult following for his concerts. The audience responses were growing more and more enthusiastic, but his managers didn't seem interested in this fact. They were more concerned with his record sales. Billy complained, "Nobody paid attention to the road trip. See, to me, the essence of what we do is the road. Records are secondary. No matter how many you sell, no matter how big you become. Because the reason I'm doing what I'm doin' is not to become a recording star—it's to go out on the road and play music. So performing beforehand with management was always: 'If the record didn't happen, well, then, to hell with the road tour, we'll just go in and make another record.' That's the formula."[18] Billy saw himself as more of a performing "artist" than a recording star. That wasn't how the record company saw it.

Okay, it was time for a new record, but what direction was this album to take? *Streetlife Serenade* was released with mediocre results at best, so it was time for a new formula to be tried. The first question was, "Who is going to produce it?" The second question was, "Who was going to be in the band?"

At the time, Elton John had one of the hottest performing bands around. And, he also recorded with these same musicians as well. Elton's group included Dee Murray on the bass, Nigel Olsson the drummer, Davey Johnstone playing guitars and mandolins, and Ray Cooper on the percussion instruments. All of a sudden someone at Caribou came up with the brilliant idea of having Billy record his next album using Elton John's band to play behind him.

Well, Billy was willing to give it a try. "I was with Caribou Management, which was a company run by [Jimmy] Guercio and a manager named Larry Fitzgerald. I didn't particularly want Jimmy to produce *Turnstiles*, but they were pushin' it. They figured, 'Billy Joel, piano player. Piano player, Elton John. Use Elton's band: great!' . . . Elton's band was really nice—Nigel Olsson's a great guy," Billy recalls. Unfortunately, he hated the results: "We cut half an album, threw it out."[60]

Then there was the matter of Michael Stewart. If it were up to Stewart, he was happy to record Billy's next album using professional studio musicians again. However, Billy would have nothing to do with it: "The only time we ran into a problem was when it came down to, I had a band together that had been on the road for two years and he didn't want me to use them on the recordings. That's when I parted ways with Michael Stewart."[18]

When he had relocated back to New York, Billy had to get some new musicians he could play with. He couldn't fly everyone to New York every time he wanted to rehearse. Even more than that, before he went into the recording studio, he really wanted to redefine his sound all together. It made sense to him to polish songs on the road, then record them in the studio with the same musicians.

As he recalls, "It goes back to the guy who does my sound, Brian Ruggles. It was time to put together a New York band, and Brian suggested Doug Stegmeyer, a bass player he knew."[60] In rapid succession, Billy put together the core of his new East Coast–based band from a group of musicians who were all from Long Island where he grew up. There was an instant chemistry among them. They grew to include Doug on the bass guitar, Liberty DeVitto on the drums, Russell Javors on guitar, and Richie Cannata playing the saxophones and any horn or additional keyboard parts that came up.

For his entire career from this point onward, Billy would always be associated with Doug, Liberty, Russell, and Richie. Stegmeyer, Javors, and DeVitto were on the first album that Billy recorded after moving back to New York: *Turnstiles*, and Liberty and Richie were both on his final rock album of the 1990s: *River of Dreams*. He has never done a full rock & roll concert tour since that point without one of them accompanying him in his band.

Richie, Liberty, and Doug were to be the center of Billy's band for the rest of the decade, which was the most crucial time in his career. Musically, they all got along incredibly well from the very beginning. They had the same interests, they were all very much into their music, and they were all at a point in their respective careers where they were courting rock & roll success.

Before Billy came into the picture, Doug Stegmeyer and Liberty DeVitto had had jobs as members of a house band at a local Long Island catering hall. Another member of the band was a musician by the name of Frank Sagarese.

According to Sagarese, "Back in the early seventies, Liberty, Doug, and myself were all working at a place on Long Island, a catering hall, in different bands and things. Occasionally we would get together for a project that we had going, separately from that. So that's how I got to know Doug. I play the trumpet, and at the time I was playing piano and trumpet and fronting the band, and my brother Michael was in the band as well. We had our own catering hall band at the Narragansett Inn. Liberty and Doug were involved in another band at the same place. That was our primary location for gigs at the time. We were all like house band people.[61]

"Doug himself was a great guy—laid back. No muss, no fuss, just easy-going. He was a great musician. Doug was the one person who was working with Billy before Liberty went with Billy. And Doug would like disappear and do concert dates in upstate New York, at the colleges with early Billy Joel. And, Doug was the guy who actually had the contact with Billy Joel."[61] It was Doug who introduced Billy Joel to Liberty DeVitto.

Frank Sagarese watched his dream band disappear when Billy Joel took Doug and Liberty to be part of his new band. "We were actually putting together a little Las Vegas–type show to work in Vegas. We had an audition with someone I had made a contact with. And, right at that time is when they all went with Billy," continues Frank.[61] Eventually Sagarese gave up on his Las Vegas dreams and instead chose a fulfilling life of teaching music to elementary school students. Ironically, he even taught Liberty DeVitto and Russell Javors's children at one point.

"Doug had a great sense of humor," recalls Liberty. "He was funny. But he was negative. He saw the glass as being half empty. He loved playing the bass. It was his life. I have known Doug since I was eighteen or nineteen years old and playing at the Village Gate with this guy, Richie Supa."[62]

Liberty DeVitto was an important part of the Billy Joel band and Billy's personal inner circle for more years than any other musician. One of the reasons that they had such a long-running friendship was that they shared a love of their music, and had very similar backgrounds. Liberty was born in 1950 and is just a year younger than Billy. Liberty's parents were first generation Americans. "My mother's side is from Palermo, Sicily; my father's side is from Naples," he says. Liberty vividly recalls his modest childhood. His family couldn't afford a crib when he was born, so he slept in an open dresser drawer as an infant. "My father became a policeman, after running with the criminals. He's got pictures. He'd say, 'See this guy, he went to prison. See this guy? He went to prison.'"[63]

Also, like Billy, Liberty grew up loving music of all sorts. Then, as with so many baby boomers, his musically defining moment came when he saw the Beatles on *The Ed Sullivan Show* in 1964. "That's it, when I saw the Beatles on TV. That's when I knew I wanted to get chicks by being a musician. I didn't play sports, that's for sure."[63] After that, Ringo Starr became Liberty DeVitto's hero.

What was it that made him gravitate to the drums? "I don't know why drums," he says. "My mother had rhythm, she loved to dance. I don't know why the drums. There's like a gap there. My parents say it's because I had a lot of energy. Because, if I was a kid today, they would be giving me Prozac. Instead, they gave me drums. I started when I was twelve. I was thirteen when I saw the Beatles on TV, on *The Ed Sullivan Show*, the one that everybody saw."[63]

According to Liberty, "I didn't go for lessons. I tried to go for lessons, the guy told me, 'You want to play jazz?' I said, 'No, I want to play like Ringo.' The guy said, 'Why do you want to play like Ringo for, he sucks.' I said, 'I saw him on TV last night, he's got all these girls screaming for him, and I don't see any girls beating down your door.' Well, that was the end of my drum lessons, so I am 'self taught.'"[63]

Also paralleling Billy is the fact that Liberty's last year in school was his senior year. After he received his diploma, he turned his attention to his music. "High school, that was it. I was the kinda guy, I went for 'the groove.'"[63]

Like Billy, from the time he was a teenager, Liberty was in a succession of local Long Island bands. "I was in a band when I was seventeen. I started in bands immediately, but when I was seventeen, I was in a band that we started to do recordings with Shadow Morton, who was the producer for Vanilla Fudge at the time. I became friends with the members of the Vanilla Fudge. They would take me out of high school. The producer and manager used to come to my school, and take me out of school. The principal was like, 'Well, that's cool, 'cause it seems like this is what this kid wants to do.' Then as soon as I graduated—I graduated in June—in

August of 1968 I turned eighteen years old, and in November of 1968 I was on the road with Mitch Ryder and the Detroit Wheels. I did six months with Mitch, because his drummer got very sick. That drummer was Johnny Syomis, who has since passed away. But, he became the [Peter] *Frampton Comes Alive* drummer—he was on that huge album."[63]

Mitch Ryder and the Detroit Wheels were Detroit rock & roll legends. With a repertoire of hard-driving hits like "Devil in a Blue Dress," "Jenny Take a Ride!" and "Sock It to Me Baby," their live shows always had an extra jolt of electrifying excitement. This gave Liberty a great opportunity to really show off his drumming expertise and boundless, hard-rocking energy.

Growing up in the same neck of the woods on Long Island, and hanging out at the same rock clubs there, Liberty and Billy were bound to have their paths cross. Liberty remembers, "I was with a band, the New Rock Workshop, and we used to play at My House, which was the same club where the Hassles played, so Billy was there. Well, I used to know Billy just in passing, to say, 'How are you?' It was in Plainview, and Russell Javors lived in Plainview. Doug Stegmeyer lived in Syosset. They were friends, and they used to come to the club, My House. That's when they used to see me playing drums. And, that's when Russell and Doug said that they would one day be in a band with me."[63]

Recalling the club, My House, Liberty explains, "It was for kids. It didn't have alcohol. No alcohol, but it had major acts who would go there, like The Crickets who had 'Younger Girl' out. They played there. Jackie Wilson played there. That's actually where I met Russell and Doug. I was seventeen, Russell was probably fifteen then. Doug was sixteen. Billy was eighteen by then—he's a year older than I am. But that all came about after the Mitch [Ryder] thing. I went out and did Mitch, then I went out with Richie Supa, who was in the Rich Kids—a band on Long Island. We did an album with him—the first album I ever did was called *Supa's Jamboree*, which was on the Paramount label. I met all the guys. We did it down south at Studio One in Atlanta. And, the Atlanta Rhythm Section, they were actually the Classics IV, with Dennis Yost as the lead vocalist. Then they became the Atlanta Rhythm Section later on."[63]

"Eventually we did get to play together: me, Russell and Doug. We were with this guy named Howie Emerson, and we became a band called Topper. Russell was writing all of the material. Doug got the call to go with Billy, because he knew the sound engineer. Doug wasn't on the album *Streetlife Serenade*, but he was on the tour. That's when Billy had decided that he was moving back to New York, he had *had* it with L.A. He was taking Doug with him, because Doug was from New York—leaving the rest of the band behind. Billy [came] to New York and wants a New York–style drummer—and it was me. We go into the studio, we start *Turnstiles,* and we need a guitar player: 'Let's get Russell and Howie.' So, Topper eventually becomes Billy's band, with the addition of Richie Cannata playing saxophone."[63]

Ironically, the kind of music that Billy was playing at the time was not exactly what Liberty would necessarily gravitate toward. Was he critical of it? "Very critical of it," he claims. "The funny part of it is that I was always into Hendrix and Cream and all that stuff, growing up in the sixties. I loved R&B, loved Aretha Franklin, loved Sam & Dave, and all of that kind of music like that. And, here comes this guy writing these songs about California, and I'm practicing, because I know I have an audition. And, my mother comes downstairs, and she hears 'Piano Man,' and she says, 'You're not gonna play for that guy are you?'" He laughs.[63]

Richie Cannata also grew up on Long Island, a contemporary of Billy Joel and Liberty DeVitto. Although he hadn't amassed a lot of recording credits, he was undeniably an accomplished musician by the time he met the Piano Man. "Well, keep in mind that, number 1, I was in my twenties. There wasn't a great discography before Billy," Cannata says. "But, certainly at six years old, I was making music. It started there. I was doing Broadway shows, and I was on *Wonderama,* a TV show in New York. I was playing in Dixieland bands. I was moved very quickly through my middle school and high school. [When I was just] an elementary school kid, they brought me to the high school to play clarinet. So, I moved very quickly through that. And, I was very involved then. At some point someone put a tenor sax in my hands, and I never looked back."[44]

Wherever he could go and showcase his saxophone playing, Richie was there: "From that point, what I was doing was teaching kids, and I was in my own band. This was back in the day before there were huge sound systems in clubs. There was music in all of the clubs. Especially, in this metropolitan area in which I lived, there were lots of people and clubs to choose from. There were these pockets in the Bronx, in Brooklyn, in Manhattan, on Long Island, New Jersey, the Jersey shore; there were all these great places with strips of music places. If you wanted to hear music, there was music playing all over. I was in that. I would be able to work from a Tuesday or Wednesday, right into Sunday—solid. I was making more money than I ever thought I would make, playing the saxophone. And, I had these bands," he recalls.[44]

It was one thing to become a master musician, but it was another thing to actually have a good understanding of economics as well. Richie's father saw to it that he had a well-rounded education. "I went to school. My dad told me not to go to school for music. Because he knew that no one could teach me what God gave me. You either have it or you don't. My dad recognized that, even though he didn't know any music. He said to me, not to go the educated route—you know, to learn the Baroque period and learn education and child psychology—so I can go out and teach kids who really don't give a shit about learning. And, here you are, you are stuck in some school district, and you are some great sax player. He said, 'Let's do something where you can parlay your music into something. Because, you could be in our basement until you are thirty-five years old, playing, and no one's gonna know you are playing.' So, I went to school for marketing research and business economics—a business degree. It kept me from being 'that jazz guy.' I was studying with this guy, Joe Allard, who was the greatest saxophone player. Myself, Mike Brecker, and David Sanborn all studied with him at the same time. This guy was great, and I was learning all these patterns and licks and stuff, and I was getting real good. But my business degree kept me in the real world."[44]

Richie claims that his enthusiasm for playing music became his passion. "You know: 'Let's go back to the dorm' and 'Let's go play some more jazz.' And, 'Let's go back to the dorm and play more of this.' While we were all so good, and everybody's stroking each other."[44]

In addition to promoting the value of education, what his father instilled in Richie was a very strong economic sense. "Then there's the business degree. My dad was very smart, he had me realize about managing money, investments, basic accounting, which I try and instill upon Eren, my son: 'If you make a dollar, don't spend a dollar fifty. If you make a dollar, invest it. Put half of it away, and live on that fifty-cent lifestyle.' Sometimes you will have to go back to that money you've saved. What we need is musicians who have the free time to write, and to make good business decisions. Because, if you don't, you are forced to, then you are in a wedding band. Then you're doing something else. Or, you are working a day gig so you can have the time to write and make music.[44]

"That's how it started for me. So, I was doing very nicely. And I was doing recording sessions. I had done something for Joe Cocker. I was still in my twenties then, and I had done a couple sessions here and there, that I was really excited about. This was in the early seventies. I graduated from college in 1971. So, it was right about that time, 1971, that I started to get out there and play, and I started to relearn the saxophone, and do all of that. I had that band I was telling you about, and I had a few college gigs. Then I had this recording session and, I think it was for *Sesame Street*. It was called 'The Meter, the Liter, and the Gram.' I got a call to play saxophone on it, and, I went there. The engineer was Doug Stegmeyer's brother, Al Stegmeyer. And Al said, 'Wow this guy's my brother, and Liberty DeVitto—the drummer—just did this basic track. And we need you to play saxophone on this track.' I said, 'Fine.' So I did, and he said, 'It's great. You know, they are looking for a saxophone player.'"[44]

Billy was just putting together players whom he could record with, as well as tour with. Richie Cannata seemed like the perfect person for the job. Richie explains, "At that time, Billy was performing 'Piano Man,' and the *Streetlife Serenade* album—the sophomore record—came out and didn't do great. So, he was kinda looking. He had Johnny Almond of the Mark Almond Band. Johnny Almond was playing sax and keyboards, and something didn't click. Anyway, Billy was fumbling with management, with band members. I know that he had gotten Elton's band, his management—Jimmy Guercio—put that together. Then he went out to Caribou. Jimmy Guercio and those guys wanted him to work with Elton's band, and I think they tried to start the *Turnstiles* record, and absolutely hated it. Then they came back [to New York], found Liberty, and found Doug—they were in a band [Topper]—and this guy, Russell Javors, too. They had a band, and they liked that band, and they were going to use that band to recut the album. They were gonna hide out, and Billy was going to produce the *Turnstiles* record himself.[44]

"So, they dabbled with the Mark Almond Band guy, and here I came into the picture. They were looking for a sax player who could play keyboard and sax. And I said, 'I kinda do that.' And I said, 'Who is this?' And he said, 'Billy Joel.' I said, 'Oh, "The Piano Man." Where do I fit into "The Piano Man" guy?' At that time he had 'Piano Man' and 'The Entertainer'—two songs. Great songs, no doubt about it. But, 'Where's my part in this?'"[44]

Whether it made any sense or not, Richie heard from Billy's camp: "They contacted me, and they sent some guys out here [on Long Island] to come and hear me. I was doing this other thing in a funk band. We got through the fact that they liked the way I played. They said, 'Why don't you come over to the studio? We are doing this record. Check out what is going on.' I said, 'Where are you guys?' They were in Hempstead, at Ultra Sonic Studios, and Liberty, Doug, and Billy were there. And, John Bradley was the engineer. I walked in, and they were doing 'Angry Young Man.' And, I went, 'Whoa, that is not "The Piano Man!" This is really cool.'"[44]

Like the rest of Billy's newly formed band, Billy, himself, wanted to know what his players felt inspired to play on specific tracks that he was working on in the studio. As Richie Cannata explains it, "We established that I was gonna be in the band. Billy had asked me, and I said 'Okay.' I wasn't sure yet. He told me, 'There's a song I want you to play on.' Then he played me 'New York State of Mind,' the basic track. I went, 'Okay, okay, I can play on that. Yeah, I could see that!' He said, 'Well, we aren't gonna record it here.' I said, 'Aw, darn, I live right around the block from here.' He said, 'No, we are going to go out to Caribou Ranch, because that's where my management is, and that's where they want me to go. So, I'll sing my parts, and you will play your parts out there.' So, I said, 'Okay.' So, the band went out there, and I played my parts. One of the first solos that I played with Billy was 'New York State of Mind.' And, that was on the *Turnstiles* record, and he said, 'Let's go out and do a small, little tour.'"[44]

Since Billy had in his mind a strong concept for the kind of music he wanted to record, he wasn't willing to defer to Michael Stewart's production ideas this time around. Instead, he decided to produce the album himself. The majority of the album was actually recorded at Columbia Recording Studios on Thirtieth Street in New York City, not far from Madison Square Garden. Then Billy flew his band to Caribou Recording Studios in Nederland, Colorado, to complete it.

Richie Cannata recalls, "I think that Billy was named 'producer' because there was nobody else. It was his music. He knew what he wanted, and it just was that. He was trying to get away from somebody else coming in and telling him that it should be black when it was white. Just for the fact that, 'I'm producing your record, so I've got to tell you something. Listen to me or I can't be your producer.' It was by default. It was great, because we were the band. John Bradley was the engineer. What we did was, we transferred all of the sixteen tracks—there were only sixteen tracks at Ultra Sonic Studios—and then we transferred them to twenty-four [tracks]—and another engineer came onto the scene and his name was Bruce Botnick. He came and he worked with John Bradley. That's when Billy and I did our stuff at Caribou, and Bruce and John Bradley mixed it together. So Billy *was* the producer."[44]

Billy and the band were thrilled with the album that they had recorded. It took Billy Joel out of the Nashville-flavored tracks that Stewart was directing him into and showed him off in more of a jazz-rock kind of light.

He was finished having the steel guitar on his albums: it was good-bye blue-grass, hello rock & roll.

Next, the band went out on the road and tried their new music out in concert. Says Richie, "Then we took this stuff, and then went out on a tour. There was really not a lot of support from the label. The label, at that point, was ready to drop Billy, because it wasn't working. *Piano Man* was a great record. *Streetlife Serenade* was a good record. *Turnstiles,* they weren't sure what to do with it. We had management. Management was Jimmy Guercio and Larry Fitzgerald."[44] This was all before the *Turnstiles* album was released.

Also making their first appearance on one of Billy's albums were Howie Emerson and Russell Javors. According to Russell, it was the whole Topper connection that got him into the Billy Joel camp: "I put the nucleus of the band together. I met Liberty when I was fifteen. The second I saw Lib play in a club, I wanted to start a band with him. Lib played with attitude. When Harry Weber left the Hassles, Harry and I tried to start something with Lib, but nothing came of it. I was friends with Harry—even though he was much older than I was—but, I was still a baby. Anyway, I also knew Doug and Howard Emerson. I was writing songs, so I put all these guys together to work them out. We called the band Topper. I didn't want to play in a jam band. I wanted to play and record original music. It was obvious from the start that we had a lot of chemistry together. We did tons of demos and spent a lot of time developing our sound. I think that focus and chemistry found its way to Billy's records." [64]

Remembering his days with Topper, Russell Javors says, "Frankly, we were a band before Billy. I think, part of what Billy saw is that it worked. It wasn't a band like it was with Billy. I was a songwriter—I started writing songs, and that's how I got together with Lib, and I always had this kind of passion to do that stuff. And I just wanted to have a recording band, so we didn't play like normal. When we played clubs, the club owners hated us because we played original stuff. We played all sorts of crazy stuff. The night before we went on the road with Billy, the club owner said we were the worst band they ever heard. They hated us. We changed our name all the time. The last one was Free Buffet. That finally brought them in a little bit."[65]

Before joining Billy's band, they frequented at bars and clubs on Long Island. "We played the Tavern Ale House," says Russell. "We played a bunch of gigs and stuff. Some nights we were awesome. But usually the bar tab was bigger than what we made for the night! We were just doing it. We were just putting it together as a band."[65]

Like every other bar band on Long Island, they were all hoping for that magical recording deal that was going to make all of their dreams come true. Explains Russell, "Me and Howie, Lib and Doug, were together forever. We did so many demos, and so much stuff." According to Russell, he had central vision, and Liberty, Doug, and Howie worked well together as a unit. "It was scary; when we were 'on' it was scary," he claims. "I mean, ask Liberty what it was like. When we nailed it, it was crazy. I don't think we ever caught it on tape."[65]

One by one they were recruited to be part of Billy's backup band. As Russell remembers it, "Doug was already in the band. Doug left [Topper] first. Billy needed a bass player. He went to California with Billy and was there for a while. So it was Doug that really brought us into this situation. Liberty first, then me and Howie. To be honest with you, Billy didn't have that much money back then. I don't think that he even wanted me. It was my band, and Howie was the only one who had the balls to say, 'Guess what, it's Russell's band, and without Russell, I'm not playing.' By Howie opening his mouth, that's the only way I got there, because nobody else opened their mouth. . . . I did the *Turnstiles* album, the tour."[65]

Russell recalls having followed Billy's career from the very beginning: "I started seeing Billy play in clubs when he was with the Hassles. It was obvious that he was very talented. We never really hung out in those days. I was closer to Elizabeth's brother Harry, and [to] Jon Small, but you could see that Billy was putting it together while he was with the Hassles. Billy actually replaced Harry in that band. When I started playing with Billy, I was impressed by the way he could take control of a room. He worked hard at shaping the set, and developed and polished the things he said in between songs. He spent a lot of time honing his act. I admired his professionalism. He had a killer instinct onstage. It was exciting to be a part of it as it evolved."[64]

Billy had made so many changes in this past year, yet there was time for one more major shift. He had moved back to the East Coast, fired Irwin Mazur, moved Artie Ripp off to the side where he had nothing actively to do with him, turned down Michael Stewart as his producer . . . and now he was unhappy with his managers.

Elizabeth Joel had been observing all of this very closely, and she wasn't happy, either, with what the Caribou Management team was doing with her husband's career. She was primed and ready to grab the steering wheel. Says Billy, "I was with different management companies and always being told what to do. Nothing much was happening, so there wasn't much to lose."[12]

The last straw between Billy and the Caribou managers came in 1976 when they called and offered him a gig opening for the Beach Boys at Nassau Coliseum, and told him he would be paid a mere $2,000 for doing the date. That was it. Elizabeth dialed them up immediately. According to her, "I told the guy on the phone, 'Go to hell. You're fired!'"[21]

Then a lightbulb clicked on in his head. Billy recalls, "I turned to Elizabeth half jokingly and said, 'Why don't you manage me?' We had moved from Highland Falls to Manhattan, and the very next day, there were phones and shelves and typewriters and secretaries in our apartment. She'd seen managers and agents come and go. She knew what had to be done. Also, if you can't trust your wife, who can you trust? And I figured this will be the first case of Artist-Screws-Manager," he laughed. "Really, I knew she was smart. I knew she could do it. It was funny. The record company considered her just another rock & roll wife. A lot of people underestimated her. They didn't know what hit them. It worked to our advantage. She did a really good job while they were thinking she was this dumb chick who could be conned and not know it."[12]

Elizabeth christened her newly formed company: "Home Run Management." From that point forward, she was not only Mrs. Billy Joel, she was also his manager. At first, people would dismiss her as a harmless presence: "I was regarded as Billy's girlfriend, a 20-year-old with long hair and a mini-skirt."[21]

It wasn't long before she was flexing her muscle as a manager. Recalls Billy, "She renegotiated my contract with Columbia, and renegotiated my publishing copyrights and a better record royalty rate. Since my albums hadn't done much, everyone sort of wrote me off. She saw that I was doing great live, selling out 5,000-seaters. We were blowing away headliners. We'd come on first and have only 40 minutes, so we did what we call our kamikaze show: Bam! We'd hit them with our hottest stuff and be gone. They'd say, 'Who was that guy?' We became show stealers. No one wanted to play with us. We didn't do it on purpose, but we just played our best. So, we came back as headliners."[12]

Richie Cannata tells it from his perspective: "Elizabeth came in and she took the reins. I think what happened was that Elizabeth was always in the picture as a personal manager for Billy. They put us on the road, and they had us open for the Beach Boys. And, I got about a good fifteen years playing for them. We found ourselves opening up for the Beach Boys at these strange venues, where we would go on at four in the afternoon. And, there's Billy in a jacket and tie, and we are all kinda in black, you know: New York guys. Billy used to poke fun at the fact that here we are singing, 'Some folks like to get away,' *boing!*—he gets hit in the head with a beach-ball. The whole audience was like, 'Where is seat Number 14, Row J?' And, 'Oh, you guys suck! Where are the Beach Boys?' The thing was that the Beach Boys and Chicago were all managed by Jimmy Guercio and that bunch. We got to jump on that. We went out there and opened up for these acts, and it was horrible. We were in Chicago and we were at the White-hall Hotel; it was a very sobering moment for us. It was kind of like, 'Well, what do we do next? Let's just end this thing. Let's just go out on our own: small theaters.' So, Elizabeth came into the picture with Dennis Arfa. It was called Home Run Management, Home Run Entertainment, and everything was kept at home. It was self-contained; the nucleus was very tight. It was just all us people from Long Island or the New York area, and we were gonna go and do this ourselves. We were going to go out there and get gigs with or without the record company. 'Who cares? Let's just get out there, and play and see what happens.' Nobody [in the audience] knew any of the songs, except for 'Piano Man,' and maybe a little bit of 'The Entertainer.' But, we kept building."[44]

It seemed that Elizabeth was quite successful at bolstering Billy's flag-ging career right off the bat. In renegotiating his publishing deal she gar-nered for him what *Rolling Stone* magazine reported was "one of the most lucrative royalty deals in the industry."[17]

She was instantly effective as his new manager, but how did this impact their marriage? According to Elizabeth, "At times we got along better as manager and artist than we did as man and wife."[21]

In May 1976, Columbia Records released Billy's fourth solo album, *Turnstiles.* From the very start of *Turnstiles* it is clear that this is a whole new sound for Billy Joel. Here he sings with much more passion and authority than he had in his previous releases. His voice in this record has a confi-dence to it that is both strong and engaging. The lyrics he wrote for this album have so much more to say, and so much more depth than the casu-ally constructed format of *Steetlife Serenade.*

The opening track, "Say Goodbye to Hollywood," was clearly an hom-age to the legendary producer Phil Spector. Years before he was embroiled in a twenty-first-century Hollywood murder scandal, Phil was looked at as a brilliant and original producer who ushered in what he called his "Wall of Sound." According to his 1960s recording formula, he would regularly double, triple, and quadruple multiple music tracks to make his records sound as if he was in the studio with a hundred musicians, instead of a dozen. Spector's top roster of groups included the Crystals—with LaLa Brooks, the Ronettes, Bob E. Soxx and the Blue Jeans, and Darlene Love. At the height of his productivity, his right-hand man was Sonny Bono, who often brought his teenage girlfriend into the studio with him. Her name was Cher. He was also famous for recording songs with several other recording stars as well, including the Righteous Brothers ("Unchained Melody"), Ben E. King ("Spanish Harlem,"), and half of Ike and Tina Turner's incredible 1966 *River Deep, Mountain High* album.

LaLa Brooks of the Crystals claims, "With 'Say to Goodbye to Hollywood,' Billy Joel really captured the Wall of Sound feeling that Phil created back at Gold Star Studios in the 1960s. It was a fitting tribute to the kind of music that we recorded back then."[30]

Billy especially loved the Spector-produced songs by Phil's wife, Ronnie Spector, and her group the Ronettes. Their most famous recordings include "Walking in the Rain," "Be My Baby," "(The Best Part of) Breakin' Up," and "Paradise." These recordings were excitingly larger-than-life in sound, with driving percussion and horns.

This was totally the sound that Billy achieved on "Say Goodbye to Hollywood," which kicks off the *Turnstiles* album brilliantly. From the very start, there is no mistaking the Spector influence. Beginning with Liberty DeVitto's crisp drumbeats, this song ushered in a whole new sound for Billy. On this track, his keyboards sound huge and magnified. Richie Cannata's sizzling sax solo in the middle of the song completely transforms it to a whole new level of jazzy excitement.

One of the many allurements to "Say Goodbye to Hollywood" is its polished yet raw recording sound. Billy's singing voice has a nice echo to it that makes it sound bigger and fuller, to match the depth of the musical track. If you listen closely to the song, four minutes into it you can hear Billy in the background shouting instructions to someone in the studio: "Hey! Where you going? What are you doing?" This unconventional fade out gives the song a live-in-the-studio feeling to it. Liberty's drum solo at the end finishes this perfectly affectionate salute to the eccentric Mr. Spector.

Interestingly enough, Ronnie Spector returned the compliment in 1977 when she recorded her own version of Billy Joel's "Say Goodbye to Hollywood" as a single issued by Epic Records. She recorded it with Bruce Springsteen's band as her musicians on the track. Billy claims that he was absolutely thrilled by this.

Billy was later to say, "I loved Streisand doing 'New York State of Mind,' and Sinatra just did 'Just the Way You Are,' but the biggest kick was when Ronnie Spector cut 'Say Goodbye to Hollywood,' 'cause I heard Ronnie in my head as I wrote the lyrics! It was wild! And then to have Miami Steve Van Zandt and the E Street Band back her up was the best. God, that made me truly happy. That's jukebox music, man, good car-radio music! And I helped make it happen!"[14]

The track also includes a blistering sax solo by Clarence Clemmons. Recalls Steve Van Zandt, "That was only the second record I ever produced. I literally got Ronnie Spector out of retirement for that. I love that song."[66] It is considered a classic and was later included on Ronnie's greatest hits album, *Dangerous 1976–1987.* Billy still raves about how much he likes this recording.

"Summer Highland Falls" is a subtle and beautiful ballad that finds Billy in a reflective mood. With his classically trained piano work in full blossom, this is one of the most beautiful and introspective songs of his entire career. With his intricate piano work flowing throughout, and Liberty's propelling drum work, "Summer Highland Falls" is a perennial favorite that Billy still performs in concert from time to time. Here he sings that life is comprised of abject sadness or sheer euphoria, and that in all relationships there is always one person who doesn't fulfill all of the fantasies of the other party, yet they somehow make the best of it and celebrate their similarities.

According to Liberty DeVitto, his drumming on this track was inspired by Joni Mitchell: "After reading about Joni's love for art I went back and listened. It's amazing how her songs are in colors and textures. At the time I recorded *Turnstiles* with Billy I was dating a woman that was totally into Joni. So just for her, I did a drum fill in the beginning of a song called 'Summer Highland Falls,' which is the same drum fill that is at the beginning of Joni's 'Help Me.'"[67]

Many of Billy Joel's fans count this as being among their favorite Billy songs. "I can so completely identify with the lyrics of 'Summer Highland Falls,'" says show business photographer Derek Storm. "When he sings about 'these' not being the 'best' of times, it really triggered something inside of me. It is not an optimistic view. It is not a pessimistic view. It is a realistic view of the world. It is one of my all-time favorite Billy Joel songs because it really stripped down this emotion to a universal thought: we all have to make the best of what life hands us, no matter what. From that point on, Billy Joel's music really spoke to me."[69]

BILLY JOEL

"All You Wanna Do Is Dance" is a reggae-flavored tune complete with a steel drum solo in the middle of it. In the lyrics of the song Billy reminisces about the days when he heard rock & roll on the tiny three-inch speaker of a portable radio, and when he used to get sick drinking beer with his buddies. He also laments in the song that he still can't figure out why the Beatles don't get back together again.

The next song on the album is one of Billy's true masterpieces, the beautiful "New York State of Mind." With an extensive and intricate piano solo introduction, Billy Joel shows off his classically trained piano skills to full advantage. It is his beautiful piano work that propels this track. This still stands as one of Billy's all-time great jazz classics. It is no wonder that this is one of his most "covered" songs.

When you listen to "New York State of Mind," and you hear that brilliant sax solo in the middle of it, it is 100 percent the musical invention of Richie Cannata. "All the parts," Richie confirms. "Billy was great, he said, 'Here's the music, you guys fill in the holes.' He was never someone who said, 'You've got to play that note.'"[44] This beautiful six-minute-long song set a new high water mark for Billy's recording career, not only as a performer, but as a songwriter.

"James" finds Billy pondering the fate of one of his childhood friends. Singing here to electric keyboards, Billy muses about whatever happened to James. Did he ever finish writing the novel he always wanted to write? How is his life going? The lyrics make one think that the singer-songwriter is, himself, pondering his own fate as well. Billy gave up his academic studies to have a life of touring on the road, and now he wonders how his choices stack up to the ones that James made in his life.

"Angry Young Man" is another piece that became a signature song for Billy. It opens with a rapid-paced piano solo, and all of the excitement that his newly formed band can muster. The song begins with an instrumental "Prelude," which is much more passion filled than either "Root Beer Rag" or "The Mexican Connection" on his previous album.

After a minute and a half, the Piano Man and the band formerly known as Topper really swing into action. As Billy tells in third person about an "angry young man," one cannot help but wonder if that young man is in reality Billy Joel. He sings here that he has reached the point where he is able to control his rage. But is that really true?

In "I've Loved These Days," Billy sings of soothing his soul on the four indulgences that begin with the letter *c*: champagne, Cabernet, caviar, and lines of fine cocaine. Ah, yes, this was the 1970s, when cocaine use was coming into full flower. By now marijuana and acid were looked upon by the elite rockers as things of the past—a holdover from the hippie-centric sixties. Thanks to nonstop touring, Billy was beginning to feel the advantages of life in the fast lane, and here he rhapsodizes about what his first taste of what rock & roll success has brought him. He sings this grandiose and metaphor-filled song, accompanied by strings and drums, as an ode to all of the indulgences that money could buy.

"Miami 2017 (Seen the Lights Go Out on Broadway)" is Billy's view of what would happen if his beloved New York City indeed did go broke and fell into ruin and flames. According to Billy, "I wrote that when I got back to New York from L.A. This is when the city was on the verge of bankruptcy and they thought it might default. A lot of people in Los Angeles were kind of gleeful about that: 'Ha, ha, New York's going down the tubes.' I got very defensive, and I wrote this song as a science fiction song, projecting into the future—in the year 2017—about me being an old man telling my grandchildren how I saw the lights go out on Broadway, and I saw the mighty skyline fall, and saw the ruins at my feet. It was an apocalyptic vision."[50] In retrospect, this song is all the more haunting, knowing what would happen on September 11, 2001.

To fully drive home the "I'm in love with New York" theme of the new album, Billy was photographed in the most New York of settings: at the turnstiles of a subway station. Wearing a loosened necktie over a white dress shirt, behind him are eight assorted straphangers, including Elizabeth's young son, Sean.

Although the album contained only eight songs, these were among the most powerful ones of his career. The critics were quick to pick up on this artsy new little masterpiece that Billy had created with his *Turnstiles* album. Stephen Thomas Erlewine in the *All Music Guide* wrote, "The key to the record's success is variety, the way the album whips from the bouncy McCartneyesque 'All You Wanna Do is Dance' to the saloon song 'New York State of Mind,' the way the bitterly cynical 'Angry Young Man' gives way to the beautiful 'I've Loved These Days.' . . . No matter how much stylistic ground Joel covers, he's kept on track by his backing group. He fought to have his touring band support him on *Turnstiles*, going to the lengths of firing his original producer, and it was clearly the right move."[70]

In spite of the artistic strides that Billy and his new band made on the *Turnstiles* album, in terms of sales, it was a total bust. Having scored two consecutive albums in the top 40, *Turnstiles* peaked at a dismal number 122 on the *Billboard* magazine Hot 200 Albums chart. It never even broke the top 100. There were no American hit singles released from the album, although "Say Goodbye to Hollywood," "New York State of Mind," and "Summer Highland Falls" all became staples of FM album track radio stations.

However, Billy was beginning to garner many fans in Europe, and particularly in Holland. Columbia Records division in Holland released two singles from the *Turnstiles* album and marketed them as "picture sleeves" that are now considered collector's items. Those two seven-inch Dutch vinyl singles are of the songs "Say Goodbye to Hollywood" and "James." There was also a British single version of "Say Goodbye to Hollywood."

To say that Columbia Records in the United States didn't know what to do with the album is a total understatement. Was Billy's music now jazz-rock? It certainly wasn't like the country rock music that Jackson Browne, Linda Ronstadt, and the Eagles were creating and placing on the charts that year. That had certainly been the sound of much of his last album, *Streetlife Serenade*. Unfortunately for Billy, this album just languished on the charts and then disappeared.

While promoting the *Turnstiles* album, Billy Joel and his new band performed on television's *The Mike Douglas Show*. It is one of the best glimpses of the band as a unit, and to see and hear the impressive and fast-paced piano work of Billy himself. Performing "Angry Young Man" and "New York State of Mind," they demonstrated the mesmerizing chemistry that they had developed. Liberty, on the first track, sets that lightning-fast tone of the song. In "New York State of Mind," Richie Cannata is heard showing off his heavily jazz-influenced sax in a spotlight solo. In the vintage clip, Billy appears fresh faced, and his singing is energetically heartfelt on this, which gave him one of his first major tastes of national TV exposure.

On *The Mike Douglas Show* it is quite evident that this whole band concept is very tightly in place. When it came time for Richie to do his sax solo, the camera did a close-up on him. When there was a drum segment, Liberty was suddenly given a close-up on camera and, for those segments, Richie and Liberty were treated like stars as well. This was the point in time where Billy, Liberty, Richie, and Doug really were a band. It wasn't just Billy and a bunch of guys.

Liberty recalls, "It was a bunch of guys who had nothing. Nothing. We went out and played, and just *killed* people. *Killed* people. Because it wasn't a business yet to us."[62]

Did Billy ever say, "We're all gonna share in this. We are all gonna be stars. We are all gonna help each other" to his band?

According to Liberty, Billy said to them, "'I'll make money, and you'll make money.' Yeah. Elizabeth was the one that told me, 'Billy will never make you rich. He'll take care of you, but he'll never make you rich.'"[62]

Like he had done before, Billy went out on the road and did an immediate concert tour to promote the album. As Liberty explains it, "That band went on the road for eighteen months playing *Turnstiles* and Billy's old albums: *Streetlife Serenade* and *Piano Man*. We *kicked ass* on everybody. People that hated the band, or hated Billy Joel, walked out of concerts— or—they became fans after they saw us play live. Because that was the powerful unit that Billy had that was there."[62] It was "make it or break it" time for Billy Joel and his group.

Since he was openly showcasing the material that was on the new release, Billy and the band needed financial support from Columbia Records to stay afloat. "Walter Yetnikoff kicked in $80,000 to save the *Turnstiles* tour," says Liberty. "We were struggling to make ends meet out on the road."[3]

On this particular tour Billy and his new band were able to reach a much wider audience. They headlined at several of the prime showcase clubs across the United States, including the Bottom Line in New York City, the Cellar Door in Washington, D.C., and the Ritz in Memphis. What this also enabled them to do was to travel out of the country as well. There was suddenly a great deal of interest in Billy and his music in Australia. Columbia Records' Australian division flew the band down there to do three days of press interviews and some concerts. He was really starting to make a name for himself internationally. It wasn't long before his growing popularity in Australia soon spread to Japan, too.

Years later, after he had achieved massive success on the record charts, Billy looked back upon this era of his first three Columbia Records albums and commented: "I've never had a concept of what I sound like. I can never compare myself to other artists. *Turnstiles,* I think, had a certain sound. The albums before that, though, *Streetlife* and *Piano Man*—I can't stand to listen to them. The tone of my voice, the production; they're all so self-indulgent. On *Streetlife,* I was trying too hard to write like Debussy. It was all so arty and undisciplined. I think I was lulled into that California state of mind, which was a big mistake for a native New Yorker like me."[59]

However in 1976, with his *Turnstiles* album, Billy had assembled the kind of band that he had for so long wanted to tour and to record with. With Doug, Liberty, and Richie, he had the core band he had been seeking to find. And, clearly his writing and musicianship had improved incredibly since his first two Columbia albums. Now he had the confidence, the drive, and the right band to make what was to become the biggest forward leap in his career.

8

THE
STRANGER

IT HAD ALWAYS been Billy Joel's dream to be a legitimate song-writer, one to whom great singers would flock. Well, that suddenly started to happen in 1977 when Barbra Streisand recorded her own interpretation of his composition "New York State of Mind." The critics unanimously loved what she did with this song. She truly helped to draw attention to his songwriting career. Since that time, "New York State of Mind" has gone on to become one of the most covered songs in Billy's entire catalog. Since then it has also been recorded by dozens of song stylists and jazz artists, including Mel Torme, Shirley Bassey, Oleta Adams, Diane Schuur, Marlena Shaw, Carmen McRea, and Tony Bennett.

The album that Streisand recorded it on, *Superman,* released in June 1977, hit number 3 on the American album charts, and by August it was certified platinum for sales in excess of a million copies. Because of this, Billy started accruing royalties for having his composition on this album.

Billy was terribly flattered to have Streisand sing his song, and to hear her take it to a whole new dimension. "It was amazing. She sent me an album and inscribed it: 'Dear Billy, Thanks for the song, hope you like it. Love, Barbra.' I still have it in a frame. My mother came over and saw it; all of a sudden, I became legit in her mind. The fact that Barbra did the song made other people pay attention."[12] This became his first song on a top 10 album of any sort. Now what he had to do was get one of his own albums to hit the top 10. That very feat was his big goal.

Billy was already writing a new batch of songs for his next album, and he was actively working them out with his band during their concert appearances. Richie Cannata explains, "We started to write on the road. Billy had these songs. Then we started to do *The Stranger* record on the road. We started to put together songs like 'Scenes from an Italian Restaurant,' and some other songs started to develop."[44]

Billy and Elizabeth sincerely felt that the key to taking his recording career to the next dimension would lie in the hands of whoever they chose to produce the next album. With that in mind, he met with the man whom he felt would be the ultimate record producer for him: George Martin. Since Billy's favorite rock group of all time was the Beatles, what could be more natural for him than to have his next LP produced by the man who did all of the Beatles' albums?

Richie explains, "We had asked George Martin to audition us, so we invited him to see us. I think it was Seton Hall University, and it was probably a hundred and fifty degrees in this gymnasium, in August. The kids were sweaty, and they loved it. Well, the acoustics were horrible, but he came to see us play. But he reneged. He passed on us. We were so stunned: 'How could he pass on us?' We felt that we were on the edge of this great career, and he just said he 'wasn't interested,' for whatever reason."[44]

Reportedly, George Martin personally loved Billy when he met him. He also loved Billy Joel's song ideas. However this dream pairing didn't quite turn out the way the songwriter had hoped. Martin was completely opposed to the idea of using Billy's new New York–based touring band in the recording studio. Billy felt confident with them, so much so that he was insistent they record with him. That became the deal-breaker. It was an instant stalemate. So it was back to the drawing board.

If George Martin wasn't going to produce Billy's *The Stranger* album, who was the right person for the job? Then, the name of Phil Ramone came up. Billy recalls, "I knew it was the right thing to do, even though it looked bad on paper. Elizabeth put me together with Phil Ramone, she set the whole thing up.[18]

Phil Ramone had been in the music business since he was a kid. He started his career as a thirteen-year-old classical violin student at the prestigious Juilliard School of Music in New York City. At the age of seventeen, however, he was thrown out of Juilliard for playing rock & roll and jazz

instead of the classics. He ended up taking a job in a recording studio, first as a demo engineer and eventually as a full-fledged recording engineer. He worked on several of Dionne Warwick's recordings for Burt Bacharach and Hal David—including the majority of the tracks on her *Promises, Promises* (1968) and *I'll Never Fall in Love Again* (1970) albums. He worked with several songwriters, including Ellie Greenwich and Leiber and Stoller. He then moved on to do engineering work on several jazz LPs for Creed Taylor's CTI Records.

In 1975 Ramone was a coproducer on Paul Simon's album *Still Crazy After All These Years*. On the disc he shared production credits with Simon. The album ended up being a huge success on the record charts and yielded four top 40 hits: "Gone at Last" by Paul Simon and Phoebe Snow, "My Little Town" by Simon and Garfunkel, "Still Crazy After All These Years," and the number 1 "50 Ways to Leave Your Lover." When the *Still Crazy After All These Years* LP ended up winning Simon and Ramone the "Album of the Year" Grammy Award, it elevated Phil Ramone to the top of Billy and Elizabeth's "wish list." Who better to produce the next Billy Joel album than Ramone? He was obviously in touch with what was happening on the charts.

During this same era Ramone truly became a hot new music producer in the business. He coproduced the soundtrack album for Barbra Streisand film *A Star is Born*—complete with the Grammy Award–winning "Evergreen" single he produced along with Streisand. Also he shared production credits with Bob James, on Kenny Loggins's debut solo album, *Celebrate Me Home*. To top it all off, Snow, Simon, Garfunkel, Streisand, and Loggins were all signed to Columbia Records at the time.

Says Ramone, "When I first heard the music of Billy Joel in 1975, I immediately joined a group of loyal fans. Most of his songs weren't big hits on the radio then, but we knew if they were something special. A year passed before I was invited to see Billy and his band in concert at Carnegie Hall. I was prepared to see the newest singer/songwriter in the old balladeer tradition. But what I observed was a first-rate rock & roll band. The interplay between Billy and his band members was extraordinary. They had much more than just raw power; they had a certain joy in playing together, without ever losing sight of the meaning of the material."[71]

He claims that he immediately noticed the great contributions of Liberty DeVitto as Billy's drummer, "I saw Liberty play with Billy Joel and I went crazy," recalls Ramone, "I just thought, 'What a great musical animal.' I met him about a year later when Billy and I talked about making music together. I said to Billy, 'You know, I'd really love to have your band. I think it's got a driving energy I haven't heard in the studio in a long time.' Liberty brought something to the sessions. He could play heavy-duty, straight rock & roll, and he could play it sensitively. I call him a 'song drummer.' He knows when to stay out of the way of the lyric and yet keep the beat hard and heavy."[72]

Meanwhile, Billy and his band were out on the road, polishing the new songs that they had put together. Richie Cannata explains, "We kept building a fan base, and more and more people heard about us, and our consciousness became stronger and stronger, until we ended up doing our own thing for five nights at Carnegie Hall, as the headliners. Elizabeth put this together with Dennis Arfa. Elizabeth was really amazing."[44]

Richie remembers that it was Ramone's seeing Billy and the band in Manhattan that cemented the deal. "Phil came to that show," he says. "He came to the Carnegie Hall show, and flipped out. He called the Record Plant [recording studio], and he said, 'Get a truck over there tomorrow, I want to record these guys.' We were just shuffling around then, we didn't know what the hell we were doing. We were out there playing music—just a bunch of Long Island guys. All of a sudden Carnegie Hall and Phil Ramone and the Record Plant. I knew all of those names: 'They are interested in me, and the band, and Billy. Wow, this is different!' So, [Ramone] heard this stuff that we were playing, because we dabbled into doing some of the stuff from *The Stranger* record. He absolutely loved it, and he said that he would love to produce us. I think that what we did, was during that tour, where we left the Beach Boys, and were doing some college concert dates."[44]

When Phil Ramone came to the show at Carnegie Hall, what he witnessed made him envision the kind of album that Billy needed to move his career toward mainstream success. "Then, Billy and I met for lunch with his wife and manager, Elizabeth, and discussed the possibility of my involvement as producer of the next album," says Ramone. "To my surprise, I learned that no one in the past, except Billy, had wanted to use his band in the studio. In those earlier years, record companies were run with very little freedom for the artists. Perhaps it was Billy's rebellious style of playing and constant willingness to risk everything that was suppressed by the old rules. But those rules never applied on stage, and there was never a doubt in my mind that Billy and his band should record together."[71]

According to Richie Cannata, Ramone's reception to the band's music was totally different from what George Martin had heard. "But Phil, on the other hand, he saw the potential," Richie claims.[44]

Billy's side of the story is this: "Elizabeth got me together with Phil Ramone. I wasn't a good producer at that time. I couldn't translate things correctly onto the record. And I couldn't really work with other producers who wouldn't let me use my own band. Phil had been an engineer on a lot of records like Paul Simon and somehow Elizabeth knew we would hit it off. She put us together and it was magic."[12]

Billy recalls the first day of working with Ramone. "Phil walked into the studio, saw the band, loved 'em: 'Wow! These guys are great, they've got road chops.' It wasn't a matter of just allowing them to do it; he was turned on by them. And they were, in turn. Because they'd been through different producers turning them down. They thought they were under the gun. When they found out the guy liked them, they grew, flowered, they blossomed," he claims.[18]

"It was funny when we met in the studio for the first time," remembers Ramone. "We were very polite, treading softly to make sure the ground was safe. My friend, Jim Boyer, used his engineering skills to help make the players as comfortable in the studios as they were on stage, and it didn't take long to find out that my group [of recording engineers and additional musicians] was just as crazy as Billy's."[71]

One of the first things that Phil Ramone noticed about Billy in the studio was what he carried around with him at all times. "This high school kind of notebook, like a lucky charm," Ramone remembers.[73] It was the notebook in which Billy jotted down all of his song ideas and lyrics. If someone made a suggestion, Billy made a note.

According to Billy, "The band had been under the gun with other producers, having to prove themselves, and also, there were always studio players, who were good but who weren't me. Phil liked my guys right off the bat. He heard them play the songs and said, 'Don't play any different than you play on the road—be the rock & roll animals that you are.' We did songs in five takes instead of 15 or 20. He was one of the guys. We'd throw around ideas, kick the songs around, try them different ways and get them right. Sometimes we'd throw pizza at each other. That's how it was with Phil. He also has a great sense of what's right. I was originally going to do 'Only the Good Die Young' as a *reggae* song. Phil heard it and said, 'Try to play in as a shuffle.' It worked. He got us to try 'Just the Way You Are' as sort of a backward samba. That's the way the songs develop. It's a communal thing in the studio. It was inspiration! We created heat in the studio."[12]

Ramone was used to recording artists like Paul Simon, who wrote and worked out his songs as a solo composer, and who would then show them

BILLY JOEL

to his band. In the case of Joel, Stegmeyer, DeVitto, and Cannata; Billy may have written the tune, but as a band they had already worked the songs out on the road. As Ramone explained it, "It's different with a group that plays together every day, a band, for example Billy Joel's basic rhythm section is just a bass [Doug], a drummer [Liberty], and a saxophone player [Richie]. But a guitarist has always been an outsider. The way I have found to record them was to work them together as close as possible, in about the same proximity as they work on stage where they can hear each other and feel it. So when they put the earphones on, there's no major change. Just a little more detail, and a little more clarity, so they can hear each other better. The thing about working physically close is that you play to the level of what you're hearing. That's not to say the drummer *cannot* play soft when somebody's playing an acoustic guitar. When the beat of the song is that heavy, why should he play ridiculously light? He just can't do that."[74]

As though he had been gambling for years without a win, Billy Joel was about to hit a major jackpot. A large degree of the success of this particular album was based on the songs that he chose to record. He had used his last four albums for polishing his craft and developing his own unique style. Now it was time to show off what he had learned.

One of the most winning parts of the formula on *The Stranger* album was the interplay between Billy Joel's piano, Liberty DeVitto's drums, and Doug Stegmeyer's bass. Says Liberty, "Doug was definitely an intricate part of the whole thing. We started recording: 'Bass, drums, and piano.' That was it. The mixes, up until I just left, the sound guy would always say, 'Bass, drums, and piano that's it.' Once he had those, it's done. Everything else is on top of that. So, it was me—the rhythm. Bill was the lead. And Doug held both of those together."[62]

In their recording sessions, the basic tracks consisted of Billy, Doug, and Liberty. According to Liberty, then Richie would come in and "overdub his horn parts, and then the guitars would come in and overdub, too. In the beginning."[62]

Liberty explains of his concept of music, "You take a slice of pizza, and you eat a slice of pizza, because you love pizza. If it was music, and I was biting the pizza, I would look at it as tomato sauce, cheese, bread, pepperoni. I know that there's parsley and basil in the sauce. I hear it in layers like that—like pizza. I hear music in layers."[63]

He further claims, "I can walk into music. Sometimes I play it so loud—and I used to say this when I used to get stoned—you can walk into music, and then you hear it around you. That's what you do when you are creating stuff. You are walking into the song. It is all around you now."[63] Liberty DeVitto's unique perspectives on music were an instant plus when it came to putting Billy's music on record. He could conceptualize the structure of a song so that there would always be layers of sound. If he heard a spot in a song that needed a little flourish, he would tell Billy that there was something missing, and then he would make suggestions of how the problem could be solved.

Richie Cannata recalls immediately hitting it off with Ramone as well: "Phil was a New York guy, he knew the cabs, and Broadway, and the city. He felt 'Scenes from an Italian Restaurant,' and he felt he knew all of us players, and all these great songs, so he fit right in. Phil Ramone is not a guy who tells you what notes are in a G-minus seventh chord. He won't tell you that, but he will pause and randomly whistle, so that you go, 'Oh, that's what you want?' His aura is great, and he brought us to the next level. And, Billy stayed with us. Again, he could have brought in Steve Gadd, who Phil was using for all of those great records for Phoebe Snow and Paul Simon. He could have brought in Steve Gadd and Ralph MacDonald. Actually, Ralph did come in and play on a couple of things. Billy wanted his band, wanted us, and when he heard us play, he said, 'Why would I change? It's their music, too.' Like on 'Scenes from an Italian Restaurant,' those are my lines, too. You get some jazz guy, like David Sanborn, and it's gonna be different—a whole other thing again. Like, Gerry Rafferty had a sax line ['Baker Street'], and everyone can play that line, but he's the guy who played it like that. He is the winner. Stop the calls. So, I was basically that guy, and so was Liberty, and Doug. Phil Ramone recognized that, and he was very smart, too; it kept Billy happy. And, it kept the cost down. We are not 'triple-scale' guys. We didn't even know what scale was or is. We didn't care. We felt, 'When we are done with this, we're going out on the road.'"[44]

Richie especially remembers how smoothly their first sessions went with Ramone as producer. "It was so easy, because we would get to the studio in the late morning or early afternoon, and by seven or eight o'clock we were done, and we were productive. We did *The Stranger* record in a month's time," he says. "Every day, we were productive. And every day Phil would order the same Chinese food for us—every day. Every day we walked in, and it was already there. It was great: 'Wow, Chinese food!' We didn't change a thing—like ball players. We had a routine. Sometimes we'd get picked up by a seaplane sometimes, and get flown in to Twenty-third Street from out here [on Long Island]. Other times we would just find our own way into the city. But it was a routine that worked. It wasn't broke, why fix it? Phil was great. The songs were basically already written, because we had rehearsed them; because we had tried them out on the road. So we set up everything. What we did do is to add guitar parts. We added Steve Khan, Richard Tee, and Hugh McCracken to *The Stranger* album. We set up and played. I had a B-3 set up, and all of the keyboards set up. I would do my solos right then, it was a no-brainer: 'Let's just play the songs like we did them live!' They added a real great taste to all of the songs. Steve Khan is great; Hughy McCracken is great, too. We set up, and Billy was there just massaging us to go this way and to go that way. Look what happened: *The Stranger* was one of our biggest albums!"[44]

It was Billy Joel's fifth solo album, *The Stranger,* which changed the course of his career. Now he was no longer just the troubadour singing songs about everyday life, he was officially a rock & roller. The album opens with a song about independence from one's family, which instantly struck an identifiable and common chord with teenage record buyers: "Movin' Out (Anthony's Song)." The lyrics are all about a colorful cast of characters in New York City's Little Italy, complete with relatives who moved out to suburban New Jersey. The song has a great rock beat, with crisp layers of sound, just like the way Liberty parallels layers of music to assembling a slice of pizza. It kicks off the album with energy and sass.

Recalls Liberty DeVitto, "That song came about when we were playing all of these clubs on the *Turnstiles* tour. Richie and I would have this running joke. We would sit around the swimming pool at whatever place we were staying. Billy would come down to join us, and we would go into these characters, like we were an aunt and uncle visiting him in the suburbs. It was like when you go and see your cousins who have moved out of the city, and you say things like, 'We just love what you've done with the place.' That became the basis for what Billy wrote about in 'Movin' Out,' when he sings about buying a house in Hackensack, and the characters of 'Mama Leone' and 'Mr. Cacciatore' on Sullivan Street. Then, at the end of the song, when you hear the sound of tires spinning out, that was actually Doug Stegmeyer's Corvette that we used for that. I remember it was burgundy on the outside, with a cream-colored interior. We strapped the microphone to a cassette recorder to the back of the car to get that noise. I still have that cassette tape sitting here somewhere."[75]

"The Stranger" is one of the most distinctive tracks on the album. It starts out with Billy's piano, and his whistling solo. It conjures an image of a smoky jazz club, or a dark and deserted street. Then the song kicks into high gear with several layers of sounds to a snappy beat. Here Billy sings about the different masks we all wear, and all of the personas that we adopt in life. Do we ever face the stranger that lives inside of us? This song perfectly asks that question.

Explains Liberty, "Billy wrote that song on one of those little Casio electric keyboards. They had all of these buttons on them where you could be accompanied by a rhythm track. Well, he pushed all of the buttons at once: 'Bosa Nova,' 'Rumba' and 'Rock & Roll.' That was how that song came about. And the whistling on the beginning of it is Billy. Russell Javors heard that and thought that the photo on the cover of the album should be like that famous pose of Frank Sinatra leaning against a lamppost with his raincoat over his shoulder: *Ol' Blue Eyes Is Back*. Well, since Billy had such odd eyes, Russell claimed that this album should show Billy in the same pose, and it should be called *Ol' Bug Eyes Is Back!*" He laughs.[75]

"Just the Way You Are" was destined to become another of Billy Joel's classic songs, written for his wife, Elizabeth. A beautiful and moody love ballad, it expresses such a simple but heartfelt sentiment about love. It carries a strong sense of devotion and acceptance that it has been a perennial favorite composition in the Billy Joel catalog. In this particular instance, several top-session musicians were brought in to add their musical touches to this track, including Hugh McCracken and Steve Burgh on acoustic guitar, Ralph MacDonald's percussion, and Phil Woods playing the alto saxophone.

Originally, Richie Cannata was supposed to do the sax solo on that recording, but he was replaced at the last minute. Says Richie, "Now, 'Just the Way You Are.' Let me tell you something about that. I first did the soloing on that, and we were in the studio, and Phil Ramone said, 'Phil Woods is next door, who was Charlie Parker's sax player.'"[44] Well, that was the end of Richie's saxophone solo on that recording. Cannata was taken off that track, and Phil Woods did it instead, just to have his name associated with the project. This did not make Richie especially happy, but he wasn't given a choice in the matter.

Liberty DeVitto points out, "Phil Woods is a big name. Phil Ramone didn't want to hurt Richie's feelings, but he didn't want to lose the song or miss the chance to have Woods on the record."[62]

At one point in the song, Billy sings of his own longing to be believed in, the way he concurrently believes in the object of his affection. According to him, "That edge of anxiety made it a more meaningful song."[19] It was such a heartfelt and touching lyric that "Just the Way You Are" was to go on to become one of Billy Joel's most covered song compositions, and one of his most beloved hits. At last count, more than two hundred versions of "Just the Way You Are" have been recorded.

"Scenes from an Italian Restaurant" is a trilogy of narrative songs about characters who live on Billy's beloved Long Island. It is sort of a soap opera. According to Billy, "It was actually three different songs that I sewed together. One song was called 'The Italian Restaurant Song,' because I wrote, 'Bottle of white, bottle of red,' and from there I went 'perhaps a bottle of rosé instead.' I'd never write that now [1996] because I can't stand rosé. But at the time I was just being introduced to rosé. So obviously, it's in an Italian restaurant, there's a couple talking, there's some kind of reminiscing going on, it's a little slice of life."[31]

When he comes to the lyrics about things being "O.K." with him, Billy explains, "That was actually another song I wrote, a little piece of a thing called 'Things are O.K. in Oyster Bay.' I was living in Oyster Bay and it was one of the first apartments I ever had. It was like a hippie crash pad, but I really dug it. I was living with this guy, Bob, who was another bum. But he was my good friend. We were all bums. 'Things are O.K. in Oyster Bay, Me and Bob and a meatball hero, da da da. . . . Playing on the piano all day, There's the L, It's the doorbell, Brian's there with a bottle of whiskey, Get in the mood for Chinese food. . . . ' Something like that. It was one of those dopey little songs. So I said, 'Ah, it's just this cutie pie little tune, it's not worth anything.' So then I needed to get from the instrumental section and I recognized we're going somewhere with this. You know where we're going? We're going to Brenda and Eddie. That's what they're reminiscing about. The story just told itself to me as I was going along."[31]

Regarding the segment of the song where he sings about the characters of Brenda and Eddie, who were high school sweethearts, Billy says, "That was another song called 'The Ballad of Brenda and Eddie.' It was sort of my ode to the king and queen of the high school in Long Island, New Jersey, New York environs—the legendary couple in school, which I think is a universal concept."[31] Finally the third part of the song finds Billy lyrically bidding Brenda and Eddie good-bye, and returning to the fabled Italian restaurant.

There is a lot of controversy about exactly what restaurant on Long Island Billy was singing about. Liberty DeVitto claims, "People assumed that it was Christiano's that was the inspiration for 'Scenes from an Italian Restaurant,' because Billy went there all the time. However, there wasn't one particular restaurant. Billy went to a lot of them on Long Island, so in reality it's a conglomeration of any of them."[75]

"Vienna" is a piece that Billy Joel wrote for his father. It is about his dad's flight from the United States to Austria. Clearly it addresses some of his frustration about his still-unresolved relationship with his father, and his father's passion and pride. A slow and romantic song, it has the slow beat of a Viennese waltz. In the lyrics he asks his father why he is always in such a hurry to run off, because Vienna would wait for him to return to it.

Regarding the origins of the music of this song, Liberty says, "There was a song by our former band, Topper, we called 'Give It All Away' or 'The Topper Song.' Billy walked into the studio one day, and he heard us doing this. It's just like the beginning of 'Vienna.' The next thing we knew he had written it in 'Vienna.' The end blues lick was my idea."[75]

Billy confesses that in his mind "Only the Good Die Young" originally started out as a reggae tune. It was DeVitto who is responsible for changing that: "Lib said, 'I hate reggae. I'm not playing on that.' We play great shuffles, so we tried it as a shuffle."[60]

The beginning of the song's lyrics find Billy attempting to convince the object of his adolescent crush, Virginia Callahan, to have sex with him. When it was released as the third single from this album, it caused a huge public uproar and was banned from several radio stations. Naturally, that helped to make it an even bigger and even more controversial hit.

Billy says, "I didn't have a problem with the Catholic Church, the Catholic Church had a problem with me. What happened was the song came out on *The Stranger* album, and it was no big deal. And then, Columbia [Records] decided to put it out as a single. That's when there were some problems. There was a radio station in New Jersey—they banned it. Then it was banned by the archdiocese of St. Louis. Then it got banned in Boston. All these archdiocese areas starting putting pressure on radio stations to ban it. And the record as a single had been out a short amount of time and it wasn't doing that well. The minute they banned it, the album started shooting up the charts, because there's nothing that sells a record like a ban or a boycott. And I speak from experience, because this record would have died out, nobody ever would've heard it if they hadn't tried to cut people off from it. As soon as the kids found out that there was some authority that didn't want them to hear it, they went out and bought it in droves and it became this big hit. Then I did it on *Saturday Night Live* and everybody was all freaked out about it, saying, 'You can't do that on TV.' I said, 'Why not?' I think some people took offense at it, but there were all these novels written about Jewish guilt, so why not write a song about Catholic guilt? Every Catholic I know is still recovering from this incredibly guilty upbringing they had. It was supposed to be lighthearted. It was taken out of context with the rest of the album."[31]

The slow "She's Always a Woman" is another Billy classic from this album. A beautiful piano-led love ballad, it was another praiseful song about Elizabeth. According to Billy, "'She's Always a Woman' is about women, but the song was misinterpreted. People said it was sexist, chauvinistic, but they missed the whole point."[12]

Like many of Billy's songs, "She's Always a Woman" was a composition that went through a few incarnations before it became what ultimately appears on this album. He explains, "I remember the melody started being written as 'The View from the 35th Floor' I was living in a high rise on the East Side of Manhattan and it was one of those 'look out the window' songs. As I was writing it, I thought, 'Well, I know it ain't gonna be about that.' But that was the 'bail out' lyric. I just needed a lyric to carry a melody until I decided what the lyric would be. It was really written as a folk song. This was during a time when my 'ex-wife Number One' was managing me in the music business. In those days, if a woman was too aggressive or too effective in business, she was looked on as a bitch, and I wanted to comment on that whole syndrome. You know, a woman can be effective and it doesn't make her any less of a woman. That was the point of the song, but some people took it as a misogynist song. They kept referring to it as 'She's *Only* a Woman.' I said, 'No, no, no, that's *your* title. My title is 'She's Always a Woman.' Misogyny is in the ear of the beholder, I guess."[50]

"Get It Right the First Time" is a medium-tempo rocker about first impressions; Billy's attempting to get a girl's attention in this song to something of a salsa beat. Phil Ramone recalls that this number had a long and drawn-out birthing process: "It's almost guaranteed that in every album there's at least one ball-breaker of a song, a tune that says, '*If you think I'm gonna give up my lyric and my melody to you so easily, you've got another thing coming.*' Billy Joel's 'Get It Right the First Time' was such a song. It's got a tricky beat, and no matter how hard the band tried it just wouldn't come together. We'd try it, then put it aside and work on 'The Stranger' or 'Movin' Out.' We'd go back to it, and then try 'Only the Good Die Young.' At the end of the date I'd say, 'Let's try "Get It Right the First Time."' We did it over and over again, day after day. It got to where the guys would anticipate coming back to the problem child and moan, "*We're not doing that again, are we? Pain-in-the-ass song doesn't wanna be born.*" One day we tried it and it slipped into place. I'm pretty sure we cracked a bottle of wine and said 'Amen' after *that* session!"[76]

The album ends with the upbeat and inspiring gospel song, "Everybody Has a Dream." It starts out slowly with Billy singing solo lines about dreaming of finding a new inspiration in his life. By the end of the song, an all-star choir of voices supplies a gospel background for inspirational support. The background voices here consist of the quartet of Patti Austin, Gwen Guthrie, Lani Groves, and Phoebe Snow—all well-known voices in their own right. Patti had a huge number 1 hit with "Baby Come to Me," a James Ingram duet in 1982. Gwen had a hit called "Nothin' Goin' On but the Rent" in 1986. Lani was one of Stevie Wonder's prime background singers on *Innervisions* and *Talking Book*. Phoebe was already an established hit-making star in her own right when this album was recorded. The result is a very effective and spiritually exalting song, which completes the album on an uplifting note.

After the gospel choir finishes, the album ends with a reprise of the whistling track that distinctively started off the song "The Stranger." It brings the music contained on this album full circle. "I'm a big melody freak," Billy later said of his music at the time of his fifth album.[26] Indeed, his work on this LP created some of his most memorable melodies yet.

Although the song "Just the Way You Are" was to become the biggest hit single to come from *The Stranger,* it almost got eliminated from the album. If it wasn't from the insistent prodding from another singer—or two— whom Billy admired, it may never have been released.

There are two distinctly different sides of this story, and the main outside party in this case was singer Phoebe Snow. Phil Ramone, along with Denny Cordell and Dion Airali, was responsible for the production of her dynamic 1975 debut album on Leon Russell's Shelter Records, *Phoebe Snow.* When her first single, "Poetry Man," had become a top 10 hit, everyone predicted a huge career for her.

One of Ramone's first opportunities to be a sole record producer was Phoebe Snow's next pair of albums for Columbia Records: *Second Childhood* (1976) and *Never Letting Go* (1977). For a time being, in the mid-1970s, Phoebe and Billy's careers were closely intertwined. Not only was she issuing a string of albums that were produced by Phil Ramone, but she was also an artist who at the time was being managed by Billy's wife, Elizabeth.

Since Phoebe had just scored a top 10 hit with "Poetry Man," and Billy had yet to achieve such a feat on the record charts, she was a much bigger name in the business, and therefore someone to pay attention to when she gave advice. According to legend, it was Phoebe who was instrumental in the success of what was to become Billy's biggest hit, "Just the Way You Are."

Billy Joel has repeated several times in the press the following story about the song. In *Performing Songwriter* magazine in 1996, he claimed, "I didn't like it very much. Liberty [DeVitto] hated playing it because he felt like a cocktail lounge drummer. I listened back to it and I thought, 'Aah, it's all right.' It just goes to show to you what musicians know really about what's going to be a hit or not. I tend to like the really obscure stuff that nobody ever hears. We were in the studio listening back to it and I was not even gonna put it on the album, and then Linda Ronstadt and Phoebe Snow showed up at the studio and they said, 'You've got to put that on the album!' I said, 'Yeah, you think so? We didn't like it that much.' And women just pleaded with me to put it on the album. So I'm going to listen to what women say. I put it on the album."[31]

Apparently both Billy and Ramone were in a quandary as to whether or not the song was going to be released as the first single from the new album, or if it was too "piano bar" sounding to include on a release that intended to be a rock & roll release.

"Billy never gets this story right," proclaims Phoebe. "Linda was not there! I don't know why he can't remember this story correctly. It was just me there. It was 1977, and he did not know Linda Ronstadt back then. We were in A&R Studios on West Forty-eighth Street [in New York City]. Phil was producing Billy and I at the time. They were playing me rough mixes [of the songs]. Billy and Phil wanted me to hear the singles. I was surprised to find that he was actually a bit embarrassed and apologetic as he prepared to play me the song 'Just the Way You Are.' He got rather self conscious: 'This is a little cheesy.' he said. 'In ten years Vikki Carr is gonna record this.' 'I'll be very objective,' I said to him."[77]

According to Phoebe, Billy and Phil proceeded to play the rough mixed tape for "Just the Way You Are." She was transfixed by what she heard. "I burst into tears!" she recalls. He was stunned to see tears streaming down her cheeks, and he asked her "Is it *that* bad?"

"This is the greatest thing I've ever heard. I'm weeping with joy!" she claimed. "Billy this is *really* good."

Furthermore, she insisted: "'That's the hit single. That's the one! I am never wrong about this.' He gave me this look like: 'You are one crazy bitch.'"[77]Yeah, Phoebe is crazy indeed—crazy like a fox.

Once all of the final tracks were in place, Billy was absolutely thrilled by the results of *The Stranger* album. He said of Phil Ramone, "He's got spontaneity; he's as nuts as any other musician; he's as crazy as I am. He doesn't come on like, 'I'm a superstar producer.' And he doesn't go for technical perfection; he goes for 'feel.'"[18]

Right after Ramone finished producing Billy's *The Stranger* album, he was interviewed by *Recording Engineer/Producer* magazine about the technical aspects of the recording process. When asked if he specifically produced rock music that would translate to the stage, Ramone explained, "Well, to answer that honestly I think you have to deal with what kind of artist you're doing. I mean, if one was producing Queen—an act like that—it's pretty hard for them to perform what they do on record. It's almost impossible. Or, even 10CC, and yet I've seen those acts in person, and it's believable. . . . For instance, in Billy Joel's new album, you can listen to it and see that everything is performable. In other words, if strings were needed to support something, or a horn line, then I used them, but I think of the song first and what the artist is about, and I tend to try to stay away from clutter. In general, for my taste, when you listen to it back after five or six times it just doesn't wear well when you've got too much going on. It tends to get boring if it's done to fill a track. And I refuse to do that."[74]

The point is well taken. What Phil Ramone helped Billy come up with was an album that was a collection of finely crafted songs, one that could be perfectly translated to the stage. Billy Joel and his red-hot band could be seen in concert, and this would inspire the ticket holders to immediately go out and purchase *The Stranger* LP, knowing that they would be purchasing the exact same music they had experienced on stage without tricks or overdubbing.

One of the arguments of the day, especially with the advent and popularity of "disco" music, was that a lot of the more popular recording artists were relying on prerecorded tracks to simulate real musicians. *The Stranger* did not adhere to that mode at all. It was real music performed by real rockers. What Billy, Richie, Liberty, and Doug created was not a product of programmed or simulated rock, it was the real thing.

The cover of *The Stranger* featured a stark and moody-looking black-and-white photo of Billy with a pensive expression on his face. He is dressed in a suit and tie and is looking into the eyes of a carnival mask. On the wall behind him hangs a pair of boxing gloves, as an homage to his former days of being in the ring. On the back of the album is a photograph of Billy, his band, and Phil Ramone, in what looks like someone's kitchen. Doug, Richie, and Billy are all seated at a dinner table, and Ramone and Liberty are standing right behind them. It truly looks as if five old friends are hanging out and sharing a couple bottles of wine, like a scene from an Italian home. This was the point: they were indeed five friends with bright and hopeful futures ahead of them, and a common goal.

The album *The Stranger*, which was released in September 1977, represented the big breakthrough for Billy. The years of frustration and struggling were about to pay off for him in such a big way, it was almost unfathomable. The brilliant collaboration of Billy Joel and Phil Ramone on *The Stranger* kicked off a decadelong association between the two of them. This milestone album was truly the one that made a superstar of Billy.

This time around, the reviews were instantly favorable. *Time* magazine writer Jay Cocks proclaimed of Billy's career, during the era of *The Stranger* album, "Joel's best songs have a brash humor, the sad, sometimes lavish sentiment that still stirs faint echoes of the boys down on the corner, harmonizing to the Top 40. . . . Under the direction of gifted producer Phil Ramone, the new record has a harder, more astringent sound. Joel's lyrics can be lilting, wistful or full of bite. He is at his best taking unsentimental trips back to home territory, exploring the dead ends and defeats of middle-class life in a song like 'Scenes from an Italian Restaurant,' a melancholy, hard-driving chronicle of the battered future high school sweet hearts, Brenda and Eddie. . . . Billy Joel is writing and singing some of the best pop music in the neighborhood. It might even make Virginia Callahan think twice."[26]

In *Rolling Stone*, Ira Mayer gave it a strong review, claiming, "This is the first Billy Joel album in some time that has significantly expanded his repertoire. While *Streetlife Serenade* and *Turnstiles* had occasional moments, the bulk of Joel's most memorable material was on *Cold Spring Harbor*—despite its severe technical flaws—and *Piano Man*, which gave him his only major single success. This time, while such songs as 'Movin' Out' and 'Just the Way You Are' are forced and overly simplistic, the imagery and melodies of *The Stranger* more often than not work. Together with producer Phil Ramone, Joel has achieved a fluid sound occasionally sparked by a light soul touch. . . . Ramone's emphasis on sound definitely lessens the impact of the sarcasm, which in the long run may help boost Joel's career immeasurably."[78]

This was the album that really built his fan base. New York press photographer Derek Storm claims of *The Stranger*: "Possibly one of the greatest albums ever executed in music history. Billy has his band that will stay with him including Liberty DeVitto and producer Phil Ramone."[49]

The month that *The Stranger* was released, Billy Joel went on the TV show *Saturday Night Live* and introduced his first single from the album to an estimated 20 million viewers. The result was *The Stranger*'s hitting number 2 on the American record charts.

The album also yielded a successful string of hit singles, including "Just the Way You Are" (number 2 in the United States and number 19 in the United Kingdom), "Movin' Out (Anthony's Song)" (number 17 US/number 35 UK), "Only the Good Die Young" (number 24 US), and "She's Always a Woman" (number 17 US). *The Stranger* was certified platinum by the RIAA (Record Industry Association of America) to signify sales in excess of a million copies in January 1978.

The Stranger album went on to sell over 10 million copies, surpassing the record set at Columbia Records by Simon and Garfunkel's *Bridge over Troubled Water* LP. Ironically, these are all acts that—in one configuration or another—were produced by Phil Ramone during this same period. Not only did he produce Paul Simon's *Still Crazy After All These Years*, but he also produced Art Garfunkel's popular *Watermark* album (1977). Billy's record for having the best-selling album in Columbia Records history held until 1984, when Bruce Springsteen's *Born to Run* surpassed it in sales.

The success that Billy was experiencing on the radio and in the record stores soon spilled over to his concert tours as well. Says Billy, "From 1971 to 1976, we averaged about 9 months of touring a year. During this period, the only records which achieved any significant recognition were 'Piano Man,' a modestly successful AM radio hit, and 'Captain Jack,' which became popular due to extensive FM airplay. Until the release of *The Stranger* album in 1977."[71] Suddenly he had reached a whole new level.

When Billy and his band hit the road to promote *The Stranger* album, he finally felt that he was being seen and heard in the right setting. According to him, "Elizabeth set things up so we could be booked properly. Once somebody put us on a tour with Olivia Newton-John. We called it 'The Snow White and Lenny Bruce Tour.' It didn't make sense at all. She was playing the big coliseums full of Sunday-go-to-meeting crowds and I'd be doing 'Captain Jack.' Instead of singing, 'You just sit at home and masturbate' in 'Captain Jack,' I would sort of slur the words: 'You just sit at home and *contemplate*.'"[12]

Suddenly he had made the leap to twenty-thousand-seat arenas. And, no more touring with middle-of-the-road acts like Olivia Newton-John. As Billy analyzes it: "The audiences got louder; that's about it. We always put on a good show, so that didn't change. People knew the songs, which was nice. And we were ready for it. A lot of groups have a big record but have no road experience. They have only one album's worth of material. They're on, they're off. And nobody's going to come back to see them again. We had four albums' worth of material and seven years' road muscle. We went to the coliseums and people thought they were going to hear 'Just the Way You Are,' but we had rock & roll from 'Captain Jack' to 'Piano Man' and 'Say Goodbye to Hollywood,' stuff people had vaguely heard of before: 'Oh, so that was his song.' Audiences got their money's worth. They felt they got a bargain."[12]

This was when Billy Joel started using his trademark concert-ending statement to the crowd: "Don't take any shit from anybody!" When he was asked by the press for an exact first time he shouted that from the stage, he replied, "I don't know, around the same time I started wearing a jacket and tie on-stage, about 1977. If you're really good at what you do, you really don't have to take any shit from anybody. But you have to be in a privileged position. It also means not giving any shit *to* anybody. I really believe it. I love swimming upstream."[12]

Billy was in contact with his father around that same time as well. When Billy told his dad that he had a huge hit single on the charts, Howard Joel was quite unimpressed with something so frivolous as rock music. As Billy explained, "I get the feeling that he don't know rock & roll. 'Just the Way You Are' was a big hit. He called me and said, 'You've written better songs than that.'"[14]

On one occasion during this time, Billy and his band encountered Howard Joel while they were on tour. Liberty DeVitto was quite startled when he met Billy's father, who was already totally bald at the time. According to Billy, "He doesn't have any hair. Liberty, the comedian in our group, called me 'Herr Joel,' and him 'No Hair Joel.' My father just looked at him and said, 'Fuck you!'"[12]

With the success of *The Stranger*, Billy made the transition from being a cult performer into being a music business superstar. When the whole world seemed to be going disco crazy, Billy was able to score a huge hit album that was anything but disco. It also set him on his path to being a bona fide rock star, and a songwriting legend.

No one was more surprised than he was about the reception that *The Stranger* received, and the effect that it had on his career: "I made a record-ing and it ended up being: 'rock star!' Which I still think to this day is very funny. I look in the mirror every morning and go, 'You're a rock star, ha ha ha, pretty funny.' I set out to be a [song]writer. But don't get me wrong, it's a great gig. But it really wasn't what I had in mind."[31]

One of the things that happened to Billy, because of the success of *The Stranger* album, was his rise to the status of "local hero" on Long Island. He was truly looked upon as the local-boy-made-good. Cheryl Khaner, who grew up to become a record industry executive at both RCA and Columbia, recalls growing up in awe of Billy. According to her, "I grew up in Cold Springs Harbor. We used to see him all of the time. He used to play at a restaurant called Café Brian, which had a big white piano, and it was in Cold Springs Harbor. On one of my very first dates, with my very first real boyfriend, he was there playing. We were huge fans. Since 'Scenes from an Italian Restaurant' was about a restaurant in Syosset where I grew up, we used to see him and his wife around—his first wife, Elizabeth. I was madly in love with him. He was like a hometown kid for us. I had his vinyl albums. That whole area of Long Island knew about him. He was a local hero, there was no doubt about it."[79]

She also distinctly remembers seeing he and Elizabeth in the eatery that was accredited as the inspiration for the song "Scenes from an Italian Restaurant." According to Cheryl, "We used to see him in Christiano's, which is a restaurant. We used to see him at this restaurant, that is no longer there, but it was right on the water and it was beautiful. We did see him and his wife around, and he was never not friendly. He was friendlier much earlier on, which kinda comes with the territory. But . . . his wife was never friendly. I remember saying hello to him very, very early on. *The Stranger*—with 'Scenes from an Italian Restaurant'—for us was like a seminal album. It is one of those albums I must have listened to 900,000 times. I went up to him one time when he was hanging around Syosset; right near where I went to high school was where the restaurant was. I said to him, 'I'm such a huge fan.' He said something like, 'Thank you very much,' but nothing dramatic. He wasn't cold, but not a lot of warmth from him."[79]

Cheryl remembers of the significance of Joel's music at the time of her high school graduation. "He was absolutely a hero for everybody who grew up in that area, at that time. We are talking about the seventies, and he couldn't have been bigger. It was right when he 'broke.' 'Only the Good Die Young' was like an anthem for my generation. When we were to graduate, that was the song we were going to play. And, the principal said, 'No.' Because it wasn't a great message. We had to pick another Billy Joel song," she says with a laugh.[79]

Although things were all going well for Billy Joel's career on the outside, all was not perfect within the band. Billy was making a fortune at the time.

Between record sales, and songwriting royalties, and concert grosses, he was suddenly rolling in money. His band members were not in the same position. The band was paid for their actual recording sessions, and they were paid for each concert that they performed at; however, they were not even near the income bracket that Billy now found himself within.

Liberty DeVitto recalls, "I don't think we ever got paid for recording *Turnstiles*. For *The Stranger* we were paid 'double session' and 'double scale.' Starting with the *52nd Street* album, we were also paid a $10,000 bonus for every million albums sold. That gave us an added incentive to really play great onstage, knowing that we were helping promote the album we would be sharing the profits on."[37] Uncontracted money arrangements, like these bonus payments, were later to cause problems in the band.

A studio working pattern had been set with *The Stranger*. Although Billy, Liberty, Richie, and Doug had all been in on the creation of these songs, it was Billy Joel who owned all of the rights to them, their sales, and their publishing. Furthermore, the band members did not have contracts with Columbia Records. Says Liberty, "There were contracts, but a lot of it was just like by word-of-mouth. It was always album to album and tour to tour. Being a drummer, you get the short end of the stick because, unless it's up front and 'in' on writing or creating the song, you don't have any melody. We were the most powerful people in the band, because we are the ones who get people up to dance. I believe that a band is only as good as its drummer. But, because we're so powerful, and everybody has to listen to us and play to us, we've been cursed with one note. We have no melody. And, melody is money.[63]

"So, when you create these drum parts, and people come up to you and go, 'If it wasn't for that drum part . . . that's the perfect part for that song.' But that's it: you are paid for that day you are in the studio, and that's it. Steve Gadd didn't get any more than union money to do 'Fifty Ways to Leave Your Lover,' but it *made* the song."[63]

At first, it was just a gig, and everyone involved was having a good time in the studio. It wasn't until later, when millions of dollars were suddenly at stake, that any of the musicians began to think of asking for royalties from record sales. But by then, the pattern was already set. Richie Cannata recalls, "Who knew back in 1975 that we should copyright every note that we could play? We were just in a band, and we were just playing these notes and having fun."[44]

Already, at this point in Billy's career, there were allegations that his songs were inspired by the work of other musicians. Russell Javors wrote a song called "Poor Boy." According to Liberty, "Russell remembers after the *Turnstiles* album, before *The Stranger* album, bringing Billy into the studio and playing that song for him. It was like, 'I'm a poor boy, I've been looking for a fight all my life. I been low down, but that's all right, you don't have to let me in.' You know, that kind of thing. 'I stuck it out, because only the good die young.' That was the line from the song. And the next thing we knew, on *The Stranger* album Billy had a song called 'Only the Good Die Young.'"[62]

Indeed, missing from the recording sessions of *The Stranger* album was guitar player Russell Javors. After Phil Ramone got to know Javors, he was convinced that he, too, could become a star. Russell says, "At the time of *The Stranger*, I had my own deal going. And actually Billy played on my demos, at Ultrasonic [Studios] the same place that he did *Turnstiles*."[65]

The plan was to give Russell Javors a solo recording career, as well as a record deal for his band, Topper. In this way, there was a bit of a tug-of-war between Billy and Russell, as to whose band Cannata, DeVitto, and Stegmeyer would be part of, and who would be left behind.

Explains Russell, "Mike Appel was my manager. He was the guy who was Springsteen's person. We did these demos with Mike. And he really didn't want me to play with those guys: 'They don't give a fuck about you!' The only thing that I wanted to do in my life was to be part of a band. And I knew I had a really good band. I tried it. I tried working with other guys, but I just never felt the chemistry that I felt with these guys. I was kinda naive a little bit. I never thought about money. I was totally gonna make a ton of money. Who gives a shit?"[65]

Russell Javors hoped that he would have his career spin-off on its own, and Topper would have its big break. However, that was not how it happened: "First of all, I had this stuff that was not mainstream like Billy. It was kinda quirky and odd. And I figured there'd be people who would love what we do, and there'd be people who would hate what we do. It's real. It's got its own thumbprint. It's valid, and it is what it is. I thought, if I had a little interesting something, and I made a good living, and the people that liked what we did were very passionate about it. But I couldn't see why everything couldn't peacefully coexist. But Billy was not at all supportive of it. Phil Ramone was very supportive of it, and Phil always included me in stuff. I think Phil wanted to produce me. I know he did, but Billy didn't want him to.[65]

"It was funny. It looked like my thing was just gonna get going, and then I think that everybody started to realize that it was the band that was starting to take off with Billy, and rightfully so. Billy was about to explode. And, my stuff, even if it went, wouldn't have exploded. It would have been what it was, but it wasn't like what Billy was doing. . . . My dream was to have my thing go, or have our [Topper's] thing go as a band. But it wasn't gonna happen that way. That's life."[65]

According to Liberty DeVitto, at this point in time there were already plans underway for Topper to get their own recording contract. "Topper was gonna get a deal. Billy was gonna get us a [recording] deal. At my old high school we had done a benefit, and CBS was all ready to sign up the band, Topper. Billy stopped it. Billy burned us," he insists.[62]

When it is pointed out that "Liberty blames Billy for ruining Topper's chance at getting their own contract," Russell Javors replies, "I think even Elizabeth would vouch for that."[65]

After that, Russell returned to Billy's band and was a permanent fixture on Billy Joel's albums and concerts for the next decade. "I didn't play on *The Stranger,* although I did the European tour. I came back in the band for the end of *52nd Street.* Like, I did some overdubs on some of the songs on *52nd Street* and everything after that."[65]

During this same period, Liberty met his first wife: "The first time I got married was right after *The Stranger* came out. We were big at that time. I married this woman from New Jersey named Susan. I met her when Richie was going out with a girl named Nancy. Nancy Morris, I think her last name was. And it was after a show. These fans were running after us and stuff like that. So, I got out of the car and these girls with albums in their hands were running after us: 'Liberty, Liberty, Liberty!' So Richie was walking with Nancy and Susan up ahead of me, and I ran up to Susan and put my arm through her arm and I said, 'Make believe you're my wife.' And we just walked off. Then she actually did become my wife!" He laughs.[62]

Was it a good marriage? "No. I married a drinking buddy. That's what happened."[62] It ended up lasting five years, and they had one daughter.

Meanwhile, Billy was making more money than ever before. He was on his way toward becoming part of the upper echelon of rock stars. As *The Stranger* album was peaking, in 1978, he and Elizabeth were living in a one-bedroom thirty-fifth-floor apartment on the East Side of Manhattan with a view of the Fifty-ninth Street Bridge. According to a profile on him in *Newsweek* magazine, "When Billy could finally afford a grand piano for his New York apartment, he insisted that he and Elizabeth spend the night of its arrival sleeping underneath it."[15] Their midtown apartment was also

BILLY JOEL

equipped with a small studio setup in case he had any song ideas he need to capture for future compositions.

By now Billy Joel was officially an up-and-coming media star. In March 1978, he was profiled in *People* magazine, which in itself signaled his ascension into the mainstream of pop culture in the United States. In the article, Billy claimed that it was Elizabeth who was the financial mastermind between the two of them: "She's the family capitalist. She knows if I get my hands on bread [money], I'll blow it. My management doesn't know that I still have a credit card. If I can pay the bills, eat in nice restaurants twice a week and live in a nice place, that's enough. Sure, it's easy for me to say now that I don't give a shit about money. But I've been poor and happy."[80]

Thanks to *The Stranger* album, Billy had officially arrived. Because of his moxie and his tenacity, he was able to score that big top 10 album he had been striving for. Now he was living in the lap of luxury. He was having his first taste of the big time, and he liked it.

9
JAZZ ON FIFTY-SECOND STREET

ALTHOUGH HE HAD previously complained about the endless cycle of recording an album, and then immediately leaving on an extensive concert tour to promote it, that was to be Billy's life for the next several years. With the huge success of *The Stranger*, the pressure was now really on to not only match the success of that album but to surpass it.

While on the concert tour to promote *The Stranger* with his band for several months, Billy and his musicians had the time and the opportunity to begin mapping out new songs for the next album. Clearly the winning formula had been found, as witnessed on his fifth solo album. He had found the writing style, the sound, the musicians, and the right producer.

Suddenly Billy Joel was looked upon as a triply talented new recording star–concert performer–songwriter to watch. His rock & roll success on the record charts represented only part of his appeal. He was also building a strong legion of fans who loved the rocking energy of his live shows. And then there was the versatility and the appeal of his songwriting. Not only could he write a raucus rocker that was perfect for the radio, he was also a highly sensitive songwriter who was seen as something of a talented jazz master as well.

Since he was the hot new kid on the block, journalists took great delight in asking Billy about his approach to writing a song. The press coverage that he received around this time started out in a chatty and entertaining dialogue. However, before long the tone of his public statements would shift extremely as Billy would find himself having to publicly defend his sources of songwriting inspiration.

Speaking of his piano playing during this period, Billy stated, "My style is mongolized. I have a lame left hand and I've forgotten a lot of theory. I don't play just with my fingers, I put my whole body into it. I want to hear the piano scream. I'm always breaking piano strings—and you're not gonna find a lot of piano players who do that."[15]

According to him, he had struggled for a long time before he had defined his own personal sound. "There's a certain kind of elitism," he said. "Like if you're from the city and you just do urban music, it's cool. If you're from the country, the mountains of Tennessee, you're authentic. But if you're from the mainstream, you're vanilla, you're nothin.' Which is bullshit because . . . a lotta people are."[18]

What was it that Billy was trying to project? What was it that was his message? "I'll tell you the truth, when I'm writing, I'm not aiming toward an image. I'm not aiming toward a certain message in what I say. I don't know what the hell I'm doing when I'm writin.' I'm just goin.' I work myself up into this state. For weeks, I'm empty. I got nothin,' I'm dry, I walk around, I'm the worst person in the world, I got stubble, I smoke, I drink, I get bombed, I curse at everything, I throw things, I think it's all over. And then I click. I don't analyze it, I don't intellectualize it, I just do it."[18]

He was also finding that his music was touching people in ways that he couldn't imagine. "Sometimes somebody will come up to me after a show: 'You know, when you said *that*, it meant *this* to me.' And it'll educate me. But I don't sit down and write suburban troubadour balladeer stuff. I go with the moment," he said at the time.[18]

When asked about his musical inspirations and influences, he said, "I like all kinds of music—jazz, country, rock, you-name-it. If I write a soft ballad, the next song I'll write will be a hard rock & roll tune. I don't want to keep writing the same thing. I want to interest myself."[15]

Still, he insisted that the lyrics, which critics and fans found so poignant and universally touching, were nearly an afterthought to him. "Dylan was the only one who could get away with not having the music as complete as the lyrics. A lot of times, I just write words for the sound of them to complement a particular key or a particular pattern of notes. Not to take anything away from the importance of lyrics, but the melody has to be complete first. It has to stand up alone. If my words don't emotionally match the music, that's because they are made to fit in afterward—and I guess that's backward from classic songwriting. You're supposed to write a poem or something and set it to music."[12]

He claimed that the words were secondary. It seemed that critics and fans were constantly looking for hidden meanings in his lyrics. Had he ever written the lyrics to a song, and then came back and wrote the music? "I tried it. It ends up as a pretentious pile of garage. I'm not a poet. When everybody was trying to figure out the hidden meanings behind The Beatles' songs, I was just listening. When 'Lucy In the Sky With Diamonds' came out, I didn't think of LSD. I said, 'Well, that's a nonsense song. That's O.K. The words sound *really* pretty. A lot of people I knew were having stoned discussions about what the songs meant; they were playing the records backward and turning the album covers upside down, and I used to sit there and go, 'You're all full of shit. It doesn't mean anything more than that it says.'"[12]

When Phoebe Snow had first met Billy Joel, prior to the release of *The Stranger* album, she was the one with all of the critical acclaim, and a top 10 hit. Once "Just the Way You Are" became the biggest smash hit of his fledgling career, it was he who was the bigger star. Phoebe recalls, "A year and a half later I visited them in this mansion on Long Island. I was meeting with Elizabeth, who was still my manager. At one point she said to me, go see Billy in the other part of the house, he is working on songs for his new album."[77]

Phoebe went into the room where Billy sat at his new grand piano, and he made motions like he wanted to be alone. "Elizabeth sent me in to see you," she explained.

"Okay, sit there for a few minutes," he relented.

"He was working on the song 'Rosalinda's Eyes,'" Phoebe remembers. "He had no lyrics yet. I said to him, 'I love the music. It sounds like Leonard Bernstein.'"[77]

As they sat there, finally Billy acknowledged Phoebe's brilliant perception about the song "Just the Way You Are" as being a hit. Says Phoebe, "There was a short pause and he looked up at me and said, 'How did you know?'"[77] She just smiled.

In 1977 Billy and his band were already working on the next album. According to Liberty DeVitto, "All of Billy's albums have specific themes

BILLY JOEL

to them."[81] Following that recipe, the album *52nd Street* was one that most successfully melded jazz music with his sound.

Richie Cannata distinctly remembers the sessions for this, the sixth Billy Joel solo album, which would ultimately be entitled *52nd Street.* "It was just a good mix of guys. And we were," he says of the recording atmosphere in the studio this time around. "And, you know what the truth is, if you listen to the radio today, these songs are still good to listen to. It's amazing. Billy, as a writer, just gave us that freedom."[44]

How was it decided where a sax part was needed in a song? Says Richie, "Whenever I had a spot to play. I was never told what to play. And, most of the stuff that I played was one of two things. The only thing that I worked out was 'Big Shot.' That was an ensemble. 'Soli' it is called, not a 'solo,' because it has three parts. I worked that out at home. But I had enough information in life, because that song was about Elizabeth and their lifestyle, and what they were doing. I knew Elizabeth, she was my friend, and she was our manager. So, I thought about that, what she was, and what I needed to play for that section. The fact was that we were really good together in the studio. Billy would have something nearly completed, or nothing. By the end of the day, we would have something. Phil Ramone was really good with that."[44]

The very name of the album had a jazz connotation. In the 1930s, '40s, and '50s, the actual Fifty-second Street in New York City was the location of several notable jazz clubs. One of the primary ones was the legendary Birdland. It was the street where you could go into a small nightclub and see the likes of Billie Holiday, Sarah Vaughn, Chet Baker, Dinah Washington, Charlie Parker, Count Basie, and Miles Davis appearing onstage. The Fifty-second Street strip of clubs would frequently attract the show business elite, including Frank Sinatra, Ava Gardner, Marilyn Monroe, Marlene Dietrich, and Sammy Davis, Jr. By the 1970s CBS Records, the parent company of Columbia Records, was also located on Fifty-second Street, as well as the studio where this album was recorded. So, the album title had a lot of significance to it, and obviously a lot of good karma as well.

Of the recording of this album Richie explains, "*52nd Street:* Billy always liked to change. And he really wanted to do *52nd Street* different. So, you remember on the cover of that record, he held a trumpet in his hands. Fifty-second Street was 'Swing Street.' That's where all of the jazz clubs were. And, oddly enough, that's where A&R Studios was located, where we were recording. Where he took that [album cover] picture with the trumpet was right in the garbage area where we used to go into A&R Studios. It was typical New York, where you had to walk through all of the garbage and the rats to get there, and go upstairs. So, he wanted that record to be different, and my participation was greater, and I had a really good time on that record, because I got to play some more clarinet. We had a song called '52nd Street' on there. 'Zanzibar' was on that record. That was Freddie Hubbard who played the flugelhorn solo on that."[44]

That was just one of many guest appearances by jazz giants that became part of *52nd Street.* In addition to Hubbard, Phil Ramone invited several other noted jazz musicians to participate on this album to fully give it an authentic jazziness. They included Hugh McCracken (guitar), Dave Grusin (horn orchestrations), David Spinozza (guitar), Ralph MacDonald (percussion), Eric Gale (electric guitar), Randy Brecker (trumpet), and Michael Brecker (saxophone).

By adding this sparklingly authentic jazz aspect to the *52nd Street* album, Billy took the winning formula used on *The Stranger* and took it a step further. "Listen, it's a definite temptation to repeat a successful formula," he explains. "But I have never done the same thing twice. I don't care what anybody says! After *Stranger,* I could have done *Son of Stranger,* but I've never done that. To keep me interested, there always has to be something new, something different. When I come up with a melody, it is not calculated. It's like an erection: It happens. There's no formula. I do try to write complete melodies; that's a constant. Because there are only so many notes and so many combinations, it gets tougher all the time to stay away from what's been done before. But everything I've done is different. The proof is that some people think I'm a balladeer, others think I'm a rock & roller, still other's think I'm the 'Piano Man.'"[12]

The *52nd Street* album opens with one of Billy's more raucous rockers, the self-examining composition "Big Shot." The music for this has a tasty and raucous rock & roll excitement to it. Led by wailing guitars and drums, Billy sounds confident, defiant, and insistent as he sings the lyrics in an accusatory tone of voice. In the song he is heard admonishing himself for mouthing off, doing too much coke, and acting like a smart-ass. According to him, "It's about anybody who has ever had a hangover. Wake up in the morning and you can't move and you're so hungover, saying, 'You stupid idiot. You had to be a big shot.' I did a *lot* of personal research for that song."[12] As the song progresses, he sings of all of the people who were impressed with all of the celebrities he knew at famed Elaine's restaurant on the Upper East Side, and at the way he had to command the spotlight all evening. As the first track on this blockbuster album, Billy Joel and band kick it off in grand style.

In a way, the stance of "Big Shot" was the rock & roll version of the West End/Broadway song "What Kind of Fool Am I" from *Stop the World I Want to Get Off.* It actually prompted several reviewers to draw a parallel between Billy Joel and Anthony Newley.

Just as he has explained, the next track needed to be a juxtaposingly slow song to contrast "Big Shot." Here Billy presents his centerpiece romantic ballad "Honesty." It is this album's counterpart to "Just the Way You Are." According to Billy, had it not been for drummer Liberty DeVitto, it might never have lyrically turned out the way it did. "A lot of times Liberty will get me to write stuff, because I won't have lyrics, and he won't record with me unless I have lyrics, because he plays to the lyrics. Or he wants to sing along. That's how he remembers things, because he doesn't read music. So what he'll do to motivate me to write lyrics, he'll make up the filthiest possible lyrics he can think of, which are really good and the song will live forever like that unless I come up with some lyrics real fast. When I wrote this song, 'Honesty,' originally it was called 'Home Again,' 'Home again, Get me out of here.' We were in Europe or on the road for a long time and I just wanted to go, 'Home again, Get me out of here.' And, I didn't write any more lyrics, so Liberty started writing his own lyrics: 'Sodomy, It's such a lonely world.' Everybody started singing that whenever we'd play that song, and I realized I better come up with some lyrics pretty quick. It's a good way to motivate somebody. Humiliation is a terrific motivator."[31]

If "Big Shot" is the "why-did-you-make-an-idiot-of-yourself?" track, then "My Life" is this album's perfect "mind-your-own-business" song. Here, the background chorus sounds very Beatles inspired, from their period of "I Am the Walrus"—very echoey and reverberating. Describing this song, Billy remembers, "I wrote that one night when I was thinking about a young person leaving home and telling his parents, 'I don't care what you say anymore, this is my life.' And the parents turning around and saying right back to the kid, 'Well, go ahead with your own life and leave me alone.' It's kind of a mutual, 'See you around. Don't let the door hit you in the ass.' There's still a line in there that I still strongly believe in: 'Sooner or later you sleep in your own bed/Either way that's O.K. you wake up with yourself.' You still have to be able to look at yourself in the morning. You are the one you wake up with first."[50]

Billy also recalls that his dad, Howard, was there in the recording studio with him. He was quick to note that his father has never quite "gotten" the whole idea of wanting to be a rock star, instead of a classical pianist. He said at the time, "He's been in recording sessions. He was there for 'My Life,' and he said, 'You're making the piano sound out of tune.' And I said, 'That's the idea, Pop.' You can't explain Elvis Presley to my father."[14]

If *52nd Street* was to be Billy's tribute to jazz, then "Zanzibar" is its centerpiece. With its references to sports blaring from a TV screen in a neighborhood bar, this is somewhat the upbeat jazz version of "Piano Man." Here, Billy Joel is narrating the scenario in a bar by the name of Zanzibar. In this instance it is a sports bar, like the ones you can still find on Seventh Avenue just south of Madison Square Garden. Freddie Hubbard's sax solo is stunning in the middle of the smoky and moody song. The jazz guest star solo turns on this album were clearly added to this piece to elevate Billy's stature in the business, and to garner attention to the album. Especially in this song, the result is brilliant.

While composing the song Billy says he had the word "Zanzibar" on his mind, but at first he was still thinking of it as being the country. It never dawned on him that the title might be something of a pun: "Zanzi Bar."[2] "Phil walked by and said, 'Yeah, I can just see the guy, sitting there, at the bar, havin' a drink.' I said, 'What?' And it hit me: 'Right! Zanzibar is a bar.' It came together then; I could picture this guy drinking, watching sports on TV. Much more interesting than what I'd been doing with it—trying to write about the mystical nation of Zanzibar."[60]

After that, the bar scenario blossomed forth. "There was an Ali fight, I think it was one of his last fights in the '70s," he explains. "I don't know whether it was [against] Joe Frazier or George Foreman, but there was an accusation that he took a dive, that he went down too easy, which is where I got 'Ali don't you go downtown.' 'Going downtown' means you took a dive. I just came up with that word 'Zanzibar.'"[31]

Billy also recalls something profound that Doug Stegmeyer said to him following the "Zanzibar" recording session: "They used to say rock & roll guys couldn't play jazz—we don't have the chops. But we tried on that particular track. After we recorded that, my bass player looked at me and said, 'Now I feel like an adult.'"[1] An unedited version of the song "Zanzibar" appears in the *My Lives* boxed set, where the jazz jamming at the end extends the track to a full six minutes and forty-six seconds.

"Stiletto" is a medium-tempo but raucous number about a sexual dominatrix of a woman who will "cut" you literally and physically if you don't

Internationally acclaimed artist Mark Kostabi's portrait of Billy Joel, painted exclusively for this book. He will forever be known as the "Piano Man." *[Courtesy of Mark Kostabi]*

Liberty DeVito   Doug Stegmeyer   Billy Joel   Richie Cannata

Billy and his band of brothers: Liberty DeVitto, Doug Stegmeyer, Billy Joel, and Richie Cannata.
[Courtesy of Liberty DeVitto]

Phil Ramone took Billy Joel's music to a new level of success as his producer.
[Courtesy of Bobby Bank]

The band of brothers before Billy Joel: Doug Stegmeyer, Russell Javors, and Liberty DeVitto in their band Topper in 1970.
[Courtesy of Suzanne and Russell Javors and Liberty DeVitto]

Billy Joel and Richie Cannata share the stage on October 16, 1976.
[Courtesy of Jay Pomerantz]

Billy Joel once considered becoming a professional boxer.
[Courtesy of MJB Photo Archives]

He is known as the "Piano Man," but he is also an accomplished guitar player.
[Courtesy of MJB Photo Archives]

Billy Joel is classically trained, but his heart is in rock & roll.
[Courtesy of MJB Photo Archives]

Billy Joel sold out his concert debut at Madison Square Garden in 1978, NYC.
[Courtesy of Jay Pomerantz]

Billy has taken his life experiences and used them as inspiration for his Rock & Roll Hall of Fame–heralded career.
[Courtesy of Jay Pomerantz]

Billy's albums *The Stranger* and *52nd Street* made him a superstar. *[Courtesy of Bobby Bank]*

In 1978, Billy Joel was one of the top hit makers in the music world.
[Courtesy of Jay Pomerantz]

Billy in concert, November 15, 1979. *[Courtesy of Jay Pomerantz]*

Billy, seen here in 1980, has always had a passion for airplanes and yachts.
[Courtesy of Richard E. Aaron / rockpix.com]

Joel in concert, 1980.
[Courtesy of Richard E. Aaron / rockpix.com]

Billy Joel during his Long Island Charity Begins at Home fundraiser for WBAB in 1987. *[Courtesy of www.DerekStorm.com]*

Billy Joel and Ray Charles in the studio recording the song "Baby Grand." *[Courtesy of MJB Photo Archives]*

Billy Joel during the Millennium Show at Madison Square Garden, New Year's Eve, 1999. *[Courtesy of www.DerekStorm.com]*

Billy Joel and Elton John at the Hartford Civic Center, Connecticut, February 6, 2001. *[Courtesy of www.DerekStorm.com]*

watch out. This succubus of a devil woman—presumably in black leather—is someone who would make you not want to turn your back on her, for fear of what she will do next. Although some women's groups blasted this song as being misogynist in nature, it is just a turn of the tables from some of the songs in which women criticize their men, for example, Pat Benetar's accusatory "Heartbreaker." Here the jazz mood continues, with Billy effectively using his piano downbeats, Liberty's drums, Richie's horn, and amplified finger snaps to play off of and sing to.

While it is filled with all sorts of exotic Hispanic/Cuban references, "Rosalinda's Eyes" is not about a Spanish sweetheart at all. Liberty DeVitto reveals that the song is actually about Billy's mother's eyes: "Listen to the lyrics; it is about his mother. Rosalinda is in reality Rosalind Joel."[37]

"Half a Mile Away" is Billy's 1950s homage. Here he sings with doo-wopping background voices and a solid horn section. The lyrics are all about his rebellious teenage days when he used to go to his bedroom, slip out the window, and go running through the streets with his hoodlum buddies. Here he sings about a particular party and all of the excitement being just a half-mile trek from his house.

"Until the Night" is a dramatic sweeping ballad that sounds as if it is straight out of the Phil Spector songbook. This was written as Billy's tribute to the great harmonies of the Righteous Brothers. That singing duo's most enduring hit was the Spector-produced "You've Lost That Lovin' Feelin'" (1964), and this very successfully emulates that song's dramatic sound. Richie Cannata's sax solo in the middle of this number continues the jazz theme that threads its way through this potpourri of rock and pop tracks.

The album ends with the title song, "52nd Street," which offers the kind of music to which Bob Fosse might choreograph a dance number. Here Cannata sets down his trusty sax to perform a jazzy clarinet solo.

In addition to all of the guest musicians who appeared in this album, there were also several guest singers. On *52nd Street* the voice of Peter Cetera of the group Chicago can be heard in "My Life," and Ray Simpson of the disco group Village People vocalizes on "Half a Mile Away."

Critically speaking, the reviews for the *52nd Street* album were very mixed. *Rolling Stone* magazine utilized their review as an opportunity to create more of a character assassination than a critical essay of his latest LP release. In his critique in that publication, Stephen Holden claimed, "Billy Joel is the quintessential postrock entertainer: a vaudevillian piano man and mimic . . . able to caricature both Bob Dylan and the Beatles as well as 'do' an updated Anthony Newley, all in the same Las Vegas format. . . . A bantam, hyperkinetic Rocky Balboa onstage, Joel works audiences into a lather of adulation with the snappy calculation of a borsch-belt ham. As cockily aggressive as Sammy Davis Jr., he lards his performances with schtick. . . . Neither a great singer nor a great writer, Billy Joel is a great show-business personality in the tradition of Al Jolson. . . . Joel's songwriting forte is pop pastiche. . . . Billy Joel would probably still be only a cult figure, idolized in concert but poorly represented on record, if he hadn't found the perfect studio collaborator in producer Phil Ramone."[82]

After slamming Billy personally, Holden finally addressed the album at hand by stating, "Here, Joel's saxophonist, Richie Cannata, becomes his foil in a Clarence Clemons/Bruce Springsteen sort of relationship. The rhythm is powered by a streamlined, Elton John/Wingsstyle propulsion, and everything is mixed hot. The result is as perfect and flattering a studio presentation as can be imagined . . . *52nd Street* evokes the carnivalesque neon glare of nighttime Manhattan, using painterly strokes of jazz here and there to terrific effect. . . . The artist's fault-finding songs are among his least interesting, and 'Stiletto,' a psychologically trite bit of misogyny, is the LP's one outright failure. . . . 'Until the Night' is the formal pièce de résistance of an album that, though far from great, boasts much of the color and excitement of a really good New York street fair."[82]

Monthly rock magazine *Creem* was similar in their critique of *52nd Street*. They, too, turned it into an essay more about Billy Joel than about his music. Reviewer Richard Riegel wrote, "Top 40 anchorman Billy Joel is posing on the cover of his new album as the young-man-with-a-horn of '50s hipster lore, to tickle the jazzy fancies of his more rabid fans . . . the cover photo is a giveaway, as Joel doesn't play any trumpet within, and as *52nd Street*, for all its jazzed celebration in the title tune, also happens to be the corporate address of Joel's employer, the CBS conglomerate." Yet when he finally gets down to talk about the music, Reigel saw the hit potential: "'Big Shot' is the biggest hit so far, but 'My Life' is coming on strong, and I expect to hear 'Zanzibar,' 'Stiletto,' and maybe even the Righteous Bros.-inspired 'Until the Night' on the radio before this album has run its course."[83]

However, true music fans pay little attention to what a reviewer says or thinks. Billy had started a groundswell of a fan base with *The Stranger*, and they instantly snapped up copies of the new album, the minute it hit the racks of their local record shop.

The *52nd Street* album was released in October 1978. By the week of November 18, 1978, it topped the *Billboard* album chart in America—a first for Billy Joel. In the United States, it sat at number 1 for the next eight weeks, into 1979. In England it ultimately hit number 10. In its first month of release, the album proceeded to sell over 2 million copies in America alone. The album yielded three international hits: "My Life" (number 3 US/number 12 UK), "Big Shot" (number 14 US), "Honesty" (number 24 US), and "Until the Night" (number 50 UK). "My Life" sold 2 million copies as a 45 rpm single in the United States, Billy's second million-selling single release.

On February 15, 1979, the twenty-first annual Grammy Awards were presented, and Billy picked up his first pair of the trophies. He won the Song of the Year award for penning "Just the Way You Are." And, he and Phil Ramone received Grammies in the category of Record of the Year for the single release of that song.

Richie Cannata remembers what an exciting time it was to be a part of the whole Billy Joel phenomenon: "*52nd Street:* that was a great record! Some of the stuff was written out on the road. By this point we were a band. We were a band, and we knew our strengths. We knew our weaknesses. We knew what we could do. We had proven that we could take it to the coliseum level. It was really happening. We did *Saturday Night Live.* There's *Billboard, Cash Box,* and *Record World:* Here we go, we start the next record—*52nd Street*—number 1 across the board in all three magazines. It was amazing. But, we didn't understand it. I remember [booking agent] Dennis Arfa coming out on the road, and I go, 'What's really happening? Number one, what is that?' He said, 'You're number one in the industry right now!'"[44]

The week of May 13, 1978, Billy Joel was represented by three totally different singles on the *Billboard* magazine Hot 100 music chart in America: "Just the Way You Are," "Movin' Out (Anthony's Song)," and "Only the Good Die Young" were all on the chart at the exact same time. There was a major concentrated push by Columbia Records to establish Billy as a rock & roll superstar.

When Billy and his band went out on tour in 1978 he found that his demand was now suddenly growing. The year before, in 1977, he was still working in small clubs. Now he was headlining fifteen-thousand-seat auditoriums. It was during this period that several Billy Joel traditions were born. One of his first precedents was to not allow any of his shows to have intermissions. As he explained it, "For me, an intermission is coitus inter-ruptus. When you get on a roll you should go! A lot of rock groups are just on automatic pilot. I like to play. It's great to leave the stage knowing the audience wants more, and if they want to listen, I'll keep playing."[15]

From this point forward, he took up the habit of juxtaposing his slow and more personal songs with his more raucous rockers. This way, his shows became a smorgasbord of divergent musical tempos and styles. His rationale: "For me, it's gotta be a tension and release. I hate shows where it's just 100 percent noise."[15]

In 1978 he vowed that he was going to always keep his concert ticket prices at the lowest possible level that he could. That way, his fans could always afford to come and see him. It is a habit that exists to the present day. He said at the time, "I've found audiences over the years have been used to accepting shit from performers; one token encore, then the announcement: 'They have left the building.' The jive performers give an audience—people pay $9.50 a ticket, the group goes on-stage on automatic pilot. I've been on the road for eight years. I've met a lot of rock stars. A lot of 'em have a lot of contempt for their audience. They really think they're a bunch of jerks. When I'm on-stage, the main thing I'm thinking about is, I want them to feel like that $9.50 was worth 18 dollars, 19 dollars. Like they walk away 'up.' Like I didn't jive them. I didn't give them no shit. I happen to think that if they're into me, they have a certain amount of intelligence. I don't know, maybe I'm idealistic. I like to think that people are smart."[18]

Billy Joel made a lot of his concert structure choices from watching other acts, and figuring out what he liked and did not like. Says Billy, "The Grateful Dead—a lot of people like them, but I never got into them. I went to their shows. I tried, I got stoned, I did everything I was supposed to do. Look, I like guitar playing: Jeff Beck, Jimmy Page, Hendrix, Clapton. I like intelligent guitar work. I don't like mindless boogie jams; it nauseates me after a while."[84]

He instead emulated the best aspects of idols. "If there's anybody I've modeled myself after, it's Paul McCartney," he revealed during the late seventies. "And it's never been picked up on. I see critics compare me to Elton John, I see Harry Chapin, and I go, 'No, no, no, it's McCartney!' I go back to all of them, though; I'm a sponge for all kinds of stuff, I suppose. A song like 'Earth Angel' in the '50s [by the Penguins]—now that's a rock & roll song, but if it came out now, they'd call it MOR or a ballad. But it was rock

BILLY JOEL

& roll to me. When people say I'm a perfect imitator, I say, 'Who isn't?' You all come out of a certain era and make your little changes."[84]

He put a lot of thought into his choices. Billy claimed that he was more in touch with the "regular Joes" on the street than many of the other performers he had seen. "When I had regular blue-collar gigs in the late '60s, they gave me this amazing insight into how elitist a lot of people and music are. Most people aren't pop stars; most people aren't celebrities, and there's this deification of people like that which I think is totally misplaced. I have a real cynicism about this whole star thing. I don't think I'm so special—I just do what I do. I put myself down on-stage, I kid around. I've read where that 'cheapens my persona.' But I do it because I want to demythify myself. 'Hey, I'm a human being, just like the rest of you.' There's an edge to success that makes me not trust it or dwell on it. The minute you've made it, you start to become extinct, especially in rock & roll; rock & roll doesn't forgive. That's the nature of this business: new blood, all the time. The bigness of this last year, I don't understand. It's a manager's game, an agent's game, a numbers game. It may be the American ideal of success, but I never bought that. I don't feel that much different. I've always liked what I do; I still like what I do, and I hope to God I can keep it in perspective. I am going to be a musician my whole life. I look at Coliseum rock groups that I think are horrible, and they draw millions of people. Now is that success? As long as I got my self-respect, that's all I care about."[84]

Not long after Billy Joel had finally hit the big time, he had the first of his major career lawsuits. This one involved a songwriter who claimed that the song "My Life" was stolen from a demo tape that was sent to Columbia Records but was rejected by the company.

Fighter that he was, Billy launched into a bitter court battle to claim that his song ideas were all his own. According to him, "There was a case where this guy alleged that I stole his song, which I didn't. And I was advised by my then manager, who was also my wife, and other people, that I might as well just settle it because I could lose the song. And I thought, 'That's absurd!' It's like, if you have a kid, somebody comes along and says it's their kid, well you should give them money so they don't take your kid away. That's the way the system works though. You'll end up paying more in legal fees and you won't win any money, you'll just be out money. So it's a nuisance suit. . . . If somebody ever accuses me of stealing a song, I will sue them back, I will fight. I will go after them with every gun I can get.

Because these are my children and I will not have my children taken away from me. But I got mad."[31]

Billy Joel wasn't about to take this lying down: "Based on the fact that I wrote the same kind of song and the fact that Columbia had his tape, he said I heard his tape and stole the song. When I heard about it, I said, 'Let's go to court. Let's kill him. I want to *kill* him.' But the lawyers said, 'Look at it this way. You're going to go to Reno, Nevada. You're a big successful rock star. Here's this poor little *schlump*. The jury's going to be from Reno. We'll have our musicologist, he'll have his musicologist. Who's to say? You can lose.'"[12]

In an interview with *Playboy* magazine, Billy became indignant: "I said, 'How can I lose? I wrote the song! I know I wrote the song! My wife is a witness!' 'Your wife can't testify.' "But she was there! I went through all hell writing this damn thing!' Anyway, they told me I should settle out of court. I said, 'What! Why should I settle? I wrote the goddamn song!' But they advised me to settle, because life is not fair. So they settled for the minimum amount of money. After everything, the guy probably got $5,000. It was a nuisance suit. But by the agreement, we were supposed to get a letter saying that I did *not* steal his song. I was totally against it, but I went along with the lawyers for once. So I'm supposed to have this letter. I've never seen this letter. And I hear that the guy does an act now and says, 'This is a song I wrote that Billy Joel stole.' So I'm going to kill this guy. I want to break his legs with my own hands. . . . If I ever meet that guy, I'm going to break his legs, I'm going to break his face. That may sound real macho and stupid and brutal, but I don't care: Don't take my child away. That's it," said Billy.[12]

Although Billy's career had hit a new zenith of success, not everyone was cheering him on from the sidelines. The press was regularly portraying him as something of a spoiled star who was a pain-in-the-ass to deal with. In a 1978 feature in *Rolling Stone,* writer Dave Marsh said of the singer: "A lot of people seem to think that Billy Joel is an obnoxious person. I couldn't deny that he is belligerent, rowdy and uncouth, although it seems to me these qualities are attractive in a performer."[18]

Marsh also reported that the two of them had gone together to a concert in Chicago, and midshow Billy kept announcing the baseball scores of two competing teams. When he announced that the New York Yankees had indeed won the game in question, several of the other team's fans booed them. It was reported in *Rolling Stone* that Billy raised his middle finger and flipped the crowd "the bird" to let them know how he felt about anyone booing the Yankees.

Back at the hotel Billy was staying in, Marsh recounted that at four A.M., he and the singer disturbed a couple of the hotel's other guests. When one woman opened her door to complain, Billy told her to "Shut the fuck up." When another door opened in protest, he yelled in its direction, "You wanna get into it, too?"[18]

This became one of the articles that did some notable damage to Billy's public character. He was garnering a reputation in the press for being an obnoxious and feisty loudmouth. Whether it was fair or not, this particular issue of *Rolling Stone* certainly presented a negative view of him as a spoiled and demanding star.

To voice his own distaste for some of the press reviews that he was receiving, Billy took to holding up articles about him onstage, and shredding them in front of concert audiences. He later said, "I supposed I overreacted to some reviews. It probably wasn't the coolest thing in the world to do. I don't regret my impulse, but I regret acting on an impulse. It just drew more attention to the negative review than there would have been normally. Also I was taking it too seriously. But then again, some times I had to, because the reviews questioned my motives, my integrity. A lot of reviewers, they don't review the album, they review me. Everything is colored by their perception of Billy Joel. Therefore, the album never really gets an objective look."[40]

Comparing his two most successful albums to date in 1978, Billy claimed, "There's been an evolution in my music. For instance, *52nd Street* is a much different album than *The Stranger*. It had a harder edge, although there was still orchestration on it. But I think people thought we were going to go into a jazz vein in, say a Steely Dan sense. I was getting hung up on public reaction to my work. But, hell, I've got a lot of good friends and success, so what am I complaining about?"[14] In reality, he had nothing to complain about whatsoever—his career was red hot at this point.

From March 3 to April 24, 1978, Billy and his band were on the international leg of his *52nd Street* world tour that took them to Amsterdam; Brussels; Frankfurt, Munich, Stuttgart, and Bremen in Germany; London and Birmingham; Perth, Adelaide, Melbourne, Brisbane, and Sydney in Australia; and Tokyo and Osaka. From the fall into December of that year, they performed in the United States to support the new album. The American tour ended up with Billy's first sold-out engagements at New York City's Madison Square Garden.

Reviewing the show in the *New York Times*, John Rockwell wrote, "Billy Joel came home Thursday night, and it was a triumphal occasion for him.

Not only was it his debut at Madison Square Garden, but it was also the first of three shows that had sold out almost as soon as they went on sale. . . . His success should make New Yorkers feel good for two reasons. One is the obvious hometown-boy angle. Beyond that, Mr. Joel in his music and his manner epitomized the sort of street-smarts that form the country's image of the city, and the fact that he's so popular speaks well for how the rest of the United States regards the city. Mr. Joel has encountered some resistance from rock critics. Although his music is far more jazzy and balladic. . . . His touring band was in fine form, too, and it should be noted that all but one of them come from Long Island as well: Richie Cannata, winds and keyboard; Doug Stegmeyer, bass; Liberty DeVitto, drums; and David Brown and Russell Javors, guitars."[85]

Similarly, Geoffrey Stokes in the *Village Voice* at first critically complained about Billy and then conceded to the success of the show: "The Garden last week was sold out long before his current L.P., *52nd Street*, began to roar up the charts. At first listening, the new album struck me as an excessively mixed blessing . . . Joel's voice is thin, and on his records it's often heavily sweetened with strings, but accompanied by just his five touring musicians, he was forced to rock rather than croon. It worked. After two years of heavy roadwork, the band is wondrously right, and Joel plays off Richie Cannata's horns the way Springsteen plays off Clarence Clemmons's. The key, however, is drummer Liberty DeVitto; he is as maniacally propulsive as Keith Moon, as melodically precise as Nigel Olsson. With Joel's pounding piano serving as another percussion instrument, the band hit high gear in the night's third song, 'My Life,' from the new album, and didn't stop coming until the fourth encore."[86]

Performing the lively music from his newest albums certainly invigorated the energy level of his concerts. Billy admitted, "Playing all that rock & roll was fun. One rock & roll song kicked off another. Also, I started to jump around on-stage more. I used to stay behind the piano."[12] He and his band were now known for putting on one of the liveliest concert shows around.

Now that he was selling albums by the millions, and filling arenas and concert halls around the globe, it was the first huge wave of success for Billy Joel. The press was viewing him as an unlikely but undeniable overnight success story. Of course, in show business, from the outside it looks like fame and fortune came quickly. The singer was constantly asked how he felt now that he was in the winner's circle. According to him at the time, "Everybody assumes—especially nowadays—I get this a lot: 'Boy isn't it great you're successful. Doesn't it feel good? Isn't it wonderful? It's really paying off for you now?' I've been trying to say for years, 'I've been successful for a long time, because I have been able to support myself as a musician since about the time I was 20 [he was twenty-nine at that point]—which is a miracle in itself. There're very few musicians who can support themselves just being musicians. So that's success. If you can support yourself being a musician, it's a miracle."[18]

Underneath the lifestyle of champagne and limousines, Billy claimed that he was still that same scruffy street kid from Hicksville. "I'm still just another heavy hitter off the street. But I've matured to the point where I don't kick over garbage cans," he told *People* magazine in their first major article about him.[80]

Although he and Elizabeth were living in the lap of luxury in Manhattan, he tried to maintain a connection to his roots: "I try to go back to Long Island and just talk to people, but they talk to me like I'm superhuman. I try to say, 'Hey, it's me, remember me? Just give me an hour and I'll get as drunk as you.' But people act like I'm totally different."[57]

He even went so far as to complain publicly about the pressure that fame brought to him. "To a certain extent, some of this new success that I've run into, some of it's a real pain in the ass, because money creates a leech/parasite syndrome: 'Oh, you have to come up with the commercial success again.' I never bought that crap," he claimed.[18]

What a wild ride to the top the last couple of years had been for Billy Joel and his troupe. In the space of two and a half years and a pair of multimillion-selling albums, his name was now equated with the term *superstar*. This was a time when albums still sold for $5.99, and concert tickets for a face value of ten to twenty dollars. And yet, between recording sales, songwriting royalties, and performance grosses, Billy Joel was personally making millions.

Although Billy was portraying himself publicly like a fair-playing blue-collar "everyman," sources close to him were starting to notice that he was both "cheap" and "greedy" in sharing the wealth. Even Elizabeth was telling members of his band not to expect any great raise in their paychecks simply because Billy was now wealthy.

It was starting to become clear to Liberty, Richie, and Doug that a slightly askew pattern had been set in their working relationship with Billy. There were no formal printed contracts, and everything was still handled on a handshake kind of an agreement. When it came time to record an album, the musicians in Billy's band were paid an hourly salary of "double scale," which is twice what the Musician's Union mandated as the minimum wage at that time. Billy's way of working in the recording studio was to bring in scraps of songs or melodies. He would ask for musical contributions from the members of his troupe, and they would create their parts. At the end of the day they all had technically contributed to the musical creating and recording of the songs, yet only one person was getting full songwriting credits. And, it was Billy Joel who also reaped all of the monetary rewards when other singers performed these songs.

Liberty reveals, "According to a 2002 covered earnings report from the Musician's Union, Local 802, I grossed $5,789.76 in 1978. I would think about $3,936.00 of it was for recording *52nd Street*, plus we got $10,000 when it was turned into CBS Records, and $10,000 every time it sold a million copies. Singles and overseas sales were not included."[87]

On tour, the band members were paid a set fee for the specific concert dates. In between tours, Billy continued to be paid for his record sales. The band went unpaid during these periods while Billy would write or relax or vacation. In a group like Fleetwood Mac, each of the members of the band is signed to a recording contract. This was not the case for Liberty, Richie, and Doug. Although these three men were the official core of "the Billy Joel band," there was no recording deal for them.

Liberty DeVitto reveals that this was the beginning of a huge dispute that was brewing underneath the surface within the Joel camp: "After the release of *52nd Street*, Doug and I were already hip to the fact that we were underpaid for our contributions to the music on that album. So, we went to see a lawyer. The lawyer said to us, 'Are you willing to quit the band?' We looked at him and said, 'No.' He said, 'Bye. Meeting's over.' That was that. With no contracts with Billy, we were considered nothing more than just hired session musicians."[3]

While Billy was onstage singing "My Life," night after night in front of his band members, his band was doing some thinking about those exact same words. It was their lives, too, and they knew that they were not being paid half of what they felt that they deserved. However, for the time being, they were all aboard a fast-moving train riding at the top of the charts, and no one was about to get off of it. At least not yet.

10

PEOPLE WHO LIVE IN GLASS HOUSES

MARCH 1979 FOUND Billy exploring fresh territory, in a geographic sense. He was one of the performers to be part of an American-Cuban musical cultural allegiance that was billed as Havana Jam. The idea behind it was very humanitarian, or so it seemed on the outside. It was to be a musical presentation of contemporary American music to the people of Cuba. On the bill were the American performers Stephen Stills, Weather Report, John McLaughlin, Bonnie Bramlett, Rita Coolidge, Kris Kristofferson, and Billy Joel. There were also several Cuban performers in the lineup for the three days of shows, including Sara González, Pablo Milanés, Orquesta de Santiago de Cuba, Elana Burke, and harmonic male group called Manguaré.

Another of the American groups, the salsa band known as the Fania All-Stars, had two members in it who were Cuban expatriates. While in Cuba they were able to visit family members they hadn't seen in two decades.

This was the first official envoy of American performers who had gone to Cuba to perform in over twenty years. When he was asked if he felt inspired by going on this supposedly diplomatic tour, Liberty DeVitto says, "I was too young. We were too young. I was twenty-eight. We're in

Cuba. You are first blown away by how poor they are, and only eighty miles from America."[62]

Richie Cannata remembers being startled by all of the 1950s automobiles that were still being driven on the streets of Havana, as if the performers had embarked upon some sort of trip into the past. He claimed he was "freaked out by the time warp."[88] Also, some of the humanitarian overtones were apparently lost on the American musicians at the time. *People* magazine claimed that some of the intended goodwill of the visit was eclipsed by some of the musicians' nonstop partying.

Then there were the purely commercial aspects of this trip, which caused a conflict in the Billy Joel camp. CBS Records put this whole thing together, and it was their intention to record both audio and visual tapes for use in a series of albums, and a TV special. Ultimately two albums were released: *Havana Jam I* and *Havana Jam II*. In other words, this was to look like something of a diplomatic mission, so the acts all donated their time and their performances. Yet, the record company was going to turn a profit for organizing the event.

However, Billy is nowhere to be found on those two albums, because he refused to sign the agreements to allow his music to be used. Reportedly, it was his wife and manager, Elizabeth, who went ballistic when the decision was made for CBS to exploit the video footage, and the audio tracks of Billy and his band from the Cuban festival. She was instantly labeled as being a "difficult" character in the Billy campwhen she "nixed" the project.

"It coulda been her. It coulda been him," says Liberty. "I remember Billy told me, 'Why should we be selling an album with a bunch of people that aren't selling albums? Because we're the hottest thing right now.' He didn't want to. He said, 'No. We *don't* want to be on it.'"[62]

As Billy explained at the time, "We wanted to see what it was like playing in Cuba. When we were asked to play there, we were really excited. My father had lived in Cuba, so I was interested for that reason, and we were just leaving Europe, where it was cold and wet and we thought, 'Cuba, what a nice idea!' It was a special concert that included other performers organized by CBS Records. We were told it was just to bring American music to the Cuban people. We understood before we left that we were only going to play—not be taped or recorded. Then, when we got there, they had all these plans to tape the entire show. We said, 'No,' we weren't going to be on a record we had no control over. We were not going to help bail CBS out for what it spent on this thing and rip off the Cuban people. We were there to play, not exploit it. Then all these stories came out about how we ruined it for everybody because we wouldn't let them tape our part of the show. The stories said that Elizabeth was giving everybody a hard time and we were prima donnas. Well, that's the press again."[12]

At the mention of this whole Cuban adventure, Liberty DeVitto laughs, "'The Bay of Gigs?' Russell Javors coined that phrase: 'The Bay of Gigs.' Cuba was unbelievable. Unbelievable! We played in the Karl Marx Theater in Havana, a small little theater, a hundred fifty people from America. It was five days. Weather Report went on first. We went on last, at the end of the show, because we were the most popular band; *52nd Street* was out then. For every American band, there was a Cuban band. An American band went on, a Cuban band went on, an American band, a Cuban band. Everybody had to go to all the shows. If you wanted to stay at the hotel, forget it. But, it was good."[62]

Richie Cannata had a great time and made some valuable contacts during that trip: "I met Kris Kristofferson and Rita Coolidge when we went to Cuba. We didn't get paid anything for it. We got the trip there. For us, to look at it, we go: 'Well, someone made a lot of money.' It's Cuba! We got to play for Castro, and we played the Karl Marx Theater. I saw the Tropicana, I met Rita and Kris, and I ended up playing on one of her records, and producing one, and [later] ended up going to South Africa with Rita Coolidge. I made some money, and I made a great connection."[44]

The concerts were held at the forty-eight-hundred-seat Karl Marx Theater, located west of the downtown area of Havana. Reportedly the events were lengthy all three evenings, up to five and a half hours each night. There was a lot of good-spirited camaraderie in Cuba among the musicians involved with the project. According to several sources, in addition to everyone smoking Cuban cigars and drinking Cuba Libres, there were also plenty of illegal substances to be had as well.

Liberty DeVitto amusedly recalls, "It was a little bit of a coke fest, too. I don't know how they got it there, but boy, oh boy! . . . Stephen Stills was fucked up all the time. *All the time.* To the point where he was dancing on stage once, and wrapped his legs, getting caught in the guitar cord. And there was [singer] Bonnie Bramlett and [piano player] Mike Finnegan, crying at the sight of this: 'What has happened to the guy?'"[62]

In a review in the *New York Times*, critic John Rockwell wrote, "Billy Joel capped the 'Havana Jam '79' at the Karl Marx Theater here last night with a stirring performance that brought the crowd cheering to its feet. Mr. Joel's presence at this three-day festival of Cuban and American popular and jazz musicians—the only American pop performer here whose career is in full

BILLY JOEL

tide—lent the proceedings a legitimacy they might have otherwise lacked. And he drew the most fervent response of the entire festival."[89]

The crowds went crazy for Billy and his band's brand of raucous rock & roll. Reported Rockwell, "They screamed when his hits appeared, they danced in their seats, and they even tried to storm the stage at the end. It was just like home." Rockwell was also laudatory of Billy and his group of musicians: "Mr. Joel and his top-notch band seemed to play and sing with a special passion. . . . The Americans not only offered at least some first-class jazz and pop performance talents, but also proved—in Mr. Joel's set—that in the right context rock & roll has the power to be subversive."[89]

No one was more surprised at the reception that they received in Havana than Billy and his band. Says Billy, "We didn't think the Cubans would know any of the music, but they pick up Miami radio stations, so they knew the hit records. The main thing was that the kids wanted to hear American rock & roll music. We were the last group on. The kids stormed the stage. The guards were there with machine guns, trying to figure out what was going on, since the kids had been sitting politely for the other acts. You see, the other groups had gone on-stage and. . . . Well, Stephen Stills came out and made this big speech about, '¡Viva la revolución!' in Spanish. And the audience just kind of went, 'We've been hearing this stuff all our lives. We don't need to hear *this*.' They came to hear rock & roll. Now, I know the critics like Robert Palmer don't consider me rock & roll—he thinks I'm the new Neil Diamond or something—but we played a rock & roll show! The only thing I said onstage was, '*No hablo Espanol*,' then went into 'Big Shot,' and the place went like, 'Whaaaa!'"[12]

He mused upon this experience, "You know, music is something everybody has. People fall in love, people have families, people have sadness. It doesn't matter if they're Marxists or Communists. These kids want to party. They want to have a good time, to hear music. They want to dance at night. We have all these ideas about what they're *supposed* to be like. Even on the level of the Cuban kids coming up to us and asking us if we wanted to buy marijuana. We didn't. They said to us, 'But you're *Americano! Americano* want pot?' We buy what we hear about them, they buy what they hear about us. A lot of it has to do with the image projected by the press. We're fed a lot of crap. We're taught not to relate to foreigners as people. I went to Cuba to play for people."[12]

Naturally, the members of Billy's band got into the whole party atmosphere of the nightlife in Havana. One night the entourage went to the Tropicana Club to see the scantily clad showgirls in the elaborate nightclub floorshow. Liberty DeVitto was quoted in *People* magazine as remarking loudly, "Hey, is it horny in here, or is it me?"[88]

Russell Javors recalls, "Havana Jam was interesting. I think some of the jazz guys were a little pissed at the attention we were getting. As if somehow our music wasn't as important as theirs. The thing I remember most was getting to hang with Bonnie Bramlett. I was a huge Delaney and Bonnie fan, and always loved her voice. She and Rita Coolidge were on the trip, so I was really happy to meet them. Bonnie wasn't drinking, but she went with me and Lib to a bunch of bars in Havana. She was a very cool chaperone."[64]

One of Richie Cannata's fondest experiences from this trip came on the return flight back to the United States: "The good part about it was, is that I remember, Billy flew a charter, and there were only a few seats on the charter. However, however the selection went, I didn't get on the charter. I think that either management or Liberty or Doug got to go on the charter. The rest of the guys didn't. Well, I ended up sitting next to Stan Getz on the charter that we had. My dad had always played Stan Getz's music. I said to him, 'Mr. Getz. Hi, I'm Richie Canatta. I play. . . . ' And he said, 'Yes I know who you are, you play with Billy Joel.' 'Stan Getz knows who I am!' I sat next to Stan Getz!"[44]

In spite of all of John Rockwell's praise for Billy in the *New York Times*, he also devoted part of his article to bashing him, and his music as well. In that same piece he claimed, "Mr. Joel's music is busy and dense in a way that can blur to murk in big indoor arenas, where he usually plays these days; heard clearly, it takes on a significantly greater impact and intensity. And his normal, two-and-one-half-hour set seems to drag on too long; his music simply isn't that interesting. In one hour, there's just enough of it for this case—15 minutes too much, even?—and the set is pared down to his very best songs."[89]

Not only did Billy and his band go to Cuba that year, but they also took another controversial international jaunt as well, to Israel. It occurred, says Liberty DeVitto, "in 1979, around the same time [as Cuba]. The biggest thing was that when we went there, we got to Customs, and they looked at our passports. And, when they looked at Billy's passport, because he was first. They looked at him and they gave it back to him and said, 'Okay.' He said to them, 'We love to get stamps on our passports. Aren't you gonna stamp my passport?' They said, 'No, if we stamp your passport, you will never get into Jordan or anything like that.' So, Billy said, 'Screw them.' He gave them back the passport and said, 'Stamp it now.' I guess he was showing his solidarity, since he is Jewish. That was pretty cool that he would do that.[62]

"We performed in Tel Aviv and Jerusalem. We played in small theaters. Nothing big. It wasn't like a big crowd. In that era we weren't huge internationally." Liberty also recalls, "That was the first time I ever saw in my hotel on the balcony, a F14 jet fighter comes flying down the beach, almost at the same level. I was like, 'What the hell is going on here?'"[62]

Playboy magazine reported that "[Billy's] appearance in 1979 in Cuba was criticized by the 'right.' When he appeared in Israel, he was blasted by the 'left.'" Billy claimed that music transcended all of the political ramifications. Speaking of the Cuban and Israeli adventures, he said, "I got criticized in the press for playing in Israel, but it was the same thing."[12]

According to Billy Joel, "I was in Turin for this press conference and this well-dressed journalist with wing-tip shoes from a left-wing paper asked, 'Why did you play Israel?' He was trying to create controversy. I said, 'I played in Israel for the same reason I played in Cuba—to play for the people. We wanted to see what the people in Israel were like instead of listening to the propaganda we get in this country.' The people at the press conference stood up and clapped. It was the same thing: Capitalist or Communist, it doesn't matter. You can play Cuba or Israel or Hong Kong or Russia. Kids just want to rock out. At the press conference, they also wanted me to put down America: 'What do you think of all the problems in your country?' I go, 'Well, we're better off than you are here.' So, suddenly I'm a right wing fascist. Well I'm closer to a socialist. But I'm not blind. I *like* my country. I've seen a lot of places and while we're not perfect, there is none better. The hip thing is to put America down, but I don't care about being hip. I think it's the greatest country in the world. We're all supposed to hate America. That's more propaganda."[12]

Billy found himself at a very centered and self-confident place in his life during this period: "Other people have religion or Scientology or shrinks or whatever. Me, I had the nuthouse. I'll never sink below a certain level after that. I don't know what people think of me, as far as what my songs represent to 'em, but I'm one of the most self-contented, happiest people, and it has nothing to do with money or success or anything like that. I know I'm okay. I been at the bottom, I know what it's like. I'm still gonna go for the top, but If I don't hit the top, it doesn't mean I'm at the bottom, it just means I'm not at the top."[18]

Since it was already time to start thinking about his next album. Billy had found a winning formula with *The Stranger,* and he had basically replicated it for *52nd Street*. What should he do on his next album? He pondered this at the time, stating, "I think if I thought about it, and tried to figure it out, that I'd get analytical, and clinical, and cold, and start to formulize. That's the danger. Like, why did I hit with *The Stranger?* Say I sat down and figured that out. Gee, was it the way the album was set up? Was it this song? What would I do about that?"[18]

The year 1979 was a big one for rock stars getting involved in charitable causes. One of the prime vehicles for this was the series of No Nukes concerts held to protest the escalation in the use of nuclear power in the United States. This particular cause rallied together Bruce Springsteen, Jackson Browne, Bonnie Raitt, the Doobie Brothers, Jesse Colin Young, Nicolette Larson, Carly Simon, James Taylor, Raydio, Tom Petty and the Heartbreakers, Chaka Khan, Jon Hall of the group Orleans, and the trio of Crosby, Stills and Nash. They called themselves the MUSE organization, which stood for Musicians United for Safe Energy.

Billy Joel considered the concert series to be a big waste of energy. He explained at the time, "I went to the No Nukes concert at the Nassau Coliseum and had a big argument with James Taylor about that. I agreed with him about a nuclear freeze, but I told him he was wasting his time because he was playing to the people who already agreed with him. A farmer in Kansas doesn't trust rock & roll musicians, and a show like that is more apt to alienate him than get him to see your point of view. I think music has more of an international political implication. It's an international language, and we all react to it emotionally."[59]

Throughout the 1970s, a pair of hitmakers who continued to place records in the top 10 and were a beloved fixture on both radio and television were the Carpenters. In 1979 a couple of members of Billy's circle became creatively involved with the duo. It was that year that the producer half of the famed sibling act, Richard Carpenter, was hospitalized to rid himself of quaalude addiction. His sister, distinctive singer Karen Carpenter, decided to use the time to come to New York City to work on a solo album. The producer that she chose to work with was none other than Phil Ramone. The Carpenters' records were often light and sweet sounding, but now Ramone suggested a bit of an image change. It was his goal to give Karen a more mature and womanly persona on record.

Phil Ramone was still very much interested in promoting Russell Javors's musical career, so he added him to his list of studio musicians to use in creating Karen's first-and-only collection of solo recordings as well as Liberty DeVitto, Doug Stegmeyer, and David Brown. Ramone submitted several of Russell's demo tapes to Karen for consideration. Says Russell, "I did Karen's solo album. Phil produced it. Out of about two hundred songs that she picked to go through with Phil for her solo album, she picked four of mine, and two of them made it to the album.[65]

"She was very nice. I liked Karen. I was so amazed that she wanted to do my songs, because my songs are so strange and so oddball, and so not Carpenters. I guess the connection was: I kinda sound a little like Leon Russell, like I have that odd vibrato. And she had a big hit with [Leon's] 'A Song for You,' and a couple of Leon songs. And I think she kinda 'got it.' And she picked the songs. Phil was always very supportive of what I did, and I love Phil to death. She picked both of these songs, and it was a very nice experience. She was from a different world than where we were from, but she was a very nice girl."[65]

Karen was used to recording in a much more restrained atmosphere, often with an orchestra or a string section. By comparison, the band that Ramone assembled was much more raucous and rock & roll than she was used to being around. He used "the Billy Joel formula" on her. Says Javors, "We were a little rowdy. I think we scared her a little bit. She was staying at Phil's and she was really tight with Phil's wife, Karen."[65]

Russell remembers with amusement, "There was an article on her in the *New York Times,* and the guy said, 'She did this album in New York with these hooligans. And her mother freaked out hearing her daughter sing lines like . . . ,' and they quoted one of my songs: 'I remember the first time I laid more than eyes on you.' Oh great, I got through to her mom!" He laughs.[65]

Unbeknownst to the public was the fact that Karen suffered from an extreme and life-threatening eating disorder. During this decade she verged on being painfully thin. "You could tell there was a problem," Russell recalls. "But I wouldn't say that she was 'divalike.' She was very friendly, she was very precise and she had a way that she wanted to do things. But she was a very nice person."[65]

After the *Karen Carpenter* album was finished, her record company persuaded her not to release it, because it was so different than the sugar-sweet image that she usually projected as part of the Carpenters. A&M Records was afraid the change in style would alienate her fans. She went back into the studio and recorded their last album, *Made in America,* which yielded the Carpenters' final four chart hits.

On February 27, 1980, Billy Joel's *52nd Street* album won Grammies for "Album of the Year" and "Best Pop Vocal Performance, Male." That same week, Columbia Records released Billy's next album. Now that *The Stranger* and *52nd Street* had made him a star, he also had a distinctive image with the press and with the record-buying public. Not only was he "the Entertainer" and "the Piano Man," he had also cultivated the reputation for being a scrappy Long Island balladeer. However, Billy longed to have a stronger image. He wanted to be a "rock star." To prove he had the chops to really rock out, he decided that his next album would have more of a hard-rocking attitude to it. In other words, he was going to throw rocks at his own image. This resulted in him coming up with his most ambitious album to date, *Glass Houses*.

According to Billy, among his main dreams were to have Ray Charles record one of his songs one day, "and I'll hear 'New York State of Mind' at the World Series."[26]

And, he still longed to emulate the musical appeal and uniqueness that his favorite group, the Beatles, had done. He admitted, "I fashion myself after The Beatles, who had all sorts of strange, unpredictable stuff on their records. I am not a stylist like Rod Stewart or Elton John that you can recognize in a second."[57]

About that point in time, he says, "I want to make a Beatles album. Every cut was great—there was not a piece of fat. They weren't necessarily a great band—everybody can say that nowadays as far as technical musicianship goes. Who gives a shit? The songs were great, from cut one to cut end. That's what I base what I do on, it's all material, writing."[18] That was the kind of album that he longed to create.

There were all sorts of new things going on in the music business. The overproduced synthesizer sound of bands like Electric Light Orchestra and Yes, and the thumping beat of disco, were suddenly pushed to the side. It was a big transition period for the whole record business, especially in America. Everyone was going through major changes when the 1980s began. There was first of all a giant shift in what was going on politically in the United States. With the 1980 election of President Ronald Reagan, the focus of the country dramatically shifted. When the new decade had dawned, the prevailing musical style of the country had changed, too. The "party down" giddiness of disco, which had dominated the music charts from 1976 to 1980, somehow came to a crashing halt. The careers of Donna Summer, Gloria Gaynor, and Village People suddenly hit a brick wall.

According to Randy Jones, the original cowboy in the group Village People, "The musical taste of the public suddenly changed drastically, and everyone in the record business was scrambling to transition out of disco.

I completely admired the way that Billy was always able to stay one step ahead of the game with his music, and to create different styles of music with each album he did."[90]

In addition, several of the biggest musical hit makers of the 1970s suddenly found themselves chasing a new sound, and rethinking their approach to the music. "New Wave" and "punk" music was the new thing. Groups like the Sex Pistols and the Ramones were stripping away the sounds of the last decade, and suddenly everyone seemed to be chasing a fresh back-to-basics rock & roll sound. To keep up with the times Linda Ronstadt abandoned her country rock sound to produce the album *Mad Love,* featuring several bare-bones songs written by Elvis Costello. Bonnie Raitt stepped away from her blues-rock stylings, put together a hot rock band, and introduced her new sound with *Green Light.* Carly Simon very smoothly made the transition from folk-pop with her harder-edged rock album *Spy.* It was time for Billy to try something new, too.

This was the era of "My Sharona" by the Knack, "One Way or Another" by Blondie, and "Roxanne" and "Message in a Bottle" by the Police. Rock music suddenly had more of an edge to it. Similar to the way the Beatles championed the three-guitars-and-drum formula to rock & roll in 1964, everyone was about to enter their punk and New Wave phase.

Analyzing the new music that was all over the charts during 1979 and 1980, Billy explained, "New Wave songs, it seems, can only be about two and a half minutes long. That's about it. Only a certain number of instruments can be played on the record—usually a very few. Only a certain amount of production is allowed or can be heard. The sound has to be limited to what you can hear in a garage. A return to that sound is all that's going on now, so don't give me any of this New Wave—using a Farfisa organ because it's so hip. It's just a reaction to a rediscovered past, and a rejection of Emerson, Lake & Palmer using multideck synthesizers."[14]

This new music had a profound effect on Billy, an influence directly attributed by Elizabeth's son, Sean, by then a young teenager who was developing a taste for his own music. And, more important, Sean was buying these records, and bringing them home with him. Billy Joel was so affected by some of the music that his stepson exposed him to that, when the new album was released, it carried in the liner notes the acknowledgment, "Thanks to Sean for the inspiration."

According to album producer Phil Ramone, the troupe tried all sorts of audio special effects to achieve the sound that they were looking for, including the sound of shattering glass, and multitracking instruments:

"Most of the time Billy liked to avoid effects, but when we made *Glass Houses* and *Nylon Curtain* we used effects like they were instruments, thus making the technical accoutrements part of the creative process."[76]

The *Glass Houses* album opens with one of their special effects: the sound of shattering glass. "You May Be Right" kicks off the proceedings to this all-rock album in an excitingly effective way. In the lyrics Billy bitches about his lover, and her assessment of him. The song also features the tasty horn playing of Richie Cannata, who adds just the right jazzy saxophone to punctuate the track.

Russell Javors recalls making a big contribution to the sound of this song as well: "'You May Be Right' is one where Billy started playing and I fell right into that guitar part. When we were in the studio, I always tried to think of what John Lennon would have played on each song. John wasn't a great guitar player, but he always played interesting stuff that helped frame the song. There was always that rough edge to John's playing. That was always my model. The Beatles played well-constructed songs with a rock & roll attitude. I always wanted to be a part of something like that. Howard and David were great guitar players, but my attitude is also all over those tracks."[64]

"Sometimes a Fantasy" starts off with another of their concocted sound effects, this time the distinctive sound of a touch tone telephone being dialed. This was an era when the whole concept of "phone sex" had become a viable alternative to having sex with others. According to the lyrics of this song, all it takes is a phone call for your fantasy to come true in your ears and your imagination. This is clearly a song about masturbation—as being the next best thing to having an in-person sex part-ner. A guitar- and keyboard-led fast-paced rocker, "Sometimes a Fantasy" perfectly captures the whole aural ambiance of the 1980s rock sound.

"Don't Ask Me Why" is a lighter element in this album and features a more classic Billy Joel sound. Against Liberty DeVitto's snappy percussion beat, Billy here sings advice to someone who is used to getting preferential treatment in life. He claims that this person of whom he sings even does a bit of bilingual "parlez-vous Français" nowadays. A true gem on this album, the multitracking of instruments is used to full advantage. Explains Billy, "In the midsection of the song 'Don't Ask Me Why,' there are fifteen pianos overdubbed on top of each other."[91] It makes his lone keyboard sound like a whole orchestra of pianos.

"It's Still Rock & Roll to Me" is the album's biggest hit, and true cen-terpiece. Here Billy complains about what all of the rock critics say about

BILLY JOEL

rock & roll's being dead, instead insisting that all of the disco dance beats, synthesizers, funk, punk, and New Wave styles are just part of the same rock category that started back in the 1950s. He sings of the "punk" style of wearing pencil-thin neckties, as compared to the old tab collars of yesterday's shirts. With rocking guitars and pan-speaker drum rolls, Billy turns his fiery aggressiveness into an anthemic salute to good old rock & roll. As he explained at the time, "The song is an out-and-out attack on the press, so why shouldn't it try to get even? I'm totally discounting everything these guys say. I don't sit around and play footsie with the press, especially with *Rolling Stone.* I have a running battle with them. I don't know when it started, but I know I'm not about to let it drop. I'm gonna keep it going. I kind of dig it."[12]

On the surface, the Beatles-influenced "All For Leyna" is a song about a love by the name of Leyna. Billy sings about his high school years, and how he nearly flunked out of his classes. Liberty DeVitto reveals that the song is actually about someone Billy had met during the recording of the album. "I grew up with a guy named Mike Cody, he was in the Rogues with me when we were fourteen years old. He used to come to the studio when we were recording *Glass Houses,* and bring this girl with him. I am sorry but I can't remember her name. Billy went ape-shit over her: one of those 'I just want to fuck her' things. Of coarse he was married to Elizabeth. Anyway, Mike now is a photographer out in the Hamptons. This girl was also the inspiration for the song 'Sleeping with the Television On.'"[92] In "All for Leyna," Billy uses his frenetic keyboard work as the musical center of this beautiful ballad, underscoring how much he longs for Leyna.

A slow ballad about finding someone to love in New York City's famed Plaza Hotel, "I Don't Want to Be Alone" is a medium-tempo rocker with a slight calypso beat to it. Due to the erotic night that he spends at the hotel, its narrator has come to the conclusion that solitude is for the birds. As love blossoms, the pace and beat of this song picks up midsong, as though the beating of his heart—and the song—have both quickened with his excitement.

"Sleeping with the Television On" has the same feeling that was emulated in several later New Wave classics. Here the music has the same snappy appeal of 1983's "Jeopardy" by Greg Kihn, and it uses TV as a metaphor for its coolness the way that Cory Hart's 1984 "I Wear My Sunglasses at Night" did for the perceived "cool" look of sporting Ray-Ban shades after sundown. The song starts out with the familiar sound of a TV's hum after the station's broadcast day has ended and only a test pattern remains. Then it swings into a full-fledged and bouncy rocker. Billy sings about his frustration using the TV to keep him company in the presence of his lover, who doesn't seem to want to communicate with him. Only the sound of the television bridges the silent and icy abyss that lies between the two of them. The television becomes the benign mediator in a romantic war of silence.

"C'etait Toi (You Were the One)" has the distinction of being Billy Joel's one and only attempt at composing and singing a song in a foreign language. The language he inadvertently mangles here is French. In this charming ballad, one can hear the atmospheric accordion playing of Billy himself, which is used to give the track that proper Parisian street scene feeling. The song starts out in English and then evolves into French very much like the Beatles classic "Michelle." However, the song "Michelle" is able to use the language shift much more effectively than Billy does here. Although it is not a bad song, this tender ballad doesn't quite work. Reportedly, when Billy Joel performed it live in Paris around the release of the album, the French audience was not sure what language it was he was singing, because it sure as hell didn't sound like their language to them. *C'est la vie!*

Billy later conceded defeat concerning this track: "I don't think we'll ever play that song again. Although I like the song musically, I did it in French, and I don't even speak French, so I really made a mess out of that. It's not really a crowd pleaser, not even in France."[93]

"Close to the Borderline" is a snappy rocker about survival. Lyrically, it is one of Billy's strong narrative pieces. Here, instead of essaying the patrons of a cocktail bar, he chooses to examine street life in Manhattan. He sings about needing doctors and lawyers and bankers just to keep his life on track. Yet, he claims here that he prefers a life on the edge of the borderline. Featuring wailing guitars, for a large section of the song it's just Billy and the drumming of Liberty DeVitto.

Closing this highly successful album is "Through the Long Night." This song carries such an unabashedly Beatles influenced sound that it could be a believable outtake from *Rubber Soul*. It has the same kind of lilting harmonies that were so effectively used on Lennon and McCartney's "Norwegian Wood" and "In My Life." Its tempo has the same slow and deeply pensive feeling that unfolds on John Lennon's "Julia," from the *White* album. Billy had said several times at this point that he wanted to emulate the Beatles, and here he took his music into that highly derivative Liverpool direction. This beautiful ballad is about surviving the night in the Irish silence, and repairing a love gone awry.

All in all, the *Glass Houses* album effectively threw rocks at Billy's older "Piano Man" image and reconceptualized him as much more of a true rocker. He shattered many people's expectations of him musically. He broke new stylistic ground and provided himself with ten fresh songs to effectively perform on tour. They were all strong numbers that could be sung and played on the concert stage with all of the fire and excitement of the studio versions.

On the cover of the *Glass Houses* album, the singer is seen with his back to the camera, dressed in blue jeans, a black leather jacket, and leather gloves. In his raised right hand he has a large stone, which he is poised to hurl at the plate glass windows of a suburban house. It is his own house on Long Island that is in the photograph.

Billy explained about his album cover art: "The mask actually had nothing to do with the song 'The Stranger,' where I talk about faces, the sides of ourselves that we hide from one another. The *Glass Houses* jacket was the same kind of thing. I kept thinking, 'Well, I suppose people think of me as a pop star, and right up to this second, I remain uncomfortable with that tag. That rock-star thing, that was not the purpose of making this latest record. I'm going to do whatever I feel like doing, and whatever I do, I know I'm going to get rocks thrown at me.' So I figured, 'What the hell, I'm just gonna throw a rock through my window, at myself—meaning the whole narrow image people have of me.' And, that is my house, by the way. People think I've got this multimillion-dollar mansion. I paid $300,000 for it, and that wasn't even money up front; I've got a mortgage. I'm not a multi-millionaire. Frankly, I'm not really sure what I'm worth. It's safe to say I'm a millionaire—that's a possibility. I honestly don't know and don't ask."[14]

The reviews for *Glass Houses* were highly mixed. *Stereo Review* absolutely loved it. According to reviewer Peter Reilly, "There isn't one instance in which he's coasting, or repeating himself, or taking a second (easy) shot at a favorite subject or theme. . . . The ten songs here are uniquely Joel: sharp, immediate, often harshly funny vignettes about the way things are *now* with his characters, about their genuine emotional impulses, not their coy philosophizing or maudlin poeticizing about them. . . . *Glass Houses* proves that it is all there: the music is there, the ideas are there, and the ability to execute both superbly is there. Billy Joel has reached an exciting and singular moment in his career: the first big crest."[94]

This was directly contrasted by such reviews as the one that appeared in *Rolling Stone* magazine, in which writer Paul Nelson tore the album apart: "Joel . . . always comes off like a particularly obnoxious frat boy who's hoisted a few too many while trying to put the make on an airline stewardess. . . . Two rock-critic friends of mine, both part-time Joel admirers, actually like *Glass Houses* 'because there's nothing overtly stupid on it' . . . unless you consider the entire album one bald and endless bad joke—as I do—there aren't any real howlers. Just fake this and fake that. . . . In 'You May Be Right,' the singer strikes one of the silliest tough-guy poses. . . . Billy Joel writes smooth and cunning melodies, and what many of his defenders say is true: his material's catchy. But then, so's the flu."[95] A further "zap" from *Rolling Stone* magazine came when they claimed in the context of their annual Critic's Poll that the track "It's Still Rock & Roll to Me" was voted the worst song ever recorded about the subject of rock & roll.

When he was accused of copying New Wave styles for this album, Billy publicly complained, "I like Elvis Costello, but I have never tried to duplicate anyone. If I consciously try to emulate anybody, it's The Beatles. I've tried to compose in a certain style—for instance, I was thinking of Ray Charles when I sat down to write 'New York State of Mind'—but that's different. I am inspired by performers, but I don't try to copy people. We didn't set out to make *Glass Houses* New Wave. We looked at it as a rock & roll album. But we knew they would throw rocks at it."[12]

Again Billy's album proved critic-proof. *Glass Houses* made it to number 1 in the United States, and number 9 in England. Different singles were chosen on different sides of the Atlantic. In the United States, "You May Be Right" made it to number 7, and "All for Leyna" hit number 40 in England. Then, in the summer of 1980, "It's Still Rock & Roll to Me" became number 1 in America, and number 14 in England. It went on to be his third million-selling single, and his first chart-topping hit. In the United States, "Don't Ask Me Why" reached number 19, and "Sometimes a Fantasy" became the album's fourth and fifth top 40 singles from this incredibly popular album.

They say that imitation is the sincerest form of flattery. This was certainly true when parody artist "Weird" Al Yankovic took Billy's "It's Still Rock & Roll to Me" and turned it into a regularly performed comedy version called "It's Still Billy Joel to Me," in which Yankovic poked fun at Joel's gift for writing a hit song, even if—as he sings in his lampoon—it's all a piece of "junk."

BILLY JOEL

It was during this same period that Billy and his band encountered producer George Martin for the first time since he had turned down the opportunity to work with them—after *The Stranger, 52nd Street,* and *Glass Houses* came out to become huge hits. "Later on, we hooked up with him," Richie Cannata recalls. "We saw him at an airport, and he boldly said, 'I made a mistake, didn't I?' We were on, like, our third multi-platinum record at that point."[44]

Billy Joel and Phil Ramone definitely had a winning chemistry together. According to Russell Javors, "Billy and Phil had such a good thing going, and I think Phil was the right producer for Billy, and combined with the combination of he understood what we were and who we were. It's not like all of us were such great players. It's a chemistry thing. And certainly David [Brown] was a great player, and you put all those pieces of the puzzle together. I always thought of us as: 'We were the E Street Band, but maybe a little more musical.' Maybe I shouldn't even say that, but we certainly understood. We weren't being paid by the note, we didn't have a session player mentality. We went into it like a band. And I just thought that that chemistry, and that point in time, it really worked. And it's stood the test of time."[65]

At the time, there was a great sense of camaraderie that existed in Billy Joel's band. As Russell remembers, "It felt like you were a family. It felt like you were a part of this thing. You just felt it happening."[65]

To Russell, recording with Billy was very much a collaborative effort. "When he was dry, Phil would nurture it. We would nurture it. We would be natural enough to get the stuff out. Billy would be Billy, and we would frame it. It's hard to explain. Sometimes it would be the lightest comment that would move it. Liberty was great at doing it. There was just a really light air to everything. Sometimes, from the oddest places, you can make things happen."[65]

Especially in the early eighties, there was also a lot of silliness and carrying on in the studio. "Billy had to go through his 'writing process,'" says Russell. "We really didn't rehearse for the records until the end. But things were just exploding in the studio. So, we always had fun."[65]

However, Russell quickly adds, "We were very professional. But we had been together for so long and a lot of the guys were really funny guys. So we were just always out of control. And Billy's a funny guy, so we really did have a lot of laughs."[65]

Often Billy Joel is depicted as being humorless and cranky. Explains Russell Javors, "Billy's got a great sense of humor. But, he's got a dark side. I

BILLY JOEL

don't understand the guy that well. I never felt that I was that close to him. I mean, I could hang with him, and we could have a lot of laughs, but I never felt like he was my pal. I never felt that he gave a shit. Like, he's not calling me up asking my opinion for anything. I felt like he kinda internalized everything. I felt sorry for him, because he just didn't seem like the happiest guy in the world.[65]

"The worst thing that I ever saw Billy do is that he farted on a 'bag lady' once. She was digging through the garbage, and he walked up and said, 'Life's ultimate insult!'" According to Russell, "Billy does stuff that I just don't understand. He's got a part of him that's a little strange. There is a part of Billy—the part of Billy that I always chose to try to connect with was that he's very bright. He's very bright. He's talented. He can be very funny. And, business aside, that's the part."[65]

However, not everyone found Billy jovial. During this period of time, the press hounded him, and he never hesitated at taking the opportunity to complain about his reception in the media. Said Billy Joel, "What bothers me is the untruths, the lies, the slander and libel. Bad reviews don't bother me. But a lot of these critics are looking for art. I run into this all the time. [*Los Angeles Times* music critic] Robert Hillburn does this all the time, saying, in too many words, that 'Billy Joel is not an artist but a pop star.' The thing that got me about that was, people who are looking for art in rock & roll or pop are looking for something that either doesn't or shouldn't exist there. An artist is a guy with a beret who sits in a park and paints pictures, and he starves in a garret somewhere."[14]

Even Phil Ramone got into the fray by stating in Billy Joel's defense, "All the digs he gets in the press really hurt him."[14]

Twelve years later, Billy was able to look back and view his circa 1980 displeasure with the press from a new perspective: "Before that first *Rolling Stone* cover piece, I'd gotten to the point in concerts where I'd sing the line in 'It's Still Rock & Roll to Me,'—'It doesn't matter what they say in the papers'—and then I'd stop, read something from a recent review and then tear it up in front of the fans! I saw it as a press war, even though logically I knew things were not that controlled. I was feeding my own frustration and enlarging the problem. But, after that article, I calmed down, stopped ripping newspapers on-stage and took charge of my feelings. The truth was that during the late 1970s and early 1980s, I was a very pissed-off guy. I had a lot of hurt from mistakes I'd made in the past. And I had no personal life whatsoever, because I was working so much and becoming emotionally drained, psychically spent. But for a whole, being constantly pissed off made it easier for me to write, 'cause when you're mad you have a lot of confidence in arguing your point of view."[96]

Billy still prided himself on the low price that he put on his concert tickets, in favor of his fans. As he said at the time, "If you look at the marketplace, $12.50 is not in line with ticket prices, which tend to run as high as fifteen dollars or more. It's a pretty low price, and I do it that way because I want the kids to be able to afford to see the shows."[14]

Yet, while on tour during 1980, he was selling concert tickets like crazy. On June 25 of that year Billy received the "Gold Ticket" award from Madison Square Garden, for being one of the few acts who had played to over one hundred thousand people at that highly revered venue. He sold out five nights at the Garden, and it was to become known as one of his favorite places in which to perform.

That week, Robert Palmer in the *New York Times* reviewed the show and wrote about how much he hated Billy's music. In the article Palmer scaldingly claimed, "He [Joel] has won a huge following by making emptiness seem substantial and Holiday Inn lounge schlock sound special. . . . Yes, Mr. Joel has written some memorable pop melodies. Yes he's an energetic, flamboyant performer. But no, this listener can't stand him. . . . He's the sort of popular artist who makes elitism seem not just defensible but necessary."[97]

At the same time that he was headlining at the Garden, Billy was also featured in the local newspapers, in gossipy articles regarding his bid to buy an apartment at the prestigious castle of a building, the Dakota. Located on Central Park West and Seventy-second Street in Manhattan, it was made famous when the 1968 movie *Rosemary's Baby* was filmed there (it was called fictitiously "the Bramford" in the script). Judy Garland, Boris Karloff, and Leonard Bernstein had all lived there in the past. At the time it was also the home of John Lennon and Yoko Ono, columnist Rex Reed, Lauren Bacall, Roberta Flack, and Gilda Radner.

The *New York Times* was less than flattering when they reported in an article entitled "Dakota Blocks Billy Joel's Bid to Buy Apartment," that the eleven-member cooperative board of the building had roundly turned down Billy's bid to purchase an apartment that was owned by surgeon Frederic Pratt Herter. He was the son of Christian A. Herter, who was a onetime secretary of state. Their article bluntly stated that "One of the problems the board reportedly had was that Mr. Joel has acknowledged in published interviews that he is a drug user. Another objection was that his presence would aggravate the problem The Dakota already has with pop music 'groupies.'"[98]

As Billy explained it, "During the Madison Square Garden gig [June 1980], it came out in *The New York Post* and *The New York Times* that I had applied for an apartment in the Dakota, and had been turned down because I admitted to being a drug user and because I had groupies! Number One: I did not want an apartment at the Dakota; my wife did."[14]

Billy was especially unhappy about the dog and pony show that he had to go through with the building's board. "It wasn't enough for Elizabeth to apply; I had to appear," he complained. "This is typical. . . . It's typical of the Equal Rights Amendment not being passed. A wife is considered chattel to the husband. They were worried about me. I showed up in my suit. I went to the interview, I did the Dakota. The man, a heavy guy who was the deciding guy, had the nerve to have me sign albums for his daughter. There had been an interview in *Us* magazine right before we went to this Dakota interview. So, because I had said, 'Once I did this,' and 'Once I did that . . . ,' it was picked up in the [*New York*] *Times* as, 'He has admitted that he is a drug user.' I got a family, you know. I got a mother. I got a sister. I got a father. And the press is calling me 'a known drug user' because I happened to say that once I went on-stage stoned. It's like Gloria Vanderbilt getting turned down at the River House. 'Ha, ha, isn't it great that this multimillionaire got turned down?' I'm not a multimillionaire. People think I have much more money than I have. I pay high salaries. I am in no way set for the rest of my life. I make a nice living, okay? But I go into the red on the road. The salaries and the costs and the production. It's a recession, man. I'm like everybody else. I don't make any money at a gig. I go on the road because I like to play. I'm not bitching about it, but I'm constantly behind."[14]

Billy Joel was featured on the September 4, 1980, cover of *Rolling Stone* magazine. In the article, interviewer Timothy White referred to Billy as being "hapless" as a businessman. Billy was quoted as saying, "This is a business. People never expected me to be as smart as I was, and they would be totally frank because they didn't realize I was building my empire. Money is the bottom line of everything."[14]

One of the burning questions at this time was: When is he ever going to get out of the deal with Artie Ripp? According to Billy in 1980, "I don't know. I get a dollar from each album I sell. Ripp gets twenty-eight cents out of that for 'discovering me.' Once in a while I get pissed off about it, but until the situation changes, it's not really healthy to dwell on it. I deserve that money a lot more than Ripp does, but I signed the papers, so what can I do? It was the only way I could get free of his 'Family Productions,' although he wouldn't let me go entirely. And he seems willing to continue to take the money."[14]

Richie Cannata describes one of Billy's many attempts to get loose from his deal with Artie Ripp: "I remember at one point—and I don't know if Liberty talked about that—but he owed songs to somebody. So, we all made up songs to give him, and we recorded them at 'sound check.' They were really crazy songs, but we made them up just to get out of this deal: 'Hey, we wrote ten more songs. Now, we've fulfilled that. Can we move on? Now am I out of the publishing deal?' We all kind of participated in that."[44]

As to the status of his songwriting copyrights, Billy said, "I have a deal with CBS' April-Blackwood Publishing; I do not own my publishing, but I do own my copyrights now—meaning that I own, like fifty percent. Live and learn, eh?"[14]

Finally the pair of lawsuits over Billy's song copyrights were settled. He explained at the time, "Incidentally, I read recently in [the] Random Notes [section of *Rolling Stone*] about this guy [John Powers of Reno, Nevada] who said that I stole his song, that he wrote 'My Life.' Now, my initial instinct is to just go beat the hell out of the guy, but my lawyers said I can't do that. I've had more leeches and sharks preying on me over the years, and it hasn't been dramatized in the press much because, until recently, Billy Joel wasn't very interesting to people." He vehemently insisted, "I never stole anybody's song. People send me tapes through Columbia all the time, and I do not and will not listen to them. As it is, I'm getting sued; I've got lawsuits up the *gazool* [sic] which is something that disillusions me a lot about writing. I don't want to steal from anyone, because I know the feeling—my stuff's been getting ripped off all my life."[14]

However, he revealed that instead of going to court, and having this drag on and on, the matter was settled out of court. Claimed Billy, "When they question my intentions, that bugs me. Enough about that. I never stole nobody's song."[14]

Billy also claimed that his marriage to Elizabeth was quite solid, and that they had a great relationship. "I'll go to bed, and my wife and I will say to each other, 'What are ya thinkin' about?' and I think, 'I am the knight in shining armor and I want to go slay dragons.' You get to a point in your life where there aren't any obvious dragons."[14]

Yet there was plenty of gossip that their marriage was crumbling. "Yeah, I've heard rumors too: 'Are you and Elizabeth gettin' divorced?' or 'You separated?' It's like, what? Give me a break. Everything's fine."[14] Or so he said.

However, things were not going well at all. Liberty DeVitto recalls that during this year, Elizabeth became pregnant by Billy. However, it came during a period when they were fighting with each other, verbally and physically. According to Liberty, "All we knew was that she miscarried."[3]

December 8, 1980, was a day of tragedy for the rock & roll community: John Lennon was shot in front of his apartment building, the Dakota. The singer met his death at the hands of a crazed fan by the name of Mark David Chapman, who posed as an autograph seeker and then shot Lennon. It made everyone in show business rethink their security measures after that. Needless to say, Billy was relieved that he had been turned down by the cooperative board of the Dakota after all.

According to Billy's friend, radio executive Bob Buchman, Billy Joel—sadly—never had the opportunity to get acquainted with John Lennon: "Billy never met John, and it's one of his big regrets. Billy knew where John lived on the north shore of Long Island. And when he was a kid—actually after he had gotten some fame—he was boating past his [Lennon's] house one day and he was very tempted to just dock the boat, walk up, and knock on the door. And he never did, because he wanted to respect John. Of course he regrets that now, having never met him. He found out, subsequently, a story that's funny to him, he found out from a friend, that John had found out where Billy was living on the North Shore of Cold Spring Harbor when he bought that house—the glass house on the cover of the album *Glass Houses*. That house, with Elizabeth. Lennon found out that Billy lived there, and Lennon was thinking of going up and introducing *himself*, and never did. So, Billy said, 'That is really interesting. I don't think that John Lennon knows who I am.' But that's the story that never happened."[99]

The year 1981 began with signs of a big boost in popularity for Billy. On January 30 he won the American Music Award for "Favorite Album, Pop/Rock" for *Glass Houses*. The trophy was presented at a live telecast from ABC-TV Studios in Hollywood, California. The following month, on February 25, Billy's *Glass Houses* album won a Grammy Award as the "Best Rock Vocal Performance, Male."

With the huge success of his last three albums on Columbia Records, Billy found that some of his favorite compositions from his first four solo LPs were being eclipsed by his newer material. On record, several of these songs sounded slightly dated, especially in light of the more rock-oriented versions the band was playing onstage.

Phil Ramone had an idea about how to solve this problem: "As Billy and I became friends, I let him in on a secret—someday I hoped we could use his band to re-record his early material that he used to play in small clubs and halls. I figured it would never happen 'til we were in rocking chairs. But four years have flown by, and the fantasy has become a reality. It was quite exciting to be on the road with the best 'escapees from Boy's Town.'"[71]

Billy revealed at the time, "Actually, we've been taping everything from club dates at the Paradise in Boston to the Spectrum in Philly, dates in Milwaukee and St. Paul, and the Madison Square Garden shows, too. Thus far, we're doing it simply to document what we do on the road, but it could possibly wind up a live LP."[14]

What they came up with was a live concert album called *Songs in the Attic*. Billy explained of its evolution, "In 1980, after years of touring with my own band, we decided to record our live performances. We taped 15 shows covering the older, as well as the newer material. And, after listening to many tapes of those shows, we discovered the reason for that gap. Something was missing on those old records. We liked the songs but the original studio recordings didn't have nearly as much energy and joy as the live renditions. The live tapes were in fact much closer to the sound I had hoped to capture originally."[71]

With that, Billy and Phil Ramone selected the tracks they found the most successful in their new live incarnation, and came up with an eleven-track album. The songs that Billy chose to reinterpret were: "Miami 2017 (Seen the Lights Go Out on Broadway)," "Summer, Highland Falls," "I've Loved These Days," and "Say Goodbye to Hollywood" from *Turnstiles*; "Streetlife Serenader" and "Los Angelenos" from *Streetlife Serenade*; "Captain Jack," "You're My Home," and "The Ballad of Billy the Kid" from *Piano Man*, and "She's Got a Way" and "Everybody Loves You Now" from *Cold Spring Harbor*.

Said Billy, "Some songs were taped in 20,000-seat hockey arenas. Others were recorded in 300-seat clubs. Ambiance was essential in capturing the original spirit. For example, 'Miami 2017' demands the gothic reverberation of a vast railroad terminus, such as New York's Madison Square Garden. In contrast, a song like 'Everybody Loves You Now' feels more at home in an intimate atmosphere. The Bijou in Washington, D.C., puts us in close, personal contact with a small but intense group of people. Some songs have been automatically excluded here because they don't translate as well as others. 'Piano Man' for instance sounds pretty much the same live as it does on the record, so why make carbon copies? However, 'Captain Jack' plays with much more power and conviction when a roaring Philadelphia audience sets off a kind of internal explosion and the adrenaline screams through our veins—when Doug [Stegmeyer], David [Brown] and Russell [Javors] push their amplifiers into ear-bleeding overdrive and Richie [Cannata] floors the organ pedal like the accelerator on a '64 Corvette—when I feel piano strings snapping and breaking under the fingers in my left hand and Liberty [DeVitto] literally tries to smash his drums into shiny metal bits of shrapnel. When we play 'Captain Jack,' we are actually committing an act of pure brutality. Passion was a critical deciding factor here. When we play 'I've Loved These Days,' we feel something very similar to sensual pleasure."[71]

In the liner notes of the album he mentioned that performing the song "Captain Jack" was an act of "pure brutality" to perform. What did he mean by that comment? According to Billy, "That's just part of aggressions everybody feels. Our therapy, our exorcism of aggression is playing music. Liberty goes up on stage and really beats the living hell out of his drums. It's close to being in a fight with somebody. I go up on stage for two-and-a-half hours and act like a crazy man. When I come off the stage I'm one of the most dull people you could meet! I say, 'I'm O.K. now, I'm fine, I've gotten it out of my system.' I don't think about putting out an image. The most important thing is the music—not me. You don't have to like me, but hopefully the music is going to last."[100]

The band is heard at the peak of their commercial popularity, and of their musical height as well. "Our intention here is to provide a selected sampling of the earlier stuff, played the right way—with honest road muscle," said Billy Joel. "This album is ultimately a reunion with lovers past. Reaffirming the faith that we in the band and those who had been to our shows during that time had forged in the crucible of the concert stage. This is the way the band I want to play these songs. This is the way Brian Ruggles, our concert sound engineer wants people to hear these songs, and this is the way our producer, Phil Ramone, has always has always wanted to translate these *Songs in the Attic* into a record."[71]

Billy claimed that he labored over the final song choices for the album: "Since we wanted to keep *Songs in the Attic* down to a single record. We had to narrow it down to 10 or 11 songs. Everybody comes out with a double album of a whole show that retails for 15 dollars. Who can afford it? So, our time was limited as far as how much we could fit in. The more time that is on one disc, the less quality the disc has. Usually records are 18 to 20 minutes a side, and this record is close to an hour all together."[100]

Additionally, *Songs in the Attic* had the distinction of being the first live album recorded entirely on digital sound equipment. This was the same technology that was about to revolutionize the recording industry in the mid-1980s when CDs were introduced to the public. But that was still a few years away. According to Brian Ruggles, the producer of the actual concert recordings that album producer Ramone worked with, it made this project very "cutting edge." Said Ruggles, "Phil Ramone wanted to try it out, and he was approached by the 3M Company. We discussed it and both thought it would be a great idea to release the first live digital album. . . . What I notice in digital is that the sound is much crisper—there's more clarity. So with a symphony orchestra, you could probably notice it more than for some of the cruder rock bands. But for Billy's recordings, it works real well."[101]

When *Songs in the Attic* was released, it received generally strong reviews. Even *Rolling Stone* magazine cut him some slack for a change. Wrote reviewer Timothy White, "Billy Joel has brought forth a number of dusty gems from his less-heralded years (1971–1976) and given them an appealing live showcase on *Songs in the Attic*. . . . These cuts are gimcracks from a catalog that didn't catch fire until the release of *The Stranger* in 1977 . . . they show his development from intent greenhorn to creator of standards, [and he] plays them with self-absorbed vigor. It's precisely this vigor, along with Joel's canny pugnaciousness, that lifts *Songs in the Attic* above the level of a pop-rock rummage sale. . . . While I'm not a fan of everything that Joel cranks out, I love his ballsiness. And I'm captivated by the commitment of his truly exceptional bar band and his often quirky material . . . he and his unbridled musicians . . . keep cooking, inbuing great ('Say Goodbye to Hollywood,') and grating ('Captain Jack') compositions of yore with surprising color and dimension."[102]

Looking back at this release, Stephen Thomas Erlewine in *The All Music Guide* found *Songs in the Attic* to truly be dynamic: "Joel wisely decided to use the live album as an opportunity to draw attention to songs from his first four albums . . . he now had a seasoned backing band that helped give his music a specific identity—in short, it was an opportunity to reclaim these songs, now that he had a signature sound. And Joel didn't botch the opportunity . . . an excellent album, ranking among his very best work."[70]

Several fans claim that *Songs in the Attic* is one of their all-time favorite albums. Says longtime Billy Joel devotee Derek Storm, "Billy recorded this live album so that he could bring his fans his older songs the way he really wanted them produced in the first place, when he had no control over his band and studio musicians. The versions of 'Miami 2017,' 'Streetlife Serenader,' 'Los Angelenos,' and 'Captain Jack' are extraordinarily different than their studio versions and much more powerful instrumentally. 'She's Got a Way' becomes the surprise hit from this album."[49]

A reprise of compositions past, *Songs in the Attic* peaked at number 8 on the American charts and made it to number 57 in England. It also spun off a pair of top 40 singles in the United States: "Say Goodbye to Hollywood" (number 17) and "She's Got a Way" (number 23).

At this point in time, the press often referred to Billy as an "artist." However, he preferred to be called a "musician" instead. How was he different than a musical artist? According to him, "Because he's *only* after art. His special, elitist, intellectual view of how life should be represented on canvas or in music, now, when you do that consciously, I believe you're really shutting yourself off from what's going on. I do what I do because of radio. Consider Devo: my, how *artistic,* what a great *concept:* de-evolution and industrial rock for the '80s. Intellectually, the whole image of it is very well put together, but it doesn't make it on the radio. If I'm driving in my car, I'd rather hear Donna Summer—*that's* where it's at."[14]

He hypothesized, "Let's remember the essence of popular music. A song comes on. What do you hear first? Words? Nah, you hear a beat, then a melody. Take 'My Sharona' [by the Knack]. If you really liked the song, then you took the time to dig out the words, and they're pubescent, Dumbo words, but they fit the song. Journalists, for the most part, always tend to tune into a lyric. I've never wanted to print my lyrics on my LPs because the lyrics are not poetry; they're part of songwriting, they're coloring, and they have to be heard the same as the music. If they wrote out the lyrics to all these incredible Motown records, it would be rotten poetry. It's really stupid stuff. The O'Jays can go, "I love you/Yes I do." But, if they sing it in a particular harmony and do a particular hand-jive, it's okay, see? But if Warren Zevon or Neil Young wrote it, it would be, 'What a dumb lyric!'"[14]

One of the most flattering things that happened during the late seventies was that Frank Sinatra recorded one of Billy's songs: "Just the Way You Are." It appeared on his somewhat ambitious 1979 concept album: *Trilogy: Past, Present & Future.* It was comprised of three vinyl albums. One, called "The Past," contained new recordings of 1940s and '50s standards. The second one, "The Present," contained songs by contemporary songwriters of the day, including Neil Diamond, Carole Bayer Sager, Peter Allen, George Harrison, Michel Legrand, and Billy Joel. When Billy was asked what he thought of this occurrence, he said, "I thought it was great . . . I was thrilled. And I did get a kick out of him doing one of my songs. The arrangement, which is real Vegas/Tahoe swing-style, is the way we used to fool around with that song at soundchecks to make the crew laugh—just the way Sinatra did it!"[100]

By now, Billy Joel was viewed as one of the biggest rock stars in the musical galaxy. His last three albums were all million sellers, and he had achieved his goal of someday hitting number 1 on both the album and singles charts. He had officially arrived. Yet at the beginning of the eighties, he didn't yet think he had made it: "I don't feel like a rock star today. Rock stars to me are still Paul McCartney and Mick Jagger. I'm supposed to be a rock star, but I just feel like the guy from Hicksville, only I was able to get out of Hicksville. But it still takes me by surprise when people come up and do those [screeching] 'Oh *BILLY JOEL!*' things. I don't look any better than I did ten years ago. How come all these girls are coming on to me now? Where were they in high school when I needed them? I don't think I'll ever get used to it. I ride in limousines and I sit in the back and I giggle, because I really don't belong there. I don't have no three-piece suit and briefcase, like you're supposed to in a limousine. I sit in my jeans and T-shirt and smoke Camels and drink root beer. You're not supposed to let people see you when you're driving around in a limousine, but I stick my head out and go, 'Nyah, nyah!' I play with the TV and the stereo. It's fun because I don't belong there."[12]

Billy was clearly living the high life during the early 1980s. For the elite of the show business world it was a time of cocaine and parties, and he had access to it all. But for him, one of the oddest things to result from being famous, was dealing with his on-the-street face recognition. People he had never laid eyes upon suddenly came up to him and greeted him as if he was a long-lost friend. "That's kind of funny or weird, depending on the situation," he explained. "On my bike, I stop at a light and somebody will say, 'Hey, Mr. Joel,' or 'Hey, B.J.' I'm pretty shy, so it's a great way to meet the world, to tell you the truth. But it can get to be too much. One day, I found I couldn't go to Yankee games anymore. That was a drag. I wouldn't see the game. Everybody would be coming up for autographs and every time I'd look down—bam! Reggie [Jackson] would have hit one out of the park. I'd always miss it. One time I didn't shave, I wore sunglasses, I brought one of those radios, I put a bandanna around my head and I made believe I didn't speak English. But suddenly there was a whole bunch of kids behind me, pointing, singing 'Honesty.' I really felt like a jerk. On the other hand, I had some of the Yankees over to my house for dinner. That was too much. This guy with the Yankees talked to our agent and said that the players were fans of mine. I said, 'My God, these are the *New York Yankees* in *my* house!'

And they're sitting there eating, saying, 'My God, we're eating over at Billy Joel's house.' We were a bit awkward for a while, but after a couple of beers, we got pretty loose."[12]

So many other rock stars at Billy's echelon of fame had decided to become actors, either on film or on the stage. Ringo Starr, Linda Ronstadt, Cher, Paul Simon, Art Garfunkel, Aretha Franklin, Bette Midler, Mick Jagger, Don Henley, Madonna, Cyndi Lauper, and Huey Lewis were all featured in 1980s films. Did Billy have the "acting bug" as well? "People always ask: 'When are you gonna make a movie?' I don't feel compelled to be a movie star. Although it seems to be a natural transition for a lot of people in my profession. . . . But I'm not comfortable in front of a camera. I don't like taking pictures, and I don't really enjoy looking at myself. I always think I look kind of weird and stupid. And one of the requisites for being an actor is to be comfortable in front of a camera."[100]

Although he had access to a seemingly unlimited amount of wealth, the Piano Man claimed that he was still keeping it real. Was he now spoiled by his own success? "I don't worry about that. I never have," he said at the time. "You can live in a nice house and everything but still have a crazy life. It used to bug me. I read these stories about Peter Frampton's multimillion-dollar mansion, 15 Rolls Royces and all that. Who cares? It's all bullshit. What was his last record like? Was it any good? That's the question. People get hung up on the money thing. It's nice to have four motorcycles. It's fun. And I walk into the garage and go, 'Holy shit! I've got four motorcycles!' But I don't go beyond a certain point. I got the Harley Electra Glide. I looked at it and said, 'What else do I need in my life? That is it. This is all I need!'"[12]

He had assuredly been in show business long enough to know that fame and riches can be a fleeting commodity. Although in the early eighties, money was piling up in his bank account at a highly escalated pace, he also noted, "But it goes out too—pretty quick. The more you have, the more you spend. So we're also responsible for a lot of different people's income. The money coming in is creating employment, too, creating jobs. I'm not really a capitalist. I never was. I'm kind of a quasi socialist; I'm embarrassed by all the money. Elizabeth is a very good capitalist; she's very sensible. She exists in this society and she accepts it. We give money to charity. I help my family out. I kind of like that. We never had no money and now I can help out. See, I'm afraid to get too business oriented. It gets in the way of creativity. I'm not saying I subscribe to the theory that you have to be hungry to create; I don't buy that, because I've eaten a full meal and sat down to write. But I'm not doing this for the money. It's kind of weird—the values. Jonas Salk. That's pretty weird. I didn't cure polio; this guy did. I walk into a bar and a whole bunch of people know who I am. Jonas Salk probably can't even get laid. Now figure *that* out."[12]

When he was asked in 1980 where the bulk of his income came from, he replied, "Well, for the last three years the revenues have mainly come from record sales."[14] Indeed, along with Bruce Springsteen, Michael Jackson, Barbra Streisand, and Paul Simon, Billy Joel was among the upper echelon of top-selling superstars at CBS Records.

He claimed that he knew that the freight train of cash could all come to a screeching halt at any point: "I don't trust rock & roll money. I've heard too many horror stories about the guy with the cars and jets and furs, and then the next year he's totally broke, looking for work. I liked my house. I really didn't want to get into any bigger deal. I didn't even know how much money I had. I didn't want to know. I *don't* want to know."[12]

Since other rock stars—like Linda Ronstadt, the Eagles, and Jackson Browne—had jumped on the political bandwagon of late, Billy was suddenly being asked to back one politician or another. He, however, preferred to retain his neutrality when it came to politics."[59]

In 1981, he stated, "I have my own politics. I'm not overtly, as a performer, someone who gets up on a soap box and preaches. I think that's an abuse of power. People have asked me to join in all kinds of campaigns. I did work for McGovern in '72, not as a performer though, just as a campaign worker—knocking on doors and making phone calls. When he was landslided by Nixon, that was it for me as far as getting involved in a political campaign. . . . I always fall to the left, whenever I fall! But who the hell am I to push my politics on anybody? I'm just a dumb musician."[100]

For the most part, Billy did his best at retaining his "everyman" kind of stance when he was out in public. He didn't go in for acting like a star for his public: "I still eat pizza and walk around in jeans with paint on them. I wear T-shirts. I always thought millionaires looked like Richie Rich or Scrooge McDuck. How much money do you need? It can really get sick. Accumulation of too much wealth, I think, is an illness. Strange things also happen to other people when you have money. People start suing you. I don't want to know about it. I'd rather just know that I can go out and eat, live in a comfortable house and drive my motorcycle."[12]

Indeed, motorcycling was his new passion. "A motorcycle is an amusement park ride. It's dangerous. Everybody on the road is out to get you. A truck goes by and can blow you right off the road. Cars are constantly pulling out in front of you like you're not a real vehicle. I had an accident on one when I was a kid. You're constantly playing terror chess: 'What am I going to do if this guy does that?' It clears all the cobwebs out of your head. When you get off the bike, it's, 'Whew, I made it.'"[12]

His relationship to his mom was very important to him, and he said in 1980, "My mother . . . she's loving, she's people oriented, a fucking blast. She is not awed by stardom. She's not a stage mother. Her whole thing was just be happy."[14]

He also kept himself grounded by staying in touch with several of his old childhood friends. One of these was Billy Zampino, who never knew at what odd time he would hear from Billy Joel about some piece of gossip, trivia, or news. As Zampino recalls, "He phoned me one rainy night in 1980, calling from a highway phone booth in Syosset, and said he was so moved by this classical piece he heard on the radio that he *had* to find out what it was. He hummed and sang it over the receiver as I searched my record collection, until I realized it was Samuel Barber's 'Adagio For Strings,' one of the most emotional pieces in classical music, it was the music played across America when President Franklin Roosevelt died. And after that night on the highway, it probably became Billy's favorite piece of music in the world."[10]

In spite of Billy Joel's intentions at staying the same person he was before wealth and fame hit him, even a strong man has a problem resisting temptation. It seemed that everything in his world was so sound and complete. He was managed by his own wife, so assuredly she should have his best interests in mind at all times. His band, whom he spent a majority of his time with, all seemed happy in their roles as his supporting group. And, he had his health. What could go wrong? Everything.

11
THE MAN
BEHIND THE
NYLON CURTAIN

MANY CHANGES WERE in store for Billy during the early 1980s: in his record contract, his business management, and within his own band. At the same time a lot was going on in his personal life as well, especially within his marriage to Elizabeth. As the new decade began, Elizabeth Joel was feeling a bit overwhelmed at managing all of Billy's business operations. They included: Home Run System Corporation, which was the management company; Impulsive Music/Joel Songs, the music publishing wing; Billy Joel Tours, which produced the concert stage shows; Home Run Agency, that booked the venues for the tours; and Roots Rags Ltd., which was responsible for all of his merchandising, from concert programs to T-shirts.

By 1980 a shift in power was already underway in the Billy Joel camp, one that was at first unperceivable from the outside. As her interest in Billy's business and her marriage to him cooled, Elizabeth began to delegate an increasing amount of her responsibilities. The person she chose to work with her was her own brother, Frank Weber. As she proceeded to distance herself from the manager's role, Frank took on more and more responsibilities. In that way, it wasn't long before Frank had eased his way into every aspect of Billy's business and was acknowledged as his new manager. To assist him in his duties, Weber in turn hired his own brother-in-law, Rick London. Also joining the Joel/Home Run Management team was Jeff Schock in the position of director of marketing and promotion.

That year, Billy went on record as stating, "Elizabeth no longer manages me. She is involved with me: fund-raising, movie production, film editing. But she's got twenty other things going. I said, 'Enough of the strain of being wife AND manager, let's just be man and wife.'"[14] This fueled further rumbling in the industry, to the effect that Billy and Elizabeth's marriage was "strained" at best. It was becoming increasingly clear that the end of their union was near.

In 1981 an East Coast–based music retail chain, the Sam Goody company, was found guilty of counterfeiting tapes of best-selling artists and using them as "returns" to the record companies. Among the bootlegged tapes were copies of Billy Joel's albums, as well as albums by Paul Simon and Olivia Newton-John. Simon and Newton-John did not come to court, but Billy Joel, clad in a light-colored suit jacket and skinny black necktie, testified in U.S. District Court. However, he was reportedly behaving in a less-than-businesslike fashion that afternoon. As Billy stated his case as a wronged party, Judge Thomas Platt admonished him from the bench, complaining to the gum-chewing rock star, "Mr. Joel, I don't know what you're chewing, but I would advise not chewing it when you're trying to testify."[103]

According to several sources, the drug use in Billy's camp was escalating, and this was not something that Elizabeth Joel found amusing. Also, apparently Billy was quite a womanizer while he was out on the road and Elizabeth was not around. Confirms Liberty DeVitto, "Like most musicians, including me, Billy could not keep his zipper up."[3] Says Sandy Gibson, "The more he kept doing drugs, the more he kept getting pulled away by other women, the less she liked it. She really didn't like the music business."[36]

Billy was quite up front about his drug use. In an article in *Playboy* magazine in 1982, he discussed his substance abuse problems: "After the show, I'll smoke sometimes. I'll have a couple of beers, some scotch. That's it. Nothing to excess, though I've tried everything once."

Playboy: Cocaine?
Joel: Yeah, I've tried that.
Playboy: Heroin?
Joel: Even heroin.[12]

When he was asked if he thought he was in danger of getting hooked on heroin, Billy replied, "No. I saw too many people get hung up on it. I don't need it. It gets in my way. Drugs can be fun; it's something I do once in a while, but I'm not a drug addict. Although the rumors . . . I didn't want to go to the Grammys last year, but my mother said, 'Why don't you go? Nobody believes you're my son.' I went and the cameras kept poking right in my face like I was a dancing monkey or something. Everybody who saw me said, 'Man, you were really stoned, weren't you?' No, I was just mad at the cameraman and that's just the way I look, especially when I'm mad."[12]

Because of all of this, and Elizabeth's growing disillusionment with the music business in general, by the end of 1980 their marriage was officially on the rocks.

Speaking of this transition time, Richie Cannata remembers, "Frank Weber's participation was he was replacing Elizabeth after Billy and Elizabeth kinda split up. He was put in there by Elizabeth, and Billy went for it. And then, we were out on the road, and we didn't know what was going on, on the administrative side at all. We just knew that Billy and Elizabeth were splitting, and that Frank was going to take over."[44]

In 1981 Billy's record deal with Columbia had come up for a second seven-year run. He had the option of either renewing it, or not. One of the things that bothered Billy the most about his initial contract with the company had been the twenty-five or twenty-eight cents per album sold that came out of his share of the royalties and went directly to Artie Ripp and Michael Lang. By the time the record company negotiations were over, Columbia Records, then helmed by Walter Yetnikoff, agreed to continue to pay Ripp and Lang out of the company's own pockets, and not Billy's. The first album to be released from this new contract was *Songs in the Attic*.

As Liberty DeVitto describes the negotiations, "Walter Yetnikoff got back Billy's rights to his publishing for him. He went to Artie Ripp and said, 'This shit's gotta stop, or I am going to make legal trouble.' They came up with a financial settlement, and Yetnikoff gave Billy back his publishing on all of those early songs that Ripp had his hands on."[3]

Liberty recalls what a nonstop party it was to be on tour back then. "We used to have so much fun. It was *a lot* of fun! When we were at our peak, and there were girls and booze all of the time. You know, when you're young, and you are in your twenties, you feel like Superman. Even in your thirties, you're still Superman."[63]

But by the early eighties, Richie Cannata was becoming unhappy with the grind of playing the same music every night. He longed to play other music than just Billy's songs. Also, like Elizabeth Joel, he was not happy with the drugs and partying that had become a large part of being on the road with Billy Joel at the time. Reveals Richie, "Billy's thing was getting sillier and sillier for me. It was almost running away with itself."[44]

Richie's disenchantment really grew with the release of the live album: "We were on the road with *Songs in the Attic*, which was the last record for me. It was a live record, and that was really the beginning of the end for me. I realized that when we listened back to all of the tapes, and there was a lot of sloppy playing. Liberty and Doug hated what they did. They wanted to rerecord the live record again, and I said, 'That's not that fair. We tried to capture a moment.' So they wanted to do the record again at Media Sound Studios. So, I was not feeling all of that. I did all of my parts, and I'm still on record as saying: 'Why don't we use a lot of this stuff that we recorded out on the road?' A lot of good stuff did make it onto that record, the stuff from Toad's Place in New Haven, Connecticut. I know that there are a lot of older venues. So, *Songs in the Attic* was the beginning of the end for me."[44]

But when Liberty DeVitto looks back on all of this, he wonders how things started to go badly behind the scenes. He just loved the band, and being part of the band with Richie, Doug, and Russell. Then it started to fall apart. "Did you ever see the movie *Lifeboat?*" he asks. He then draws a parallel between that classic 1944 Alfred Hitchcock film starring Tallulah Bankhead and John Hodiak, and Billy's band.

"The ship sank and they're on a lifeboat. They don't know they're going to be rescued; they are hoping they will. But we know that the movie is going to eventually end. As they are getting closer to being rescued, who is getting thrown off the lifeboat? Who is going to screw who, to get saved? Well, when the bucks get bigger, and the true colors come out. You start out as a band: 'Like, this is great!'—'We have nothing right now. Billy's writing the songs, I'm playing the drums to complement his songs. Richie is playing the sax solo that will take the place of the vocal, when there is a break in the middle. Russell [Javors] and David Brown or whoever else, is playing guitars and making things great: "We're a band!" Which is great. We are one unit, we are forging ahead. We go on the road, we play live. We knock people dead. Lib's up there because Billy wants the weight taken off him. He doesn't want people looking at him all the time. He wants to bend over and blow his nose. Lib's up there playing his ass off. He sells the records. People are looking at him. Richie's up there being a star, and playing and playing and playing.' Then somebody comes up and says, 'Hey, Billy, you write the songs. It really is all about you.' You know, 'Fuck these guys!' At first Billy says, 'Well, I can't really do that.' But then, one day, one of them does something that triggers Billy off, and he goes, 'I don't like what you just did.' And then, 'Yeah, you know, you're right. Fuck him. I can live without that.' And then, once he gets rid of one, he realizes that everyone can be replaced. After you shoot your first person, the next guy is easy to shoot."[62]

It was similar to Motown Records at its height. Once they fired one member of the Temptations, it was easy to continue to fire any of the group members who displeased the company. Asks Liberty, "How did we go from 'Love me, love my band,' to 'What happened to the band?' And, the first tragedy was Richie. Richie was drowning in this huge wave that we were on. And whether anybody saw it or not was one thing, but whether anybody cared or not. If we were drowning, we were riding the wave in."[62]

Pondering upon Richie's exit, he says, "To be honest with you, I don't know if it was a matter of Richie wanting to leave or not. I know that Richie told me that he wanted more money. But, there was a thing that happened when the lighting designer and the sound man got way too much power. The guys up front, they are hearing everything that is going on out front. Now, we may think that we play great, but when it comes through the PA, they could say, 'It sounds like shit.' If that's what they say, then Billy says, 'It must sound like shit.' If they say, "It looked great that night," they must have had a great show out front. Billy started to base a lot on what they had to say from out front."[62]

When the band started, and it was time for Liberty to do his drum solo, or for Richie to do his sax solo, they would suddenly be in the spotlight— the lighting director saw to that. And the sound man would make sure that the volume on the sax or the drums was appropriately turned up as well. Liberty noted that the sound man and the lighting man each had his own power trip as well. The sound man and the lighting man found that they had the power to make the drums and the sax solos less and less showy by turning *down* the lights or sound on Richie or Liberty if they wanted to do that.

"There's always one person who becomes the 'nerdy' guy, or the one person that everybody picks on," Liberty continues. "Which was shocking to me that I became that person that everybody was suddenly turning on, and you just don't know about it, that you are the one everybody is talking about. All of a sudden, 'Wow, I'm that guy now. The Fickle Finger of Fate pointed at me now.' Well, Richie was the first person to get pointed at. It's usually jealousy that brings everybody down. Somebody's jealous of Richie. Somebody doesn't like the fact that Richie's a star. Maybe somebody is making Richie a star, but they're not getting all the credit for it. And then Richie says something wrong to the person who is flicking the lights or making him sound good."[62]

Then there was the money issue. "Billy was suddenly making a lot more money," explains Liberty, "but what about the rest of the band? "That's what Richie told me; he asked for more money. Billy actually sent a limo to his house to pick him up. He was planning a tour, and Richie didn't show up, something like that. Richie didn't want to be 'the utility man' anymore—that's what I think. Richie was playing sax, playing organ, playing accordion. The accordion was the thing that broke Richie; he would play that during 'Piano Man.' He thought he looked silly playing the accordion. And I don't think Richie wanted to do that anymore."[62]

Looking back on his career with Billy, Richie Cannata explains, "*Turnstiles* was the first one, then *Stranger, 52nd Street, Glass Houses, Songs in the Attic.* Then I just felt it was just wasn't me anymore. It was a mutual decision. I didn't ask. Billy and I had a talk. We were backstage somewhere, and [rock writer] Timothy White was there. Tim said to me, 'Hey, are you and Billy going to go out and work together again?' Billy looked back and said, 'We'll work together again someday.' And I said, 'Yeah, we will.' I just wasn't ready to do it again, and he saw that. I remember there was a long period off. I did some of *Nylon Curtain.* There were some songs on there that we were doing on the road, and I had added my parts and stuff. But then I was gone for the record, I didn't get to play on that record."[44]

Richie even claims that he had a big hand in finding his own replacement in the group. "Things and events had happened," he says. "It was time to move on. People thought that it was a money issue, and it really wasn't. I never said to him, 'Well, if I don't make X amount of dollars, I won't go out.' It was never like that. He never called me to say, 'We're moving on with somebody else.' I had this club in Roslyn. It wasn't My Father's Place, it was next door, it was called Fern's. There was a band that played in there, and there was a sax player who came in, and Doug Stegmeyer recommended this guy to me, and I said, 'Oh, good.' I met him and then I said, 'Why don't you go audition for my part, they need an alto sax player.' It was Mark Rivera."[44]

Even before he officially left Billy's band, he was already playing the saxophone or serving as a producer on other people's records. "That's when I got busy, and I left Billy, and I worked for Elton [John], and then Rita [Coolidge]," Richie recalls. "I ended up producing one of Phoebe Snow's records: *Rock Away*. I went through some of the hardest times with her. We were in the studio recording when John Lennon was shot. We immediately went over to the Dakota, with Greg Ladanyi who was my coproducing partner on that album. Phoebe was going through so much. Her daughter was born with the doctors saying that she wouldn't live, or would be mentally challenged her entire life. She defied all of the medical reasons why that little girl shouldn't be up and walking around, and coherent. She is now [in 2005] thirty years old. Phoebe went through all kinds of things. She had a continuous black cloud over her, but she channeled it into taking care of her daughter, Valerie. She is absolutely wonderful. Phoebe was managed by Elizabeth [Joel] back then, too. If you asked Elizabeth and you asked Phoebe, if it was the right combination, it might be a big question mark. But, if you asked about Billy and Elizabeth, that was the right combination. Phoebe should have been huge. She should have been looked at like another Aretha [Franklin]. She should have been up there. She is a great talent and a great singer."[44]

For a while Richie tried the West Coast as well. "I was actually out in California, I was producing Rita Coolidge then. I did a tour with her, and I did a record with her. I did four tracks for her, and who was my coproducer? Booker T. [Jones] was there for a little bit: David Anderle. It was David Anderle and myself, and Rita and Booker T. Then I joined Booker's band. I found myself in L.A. playing 'Green Onions' with Booker T."[44]

He actually found it much more interesting pursuing his musical career this way, rather than playing Billy's same music year after year. After Richie left Billy Joel's band, he found that the Billy fans were really upset that he left: "I got so much flak, man, when I left the band. People would say, 'How could you leave the band?' 'How could you let this guy play your parts?' They weren't happy with me for leaving. They wanted to see me, and I wasn't there. I had to live with that for a while, but I didn't want to go back to that. It wasn't the thing to do. I have my recording studio, and my home and my career. I got to do a lot of things. I got to play with Elton. I dreamt that I played with Elton, and I got to do that—*24 at 33*—I got to play on that record. And that was the time I was working with Rita, and Booker T., and then after that came Styx, and Tommy Shaw. Then I worked with Celine Dion, who came here to my studio to record. And Taylor Dayne. I played on all of her hits. I was on a great record with Celine, her Christmas record. That is the staple of all Christmas records, they dust it off every Christmas. If I had played with Billy for thirty years, I would have felt trapped. And, I didn't want to do that."[44]

For Billy Joel fans, it appeared that Richie Cannata just disappeared from the scene. In reality he was to be much more the master of his own fate than would any of the other guys who left Billy's band. Richie spent several years touring with the Beach Boys as their sax player and worked on several of the solo Beach Boy projects throughout the years. He invested his money well and eventually purchased his own recording studio, Cove City Sound, which he still has and runs today. Says Richie, "In 1983, 1984, I was dabbling in real estate. I had the restaurant, Fern's, in Roslyn. Then I was working on this building. I sold that, and I made that into this building. Then I had a house in Seacliff. And then I sold that house, and got my house in Glen Cove. So, I was doing all of that, and I had to be here for all of that. That's when I started this place, Cove City Sound. I had a partner and we started a restaurant as well. I invested in fast-food restaurants. I did a lot of planning so I could do music."[44]

Liberty DeVitto especially missed having Richie Cannata in the band: "Richie didn't want to play the accordion. It took two people to take his place."[62] In the interim years, Richie met a woman he fell in love with, by the name of Shirlene. Together they had a son named Eren, who is an aspiring singer and songwriter today.

Although Richie Cannata was officially out of the Billy Joel band by 1982, he is someone who continues to have a recurring role in Billy's life and career. He claims, "I was okay with not being part of the craziness. I was okay being my own person, sitting in my own studio making my own music. I was touring as much, but not spending the money. You know, not spending the dollar fifty when I was earning a buck."[44]

Meanwhile, the Billy machine continued to move onward. He had gotten Artie Ripp out of his path. Richie left the band to pursue his own music. Elizabeth was now out of the picture as his wife, and as his manager. Frank Weber, his about-to-be-former brother-in-law, effortlessly eased into the role of personal manager, so everything seemed like smooth sailing ahead.

For Billy, it was time to make a new album, and a fresh start. As Richie recalled, Billy and the band were already at work on the recordings that would become one of his most critically acclaimed LPs, *The Nylon Curtain*.

While all of this was underway, he and Elizabeth officially announced their split. "It didn't work. The hardest thing for two people who love each other to do is to break up. But sometimes it has to be done," he said.[17]

Did the fact that she was not only his wife, but his business partner as well, harm their relationship? "She was more focused on my career than

I was," explains Billy. "Her function as my manager was to make me a rock star, and I think that's where our paths diverged. I might have become a commodity to an extent, and she might have become the enemy, which is business, capitalism, exploitation. I think as human beings we went in different directions. It was fruitful and successful in terms of what the music business is supposed to be, but it was ultimately damaging in terms of a relationship."[40]

At the time, Liberty DeVitto told the press, "I think it was part of his finding himself, breaking away from Elizabeth. The sad part is that they still love each other very much. He didn't change much, but she found a whole new group of people to hang around with. They're not his type. He likes normal people; he's a Long Island guy."[17]

By the time they finally broke up, Billy was more relieved to have it over and done with than he was depressed: "A lot of people are calling up, going, 'Are you O.K.?' 'Isn't it lonely?' And I'm like: 'No, man, I feel good.' It's not a real bitter thing, at least on my part. I'm not sure how she is, but I'm not looking at despair and the end of the world. It's hard to admit defeat, but I can do it. I'm not going to drink furniture polish!"[17]

He even thought then about having children. "I've wanted to have kids," he explained in 1982. "I'm 33. I see little kids, I get a little mushy. I'd love to have a little girl who thinks her daddy is everything. A little boy I could take fishing or teach how to work on bikes and stuff. And the last 12 years, I've been on the road so much it wouldn't have been fair if I'd had a family. Some of the problems with that came up in the marriage. So in the future, I'm gonna make sure I have some time to give to a family. I grew up without a father, and I don't want my kids growing up the same way. I think the real test of being an adult is having a kid. I don't think you know what it's really all about until you have children, and therefore, I don't really know what it's all about yet."[17]

Everyone needs a hobby. For Billy, it became a newfound fascination with motorcycles. Liberty remembers when Billy first became fascinated with the two-wheeled power machines: "Right before we went to Cuba we went from England to the Florida Keys. We stayed there before we went to Cuba. We told everybody we were going to Aruba. We got on these mopeds, and that's what got Billy into motorcycles. We got home from Aruba, and Billy bought a small Yamaha. Then, because of his money, he could buy all of the toys he didn't have when he was a kid. So he went from the small Yamaha, to a 750 Yamaha, to a Sportster, to a fully dressed Harley Davidson. He had a Ducati; [an] Italian motorcycle. And then he had this Café Rosa Harley

Davidson racing bike. I rode on that a few times, and it was quick—it was really quick."[62]

On April 15, 1982, Billy was out on Long Island, riding one of his fleet of motorcycles on a spring afternoon. It was 5:40 P.M., and he was at the intersection of West Ninth Street and New York Avenue in Huntington. There was little traffic and lots of trees as Cornelia Bynum made a turn in her car at the intersection—and ran right into Billy Joel, who was riding his 1978 Harley-Davidson.

Billy recounted, "I was really, really mad. This woman ran a red light, and there was nothing I could do. There are a couple of things you can do with a bike: you can hit the brakes, you can ditch the bike, or you can take evasive action. Really, the only thing you can do is hit the brakes—and where she came out, you could hit the brakes and you'd still hit. I was really mad: 'What are you, crazy? What are you doing? NO!' And, when I hit, it wasn't, 'Oh, my God, forgive me.' I just went, 'I'm going to hit,' and then I hit. And it was such a big noise, I really thought, 'This is stupid!' I thought, 'Man, that was a big noise, that was some impact.' Then I started to flip over the car. It was like slow motion, and I said, 'I'm flip-ping o-ver,' just like in those stupid drug kaleidoscope movies. And I landed on my back: 'boom!' I had a helmet on, leathers and stuff. And I said, 'O.K., that's that.' Then I got up.[17]

"Right before I hit, I had a flood of images, jumbled up thoughts. I thought I was going to die and I was pissed off at the car, which looked the size of Brooklyn to me. I thought, 'You can't do this to me, I'm not ready to die.'"[22]

He was most startled at how fast things like this happen. One minute you have all the variables, the next minute you don't know what just hit you. "The biggest thing I learned from the accident was that when you think you have all the control in the world, suddenly someone is going to turn [on] a red light. . . . I tried to remember, almost through self-hypnosis, what was going through my mind subconsciously at the time of the accident. It's very stream-of-consciousness, and to this day, I don't know what it all means"[104]

Liberty DeVitto says, "When he had the accident, and I heard about it, I was with my first wife at the time. And, I said to her, 'He was on the Rosa.' That was the one with the small little windshield, the Harley Davidson racing bike. That was the one. But I remember Billy always used to 'jump the lights'—you know, just take off as soon as the light turns green. I'm not saying that it was his fault or anything. He certainly stopped at the red light. We thought he was 'done' then."[62]

Although he was in a bit of a state of shock, once he realized that he was alive, Billy's first instinct was to grab his motorcycle and drag it out of the intersection. However, when he attempted to use his left hand, he realized that something was horribly wrong with it. This is a man who makes his living from the dexterity of his wrists, hands, and fingers, and when he looked at his left hand, he saw that it was swollen to the size of a grapefruit.

First he was taken to a local hospital, then Billy was transported by helicopter to Columbia Presbyterian Hospital in New York City. The first fears were for his life. Internal bleeding can kill a person before anyone knows what's happening. Once they were certain he would live through this, the concerns shifted to the broken bones in his left thumb and right wrist.

Although separated from Elizabeth, she was then still his legal wife. She told the *New York Times,* "We're all highly relieved. He's in excellent spirits, he feels great, but his hands hurt."[105]

It was Dr. David L. Andrews who performed surgery on Billy Joel's right wrist and his left thumb. "The doctor he had was one of the greatest surgeons," states Liberty. Indeed, he did. Thanks to Dr. Andrews, the operations on his hands were successful. After he was finished, Andrews was confident that Billy would regain the majority of his dexterity in both of those hands. As it turned out, he was correct.

Finally, in September 1982, Billy released his ninth solo album, *The Nylon Curtain,* again produced by Phil Ramone. At this point his band consisted of Liberty DeVitto (drums), Doug Stegmeyer (bass), Russell Javors (guitar), and David Brown (guitar). The strings and horns on the album were arranged by jazz star Dave Grusin.

The album opens with "Allentown," an ode to what was going on economically at the time in Middle America. The steel mills, particularly in Pennsylvania, were all having major problems. Billy had read about this in the headlines, and he turned it into one of his most effective musical turns. With the fire, drive, and conviction of the opening number of a Broadway musical, "Allentown" becomes the anthem of the album. Rife with industrial sound effects and driven by Liberty DeVitto's relentless beat, it kicks off the disc with true rock & roll excitement.

As Billy explained, "It was written during the steel industry recession. I think a lot of people assumed that they could get the same job their father had, in the Northeast especially places like Ohio and Pennsylvania. Suddenly those jobs were gone. There was a diminishing horizon in America. I think it was the first time since the Depression that people were actually faced with limitations in the America that they know, and that was what that song was about."[50]

"Laura" is musically out of the Beatles-sounding realm, lying somewhere between "Dear Prudence" and "Maxwell's Silver Hammer." Here Billy sings about how a manipulative woman telephones him in the middle of the night to go on and on about this and that, while she is pushing all of his emotional buttons. While the initial assumption is that the Laura in the song is a friend who calls to complain and cajole, and peppers her monologue with poisonous barbs, he states in this song how his newfound bachelorhood is not as much fun as he had hoped it would be in reality.

The truly fascinating revelation is finding out who Laura really is. According to Liberty DeVitto, this song is one that Billy wrote about Rosalind Joel. "Yes, this is about his mother," says Lib. "The word 'mother' has the same amount of syllables as the word 'Laura.'"[92]

The stripped-down fast-paced rock song "Pressure" is the album's perfect New Wave–ish radio-friendly single. Direct, blistering, and written about a subject that everyone could identify with—day-to-day stress—it has a nice bouncy feel to it, led by Liberty's drums, and features Billy Joel's evocative keyboard playing.

Every one of Billy's most successful albums has had one centerpiece dramatic epic in it. In this album, it is truly "Goodnight Saigon." This seven-minute-long musical drama is all about the Vietnam War, into which the singer projects himself in the narrative role of one of the soldiers who found himself in the middle of that politically charged conflict in the sixties and seventies. Beginning with the beating of helicopter blades whirling around from above, it brings a whole *Apocalypse Now* experience to rock music. A heartfelt salute to the boys who went over there and came back, and a tribute to those who did not return, it remains an enduring Billy Joel classic. In addition to his regular band, his childhood friend Billy Zampino is heard on this cut, playing the field snare drum.

According to Billy, "I wasn't trying to make a comment on the war, but writing about the soldier as a person. The song isn't a political statement, even though it's been interpreted as one. The European press found it too pro-American, but in South Korea they won't release the record because the Government think[s] it's too anti-American.[104]

"Of course I was hesitant to write about Vietnam, because I wasn't there. But a lot of my friends fought in Vietnam and two close friends were killed. But the people I knew who fought and came back encouraged me to write it. I picked their brains and asked them what music they listened to, what they did, and how they felt. The feeling of camaraderie, of only having one another for support, was something they all still share."[104]

"She's Right on Time" is Billy's attempt at writing a Christmas song. This ballad has great drums, and although it mentions the December holiday, he actually only sings the word "Christmas" twice. It is much more about his relationship with a lover than about Yuletide issues. Still, it comes across as a very nice and passionately sung song about love and devotion.

"A Room of Our Own" is a total drug and sex song. In the lyrics it seems that he is wanting to have an affair with another resident of a rock & roll hotel. Billy sings of having razor blades, a typical coke-snorting accoutrement, and proclaims that the woman in the scenario has pills. Now, he sings, they just need a room of their own in which to get stoned and have sex.

"Surprises" is a beautiful piano ballad with some "Lucy in the Sky with Diamonds" touches to it. Here he surveys a relationship that he claims has "changed." It is pretty obvious that this song has to do with his divorce from Elizabeth. When he sings songs of warning, speaking to his opponent to "marshal" her forces for a forthcoming attack, he was most likely thinking of facing off with his ex-wife's lawyers.

"Scandinavian Skies" is very "Strawberry Fields" with its loopy strings and highly manipulated musical tracks. In this song he sings of flying through northern Europe amid what seems to be a very druggy tour. Heavy shades of "I Am the Walrus" abound here as well, complete with a "Back in the USSR"–style stereo plane landing at the beginning of the song. Apropos of the whole Beatles' late-sixties mode, the song is clearly about getting high and being stoned on drugs. He sings of the "sins" he committed in Amsterdam, which apparently involved both drugs and sex—two commodities openly sold there.

Said Billy, "What I realized after I made it, and it was just after John Lennon was killed, that I even found myself singing like John Lennon. I didn't realize I was doing it and I was writing these songs that I pictured John Lennon singing. Like 'Scandinavian Skies.' I remember Phil Ramone, who was the producer at the time in the studio, saying, 'You're really singing it like John Lennon too much,' and I didn't realize it. Then when I came back and listened to it, it was weird. And then I said, 'Okay, I'll try to sing it more like whoever Billy Joel is,' who, I'm still not sure what he sings like. And it didn't work. I had to sing it as it was written, as it was conceived to be sung."[31]

BILLY JOEL

The album's closing track is called "Where's the Orchestra?" He delivers his lyrics in a very melodic, almost Paul McCartney, singsong way. It is this slow and peculiar ballad that finds Billy going to see a dramatic play on Broadway, expecting to see a musical. Onstage, he sees a movie star taking a turn at the theater, but where is the orchestra and where is the music, asks the song's lyrics.

Billy was very enthusiastic about how this particular album came about and what it ultimately sounded like. When it was released, he spoke of it very proudly to the press. According to him, it took a lot of effort to come up with the material this time around: "I feel like I almost died making *The Nylon Curtain*. The thing you don't have control over is writing—you have to pull it out of yourself, stretch yourself. . . . You pace the room with something like the dry heaves, having no control over the muse, horrified that it won't come. You're always in the desert looking for the oasis, and all that's out there with you is the piano—this big black beast with 88 teeth. You have to lay your guts on the table and go through them eleven times on the album. 50,000 packs of cigarettes later, you start getting it."[22]

He claimed that each new LP received a new concept. *The Nylon Curtain* was no different. "On every album I adopt a different sort of character, and the character of this album is sort of a sweet person who is in love and feeling good. It's a guy enjoying the courtship rituals—making out, dating, slow dancing and the insecurities that go with it—the gamut of passions that come with romance. I wrote ten songs in about seven weeks, which I've never done before. It just came pouring out of me. It doesn't really ape anything. It just feels like it. There actually isn't a standard chord progression in the LP. It's musically pretty complex. The challenge for me was making it feel so simple."[22]

Billy said he was thrilled by the results: "I like the *Nylon Curtain* album a lot. That would probably be the album I'm most proud of making, as a labor of love."[31]

He put a lot of thought into it and had a specific era and a specific sound in mind when he went into the recording studio: "This record is very richly textured; there're a lot of orchestra instruments on it, and synthesizers and sound effects. Sort of *a la* the *Magical Mystery Tour/Sgt. Pepper* era. I always loved those records in the late '60s, even though I didn't do any acid." He called it "a very American album, aimed at the post-Baby Boom kids. [It] was very complicated. As a matter of fact, half way through it, I could have shot myself for deciding to make this quantum leap. But I'm really happy with the way it turned out."[106]

There were so many Beatles sounds, techniques, and references in this album, that they could not be ignored. Billy was the first to embrace the similarities. "I'd always thought of Paul McCartney as a bigger influence, but when John Lennon was killed, I realized he was the one who was kicking in more soul," he said analytically. "I thought about it a lot, and when I heard my vocals in the playback booth, the similarity to Lennon seemed weird, because the resemblance wasn't intended. But my producer and the guys in the band said, 'Leave it, it's right, that's the way you felt.' *The Nylon Curtain* wasn't an easy album to make."[104]

According to Billy, the very title of the album was a play on the terms for cold war isolationism that existed in the 1950s and '60s. "There's all this paranoia about the Russians, he said. "We're so cut off from the rest of the world that merely bringing people closer together is a really radical change. The title of my album, *Nylon Curtain,* meant just that. The Russians have an Iron Curtain, and we have a nylon one. It's this very sheer, Capitalist haze we all seem to have. Everything looks so rosy through it, so unreal. Making contact with another nation based on something other than what you read in the papers, or what some politician tells us, that's radical."[59]

When the press called *The Nylon Curtain* album heavily "Beatles" influenced, Phil Ramone claimed the connection was something "which wasn't at all in our minds. But it's better they put the label on it than me. . . . On *Nylon Curtain*, we were also accused of *stealing* from The Beatles, of course, and that was all junk. Everybody looks to throw flak."[73]

Even *Rolling Stone* praised Billy Joel's artistry this time around. Wrote reviewer Stephen Holden, "While 'Goodnight Saigon' is *The Nylon Curtain*'s stunner, there are other songs in which Joel's blue-collar smarts, Broadway theatricality and rock attitude blend perfectly. 'Allentown,' his portrait of a crumbling Pennsylvania mining city in which the American dream has died hard, could be a scene from *The Deer Hunter* put to music. Like 'Goodnight Saigon,' its tune, language and singing are all brazenly direct. And that directness is presumably what the album title refers to. For in one way or another, the songs on this LP are concerned with the tearing away of protective emotional filters to reveal naked truths. . . . *The Nylon Curtain* finds Billy Joel on higher artistic ground than ever before."[107]

Music industry trade publication *Billboard* claimed to love *The Nylon Curtain* "for the strength and conviction of its lyrics . . . the music again reflects the well-crafted pop-rock fusion that Joel honed in *The Stranger* and *52nd Street*."[108]

In *Creem* magazine, Richard Reigel's review read, "Thankfully *The Nylon Curtain* makes my task simpler, as it's a real good album . . . Now that the actual *The Nylon Curtain* is upon us, I can assure you that it doesn't sound like *Sgt. Pepper* . . . since [David] Bowie has more to do with the shape of our current post-modern rock than the lost Beatles can, Billy Joel is lunging ever closer to the heart of the rock & roll beast."[109]

Stephen Holden also wrote a feature article about Billy in the *New York Times* in which he further praisingly proclaimed, "With its use of sound effects, aural montage, exotic orchestration, and thickly overdubbed vocals, *The Nylon Curtain* is a far cry from the pared-down rock of *Glass Houses* and harks back to the late '60s psychedelia of The Beatles."[104]

The Nylon Curtain was quite successful on both sides of the Atlantic Ocean. It hit number 7 in the United States, and number 27 in England. The album yielded several hit singles in America including: "Pressure" (number 20), "Allentown" (number 17), and "Goodnight Saigon" (number 56). *The Nylon Curtain* very quickly became Billy's fourth million-selling album.

The songs "Allentown" and "Goodnight Saigon" were two of the reasons why this album did not become the usual international hit that his previous ones had become. Both of these songs were entirely culled from an American perspective and held very little resonance to audiences in different countries.

Two other Billy Joel recordings were also released in 1982. A song called "Elvis Presley Blvd." appeared on the "B" side of the "Allentown" single. And the nursery rhyme–like ballad "Nobody Knows but Me" was featured on the children's album *In Harmony II,* which was produced by Lucy Simon [Carly's sister] and David Levine. Both tracks were later included on Joel's boxed set *My Lives.*

When his hands were sufficiently healed from the motorcycle accident, Billy returned to touring after *The Nylon Curtain* was released. The reviews were likewise glowing:

Los Angeles Times: "Joel is fiery . . . and quite a dazzling showman. . . . Joel's apparent goal is to seize control of the hearts and minds of his fans, and he has the charisma, the vocal and musical skills and the high quality songs to pull it off."[22]

The Herald in Everett, Washington: "Pound for pound, dollar for dollar, few acts give as much of themselves and their music as the Piano Man."[22]

The Union in Sacramento, California: "Few can interweave the soft qualities of a well-known ballad with a powerful rocker just moments apart and do it so effectively. . . . He is a tough man to stereotype."[22]

By 1982 it was acknowledged in the press that the song "Just the Way You Are" was now played during more weddings than any other popular song. Billy dismissed the comment by snidely saying, "Yeah, whatever that means. I get a lot of letters that make me wonder, 'Wow, have I written "Here Comes the Bride?" Am I going to get blamed for the divorce, too?'"[12]

Speaking of divorces, he was now publicly making jokes about his own recent split from Elizabeth. "I just wanna be a blues pianist in a band like J. Geils," he claimed. "Just sit there and play the blues. Just wearing a hat, dark shades, a beard, a little Scotch on the piano, a pack of cigarettes. . . . 'O.K., Bill.' Or, 'B.J.,' or some anonymous name: 'Al.' Yeah, 'Al.' I'm always 'Al' on the road: 'Alcohol,' 'Alka-Seltzer.' In England, I was 'Aluminum.' This tour, I think I'm gonna be 'Alimony!'"[17]

In 1981 and '82, the American record charts were heavily populated by songs by superstars teaming up to perform together. Occasionally groups paired with individuals, and in other instances solo superstars came together as a duo. Among these duets were Queen and David Bowie's "Under Pressure," Aretha Franklin and George Benson's "Love All the Hurt Away," Paul McCartney and Stevie Wonder's "Ebony and Ivory," Diana Ross and Lionel Richie's "Endless Love," Barbra Streisand and Barry Gibb's "What Kind of Fool," Dionne Warwick and Johnny Mathis's "Friends in Love," and Joe Cocker and Jennifer Warnes's "Up Where We Belong."

So, where was the Billy Joel–and–somebody duet? Said Billy at the time, "Nobody asks me. I think people have this idea that I'm an inaccessible, glacial type of guy. But, I'm around all the time. Maurice White [of Earth, Wind and Fire] wanted to do something, but we never got back together. Michael Jackson wanted to do something, but he didn't get back to me. I got a call from Eric Clapton, but he didn't get back to me, either. Maybe I give bad phone."[17]

Billy continued to wage a war with the press. The singer still delighted in ripping apart unfavorable articles about him. He was certainly one to look a potential fight straight in the eyes: "Where I come from, somebody smacks you in the face, you smack him right back. You don't turn the other cheek. You hit him back as hard as you can. On-stage, I have a forum for saying what I think. Reviewers can say something bad in the newspapers,

BILLY JOEL

but they have to take into consideration that If I'm going to play a 20,000-seater the next night, I'm going to say exactly what I think of a review. The smart thing for me to do would be to forget it, not to mention it, but that's just the way I am!"[12]

His main "beef" of late was Robert Palmer, who wrote for the *New York Times*. Claimed Billy Joel of Palmer, "He's irrelevant. He is nothing. He gave away his prejudice in his review. He said, [of Billy] 'I never liked him.' So, why the hell did he come to review the concert in the first place? I mean, he doesn't fool anybody. I will not write what the critics think I should write, and *that* infuriates them the most of all."[12]

Ironically he also admitted, "Criticism is healthy. It's needed. I've been busted for things where they were right to bust me. Sometimes the show wasn't up to par and they say the show wasn't right. But if somebody doesn't like the music up front, he's not going to like the show. That's not criticism. That's just publicly stating your prejudices. There's another thing to consider. The reviewers never pay for tickets. They don't know the value of anything. They never buy the records. They get them free in the mail. They don't stand in line or pay money like everybody else. They're not going to a show because they want to, they're going because they *have* to. How do they know whether a show is any good or not. Tell them to ask the people who waited in line and paid the money. . . . It doesn't affect anything except people who are fans of critics, and I don't know many of those."[12]

Phil Ramone was still among Billy's biggest fans and supporters: "He's very disciplined. We—he, the band and I—generally get a song done in just two or three takes. And it's all part of his tough, seasoned exterior, born out of years of double-crosses. But behind his hard facade is a great, great tenderness."[14]

Billy was someone who was obsessed with the idea of not becoming pigeonholed into one particular category. He prided himself in recording each new album with a different feeling and a different musical style to it. "A lot of people who are attracted to me they haven't been exposed to black music; they think right off the bat that all black music is disco, so they think that my ballads are something to be played only on Adult Contemporary 'dentist's office' Easy Listening stations. I'm just trying to be accepted for doing a diversity of things," he claimed. "When The Beatles did 'Yesterday,' did that mean that they became an Adult Contemporary group suitable only to dentist's offices? No, that didn't stop them from doing any of the trashy rock & roll stuff they did. Same thing with The [Rolling] Stones. They did

BILLY JOEL

'Angie' and 'Ruby Tuesday,' but it didn't mean they weren't The Stones any-more or had deserted their audience."[14]

There were definitely two different phases of Billy Joel's recording career at this point. There was his early phase—up to *The Stranger*—when he was viewed as a balladeer. After the success of it, album after album, Billy was delving deeper into rock & roll, and moving away from the touching piano ballads of his young adulthood. As he viewed it, "Everybody puts things in categories. Everything has to fit into a certain bag: New Wave, next phase, dance, funk, punk. . . . Call it what you want, but it sounds like the music I heard in the early '60s. The new Wave isn't new. It's just the explosion of a lot of groups which I think is good. . . . Well, take M.O.R. [Middle of the Road]: You can hear it and not hear it. That's how a lot of music is. Rock & roll is music you *have* to hear. People say I'm not rock & roll because of my ballads, but that's not right: Take a song like 'Yes-terday,' a ballad created by a member of a rock & roll band. Is that rock & roll? If you're a rock & roll snob who hates ballads, you never would have listened to The Beatles. If The Beatles were around today, they would never make the hard-rock stations. You see, elitism of any kind is bad. You're shut-ting yourself off. Christ—Led Zeppelin and The Rolling Stones have done ballads. I think a lot of it has to do with the emotion behind it. If it's per-formed with passion and recorded with intensity, and it's written in some rock form, it's rock & roll. If I like it and I hear it on the radio and it gets me going, stimulates me, it's rock & roll."[12]

When it came time to write a hit song, Billy admitted that his frame of reference was his childhood passion for what he heard on the radio when he was growing up on Long Island: "I grew up on jukebox music, and every-body in the band has played this music all their lives, and they range in age from 28 to 31. We played the Top Forty singles in bars. Then, when *Sgt. Pep-per's Lonely Hearts Club Band* came out, everybody started smoking pot and tripping and listening to the 13th Floor Elevator. Suddenly, everything changed—all the formats for playing and recording and listening to music. You could hear 25 minutes of music on the air with no commercial break."[14]

In addition to making parallels to the music that Billy was now making, and the music of the Beatles, the press also seemed to create some sort of rivalry between the singer and his label-mate, Bruce Springsteen. "I don't think we're anything alike at all," retorted Billy. "Bruce writes his Jersey stuff and I write my Long Island stuff. I thought that guy was a friend of mine. We don't have any rivalry. There's plenty of room for both of us. Bruce is 'the Boss.' I have no pretensions to his throne. I just do what I do. I've seen Bruce. He's great. But I don't know how good I am, because I'm up there working. It's hard for people to realize you're just doing what you want to do. The press has nothing better to do than attack. I lost a lot of respect for what I read."[12]

Billy still liked the "fun" aspect of his craft. "I like to play music," he explained. "We're not in the studio to make important records. We go into the studio, the song gets mixed and it's eventually heard through tiny car-radio speakers. We also like being together on-stage. You should never lose sight of the fact that you're there to entertain. People don't pay money to see art. They don't pay money for you to sit there and be 'Billy Joel.'"[14]

In 1982 Billy Joel made recorded music history. The record industry had long been trying to develop some sort of new way of selling music to the listening public. Vinyl records were still the king of the business; however, it presented intrinsic problems. Since vinyl recordings had to be played with a stylus or needle being dragged along the indented grooves of a piece of plastic, eventually there was bound to be wear and tear. Playing vinyl recordings again and again caused surface noises on the plastic disc. Not only was there the constant hiss caused by the friction of the needle on the grooves, but any piece of dust or crud that settled on the record was also audible. The same thing was true for cassettes and eight-track tapes. Eventually the particles of magnetic compound that the tapes relied upon for sound transmission revealed audible signs of wear. But finally, a new invention had been struck upon by the Phillips Corporation, and *voilà*— the compact disc was born!

In the 1980s the record companies were all complaining that sales were down on recorded music. Well, the CD revolution was suddenly hurled upon the unsuspecting public. Since the sound of CDs is retrieved from optic lenses and laser-cut images, and no actual friction occurs on the surface of a CD as it plays, the discs instantly offered incredibly sharp, dynamic, and consistent sound. The CD technology worked brilliantly. By the middle of the decade of the eighties, every audiophile on the planet was suddenly scurrying about to repurchase an entire record collection on compact disc.

And what was the very first commercially available CD to hit the marketplace? None other than Billy's phenomenally successful *52nd Street* album. Maybe he didn't start the fire, but it truly was Billy Joel who officially started the CD revolution.

Regarding his personal life circa 1982, Billy spoke about being single again. "A lot of men my age grew up just as the sexual revolution was getting started, and now that it seems to be winding down, they are confused. I was married for a long time and living on Long Island. When I got divorced and moved back to New York City, it was a Rip Van Winkle experience. I found that the rules had changed, and in many ways my attitudes had become old fashioned," he claimed.[110]

Speaking of Billy's transformation into born-again bachelor, Liberty DeVitto told *Rolling Stone* magazine at the time, "He's found himself. He knows who 'Billy Joel' is, more than what other people have tried to make him into."[17]

With all of the changes that Billy had been through in the past year, including having survived a motorcycle accident, he was ready for a bit of an escape from reality. So he planned an out-of-the-way vacation. Little did he know when he made those reservations, that the trip was to have life-changing ramifications. It was on this holiday jaunt that he would meet and fall in love with Christie Brinkley.

Five years younger than Billy, Christie Lee Hudson was born on February 2, 1954, in Monroe, Michigan. She received part of her education at the Lycée Français de Los Angeles. Having studied art, she worked in Paris as an illustrator. In 1976, at the age of twenty-one, she signed a modeling contract with Cover Girl cosmetics. They loved her so much and she was so beautiful that the company continued to renew her contract again and again, over the next twenty years.

In 1979 Christie appeared on the cover of the annual *Sports Illustrated* magazine "swimsuit issue." She was so popular that she was asked back in 1980 and 1981, and in doing so became the first model in that publication's history to have graced their swimwear cover three years in a row. At five foot nine inches, she is considered one of the world's true beauties.

In addition, she made her film acting debut in 1983's popular *National Lampoon's Vacation* with Chevy Chase and Beverly D'Angelo. In the film Christie played the part of "the Girl in the Ferrari."

Through her television commercials and print ads for Cover Girl cosmetics alone, Christie's face and features were instantly recognizable throughout America. When Billy met Christie they both knew at once who each other was. For him—especially—it was love at first sight.

In her personal life, Christie had been married to Jean-François Allaux from 1973 to 1981. Then she began dating Olivier Chandon de Brailles, who was the heir to the Moët et Chandon champagne fortune. He was also a passionate race car driver. Olivier loved the sport and was a frequent participant on the elite race car circuit.

Regarding his first encounter with Christie, Billy recalls, "I took a week off in the winter of 1982–'83, the first vacation I'd taken in years. I was going through a separation and divorce. I had just finished a tour, and I was exhausted. Paul Simon had rented a house down in a place called St. Bart's, this island in the Caribbean, and he said, 'Look, it's great down here. It's real quiet. Just take a break.' It sounded like a good idea. When I was making the transfer flight—you go down to St. Martin, then you take a commuter plane—I saw Christie Brinkley. I recognized her immediately. She was more beautiful than she was in her pictures: 'Oh, wow, that's *Christie Brinkley!* I wonder if she knows who I am?.' So I did what I call an album cover—I tried to look like me on an album cover. I gave it every angle I could. She didn't recognize me from a hole in the wall. And then I was on St. Bart's, and I went to this bar in the PLM Hotel. They have a little piano there, and I had a couple of drinks. I was feeling, you know, a little melancholy. And there's Christie Brinkley. And Whitney Houston and another girl, Elle [MacPherson], who is now also a famous model. I met them all at the same time."[40]

At the time, Whitney Houston had yet to release an album of her own. She was amid her first wave of success, as a teenage model. Eventually Whitney ended up on the pages of several women's magazines, including *Cosmopolitan, Young Miss,* and *Glamour.* She also did some work for several print advertisements for Revlon cosmetics, and for Sprite. She was signed to the Click Models agency. She stands at five feet eight inches tall.

Like Brinkley, Elle MacPherson was—and is—still considered one of the world's most successful models. She is six feet tall, and Australian-born. Elle was discovered the year before, while she was skiing in Aspen, Colorado, and was signed to Click Models as well. Her modeling career had just begun at this point.

Here was newly single five foot six Billy Joel in St. Bart's with three of the world's most statuesque and recognizable models—all of them two to four inches taller than him. Although she was cute, he had zero interest in eighteen-year-old Whitney Houston. Nor did he fall in love with nineteen-year-old Elle Macpherson—although he found her to be very nice. However, he was instantly taken by Christie Brinkley. She was very sophisticated, and she possessed both wit and charm.

Billy recalls, "I'm sitting there going, 'I don't *believe* this.' So, everybody's having a couple of drinks, no one was feeling any pain, and we started having a sing-along. I was making believe I was Humphrey Bogart in Casablanca, and I was playing 'As Time Goes By.' Eventually a little crowd gathered, and we were singing. Christie was sitting next to me. Whitney was standing in front of the piano, singing. Elle was there. And that's how we met. I started playing some old rock & roll songs. Platters songs, Little Anthony & The Imperials, mushy stuff. She told me afterward she had just split up with a guy she had been seeing, and all of her friends were trying to encourage her to meet other guys."[40]

He knew about Christie and her affair with Olivier Chandon. He also knew that they had broken up not long before this chance meeting on St. Bart's. "They had split up months before that, and she hadn't been seeing anybody," Billy explained. "I guess she was kind of down, too. And they said, 'How about Billy Joel?' And she said, 'Nah, he's not my type.' I guess her first impression of me must have been this guy sitting at the piano with a Harley-Davidson T-shirt, looking like a bloated, puffy lobster. I had this incredible sunburn. The music was the key to the introduction. She sat down and started singing, too. She was laughing about it, saying, 'I don't have much of a voice.' And I was encouraging her: 'Oh, no, you have a great voice. Come on sing, sing, sing.' And I got a crush on her right then and there. Real down-to-earth, you know, down-home kind of girl. Not stuck up or anything, and not very self-conscious about her looks. I didn't see much of her on the island after that. We chitchatted and said, 'Well, maybe I'll see you when we're back in New York.'"[40] With that, the vacation came to an end, and everyone went their separate ways.

A couple of weeks later, on March 2, 1983, Olivier Chandon was racing his single-seater Formula Atlantic at Moroso Motorsports Park in Palm Beach, Florida. As Chandon entered turns 8 and 8A, he lost control of his car, overturned, and landed facedown into a canal filled with water. He was clocked at speeds in excess of 100 miles per hour when the accident occurred. By the time they could get him out of the car, twenty-seven-year-old Chandon had died. An autopsy showed that he had drowned.

Billy recalls, "When I was back in New York, I was living at the St. Moritz Hotel, and she was living on 67th Street by Central Park, which was right around the corner. I picked up the paper one day, and I saw that Olivier Chandon had been killed. I called her up and said, 'Look, I know you're going through a hard time. If you just need someone to talk to, I'm here."[40] Well, it turned out that she *did* want someone to talk to, and that was when the affair of Billy and Christie all began.

12

AN INNOCENT MAN

WHILE ALL OF this activity was going on, there was another side of Billy Joel that was not at all as highly publicized as his divorce, his love life, or his career accomplishments. That was his charitable causes. He may not have found a passion for such megacelebrity rock events as the 1979 No Nukes concerts, but he found his own signature causes to support. At the end of 1982, two of his last appearances for the year had both been charities. On December 27 he performed in Allentown, Pennsylvania. Since his song "Allentown" was concurrently on the charts, it was a natural move for him to aid the community that inspired his latest hit-bound single.

Then, two days later, on December 29, Billy performed a benefit concert at Nassau Veteran's Memorial Coliseum in Uniondale, New York. This Long Island event successfully raised $125,000 that would be distributed among dozens of different causes. It was all part of an organization called Charity Begins at Home, which was—and is—in reality a charitable organization that Billy helped to create.

Describing the scope of the individual charities that Charity Begins at Home supplied funds toward, Billy revealed at the time that they included, "the Rehabilitation Institute in Mineola, New York, which handles a lot of causes, and the Little Flower School in Suffolk, for orphans and kids who are emotionally troubled. There are several others."[14]

Bob Buchman is currently the program director of New York City radio station Q104.3 (WAXQ), which sponsors the annual Charity Begins at Home fund-raiser every December. When he first became associated with Billy Joel and his Charity Begins at Home organization, Buchman was at radio station WBAB on Long Island.

"In 1979 is when I started," says Buchman of his job at WBAB. "The year prior—1978—is when he founded Charity Begins at Home with a woman that—ironically enough—was something of a mentor of his. I don't know if I would call her a 'mentor' actually, but Louise Friedman was a confidante of Billy's. I didn't know them back then, but it's been put to me several times as their relationship. I don't want to say a 'confidante,' or a 'mother figure'—because Billy has his own mom.[99]

"She was someone that he could confide in. Although he has a very strong relationship with his own mother, [Louise] had her own motherly qualities. Louise Friedman was a not-for-profit person. She had nothing to do with the music business. I don't know to what extent Elizabeth Joel, his first wife, was involved at the time in the Charity Begins at Home concept. She may have been to some degree involved, but the concept of Charity Begins at Home was his personal idea. And Louise Friedman, with her not-for-profit expertise, was the woman who turned that idea into a real living and breathing charity. She ran the Rehabilitation Institute in Garden City at the time, which was a large charity. And she had the framework to house within that charity, Billy's charity. This way, Billy would never pay rent, like charities have to do. And Billy would never have to pay an executive director a salary, because she was already being paid by a different charity. So, Charity Begins at Home has, from that day forward, right to this day, been a rent-free, salary-free charity. So much of the money goes right to the people who need it. It's an umbrella organization."[99]

So many charities have such a great amount of overhead costs, that one often hears stories about how the bulk of the money never gets to the people who really need it, as it ends up whittled down in administrative costs. Buchman claims that this doesn't happen with this particular charity: "It's great. Charity Begins at Home is very simply, as Billy puts it—his slogan for it is: 'Put your money where your house is.' That's his way of saying, 'Keep it local.' There are a lot of great national and international causes. But this is about our home town. At the time it was Nassau and Suffolk [counties] only."[99]

According to Bob, it might pinpoint an individual who is in need, or it might be something that is good for the whole community. "It might be something for a whole bunch of individuals, like the homeless, which is the saddest of stories," he says. "And then it also will help fund programs in the parks. Like a musical program in a park. Maybe budget cuts may be eliminating that; well, we can fund those budget cuts. We can fund that budget, and all of a sudden there's music in the park, or there's a Shakespeare program in the park, or a fireworks program in the park. The consistent thing about the charity is that it's local. But in terms of, 'Does it help the hungry, and the blind, and the deaf?' Yes, but it also helps everybody. So, that's the whole concept in a nutshell—from its inception in '78. I got involved in '80, and I'm still involved."[99]

One of the prime inspirations for Charity Begins at Home was an organization that was started by another Long Island singer-songwriter, Harry Chapin. He had a lot in common with Billy but unfortunately was killed in a car accident in 1981. Chapin's charity, Long Island Cares, primarily addressed feeding the hungry. Buchman reveals, "Actually, Long Island Cares is one of the charities that Charity Begins at Home funds. So it's one of our eighty charities. We fund eighty different charities. I call it an 'umbrella.' That's all it is: an umbrella. We don't actually do any work, we just make sure that the people who do the good work are funded as best we can."[99]

Bob confirms that it was Billy Joel who approached him and wanted to get WBAB involved. "Yes, in 1980 we got that started with him, and it went so well, and ironically, when we got it started that year, in 1980, the marathon was being done: a hundred-plus-hour nonstop radiothon. The first one that we did, that was the window when John Lennon was killed. I remember talking for hours and hours and hours about that. He was so devastated, I mean, that was one of his true heroes—John. He was just devastated. That certainly impacted negatively our ability to fund-raise. How do you fund-raise for a charity when this incident of epic proportions is happening? So, that was how we started. Still, it was a great first effort. And he said, 'You know what? Let's continue with this. And then basically, then he jumped off—by design, and continued to support it. But, he jumped off by design, and I just kept it going," says Buchman. "But it's all about his ideal, which is, 'Put your money where your house is.'"[99]

Every year since then, December becomes the fund-raising month for Charity Begins at Home. Explains Buchman, "We choose to do it around the holidays. And it's been done that way since 1980, and it's never skipped

a year. The first year, I think we raised $14,000 on that John Lennon year. And now [2005] we raise half a million: $540,000. It's grown!"[99] Although it has always been known as "Billy Joel's charity," in reality he started it, he supports it but does not officially serve as a director of it.

Radio personality Ken Dashow has worked with Buchman and this charity both at WBAB, and now at WAXQ. "Charity Begins at Home: It is something that he and my program director, Bob Buchman started when Bob was at WBAB," says Dashow, "the idea being: 'There are all these great charities, but what if we just concentrated on whatever happens locally, even if it is a larger group.' I work with the March of Dimes, with the Hungerthon—with the World Hunger Year people that Harry Chapin started. But our own mandate [at Charity Begins at Home] is: even if it is a larger organization, a cancer organization, that all of the money be kept in the local area. I actually agree with Billy on this. It's not that you don't donate to Tsunami Relief or Hurricane Katrina Relief, but when you donate to any kind of a larger cause, 'Could we please earmark that for the people suffering from that problem, who are in my neighborhood.' It's the local church fund-raiser, it's the local potluck supper. And, it feels better when you do something locally like that. He's stayed with us, and he's always helped kick it off with us, wherever he is. He cuts the first check. He calls in, and sees how we are doing. He is actually involved. He looks over what's going on, where it's going . . . the people who organized Charity Begins at Home are still the people who he helped start it with, and know what the deal is. No, this doesn't take care of the Northeast. This is specifically for Huntington, this is specifically for Brooklyn. It doesn't have to be Long Island. But it has to be in our backyard."[111]

Analyzing the whole rock-star-as-charity-organizer phenomenon, Ken Dashow says, "There's, like, a troika of Bruce [Springsteen], Billy, [the late] Harry [Chapin] thing of people who cared so much, and didn't just do it because a manager said, 'Hey why don't you give some money to charity? It'll look good.' No, these guys just read the newspaper, with the newspaper on their left and a checkbook on their right. That's another thing for me that elevates Billy—again along with Bruce: 'Don't put my name on it. Don't do a press release. You need musical instruments? You need something? Here.' Not when it was fashionable. Not when he needed to clean up his image. They've got a picture of him at a soup kitchen, which sadly is a great deal of how the media works with rock stars. Behind the scenes—99 percent of it you've never seen or heard about what he's done, or some of these guys. It's always been a big part of their lives—these guys. It's always been a big part of their life. That's their way of giving back."[111]

As a radiothon event, there are auctions of celebrity items, autographs, and concert tickets. Says Dashow, "It's a radio marathon that we do for four days, usually right before Christmas. And we auction off signed guitars and signed memorabilia, and tickets to shows and tickets to concerts. And we just ask people to donate—even if it's just a raffle ticket. Most of it is by raffle, and there are some online auctions. I think that people like the fact, too, that they know where it is going."[111]

Like Billy's song "Only the Good Die Young," on February 4, 1983, thirty-two-year-old Karen Carpenter collapsed and died of complications of anorexia nervosa. Thirteen years later, the Phil Ramone–produced *Karen Carpenter* album was released with its two Russell Javors tracks on it: "All Because of You" and "Still In Love With You." Laments Russell, "I liked her, and I am sorry that I didn't get to be friends with her, because she just didn't stay around long enough. It's one of those bittersweet memories."[65]

It was also in 1983 that the time came for Billy to record and release his tenth solo album. It was to become one of the most popular discs of his career. He was in need of a new creative muse. What would most inspire a man who is used to writing love songs? Why, being in love of course. In the case of *An Innocent Man,* clearly the central inspiration for the majority of the songs Billy wrote was the new love of his life, Christie Brinkley.

As he had done with his previous five albums, Billy went back into the recording studio with Phil Ramone as his producer. According to Ramone, his production work does not change with Billy's stylistic musical changes: "You've got to be true to the songs, to see changes as the songs evolve. The songs are different conceptually for him, so I have to be different. I think the producer is solely responsible to make sure every inch of a record is done in the best possible fashion. And I think if it's a major hit, it's really up to the artist to remember who they worked with and have a good relationship with them. The primary responsibility is to be truthful to the artist. If you're going to sit in a producer's chair, you better take your ego and put it someplace where it doesn't interfere with what the artist or the writer or the musician is about. I think a producer's responsibility is misunderstood for people who say, 'I' a lot: 'I did this,' rather than, 'If it wasn't for Liberty DeVitto or Steve Gadd or some bass player who contributed to something at that moment, I wouldn't be a hero.' You start by getting the music right; if you have to put some kind of stamp on it, the music's probably weaker than it should be.[112]

"I pre-produce right in the studio, to be honest with you. The real pre-production is between the writer and me, and the surprise is in the first effort that a person plays, in the first 20 minutes of playing the song. You get that as your first raw architectural drawing—it's a sketch. You may perfect it or you may over-perfect it, and the people who are playing it will tend to want to overdo it, until it's past the point, maybe until it's too pristine, too clean. Billy Joel, for instance, will write sixty or seventy percent of his stuff in the studio. He doesn't go in without a song that's almost done, but he could go three days and have two songs and then be dry for two days. He likes to work where the pressure is on and the band's gonna show up and he better have a song. He doesn't want to be sitting there with mud on his face—he's gonna come up with a song. There's no star bullshit in the studio. That's true of everybody I work with, because if that becomes part of your reality, you have to get rid of all the road people and tell them to stay out. It's always a danger."[112]

According to Billy Joel, in the beginning of his career, he developed a ballad singing style quite by accident. Then it evolved. "I didn't think of myself as a 'stylist,'" he explained in 1985. "I didn't approach *Piano Man* as a rock & roll album; we started exploring that more and more because of our live shows. I started to 'rock it' a little more during those early tours."[60]

Billy explained that his songs from this era would start out as rough demo tapes that he would make. He would then work out the beat of the song with his drummer, Liberty DeVitto. Then he had his band add their suggestions for their parts. "I'll tell Lib, 'This is what I want on my drums.' I'll tell my bassist and guitarist what I want and so forth. On a lot of songs, though, it's wide open: 'Here's the way I see it, you try it *your* way.' Lib keys into a lyric. His drumming plays off my piano playing, but he also keys into me lyrically."[60]

The album *An Innocent Man* was a total homage to the early sixties doo-wop and harmonic rock & roll music Billy grew up listening to on Long Island. It produced a staggering number of top 40 hits, and many fans and critics considered it to be the most completely visualized, and most successfully executed album of his career. And that was just musically speaking. The subject matter covered in the lyrics of the songs made the album even more vital and exciting.

Billy admitted at the time that this was truly an inspired album, because he suddenly found himself in love and feeling like a teenager again: "On every album I adopt a different sort of character, and the character on this album is sort of a sweet person who is in love and feeling good. It's a guy enjoying the courtship rituals—making out, dating, slow dancing—and the insecurities that go with it—the gamut of passions that come with romance. I wrote ten songs in about seven weeks, which I've never done before. It just came pouring out of me." 22

Each of Billy's albums have a slightly different tone to them, in the sense of subject matter, and in the musical style. As he put it, "I never do the same thing twice. To keep me interested, there always has to be something new, something different."22

This circa 1983 feeling of falling in love made him feel so rejuvenated that he infused *An Innocent Man* with the kind of music that he used to listen to when he was a teenager, in the early 1960s: "I decided I wanted to have as much fun as I could have, and I wanted it to *sound* like I was having fun. It doesn't really ape anything. It just *feels* like it. There actually isn't a standard chord progression in the LP. It's musically pretty complex. The challenging thing for me was making it feel so simple."22

Interestingly enough, the way that Billy started writing material for his *An Innocent Man* album came about via an invitation he received to write the theme song for a 1983 Rodney Dangerfield/Joe Pesci film called *Easy Money*. With that, Billy Joel set about writing the first song that was included on this album, "Easy Money." He explained, "When I think of Rodney, I automatically think of soul music. I don't know why. So, I wrote a soul song. The next thing I wrote was 'An Innocent Man,' which led me to write the next song—'The Longest Time,' I think. I don't remember the exact chronology. It was about that point, though, that I said, 'O.K.—that's the new album. That's the direction I'm going in.'"60

"Easy Money" has a very driving sound with a really strong and funky horn section, like those of some of the Stax and Atlantic Records artists, such as Carla Thomas, Rufus Thomas, Wilson Pickett, and/or Sam & Dave, would deliver in the midsixties. The song was the perfect track to set the musical time frame of this, one of the most consistently exciting albums of Billy's career.

"An Innocent Man" has the kind of tight harmonies and driving beat that is very reminiscent of the Drifters' classic "Under the Boardwalk." Sung like an impassioned plea, and punctuated by his own fingersnaps, Billy Joel makes this his most heartfelt singing performance. In the song the singer pleads with the object of his affection to take him seriously. This is Billy singing to Christie Brinkley, a woman who is used to guys' "hitting on" her.

In the lyrics of the song, Billy tries to convince her of his sincerity about her. Musically the track is very minimalist, letting the lyrics and the fingersnaps carry the message.

Explains Billy, "'An Innocent Man' was written to evoke the same kind of feelings that I got when I heard Ben E. King and the Drifters. There's a high note in that recording—this was done in 1983—and I had a suspicion that was going to be the last time I was going to be able to hit those notes, so why not go out in a blaze of glory?"[113]

"The Longest Time" is sheer doo-wop, with little more than a bass line, fingersnaps, and vocal harmonies as the music of this song. This is very Frankie Valli and the Four Seasons–sounding in its execution, borrowing from other groups of the era, such as the Teddy Bears. Here Billy sings of relishing the new bloom of a fresh romance. He confesses that he hasn't felt love for the longest time, and clearly Christie's appearance in his life signaled a fresh and dramatic start to an optimistic new phase of his life.

"This Night" has the kind of harmonic doo-wop construction that Dion and the Belmonts made famous with such songs as "Runaround Sue," "The Wanderer," and "A Teenager in Love." An effectively evocative song that builds to nice vocal crescendo, it is about a love affair that takes the singer delightfully by surprise. With piano and Liberty DeVitto's backbeat drumming to propel it, Billy sounds like an innocent teenager in love. Mark Rivera's dreamy and lilting alto sax solo midway through drives the song to jazzy new heights. According to Billy's liner notes, included with the album, the chorus was actually lifted directly from Beethoven.

After this trio of romantic ballads, "Tell Her About It" kicks things back into high gear. Against its exciting ensemble-led rock & roll beat, Billy gives advice to a lovelorn lad, with early sixties-style background harmonies. Explains Billy, "The song says I'm not living in the past, I'm celebrating today. I'd never have had the fire if I'd never hung out with the wild boys and heard the old music."[22]

Looking back on this musical period, he stated, "I must admit I owe a great deal of my perceived success to having had hit singles. But what happens with a hit single is it's taken out of context of the album. It's cut out and repasted somewhere else. So you take a song like 'Tell Her About It,' which was a hit single. To me, that sounds awful on its own. It sounds like Tony Orlando & Dawn. I hate that single. But in the context of the album it makes sense, because the *Innocent Man* album was sort of a tribute to old rock & roll influences. One of those influences was Motown groups like The Supremes. And there I am doing The Supremes. But if you take it out of context, it sounds like Tony Orlando & Dawn. But if you put it next to the song that came before which sounds like The Platters or Wilson Pickett, then that makes sense."[31]

"Uptown Girl" was the album's surefire smash. With a driving beat and amusingly self-deprecating lyrics, this song is all about Billy and his love for Christie. Here he wonders how a downtown schlub like him actually caught the attention of a classy act like Brinkley.

Says Billy, "'Uptown Girl' is a joke song. It's a tribute to Frankie Valli & The Four Seasons. I did it in that style. I even tried to sing like Frankie Valli—that strained falsetto. It's a joke, but if you listen to it in the context of the album, you get it. You go, 'Oh, this is like The Four Seasons,' which were a hugely influential group in my youth. The Four Seasons, before The Beatles, were maybe one of the biggest American bands there were. But like I said, taken out of context, it's like: 'What kind of pop silliness is this?' So I don't set out to write a hit single. I write songs in response to other songs I wrote. Then when I get to about the tenth song, if I'm lucky, I'm pretty much tapped out. I've had it. It seems to have ended. The little guys in the brain close up shop. They put their coats on and their scarves and their galoshes and they go, 'We're leaving now.' They turn out the lights and they're gone. And if I have ever mentally let the shop close, it's hard for me to start writing again."[31]

"Careless Talk" is another song that is lifted stylistically from the doowop years. Here Billy sings of the local gossip that is eroding his latest love affair, which his background singers harmonize behind him. "Christie Lee" has more of a Jerry Lee Lewis feeling to it. The piano work here on this excitingly rocking track is very much out of the "Great Balls of Fire" mode. Here he immortalized Christie in this song about her being a musical inspiration for a saxophone player in a nightclub.

There was no doubt that this song was all about Billy's new girlfriend. Looking back in 1996 on his songwriting of this time he was to explain, "I remember when The Beatles were writing music, and I'd try to find who their girlfriends at the time were: 'Oh, that's about Jane Asher.' Or with Mick Jagger: 'Oh, that's about Marianne Faithful.' We all do that. I think we all play those games, and I'm not going to deny that she was the muse for a great deal of the music I wrote during the time I was with her. She was what I epitomized, what I loved about women. She was the woman I married. That was my muse. She was my inspiration. But I think to assume that everything I wrote had something to do with our relationship wasn't true. I mean I had another life. I had a family before that, I had friends before that, I have my opinions about things."[31]

BILLY JOEL

"Leave a Tender Moment Alone," which features Toots Thielemans' hauntingly beautiful harmonica solo, shifts gears to take a more jazzy approach to the doo-wop flavor of this album. Describes Billy, "You say something really tender and affectionate [and] a part of you thinks, 'I don't believe I said something that corny,' so . . . you've got to make some kind of humorous comment to cover yourself. You should communicate your feelings to somebody you're in love with, despite the insecurity it brings."[22]

Phil Ramone recalls, "We started talking about it, and he said, 'Yeah, you know it's that awkward moment when you're with a woman and you say one sentence—the wrong one—and you can't take it back.' That's where a song comes from."[73]

The album ends up with the reminiscing sound of "Keeping the Faith," a medium-tempo song featuring Mark Rivera's saxophone, and Liberty's steady distinctive drumbeat. Here, Billy sings of his teenage years in the early sixties, and he hits on many of the touchstone items that reminded him of those tough but innocent years. Among the things he reminisces about were Cuban-heel shoes from Flagg Brothers, Old Spice aftershave, fast food at the local drive-in, his dad's Trojan condoms, making out with a girl in a Chevy, and Sen-Sen breath fresheners (from the years before Tic-Tacs were invented). This song lyrically looks back on the entire era it mimics, with both fondness and optimism.

When I asked Russell Javors which songs he made important creative contributions to, he explains, "Billy wrote the songs, but I helped shape a few. 'Keeping the Faith' was one. I showed Billy the groove and the lick to that one."[64]

This album became a favorite of Billy's many fans. Bobby Funaro of TV's The Sopranos recollects, "One of my fondest growing-up memories is sitting in the backseat of a gigantic Cadillac, and making out with a girlfriend while listening to Billy Joel's 'Keeping the Faith.'"[114] On this album, Billy recorded this music to bring back the days of his youth and his first romances, and in doing so, he was simultaneously creating musical memories for another generation.

Like most of Billy's Ramone-produced albums, An Innocent Man also included several guest appearances by several famous jazz musicians, including Ralph MacDonald (percussion), Richard Tee (acoustic piano in "Tell Her About It"), Michael Brecker (tenor sax), and David Sanborn (alto sax in "Easy Money"). To accomplish the tight harmonies it took to pull off the doo-wop-style vocals of much of the album, several of the top-session

BILLY JOEL

singers were brought in, including Frank Floyd, Lani Groves, and Ullanda McCullough. Billy Zampino is credited as being the album's "musical advisor."

The album cover featured a black-and-white photo of Billy, dressed in a T-shirt, jeans, boots, and a leather jacket. He is seated on the front steps of a New York City residential building, looking like the *West Side Story*-style punk he once tried to emulate when he was a teenager on Long Island. On the back cover he and his current band—Liberty DeVitto, Doug Stegmeyer, Russell Javors, David Brown, and Mark Rivera—were photographed on the same set of steps, like a street gang on the prowl on a hot summer night.

Although Billy still relied on having his own core band throughout the periods that he was not working, when he wasn't recording or touring, his band members weren't being paid, or collecting any sort of a salary from him. Basically, he just expected them to be ready, willing, and able to jump when he said jump. Even though there might be huge gaps of several months in between albums and/or tours, he relied on their being there for him. And, they were. To fill in the gaps in their careers, and their incomes, the individual band members would find other gigs to fill in their income. During this particular era, Liberty landed a job playing the drums for Stevie Nicks.

An Innocent Man is remembered as the LP that Christie Brinkley inspired. Liberty recalls, "Billy and Christie? They were great for each other. The inspiration that Billy got from her, from that relationship, he wrote some of his best songs. I remember, when I got the [temporary] gig with Stevie Nicks, and I was on the airplane. *An Innocent Man* was just about ready to come out, and I had a tape of it. And I sat with Stevie's producer, Jimmy Iovine, and I played it for him. You know, all of the songs are about love and finding new love, and blah, blah, blah, and all this happy stuff. Jimmy Iovine took the headphones off after listening to the album, and he said, 'Those songs are really great, but I want to hear what he writes when they break up.'"[62]

When *An Innocent Man* was released in August 1983, the press reviews were consistently strong and favorable. Everyone seemed to key directly into the "fun" aspect to the music and the theme of young love that prevailed throughout the material. In *Rolling Stone*, the review given to *An Innocent Man* was used to zap Billy Joel for his previous LP, while praising this one. Wrote critic Parke Puterbaugh, "One need only think back to the brattish pedantry he pawned off as rock sensibility on *Glass Houses*, an LP whose

'rock' sounded more like something Joe Piscopo's Frank Sinatra would sing than the real thing. Unlike that record, *An Innocent Man* sounds like the real thing, or at least a real celebration of it. As Joel strolls through the archives of soul, his writerly eye hones in on one style after another until *An Innocent Man* becomes a panoramic overview of what it must have been like to be a Long Island kid with an ear glued to the radio during the golden dawn of rock and soul and doo-wop. . . . I can find no other reason to be cynical about a record that's so plainly a labor of love. *An Innocent Man* is an affectionate, spirited paean to an undefiled past that's truly forever."[68]

In the *All Music Guide*, Stephen Thomas Erlewine writes, "It was time to record an album just for fun. And that's how his homage to pre-Beatles pop, *An Innocent Man,* was conceived: it was designed as a breezy romp through the music of his childhood . . . only three songs, including the haunted title track aren't about her [Brinkley] in some form or fashion. That giddiness is infectious, helping make *An Innocent Man* an innocent delight that unwittingly closes Joel's classic period."[70]

An Innocent Man was a huge sales hit, reaching number 4 in the United States and number 2 in England. The album, which contained ten tracks, yielded six huge international hits. The initial single was his second American number 1 hit, "Tell Her About It," which sold a million copies. The song "Uptown Girl" hit number 1 in England, becoming his biggest in that country, ultimately selling over 900,000 copies in the British Isles. It also peaked at number 3 and sold over a million copies in America. Additional top 40 hits from the album included "An Innocent Man" (number 10 US/number 8 UK), "The Longest Time" (number 14 US/number 25 UK), "Leave a Tender Moment Alone" (number 27 US/number 29 UK), "Keeping the Faith" (number 27 US).

One of the keys to the success of *An Innocent Man* was the fact that Billy Joel was regularly featured on the new music cable TV network, MTV. In Canada, the station Much Music correspondingly followed suit, and it wasn't long before every major country on the planet came up with their own 24-hour music video-playing network.

It was America's own MTV that instantly started this phenomenon. On August 1, 1981, the new cable TV network began broadcasting, and it suddenly started something of a virtual revolution in the music business, and in the television industry as well. Since the 1950s, with no consistent regularity, record companies would occasionally pay to film their rock & roll performers singing their latest single releases. There are even promotional video clips of fifties acts such as Billy Haley and the Comets, and

Frankie Lyman and the Teenagers singing and dancing to their songs in front of the cameras.

In the mid-sixties, the weekly TV show *The Monkees* featured at least two performance videos per episode that had nothing to do with the actual plot. This way, videos of the latest album or single could be edited into the reruns of the episodes the following season, yet the music promotional aspect of the program would seem totally up-to-date.

When MTV began broadcasting in the summer of 1981, the first song to broadcast on the new network was—ironically—"Video Killed the Radio Star" by the Buggles. Even though that actual video clip was a couple of years old—dating back to 1979—that was the song that kicked off the beginning of the MTV revolution.

Very quickly, MTV gained momentum and became a tidal wave of a musical phenomenon. Now, all of a sudden, not only did rock stars have to sound good on the radio, they had to look good on television. And, some acting and dancing skills was a plus, too. It wasn't long before acts like Madonna, Culture Club, Wham, Cyndi Lauper, and Rick Springfield launched their careers and became huge stars based largely upon their exciting, controversial, and trend-setting video performances.

At the time that this album was released Billy had already won five Grammy Awards, and an American Music Award, and he had sold an estimated 40 million records. He was one of the most popular, and most instantly recognizable contemporary rock stars. Fortunately, as *An Innocent Man* was being released, MTV was in full swing, and Billy was at the appealing top of his game. The most famous video of his entire career was the one that was filmed to promote the song "Uptown Girl."

It is set in a garage. Billy portrays the role of an auto mechanic who dreams of a date with the pinup girl of his dreams. Naturally, this dream-girl is none other than Brinkley. Before she even appears in the video her image is already seen in one of her famous swimsuit centerfold pinup poses, hung from the back of a locker door in the garage, behind Billy. Her image is also seen on a billboard atop the garage his fictitious character works in, as she is the girl advertising "Uptown Cosmetics," clearly a nod to her concurrent Cover Girl campaign. While singing and dancing, Billy shows off Christie's photo to a couple of his co-workers, on the cover of a fashion magazine.

Then when a classic two-toned Rolls-Royce pulls into the garage for a fill-up, we get a glimpse of the undeniably beautiful cover girl herself. Dressed in a wide-rimmed black hat and a short and sexy black and white

dress, Brinkley is this grease monkey Romeo's own personal Juliet. Although she is in much of the video, she more often than not is filmed from the waist upward. Finally it comes time for her to join in on the choreography. As gorgeous as she is, she reveals that she is stiff as a board as a dancer. Although she follows each of the moves of the choreography, which is little more than kickline movements, she looks like she mentally is counting out every step of the simple routine. By comparison, as a dancer, Billy actually does quite well in this famed video.

Although critics might lament Christie's slightly stiff dance routine, the overall tone of the video is so charming that it actually works brilliantly. Throughout most of it Billy plays the part of a guy who ponders how he is going to get the attention of this babe in the Rolls. He is so appealingly cute that you know he is ultimately going to prevail. At the end of the song, Billy not only gets the attention of Christie, she ends up taking off with him on the back of his motorcycle.

By the time *An Innocent Man* was released, Billy was no stranger to filming promotional videos, having done so for the songs "Pressure" and "Allentown." So rabid was MTV for programming at this point, that Columbia Records wasted no time producing other videos to accompany this album. In the video for "The Longest Time," Billy portrays someone attending his high school reunion, accompanied by DeVitto, Stegmeyer, Javors, Rivera, and Brown as his doo-wop-harmonizing classmates. The "Keeping the Faith" video was set primarily in a rock & roll courtroom scene. In the courtroom are three girls dressed as an homage to the Supremes, and there is one shot of a Jimi Hendrix look-alike as well. Christie shows up in this video toward the end of it, as the gum-chewing girl on the back of a convertible Chevy.

According to Billy Joel, "video" was not a medium he instantly embraced. First of all, he was very self-conscious about his looks. "I became a musician partially because of my physical limitations," he explains. "I wasn't tall, I don't have Cary Grant looks. I had to transcend somehow, so when I'm in the studio and I'm free to move, I'm six-foot-six and I look like Cary Grant! So I pretty much inveigh against music videos, because to see this composition that I come with reduced to this chunky little short guy with bad hair running around—no, no, I object."[10]

He distinctly recalls filming this particular video: "'Uptown Girl' I wasn't too crazy about, because they wanted me to dance. I sort of said, 'O.K., you know, I'll give it a try.' We shot it on the two hottest days of the year. We were down on the Bowery, and all these bums kept butting in with, 'A-a-ay Chri-i-ist-a-ay!' They wouldn't leave her alone. It was a real drag. It wasn't my idea to put her in it in the first place, either. It was the production people's. I was against it from the beginning, even though they said she'd be perfect for it. I didn't want my personal life brought into it. But she was a good sport about the whole thing. She was great in it 'cause she's used to cameras. But I kept wincing, turning away from the camera. The more I watch videos, the more I'm put off by them. The abstract ones aren't too terrible, but more and more you're seeing the girl in high heels and a garter belt, with hints of ultra-violence, dogs barking and monsters and crap. It's getting depressing, and I resent it. That's just the way the system works nowadays, I'm afraid. I'm going to be doing less and less of them if I can help it."[59]

Some recording artists—Madonna particularly—loved doing videos. She, in fact, turned them into compelling film pieces and launched her entire acting career based on the success of her videos. Billy didn't share this opinion. "I hate them, hate doing them," he claimed. "I only do them because I have to promote my records one way or another. It's part of my contract, but I never enjoyed it. Still, I'd rather do a video than go all over the country, meeting every rack-jobber and record retailer, visiting every little radio station that plays my records. I never could handle that end of the business. You never know who you're talking to most of the time, which bugs the hell out of me. So I just do a video and, bingo, my end of the bargain is kept. I know they've got to be done, though, so I do try to make them good. It sucks, really, because I'm not a camera-oriented person, so there's no enjoyment in it for me. I feel there's no enjoyment in it for me. I feel there's a danger with videos in taking away the listener's imagination. I think most of them are stupid, including mine. I did one for 'She's Right on Time,' which is this sort of Christmas song that, if I'd done it literally, would've been too cornball. So I tried to do it funny, which was even worse. I should've left it corny."[59]

With regard to the "Uptown Girl" video, one of the things that was the most talked about was the fact that Christie showed conclusively that she was not an experienced dancer. According to one unnamed former Columbia Records executive, "When she did the video, it was so obvious that she had no sense of rhythm. It was horrifying. And they sent us all advance copies, and when we got them, we were spread all over the country, but we had a conference call, and we were yelling and screaming, 'Don't put that on TV! Don't put that on TV!' She's beautiful. Why didn't they just show her face. I mean, he's got rhythm at least."[5]

However, it still became the most watched, most famous video of Billy's career. Whatever he thought about the way he looked, and in spite of the fact that Christie couldn't dance well on camera, the "Uptown Girl" video was cute, charming, and totally believable. Here was Billy Joel as this loveable-looking guy asking the hypothetical musical question "How did I end up with such a gorgeous model as my girlfriend?" It was a totally believable emotion.

Having a high-profile model as his girlfriend in the picture instantly upped the ante on Billy's star quotient. He said at the time, "When I was by myself, I used to love hitting the local bars—just pop up on stage and jam a little. With me and Christie together, though, it's like double jeopardy. We don't ever get a chance to sit and observe anything, or to have any kind of situation that's real, because all you're doing is signing autographs; everybody's staring at you. It makes me real uncomfortable. People ask me if I've changed since I've become successful. It's not so much that I've changed as people's reaction to me that's changed. So my reaction to them has to change, too. I can't be real. I can't go out, have a couple drinks and get loose. Then everybody goes, 'Oh man, look, he's bombed!' Or they think I'm doing drugs. If I want to go to an amusement park, I can't. I get paranoid after awhile, with everyone looking at me, and it becomes an artificial situation. So I have to give that up."[59]

They were quite distinctive looking together, and the press cameras were always flashing whenever they arrived at a public function. Recalls entertainment journalist Marcy MacDonald, "I used to run into them together all the time at press events and parties. The difference in their height made them look like the old comic strip characters, 'Mutt & Jeff.' Christie is that much taller than Billy—especially when she was wearing high heels."[115]

As the hot new superstar couple on the scene, Billy Joel and Christie Brinkley instantly became the subject of an avalanche of press coverage. Some of it was accurate journalism, and some of it was grist for the gossip column mill.

If Billy had been instantly recognizable before, having his fiancée in tow was like living life under a microscope. "Right off the bat, the recognition factor doubled," Billy claimed. "What I found was that I didn't change, Christie didn't change, but people's reaction to us changed drastically: 'Oh, well, he married this fabulously notorious model, and now he's changed.' As if I married because she was famous or wealthy."[40]

Now that Christie was part of Billy's life, she often accompanied him on the concert road. He began the year 1984 in the middle of a concert tour to support the *An Innocent Man* album. In the February 6, 1984, issue of the *Indianapolis News*, rock critic Zach Dunkin wrote, "For three consecutive years Billy Joel graced Indianapolis with some of the best rock performances

BILLY JOEL

this town has ever witnessed. But not since November 19, 1979, had the Long Islander visited here. A lot has happened to Joel since. A divorce. A horrifying motorcycle accident that nearly killed him and required extensive surgery. A new girlfriend, model Christie Brinkley. Millions of records sold and a new status as one of today's top rock video attractions. But after his return performance last night at Market Square Arena, it was evident one thing hasn't changed for Joel: he hasn't lost his touch. . . . Joel charged through two hours of non-stop entertainment last night."[116]

Dunkin also pointed out, at the Indianapolis show, "The biggest guffaw occurred when Joel and drummer Liberty DeVitto began laughing so hard at each other they had to delay the start of 'Don't Ask Me Why.' . . . DeVitto, whose crisp, booming drumming pushed enough air around the place to make shirt sleeves flutter, was just one of four longtime Joel musicians on stage with him last night."[116]

With Christie Brinkley present on the tour, and at home in his personal life, press photographers and fans began to hound them wherever they went. Now more than ever before, fame was becoming a bit of a trap to Billy. "Now, don't get me wrong," he said at the time. "I'm not crying about this. I do have certain privileges other people don't have, because I make money and I'm well-known. A lot of people want those kinds of things. Sometimes it helps. If I want to go to a crowded restaurant, I tell them my name, and it's like, 'No problem, Mr. Joel. Here you go.' On the other hand, there are plenty of drawbacks. I can't have a quiet conversation with my girlfriend, 'cause they always want to take my picture. And, if I don't let 'em, I'm a snob. Autograph hounds keep interrupting me, so I never get to complete a thought. It's really weird. I'm always confronted with that whenever I try to go out. I don't think I'll ever get to make my peace with it. It's forced me to change my lifestyle. I have to move from where I live, it's gotten so bad. I live on the water, and every weekend there are 200 boats with zoom lenses looking right in my bedroom window. I can't lay out in my own backyard. I can't stay there. I've got to move to a more remote area. They climb over the wall, for *Chrissake*. I don't want to live like Elvis Presley, with my own personal Mafia around and guard dogs protecting me and stuff. I'll never get used to that. I'm from Hicksville, man, not Beverly Hills."[59]

That year a couple of notable Billy Joel releases hit the stores. As compact discs of classic albums continued to roll out at a consistent clip, Billy's debut solo album, *Cold Spring Harbor*, was rereleased by Columbia Records. Its 1984 version is most notable for having been remixed in the proper speed, and made to sound more consistent with his most recent recordings. When it was released in this new version, it made it to number 158 on the U.S. album charts, and to number 95 in England.

That same year, Billy also released his first live concert video cassette, titled *Billy Joel: Live from Long Island*. The performances included on this eighty-minute compilation were filmed during the *Nylon Curtain* tour, which was released by CBS/Fox Video. The following year Billy received a Grammy nomination for that release, in the category of Best Video Album.

Billy was in Los Angeles on January 28, 1985, to attend the international telecast of the American Music Awards, at the Shrine Auditorium. The night of the awards, dozens of singing stars were invited to A&M Recording Studios to record the song "We Are the World." The funds that the song raised were to assist relief efforts in famine-plagued Africa, and especially the people in Ethiopia. "We Are the World" was written by Michael Jackson and Lionel Richie and produced by Quincy Jones. They were able to get the participation of a virtual who's who of the concurrent recording world, primarily because it was recorded the night of the annual American Music Awards telecast. It was kind of like those old Judy Garland and Mickey Rooney movies, where someone would announce, "I've got a barn—let's put on a show."

Somehow it seemed, everyone—including Billy—wanted to be involved. The cast of singers included Ray Charles, Bob Dylan, Cyndi Lauper, Huey Lewis and the News, Kenny Loggins, Bette Midler, Willie Nelson, the Pointer Sisters, Smokey Robinson, Diana Ross, Paul Simon, Bruce Springsteen, Tina Turner, Dionne Warwick, and Stevie Wonder. When it was released, the recording of "We Are the World" received a tidal wave of airplay and raised millions of dollars. It became a huge number 1 hit and was heralded as the most successful "benefit" single ever recorded.

Anyone who has met Christie Brinkley is immediately taken by her charm. This included Billy's fellow band members and all of his friends. Liberty DeVitto recalls, "She was great for him. Christie Brinkley is one of the nicest women I know. If you write anything about her in the book, let her know that I think she is one of the greatest women I have ever met. She has so much class. She taught him class. I remember going to see them, when he asked to marry her. I was walking down the street with my now ex-wife. He had a couple of drinks because he was very nervous. He said, 'Come join me at the Russian Tea Room. Look what I got for Christie.' He opened up a box to show a sparkler of a diamond ring that looked like the sun just came from behind the clouds. So, we go to the Russian Tea Room,

BILLY JOEL

and he asks her to marry him. And, she's, like, thrilled. And don't you know, in that same meal we had champagne, the whole thing; great meal, caviar, everything. The guy brings over the dessert tray, with chocolate mousse cake or something like that. Billy asks, 'If I only eat half of that, do I have to pay for the whole thing?' So, here's a guy who just bought a rock for the most beautiful woman in the world, who is the most famous model in the world. So, he's up there. But he's still in his Long Island shoes saying, 'If I only eat half of that, do I have to pay for the whole thing?'"[62] With that he presented Christie with an engagement ring.

Ironically, Billy recalls a totally different version of how he asked Christie to marry him. "I popped the question," he recalls. "I think we'd been going out something like two years. I was on the road—I think I was in Dallas. I hadn't even thought about it. I'm sure it had crossed my mind, but I really didn't know I was going to do it then. We were in a hotel. I said, 'Will you marry me?' I think she was very moved by the fact that I asked. A couple of weeks after that, we were home. We had kind of not said anything after that. I got her this diamond ring. I had this whole candlelight dinner planned, but I couldn't wait. It was the middle of the afternoon. She was upstairs painting—she had a little art studio. I had the ring, and it was burning a hole in my hand. I ran upstairs, and I put it on her easel table. She broke up, and she said, 'Yeah, let's get married.'"[40]

Regardless of which of the two above stories—or which part of both of them—is accurate, the result was the same. Finally, after going together for over two years, Billy and Christie set a wedding date. Boating enthusiast that he is, they were wed on March 23, 1985, aboard a 147-foot yacht. The boat wedding was held in the New York City harbor.

Explained Billy at the time, "The reason we're going on the boat is to get away from the press. The wedding is not something we want to go public about. We're not [Prince] Charles and Di. We don't think of ourselves as royalty. We happen to be working people."[117]

Christie wore a gown by Norma Kamali fashioned of satin with lace and gold accents. As her father led her down the aisle, Christie carried in her hands a bouquet of fifty white roses. The wedding ceremony only lasted seven minutes, which is only fourteen seconds longer than the unedited version of the song "Zanzibar." Billy Zampino was Billy Joel's best man, and the music of James Brown's "I Feel Good" was worked into the ceremony. It reflected his mood that day.

Reportedly, the groom's face had a glaze of happiness during the entire wedding and reception. He quipped to *People* magazine, "A lot of people have told me I seem so happy. . . . I feel happy. I must have been a real drag at one time."[117]

Once they were married, it seemed that they were hounded by the press even more than ever before. Some of it became a true nuisance. In 1985 Billy complained, "Even if you don't talk to the press, it doesn't stop them. If they don't have anything to write about, they make it up. I'm here to tell you, everything you've ever read about me and Christie's all bullshit. Absolute, total, unadulterated bullshit. Except that we got married. What really sucks is that the crap that's written about us really hurts her a lot. They say mean things about her, and she takes it bad; about how her boyfriend died, and she immediately ran off with me, so there's no way they know what the facts are. They have us going to all these nightspots in New York. We never go to nightspots. I never go to discos. We hardly ever go out period. They have us riding motorcycles together. She hates motorcycles. She doesn't want to have anything to do with them. It's like Richard Burton and Elizabeth Taylor to them, or something. Like, give me a break already."[59]

As a rock star, Billy had rarely been in the gossip columns. Now however, he and Christie very often got ink for their every social move. "It bothered us," he said, "because it made us seem as if we were these social butterflies, and we're not like that at all. We're pretty low-key people. We enjoy very simple things. We do our own shopping, we do our own cooking."[40]

In a world-weary fashion he announced, "I'm Billy Joel-ed out. I'm not that self-horny. I did interviews for years, and I'm just not interested in them anymore. I find that analyzing my work isn't worthwhile. I don't get anything out of it. And if I don't want to talk about my work, then people ask me about my personal life. And I don't want to do that either, because it's one of the few things I have left that's my own. Whenever I do interviews, people take me out of context; they misquote me. Sometimes the guy would have the story written before he even meets me. He just wants a few quickie quotes and then I read it, and it's a hatchet job. The guy would be nice and friendly to my face: 'Thank you Mr. Joel, I really appreciate your time,' then—Bam!—he cuts my balls off. It makes you mistrust people, makes you suspicious. And I don't want to become one of those celebrities who becomes a recluse and lives in a prison. I'm battling to retain my faith in people. 'He's gone commercial,' they write. 'He sold out,' they write. You see it everywhere, and you start to doubt yourself. 'Have I?' you wonder. If you read it often enough, it does that to you. They've had a field day with me."[59] In other words, Billy's love-hate relationship with the press seemed as if it was never to resolve.

With over two dozen hit singles to his name, in 1985 Billy Joel's first "best of" package was compiled, in the double-disc set, *Greatest Hits, Volumes One & Two*. The album was a huge sales success, hitting the top 10 on both sides of the Atlantic: number 6 in America and number 7 in England. One of the most promotable aspects of this album was the ploy of including two new Billy Joel recordings that were only available on this hits set. The two new songs that were included on this album both went on to become hits in the United States: "You're Only Human (Second Wind)" (number 9) and "The Night Is Still Young" (number 34). In England, a double-sided single was released from the album—"She's Always a Woman to Me"/"Just the Way You Are"—which hit number 53 there.

The magazine *The Record* reported that when the song "You're Only Human (Second Wind)" was released, Billy donated all of his royalties to the National Committee for Youth Suicide Prevention. That publication claimed, "Joel says he was moved to do this good deed after the son of a close business associate committed suicide."[118]

Billy confessed that when he first sat down to write additional songs for the *Greatest Hits, Volumes One & Two* album, he was really drawing a blank in the inspiration department. He sat down with pen and paper and came up with: "*No-thing!* Sitting there staring at *bl-ank* paper. I'd read somewhere that Julian Lennon wrote his songs in a *cha-teau!* There are very few *chateaus* [sic] for rent on Long Island. All I could find in Manhattan were these lofts. I didn't want to work in one of those, so I just moved the car out of the garage, moved in a piano and some synthesizers. I've been working on the new songs in my garage. It has come full circle.[60]

"It's been hard just writing 'two new songs' for this album. I'm used to working in a format where I start, I write all the songs, and then it comes together. There's usually a flow to it. I realize where an album is going after I've written the first couple of songs, then build to a peak, then write a sort of resolution—a coda. It's like writing a symphony or a little Broadway play. It's a little play I write myself, actually."[60]

A consistent seller from the minute it was released, the album *Greatest Hits, Volumes One & Two* went on to sell over 10 million copies by 1999, in the United States alone. In doing so, the album earned the RIAA's "Diamond Award."

13
CROSSING
THE BRIDGE

NINE MONTHS FOLLOWING their wedding, on December 29, 1985, Billy and Christie celebrated the birth of their daughter, Alexa Ray Joel. From the moment of her birth, Billy took his role as a father very seriously. He still had very strong abandonment issues that he was dealing with, stemming from his own dad having left the family. He vowed that he wasn't about to let this happen to his relationship with his own child.

Billy said, "I missed having a father very much. I went out and did crazy things to discover what my masculinity was. I got into trouble, I got into fights. I had to go out and box to discover my masculinity. Stupid stuff. One thing I knew when I had a kid was I was going to be very much present in my daughter's life. Not just as a male, but as a father. And I don't mean in the old sense of *Father Knows Best*, with the pipe and the slippers."[40]

The name that they picked for their daughter was very much derivative of things and people that were important to them. Explained Billy, "Her name is a feminine version of 'Alexander,' and I like the fact that 'Alexa' has a particular rhythmic pattern and strong sound."[119] Her middle name had additional significance. It was Billy who came up with the name Ray, to honor his all-time favorite singer: Ray Charles.

Alexa's arrival brought out a whole new Billy Joel. He very much relished the idea of having a child of his own. Even perfect strangers who ran into him on the street noted a dramatic change in his demeanor. "I recall being in Central Park one warm spring day in 1986. I was with my friend, Marie," says Isiah James, who is the floor manager for TV's *Montel Williams Show*. "We were walking on the sidewalk through Sheep's Meadow, and I said to Marie, 'Isn't that Billy Joel coming towards us?' She said, 'Oh, my God, you're right.' There was Billy pushing the most expensive and elaborate baby stroller with Alexa inside it. He had a pleasant look on his face. As he came nearer, and we were passing him on the sidewalk, we all made eye contact, and Marie and I both said 'Hello' to him. He smiled and said 'Hello' back. He had the look of a proud father on his face, and he was very pleasant and nice to us. He was just a Dad and his daughter strolling through the park."[25]

While all of this was going on, there had been several very big gaps in the scheduled activities of the members of the Billy Joel Band. Whenever Billy took off to do things in his personal life, the band members weren't on any sort of a financial retainer. While he was confident that royalty checks were rolling in consistently, thanks to album sales, song publishing, and radio airplay, the rest of the band was not so fortunate. Several band members claimed that they were becoming very unhappy watching their own personal bank accounts fluctuate due to Billy's scheduling whims.

Billy did notice that the morale of the band was not exactly at an all-time high. Liberty DeVitto was busy looking for odd jobs—like the Stevie Nicks tour—to fill in his income. Billy recalls, "It got to a point, it became such a big business what we were doing. Rather than be friends like we used to be, we became business associates. . . . On *The Bridge* album, it came to a head."[120]

Joe Salvatto was one of the technical engineers for the recording of *The Bridge* album. He is credited in the liner notes of the album as part of the technical support staff. According to him, "I am a tech support engineer, not a mixer type engineer. I do studio and theater sound installations."[121]

Salvatto became well acquainted with Billy Joel in 1988, and during the recording sessions the Piano Man purchased a $7,000 stereo from him. As Joe recollects, "So it was at one of Billy's many pieds-à-terre that I had the pleasure of providing music for. This one on Central Park South, a newly decorated apartment. The architect had put in blue marble shelves to match the glow of the stereo. The equipment was too heavy for the shelves, and the day after I installed the equipment, he calls me and asks me to pop by. When I arrived I found the gear hanging by the wires. He explained that he just put a CD in and was carrying Alexa and turned around when the shelves buckled. So with a few high-powered phone calls, the McIntosh stereo was replaced by dinnertime. He was so happy, as we were in the middle of recording *The Bridge* and needed to listen daily. With the weeks passing he said the architect was to claim the damaged gear and had not come by to pick it up. So it was pissing him off looking at such disfigured gear. Finally Billy said to me, 'So if he doesn't show up by Friday, do you want it?' I casually said, 'Yeah!' and prayed for the few days it took to claim my $7,000 stereo, which I have in my living room to this day."[121]

While his last couple of album releases seemed to have a theme running through them, this one did not. For *The Bridge,* the only theme seemed to be one of creating an LP of contemporary-sounding rock.

Billy explained, "The only premise for *The Bridge*—when I started—was that it not be a concept album. After *52nd Street,* I felt I was being typecast as someone who I wrote and played well-crafted variety songs. My feet were being encased in cement. Because my band was a rock & roll band and we played large arenas, I needed to go for more rock & roll, and so the songs on *Glass Houses* were written to be performed in concert. The next album, *The Nylon Curtain* was just the opposite—an elaborate studio album that took a year to make and whose songs were difficult to play live. I thought of it as my *Sgt. Pepper's Lonely Hearts Club Band,* although I didn't intend to copy The Beatles. The last album, *An Innocent Man* was a complete reaction to *The Nylon Curtain,* which had been so laborious. It was a romantic tribute to my rhythm & blues roots and the discovery of love when you're a teenager."[110]

As he had done on all of his albums that were produced by Phil Ramone, *The Bridge* featured several acknowledged jazz legends augmenting the music played by Billy and his band members. This time around the jazz masters included Ron Carter on the upright bass, as well as Michael Brecker on tenor sax. After several albums had featured some of the most renowned names in the jazz world playing on the tracks, finally on *The Bridge* several of Billy's contemporary and classic rock stars appeared. There were vocal duets with Cyndi Lauper and with Ray Charles, and Steve Winwood of the group Traffic was featured playing keyboards on "Getting Closer."

Unbeknownst to everyone at the time, this was to be the last studio album that Billy would record with Phil Ramone at the helm as producer.

Together they had created the most memorable music of Billy Joel's entire career, and this was to be their swan song as creative collaborators.

From the very start *The Bridge* rocks out and becomes a memorable musical statement for Billy. "Running on Ice" perfectly kicks off the proceedings with power, beat, and an impassioned performance from the singer-songwriter. Snappy and rocking, it is about the rat race of modern life where everyone is chasing the elusive commodities of stability and security, which are dangled in front of them like a carrot. Here Billy sings of the frustrations of trying desperately to stay on top of things. He compares modern society to trying to run on a sheet of ice: lots of exhaustive action, and very little forward-propelling traction.

Every one of Billy's albums contains at least one touching ballad that tugs at the heartstrings. On *The Bridge,* that song is "This Is the Time," in which Billy sings about the fact that at this stage of his life, he is conscious that right now—1986—is the time he will always look back upon as the best years of his young adulthood. Although he doesn't specifically mention either Christie or Alexa, one can tell that they are in the forefront of his mind as he sings this highly effective and sentimental song.

According to him, the song carries the following message: "Remember this good time, because we're going to need to remember it when times get tough."[113] Things were going swimmingly well for Billy in his personal and professional life, and "This Is the Time" succinctly crystalizes that emotion.

"That's a strange song," he said, "in that part of it is the past, part of it is the present, and part of it is reminiscing about what the future will be: 'I'm warm from the memory of days to come.'" To Billy, the song is all about relationships, and hoping that they grow and blossom, "There's also a maturation of the relationship, because the character says, 'You've given me the best of you, and now I need the rest of you.' Now, I'm ready to go beyond the infatuation stage. I'm ready for more depth. The relationship has to move, it has to be constantly progressing. And there's always a danger in progression of losing some things. . . . There's a certain amount of surrender, a certain amount of acceptance.[40]

"I do believe relationships can last, I see these old people who are together in their eighties, holding hands. I think that's really neat. I think that's probably one of the hardest things to do in the world, to be a human being, maintain a relationship, be a decent person. They talk about the difficulties of being an artist and the difficulties of being successful in this business. These things you can work on. The toughest thing is to do the things that are very human and make them work, because everything

BILLY JOEL

seems to be against it a lot of the time. A lot of temptation, a lot of pressure in other directions. You know, like to think that I'll be able to live like a normal human being. I am going to be a celebrity forever. I don't have any great grand plan to be a famous personality when I'm older. I hope to retire from it somewhat."[40]

"A Matter of Trust" is the album's totally strong and straightforward rocker. Billy called this "a guitar oriented song that had some grit on it."[113] Indeed, it is. This piece is about how hard love can be in the modern world. There are loves that are deceitful, and loves that are sincere. It is hard for the heart to tell what is what with so much subterfuge in the air, and people with so many divergent agendas. This was a song that anyone who has been in love can identify with.

"Modern Woman" was actually written for the soundtrack of the Bette Midler/Danny DeVito comedy film *Ruthless People*. This particular movie was one of Midler's big screen comeback hits from the mideighties, so it was a great showcase for Billy Joel's tune, which helped promote the single on the charts. Although he later proclaimed that he didn't like this track, it is the one song that sounds 100 percent welded into the "big eighties" mode. It was an era of big shoulder pads, big jewelry, and big and boisterous synthesizer sounds. "Modern Woman" is a dramatic and bouncy tune that showcases Billy's ability to follow the audio trends of the 1980s, and to master it in a snappy and effective fashion. Although he later insisted, "I hated that thing," his fans and radio programmers alike loved it.[113] It remains one of his big top 10 hits that often gets eclipsed by many of Billy Joel's other signature songs, but it is actually one of this LP's true gems.

While "Baby Grand," wasn't a big hit, this is the song from *The Bridge* that Billy was the most proud of. It is undoubtedly due to the fact that it is a perfectly planned duet with the great Ray Charles. With a string section that is very reminiscent of Charles's biggest hit, "Georgia on My Mind," it has a unique and sentimental flavor to it. Here, comparing the devotion to the piano to a lasting love affair draws a nice and sentimental parallel for the two men to draw upon.

Not only did Billy and Charles sing the song together, but they played duet grand pianos on the track as well. Billy had always longed to have Charles sing one of his compositions. This was the blossoming fulfillment of a lifelong dream for the Long Island native: "Ray Charles was my hero when I was growing up. As good a pianist or as big a star as I could ever become, I could never be Ray Charles, who is a total natural and one of the greatest singers of all time. I've never had much confidence in my own singing. The collaboration came about because I named my baby daughter, Alexa Ray, after him. Ray heard about it from Quincy Jones, who is a friend of my producer, Phil Ramone, and sent word that he would love to record with me if I had the right song."[110]

Coming up with the right song for the two of them to record proved challenging for Billy: "I thought, 'Great.' But what the hell do I have in common with Ray Charles? He's an African-American blues singer who's had a rough life. He's from Georgia and he's been around for a long time. And I'm this schnooky white kid from Levittown, Long Island. What do we have in common? Then I realized, 'Wait a minute. The piano. We both played the piano.' And my daughter had just been born, so I had 'baby' on my mind. I thought, 'Baby grand—this would be an interesting idea to pursue.' I wanted to write a standard kind of song, and I wrote this love song to the piano, and I thought Ray could relate to it, because he's had friendships come and go, and he's had love that's come and gone, and money that slipped through his fingers, and business that screwed him—just like what happened to me. The one thing that's been consistent in both our lives has been the piano."[50]

This song was one of the easiest for Billy to conceive of and to put down on paper. "I was so excited that that very night I sat down and wrote 'Baby Grand,' and polished it up the next morning. It was one of those rare songs, like 'New York State of Mind,' that seem to come all at once—it seemed almost as though I had heard it before," he claimed.[110]

Still, he was paranoid that Charles might not like what he came up with: "I sent the tape, and I was on pins and needles to see what he thought. Then he called up while we were in the studio, and he said he loved the song: 'Let's do it.' That was fun."[50]

Then, when it came time for the recording session, Billy was on pins and needles, wanting everything to go smoothly. "A funny thing happened when we finally got together to record the song in Los Angeles. I started singing very tentatively. And Ray, assuming that's what I wanted, came in sounding like me—a white kid from Hicksville. When we started it again, I did my Ray Charles imitation, and Ray kicked in as 'Ray'—the rest was smooth sailing."[110] The resulting track is one of the most successfully satisfying ones on this album, and the one of which Billy is the proudest.

"Big Man on Mulberry Street" is the most jazz-oriented track in *The Bridge*. With all of its Italian imagery, it is hard to resist the temptation of comparing this song to "Scenes from an Italian Restaurant." Billy's piano playing is impressively sweeping, and the nice jazz beat makes it this great album's centerpiece. It is a minivignette of a swaggering macho guy who is cruising down the street in Little Italy in New York City. The song flows smoothly and captures the breeziness of a summer's day. The six-piece horn section in the middle of this five-minute track and Billy Joel's trademark keyboard work propel this song with satisfying ease. It is a kind of mini-opera about a character he encountered in a chance observation.

According to Billy, "I had a writing studio down in Soho, in this place called The Puck Building. I had ten thousand square feet where I had all this writing and recording equipment set up. . . . Sometimes I would leave the building and walk down to Little Italy, get a little food, wine, a little espresso. The walk I took was on Mulberry Street. And I just kind of invented this character who thought he was 'Mr. Cool.' The character is really kind of a nebbish, but in his mind he's king—the king of Mulberry Street."[122]

A slow, deliberate ballad, "Temptation" finds Billy lovingly lamenting about a new love. In this piano-led track, he sings about losing his sleep and his grip because of this new woman in his life. He finds himself caught up in a love affair that is wearing him out, but he can't seem to break the habit. Billy sings the song with such a pleading tone that it is one of the most strongly heartfelt and soulful performances on the album.

"Code of Silence," a duet with Cyndi Lauper, is something that Billy wrote with her. Billy explained how it came about: "I had gotten to the last song and I had terrible writer's block. Cyndi Lauper was recording downstairs at the Power Station, and she comes up with me and says, 'Billy, what's the matter? You look like you're going out of your mind. You're climbing the walls.' And I said, 'I can't get this song I want to write.' She was great. She got one of those yellow legal pads and said, 'You sit down at the piano and play, and I'll write down the . . . words you throw out.' . . . She ended up showing me this legal pad . . . and the title came out: 'Code of Silence.' . . . She actually stimulated a lot of writing and suggested a lot of things."[117]

The ultimately resulting song is unique, as it sounds more like the kind of edgy rock tune that Lauper herself would have recorded at that time. It is one of the prime highlights of the album, with its harmonica intro and its rocking beat—thanks to Liberty DeVitto's rock-steady drumming. Cyndi's blisteringly quirky vocals make a great counterpoint to Billy's more modulated voice. It would have been great to hear what two of the most influential singer-songwriters of the eighties might have done on an all-duet album collaboration.

"Getting Closer," which ends *The Bridge,* benefits from the blues sound of Steve Winwood on the Hammond B-3 organ. Winwood's solo in the middle of the song takes this track to a nice new level of interaction. Billy sounds great here; he delivers his lyrics in a sassy and very self-assured fashion, making this a fitting finale to one of the most satisfyingly consistent albums of his career.

The press reviews for *The Bridge* were highly complimentary across the board. Stated Ira Mayer in the *New York Post,* "Billy Joel's just-released Columbia album *The Bridge* is a delight . . . there isn't a track that doesn't work here." In the *Washington Post,* reviewer Jonathan Karp wrote, "*The Bridge* recalls the best of his earlier tunes. . . . If Cole Porter had worn blue jeans, he would have written like this." Dean Johnson at the *Boston Herald* reported, "Sounds like it was almost as much fun to make as it is to listen to." C. B. Adams referred to the album in the *St. Louis Globe–Democrat* as "quite possibly his finest to date."[123]

Even Anthony DeCurtis, in *Rolling Stone,* wrote praisingly, "A steady movement from polished rockers to full-blooded ballads sets the musical rhythm of *The Bridge.* . . . A smart, sophisticated collection of songs that seemingly brings us closer to Billy Joel than we've ever been before—and leaves us with a pleasant sense of expectation about the bridges we'll be crossing with him in the future."[124]

One of the most authoritatively glowing reviews for the album came from Stephen Holden in the *New York Times,* in which he proclaimed, "On *The Bridge,* his first album of all-new material in three years, his musical reach is longer and more confident than ever, encompassing everything from Gershwinesque pop/blues to jittery post-New Wave pop. After making three highly successful 'concept' albums, the singer, composer and pianist from Hicksville, L.I., has returned to what he called the 'variety' format of his late-'70s blockbusters, *The Stranger* and *52nd Street.*"[110]

The Bridge album, which was released in July 1986, hit number 7 in America, and number 38 in England. It produced four hit singles: "Modern Woman" (number 10 US), "A Matter of Trust" (number 10 US/number 52 UK), "This Is the Time" (number 18 US), and "Baby Grand" (number 75 US).

One of the most interesting gigs that Billy Joel and his band played in 1986 was the Willie Nelson–organized charity concert event, Farm Aid. Recalls Russell Javors, "We did Farm Aid with Randy Newman. [Bob] Dylan was on it, and Tom Petty, and Johnny Cash, and all these other people. 'Wow!'"[65]

Said Billy Joel in 1986, "I'm 37, and there's no point in pretending I'm a teenager anymore. That doesn't mean I don't love rock & roll, but I love other kinds of music just as much. George Gershwin was the greatest American composer because he worked in all different mediums and brought the street into the opera house."[110]

One of the things that seemed to concern him the most was that he often found that he wasn't cranking out songs as he used to do when he was younger. In fact, sometimes they were like pulling teeth. "Some people write a hundred songs a year, and choose what they like," he said. "I'm not one of them. When I'm doing an album, I only complete 10 or 11 songs. If I don't like something I've started, rather than continuing to work on it, I toss it into the trash can. There's no backlog of Billy Joel material. You'll never hear my basement tapes, because there are none. While I get ideas for songs all the time, I've found that the pressure to record has been the major motivation for me to finish anything. Once I get an idea, I write it down in a notebook. Six months later, when it has marinated, I'll look at it an probably think of something better. I enjoy catching up with myself like that. Then when I finally go into the studio 80 percent of the actual recording process consists of cutting things out, changing, revising, and editing.[110]

"I write the tunes first and then the lyrics, which are dictated by the mood of the music. Though the two have fit together, for me the language is really secondary. It's the strangest thing. I don't think about what I do. I like to be as non-thinking a writer as possible. It may take me a year to figure out why I wrote some of the songs I did, why I said some of the things I said, and what I really meant."[110]

On this particular album, he relied on his long-time producer, Phil Ramone. According to Billy, "Because I'm a songwriter, I have to imply a rhythm for the band, give them an approximation of an arrangement I want with just the piano. You see, everyone in my situation crosses over into what everyone else does. Phil [Ramone] has made songwriting suggestions: songs have been restructured, a verse substituted for a chorus. Phil will say, 'That peaks too quickly,' and things get moved around."[60] What no one realized at the time was that *The Bridge* was to become one of the last three pop-rock albums Billy Joel was to record.

In 1986 Billy projected far into the future that he and Christie were meant to endure as a couple for years to come. He said at the time, "Well, I don't see me being an entertainer forever. I don't see me being a recording artist forever. I can see me working music and composition and maybe songwriting, but sort of retiring from the forefront of the celebrity part of it. I think it's a matter of knowing, just knowing, what your priorities are. I would walk away from being a rock & roll star in a shot if it was a choice between my wife or my work. I know what's important. So does she. She never embraced modeling as some kind of successful career to strive for. She fell into it by accident, and she's never looked at it as an end in itself. She's an artist in her own right. She's a very good painter and illustrator. She has a flair for comedic acting. We have other things that we're interested in, besides the particular fields we're in right now."[40]

He claimed that he was comfortable in his own skin for the first time in ages: "I'm not afraid to be Billy Joel. I'd kind of stayed away from that on purpose after *52nd Street*. I thought he'd had his say. I think I write certain things better than I write other things, which doesn't mean that I think my main strength is ballads. I think my main strength is melody. And I'm not afraid to sing more like me now. I've gotten used to the fact that, well, that's what my voice sounds like. Let's not have to hide it too much."[40]

In the mideighties he was able to calmly look back at his prolific career, and to make some astute assessments. When asked then what his favorite album was, he replied, "I think if I had to pick an album that would be *The Nylon Curtain*, because I'm still amazed at the stuff that's in that record, the work that went into it. The stuff I enjoy hearing, believe it or not, is *Glass Houses*, because that album was written, not to prove that I was a rock & roller, as I've read in a lot of places, but to be a performance album. We were playing in these big arenas, and I started writing arena-oriented pop and harder-edged stuff because it works better in those places. I enjoy listening to that album, because I know the fun it was done in. The same with *An Innocent Man*. *An Innocent Man* was written so quickly, really, without a lot of laborious effort going into it, and I still enjoy the spontaneity of it."[40]

Now that he was a husband and a father, his focus started to change: "It still surprises me that I'm this very naive, non-capitalist type of person dealing with what is the American dream. It scares the hell out of me, because I don't know what's going on. I wouldn't know how to invest money. I've never been in a bank in ten years. I don't know what it all means. I mean, I go to a bar in Manhattan, and there are these Wall Street brokers sitting around talking earnestly, in detail, about achieving exactly the kind of thing I've achieved. I sit there thinking, "I've got more money than everybody sitting at the table, but I don't know what they're talking about.' It scares me. I'm kind of glad I've retained a lot of that innocence."[40]

Meanwhile, the lives of Billy's band members were continuing to grow and evolve as well. Liberty DeVitto changed spouses during this period: "I got divorced because I met my next wife on Stevie Nicks's tour. She was Stevie's roommate. She is from L.A. I met her. Got divorced. Married her."[62] With the divorce came payments of alimony and child support.

While everything seemed to be going swimmingly well in the Joel camp in 1986, the Internal Revenue Service had a different opinion. It seemed that they felt Billy owed them $5.5 million in back income taxes, dating back to the time of his marriage to his then-manager, Elizabeth. Because they had split their assets fifty-fifty when they divorced, Billy felt that half the bill should be hers. With that, he instituted a lien on her percentage of the publishing rights to the songs he had given to her during their legal union. This was just to be the tip of the iceberg of financial woes for Billy Joel over the next coming years.

The band that Billy had with him for the 1986–1987 concert tour included his longtime band members Doug Stegmeyer and Liberty DeVitto. They also included Russell Javors (acoustic and electric guitar), David LeBolt (keyboards), Mark Rivera (saxophone), Kevin Dukes (electric guitar), and Peter Hewlett and George Simms as the background singers. Fortunately for Billy and his whole entourage, the success of *The Bridge* meant a demand for a yearlong world concert tour. The added income of the tour would surely ease any form of financial hardship that existed. Or so it was thought.

While all of this was going on, the members of the band were all living a comfortable middle-class existence. They were playing at huge, sold-out auditoriums all over the world, yet they were not becoming wealthy. How can that be possible? When one factors in all of the downtime they experienced in between tours and recording dates, and averages out their individual incomes, their net profits were not all that substantial. It was just like what Elizabeth Joel had told Liberty years before: "Billy will never make you rich."[62] Well, her premonition was becoming a reality. As the band members watched Billy become a multimillionaire in front of their very eyes, their own lives were nowhere near as stable, and they began to resent him for it.

Also, a large amount of cocaine was being consumed by members of the entourage. They were living a life of full-tilt rock & roll, and they indulged in all of the substances that went along with it. According to a friend of Billy's, Bruce Gentile, "[They] had all the cocaine in the world with them at all times."[36]

When asked, "Was there a lot of partying on the road?" Russell Javors very diplomatically states, "Playing in a band and being on the road is a surreal situation. We certainly had a lot of laughs. I'm not about to tell you who did what or who they did it with."[64]

The Bridge tour was to be Billy Joel's first concert tour in two years, and it kicked off at the Civic Center in Glens Falls, New York, on September 29, 1986. This coincided with the release of his latest single, "A Matter of Trust," which was promoted on MTV and other video music stations by a performance clip directed by Russell Mulcahy. It was filmed on the site of the former Electric Circus, on St. Mark's Place in the East Village in Manhattan. In the video, Billy and his band are depicted in an empty loft space located on a busy and colorful street. They appear to be in a show rehearsal, and as people walk by on the street, they peer in approvingly. Even Christie is seen in the rehearsal space, walking around with little Alexa Ray in her arms. In one scene Christie and Alexa are filmed standing behind Liberty DeVitto, intently watching him play the drums.

Even though his videos were brilliant promotional tools that helped his albums sell millions of copies, Billy regularly bitched and complained about having to star in them. In his mind, it denegrated the music by depicting him as not being all that attractive to look at. "I would really hope that people wouldn't judge my music based on the videos," he said at the time. "One of the reasons I became a musician is because it had nothing to do with visual. It had to do with the imagination of the listener. When I'm in the studio and I'm creating beauty, I'm six-foot-nine and look like Cary Grant. And then I see that reduced to this nebbishy little guy with a double chin. Come on. That ain't music. Can you imagine Beethoven doing this?"[125]

As the tour continued through North America it wound its way around the entire globe. Billy was so hot in Australia that the band went back to that continent not once, but twice, during this tour. However, the really big and important series of concerts were the historic ones that Billy and his band performed in Russia.

What was happening in the USSR at that point was a new policy of what is known as *glasnost,* which is Russian for "publicity" and "openness." Suddenly there was a new freedom of speech in that country that had not existed since before World War I. The iciness of the cold war years was suddenly defrosting. In the past there had been a few midcentury cultural exchanges. There was a touring production of the musical *Porgy & Bess,* which Truman Capote chronicled. And the Bolshoi Ballet company had played in New York City in the seventies. However, it had never encompassed rock & roll. Suddenly, the Soviet government was open to allowing American rock acts and performers to begin a new form of cultural exchange. The very idea of being able to be the first Western rock star to play a full-out series of rock concerts in the Soviet Union became a quest of Billy Joel's.

In 1985 an agreement was signed by the United States and the USSR for some sort of cultural exchange between the two world superpowers. One of the very first events to test the waters of this new policy was a July 4, 1987, "free" multiact rock show that was presented in the Soviet Union. Billed as "the July Fourth Disarmament Festival," it was a musical concert of both American and Soviet acts. The concert was organized by rock promoter Bill Graham, and included James Taylor, Bonnie Raitt, the Doobie Brothers, and Santana.

Only weeks later, in late July and early August 1987, Billy Joel took his full rock & roll show into the USSR—at his own expense—and staged a series of six concerts that made history and yielded a live album, a video presentation, and even a cable television special.

For the most part, Billy's humanitarian intentions were brilliantly fulfilled. He was very heartfelt in his intentions of bringing rock & roll to a country that had been held in the stifling grip of communism for so long that it was thirsty for anything cultural from the West, and he was met with cheering enthusiasm. On one of his days there Billy visited the grave of deceased Russian folk balladeer, Vladimir Vysotsky. In addition to the obvious Moscow and Leningrad [Saint Petersburg] shows, Billy Joel and entourage also ventured into the Soviet Republic of Georgia, where they performed an unscheduled concert at the opera house in Tbilisi.

While in concert in Moscow, Billy threw what was to become the most famous—or infamous—tantrum of his long career. He was in the middle of his song "Just a Fantasy," when the film crew that had been hired to make a documentary about the Joel concerts shined lights at the audience. The Russian music fans gathered there, frozen like deer caught in car headlights. Billy took the lighting incident as a threat to the success of his show and threw a fit. He reportedly flipped over an electronic piano in the middle of the song, then swung a microphone stand over his head and crashed it to the stage floor. Such public outbursts were unheard of in the USSR.

The attendees at the twenty-thousand-seat sold-out Moscow Olympic arena had apparently been intimidated by having the lights turned on them. Instead of dancing and partying, the audience members suddenly stiffened up, fearing reprisals from the security guards. Billy wanted to keep the audience's energy level high. This situation was so frustrating for him that he felt compelled to do something to change the mood. At one point he shouted at unresponsive audience members in the front rows, "Why are you here? You obviously don't want to be here." According to Billy, "I just want to break even, but this is bigger than 'bucks.' People in the audience want to be in the dark. They want to get loose." He stated backstage after the concert, "It was a real 'prima donna' act, but I have to protect my show."[126]

The temper tantrum reportedly startled the crowd, making them uncertain if that was a scripted part of the tour or not. However, both they and Billy recovered from the outburst. By the time the show ended, the response from the crowd was enthusiastic enough to please "The Angry Young Man," who was the star of the concert. Ironically, the camera crew with the offending lights had been hired by Billy himself, to capture on film his Soviet audience. It was reported in the New York Times that the plan was for Billy to sell the documentary to TV or other legitimate distribution, in hopes that it would help him to recoup the $2 million plus price tag that the tour cost.

Columbia Records' president, Walter Yetnikoff was present for this headline-making visit to the Soviet Union. He recalls, "I went to Billy's big concert at the Olympic Sports [arena]. Billy rocked. In fact, he rocked harder than the Soviets wanted him to rock. They told him no encores, but he did seven. He sang 'Back in the U.S.S.R.,' and the crowd went wild. Fans rushed the stage. American rock & roll ripped up the Iron Curtain. Billy's non-stop performance so angered members of the Soviet Central Committee that Billy's tour manager [Rick London], fearing arrest, hid in the men's room after the show. Moscow was never the same."[127]

This unique and undeniably historic series of concerts was such big news that several press agencies sent reporters to cover it. In the New York Times John J. O'Connor reported of the resulting video, "Some unexpected headlines were made at one concert when, furious with his technical crew, Mr. Joel overtuned his electronic piano and broke a microphone stand. The incident is included here. . . . He is always in motion. When not performing, he is preparing to perform. When not being the curious tourist, he is giving press conferences or appearing on Russian television. He's pampered by his wife and stroked carefully by his musicians. He chews gum a lot and clearly likes to hear how wonderful he was last time out. Throughout, he's never less than likeable."[128]

In *Time* magazine Guy D. Garcia wrote, "Billy Joel kicked off a six-night tour of the Soviet Union that had glasnost-inspired youths dancing in the aisles. After a slow start, the Piano Man broke the ice at Moscow's 20,000-seat Olympic stadium by urging the crowd to rush the stage. As flower-tossing youths surged forward, a jubilant Joel warmed things up even more by dedicating 'Honesty' to the late Soviet folk hero Vladimir Vysotsky and then brought down the house with a blistering encore of The Beatles' 'Back in the U.S.S.R.'"[129]

Felicity Barringer, another journalist writing for the *New York Times*, stated, "Billy Joel brought his rock & roll here today and won the souls of those in a stony Soviet audience, leaving them cheering, dancing on chairs and looking around in fearful wonder as they followed the music and not the rules."[130]

On October 24, 1987, American cable TV network HBO presented its TV special, *Billy Joel from Leningrad, USSR*. A videocassette of the documentary that was made of these concerts was also released. Proclaimed *TV Guide* magazine of the HBO special, "Billy Joel demonstrates that rock & roll needs no translation (even though he has a translator on hand) in this tour, filmed over three nights in August at the V.I. Lenin Sports and Concert Complex in Leningrad."[131]

In *People* magazine, reviewer Jeff Jarvis liked the Russian TV special so much that he gave it a grade of A, and wrote, "It's *glasnost* rock behind the heavy-metal curtain. . . . Billy really gives those Reds a show to remember. . . . And yes, you get to see wife Christie Brinkley and little Alexa Ray who's wearing baby ear protectors so she won't be deafened by Daddy's roar. Here is diplomacy you can dance to."[132]

Said Billy at the time, "We think of the Russians as a monolith. We don't think of them as individuals." Of the Russian citizens he met during this history-making Soviet tour, he said, "I have dreams about them; I'd like to see them again."[128]

Looking back at this Russian adventure—and his other press-worthy foibles—from the perspective of 1990, he claimed, "It's the same thing as my going to Russia and the big story being that I threw a tantrum—'Billy's Russian Tamper Tantrum.' I still read about that. My God, I've thrown the piano about twenty times in the States and nobody said nothing. All of a sudden I do it in Russia and it's an international incident. That's not the real story. The real story is that we went to the Soviet Union. Everything that people said to me when I was over there has a much deeper meaning now. I gave my leather coat to this hippie guy who was our translator. And it was a really nice black motorcycle jacket. The guy was speechless, and I found out later he never wore it. He had it framed and put it on his wall. And I realized the importance of the relationship we had with people there is still hanging on people's walls. And it's hanging on *my* wall, too—I have the Russian tour poster on my wall in a place of honor. Aside from getting married and having a child, the Soviet trip is the highlight of my life. I can't believe I got to do it. I remember when [classical concert pianist] Van Cliburn went there back in the '50s. All of a sudden there was a thaw in the Cold War. Now look at what's going on. I'm not saying I'm the guy who did it, but I'm glad I went and saw the place, because the Cold War ended a lot sooner for me than it has for everyone else."[125]

For the members of Billy's band, it was a moving experience as well. Comparing the Soviet tour to their Cuban concert in 1979, Liberty DeVitto says, "The most obvious comparison was that the Cubans were more communist than the Russians were. Russia was such a moving experience. It was very hard to explain."[62] According to him, when Billy took a side trip to Soviet Georgia, the entire entourage was not included, but he did take DeVitto along with him, for comic relief.

In 1987, it was clear that the Russian economy was anything but healthy. The population had broken down into the haves and the have-nots. Liberty observes, "Everybody knew it. Even the people in Russia knew it. But it was such a moving experience. You know, people give you presents, bottles of booze, whatever. There, people had nothing to give you. Nothing. So when they were excited, the fact that you were there, they were genuinely excited. They could not believe that we were there. They couldn't believe that we came there to play for them."[62]

Liberty recalls watching his preconceived notion of Soviet Russia dissolve before his eyes: "I thought I was going to get off of the plane and see three headed dragons breathing fire, which was 'the enemy.'" Instead, he found something completely different. "It was like I was sitting at my grandmother's table, when I talked to them. Full of love for each other. Sharing with us whatever they had, which was nothing. That's when I realized that it's not people against people, it's government against government."[62]

Said Russell Javors, "That was one of the most interesting tours I was on. I had my wife, Suzanne and my son, Jesse, with me. I was happy that they got to be a part of it. It was exciting on so many levels. Billy did a good job of connecting with the audience under difficult circumstances. The concerts were exciting. Russia had never seen a production like ours. We were told before we left that our rooms would be bugged. I think that was true. One night I thought I heard the sound of applause."[64]

But even while this historical and humanistic adventure was taking place, the spirits of Billy Joel's band members were sinking. "Honestly I don't know what it was, or where it turned, or when it started going south," says Russell Javors.[65]

He also recalls that tensions were high between Billy and bass player Stegmeyer: "Doug started to have some problems. Whatever," Russell says in his friend's defense. "His pancreas gave out, and he might've missed one session, but he never missed a note onstage, and he was fine. But, Billy started making fun of the way he looked, behind his back, and stuff. Just little things. Then I would get pissed off. If you are his friend, either confront him, or fire him, but do what you're gonna do, but don't talk about him behind his back."[65]

Another point of contention was the fact that Billy informed his instrumentalists that they were not getting paid for doing the Russian concerts. This really hurt the morale of the band. Guitar player David Brown wasn't going for it, and for that reason he was not on the Soviet concert dates. Says Russell, "The Russian video I liked, because it was an event. But the payment wasn't there, so it's not the best concert we ever did in our lives. But it was an interestingly enough one."[65]

While the world tour was still on, the live concert album that was recorded in Russia, *Kohuept,* was released in October 1987. The title is the Russian word for "concert." The album completely skipped most of Billy's more obvious hits like "Piano Man," "New York State of Mind,"and "Just the Way You Are." Instead, it included three tracks from *The Bridge;* some of his more up-tempo rockers such as "Uptown Girl" and "Allentown"; and two ballads, "Innocent Man" and "Honesty"; and featured the unique cover tracks: Bob Dylan's "The Times They Are A-Changin'" and the Beatles' "Back in the USSR." The only other track that was exclusive to this album is "Odoya," performed by a group of Soviet Georgian singers, which kicks off the set. One of the most important things to note is that this was the first album that Billy Joel had released in the last ten years that did not utilize the talents of Phil Ramone. Instead, the production credits went to technical engineers Jim Boyer and Brian Ruggles. Also listed on the album as "executive producers" were Billy's manager/former brother-in-law Frank Weber, and Frank's brother-in-law Rick London.

In terms of sales, the *Kohuept* album didn't do all that well in the United States (number 38) or England (number 92). However it was a big hit in

Australia. In fact it was such a big hit that it facilitated a return "down under" for a second visit to that continent to meet the demand for Billy and his music. The troupe returned to the United States in September 1987. The final date for the band that year was in late December at Madison Square Garden for the benefit of the Homeless Children's Medical Benefit Concert.

The *Kohuept* album was the first LP that Billy had released in over a decade that was not instantly certified gold for selling over 500,000 copies in the United States. Whether it was the fact that there was not one hit single that was unique to this album, or the fact that there were only two new rock & roll songs on this two-disc [one CD] set, *Kohuept* was a bit of a sales disappointment. Not only was Phil Ramone now permanently out of the picture, but other major changes in the Billy Joel camp were already underway as well.

BILLY JOEL

14
FACING THE
STORM FRONT

IN 1988 BILLY should have been sitting on top of the world. He was living a jet-setting existence. He was married to one of the top models in the world. He had just come off of a yearlong worldwide sold-out concert tour to promote his eighth consecutive multiplatinum top 10 album. In November of that year he lent his speaking and singing voice to a new Disney feature-length cartoon, *Oliver & Company,* in which he vocally portrayed the character of the Artful Dodger, a canine version of the Charles Dickens's character from *Oliver Twist.* Two months later, on January 22, 1989, Billy sang the National Anthem on the live telecast of Super Bowl XXIII, while millions of people watched on their TV screens. Although his personal life with Christie and Alexa was in order, there suddenly seemed to be some sort of financial problem. Having sold 75 million albums, he found himself in a bit of a cash crunch. How could that be possible? Yet, one by one, over the last year or so, little signs began to surface that betrayed the fact that something wasn't right.

Liberty DeVitto claims that he was one of the first to spot that something was a little awry in Billy's world. He recalls one particular conversation with Billy's manager and former brother-in-law, Frank Weber: "We were at the Plaza Hotel. Frank got drunk, and he told me, 'I hate you.' I said to him,

'Why do you hate me?' He said, 'You know why I hate you?' He says, 'Because one day they'll find me out, and you'll always be here.' Now, I didn't know what to think of that. What do you say?"[62]

Liberty soon spotted another red flag: "Then [we were] at the [Nassau] Coliseum one night, and I had invited a jeweler friend of mine to come to the concert. He took a look at Frank's wife. She was wearing a sweatsuit, and she had some very impressive jewelry on. And my friend said, 'Is there *something up* with Frank as his manager?' I said, 'What are you talking about?' He said, 'Do you have any idea what a diamond necklace like that costs? And, if she wears jewelry like that with a sweatsuit, what does she wear when she gets dressed up?'"[62]

It all started to unravel after a dinner that Billy Joel had with the president of his record label, Walter Yetnikoff. If anyone knew intimately how much money was being paid out to Billy from record sales and song copyrights, it was he. Said Yetnikoff, "I remember the evening me and Billy at Fontana di Trevi on 57th Street; over fettuccine Alfredo and a river of red wine; him telling me how he had to sell his Manhattan apartment to Sting to buy a bigger house for Christie in East Hampton; me wondering why Billy Joel, whose copyrights are worth millions, has to ditch his Manhattan digs, him telling me he's strapped for cash; me telling him that I smell a rat, and he needs to audit his people; him telling me to mind my own goddamn business; me ordering more wine."[127]

But, he didn't mind his own business. Yetnikoff wasn't going to let the issue die. He got hold of Billy's attorney, Alan Grubman, to inform him that something fishy was going on with his client's personal accounts. When Yetnikoff suggested that there be a complete audit of Billy's books, he was surprised that Grubman told him no. Billy later alleged in a separate lawsuit against Grubman, that Grubman had refused to do so for fear that Weber—as Billy's manager—would have him fired as Billy's attorney.

At the time, the law firm of Grubman, Indursky and Schindler also had several high-profile clients, including Madonna, Michael Jackson, Bruce Springsteen, and John Mellencamp. When Yetnikoff informed Billy of Grubman's refusal to instigate an audit, Billy fired Grubman and retained John Eastman as his lawyer. Eastman was the brother of Linda Eastman, who was married to Paul McCartney. Eastman engaged the accounting firm of Ernst & Young to audit Billy Joel's accounts.

When Billy found out what was really going on, he informed Yetnikoff that the "rat" he had claimed to smell—that night at Fontana di Trevi—was Billy's personal manager, Frank Weber. On August 30, 1988, Billy told

Weber "you're fired," officially ending years of deceptive tactics and criminal practices. From that point forward, Billy started managing his own affairs.

Billy said to Walter Yetnikoff, "You were right. The audit was an eye-opener, I was being robbed blind. Now I'm suing. So thanks for the wake-up call."[127]

On September 25, 1989, legal papers were filed in New York State Supreme Court by attorney Leonard Marks, part of a $90 million lawsuit against Frank Weber. The suit alleged misuse of the power of attorney, misappropriation of funds, and the funneling of Billy's cash into "high-risk, low-liquidity investments." There were also allegations that claimed that Billy Joel's song copyrights were used as collateral to obtain loans with banks.

The lawsuit alleged that Frank had diverted Billy's funds—to the tune of $30 million. The suit demanded repayment of that, plus $60 million worth of damages and punitive charges. Marks claimed that an audit of the books and the evidence provided by private detectives "revealed major incidents of fraud and dishonest dealings, virtually from the inception [1980]."[133]

Apparently Weber made various investments with Billy's money, including gas and oil tax shelters, real estate partnerships, and horse-breeding farms; however, Weber had controlling interest in each of these ventures. Another investment, the development of a hotel in Richmond, Virginia, went on to default on its loans, and creditors seized $1,265,699.28 out of Billy and Christie's joint bank account.

There were also charges that Billy's videos were being produced by some of Frank Weber's other relatives, at an inflated cost to Billy Joel. This relative was Rick London, who was credited as the co-executive producer of the *Kohuept* album. There were also accusations that Weber was borrowing money against Billy's songwriting copyrights.

Frank Weber's lawyer, Daniel A. Gecker, argued, "This whole thing is an effort to avoid paying Frank royalties of the upcoming LP and tour which are due under the management contract. The only grounds upon which the contract can be broken are to claim fraud, hence these accusations."[133]

One of the most amazing things about this whole affair was that Billy had truly trusted his ex-brother-in-law. After all, he was a family member. Frank Weber was even little Alexa's godfather. Talk about "A Matter of Trust"!

Marks stated at the time of the trial that these abuses were "the worst I've ever seen." He also pointed out, "Often a manager will let the power

BILLY JOEL

that comes from associating with a megastar go to his head. It can lead to all kinds of abuse."[133]

Billy lamented to Wayne Robins of Long Island's *Newsday* newspaper, "The lawsuit itself I can't discuss. I can say I'm shocked, disappointed, I'm really hurt by the whole thing. As far as I'm concerned, it's my third burn. There was Artie Ripp, my ex-wife, now this. How many lives do I have?"[32]

He was truly disgusted at how he had been taken advantage of throughout his career. It seemed that time after time he was financially screwed over by people whom he had trusted. Complained Billy, "I go around, I'm married to Christie Brinkley, the comment I get is, 'Man, you've got it made.' I even have a wry comment in one of my songs: 'Most men hunger for the life I lead.' But you know what? Nobody really knows the inside of somebody's life. I never trusted rock & roll money, but I should have looked after it a little better."[32]

For years Billy had declined examining his own bank accounts, and this was what his negligence had gotten him. He confessed, "I *am* naive. I'm to blame for my own misfortunes. I could have cracked open the books once in a while and taken a look at what was going on. This is not rocket science."[16]

Billy later admitted that he should have paid better attention to his wife when she first voiced her concerns: "Christie's a hell of a lot more than beautiful. She's a lot smarter than I am. . . . She was trying get me to look into my business long before I did, and I should have listened to her sooner."[125]

Liberty DeVitto recalls, "Then it all blew up. It all blew up, and then it all came out in the press. I went to lunch with Billy. The first thing he did was sat there, he looked at me and he went, 'I'm an idiot aren't I?' I said, 'No, you're not an idiot. You just trust the wrong people.'"[62]

It seems unfathomable to think that Frank Weber was given carte blanche authority to steal such great sums of money, right under Billy Joel's nose. Who would hand over the controls to someone like that, and give Weber such power? Says Liberty, "Billy . . . Billy gives power to managers and to accountants, because he trusts them. That's why he got screwed out of $60 million, or however much it was from Frank. It's because he gave them the power. Billy used to run around with Frank, and Rick London. He would have one on one side, and one on the other side, and make believe he had leashes on them like they were watchdogs. 'These are MY watchdogs!' Rick London was in with Frank on the management. Billy goes for the wrong people, like a woman who goes for the loser all the time.

Some women always go for the losers. There will be a nice guy who is nice to them, and have a lot of dough, and are nice to them—they don't like them. But the loser, they go for. Billy was managed by people like that. Anybody who tells him something good about himself, no."[62]

From 1987 to 1989, teenage singer Debbie Gibson experienced an unbeatable hot streak on the music charts in America. She placed five songs in the top 10, including the number 1 hits "Foolish Beat" and "Lost in Your Eyes." In doing so, she became the youngest performer to write and record her own number 1 single and album. Also, growing up on Long Island, she was a huge Billy Joel fan. "I also studied with his piano teacher Morton Estrin in Hicksville," she explains.[134] Since the 1980s, Gibson changed her stage name to the more adult "Deborah" and became an accomplished Broadway actress in such shows as *Cabaret* and *Beauty and the Beast*. However, one of the biggest thrills she had during this era was having the opportunity to meet and perform with Billy Joel onstage.

Deborah recalls, "For my eighteenth birthday my mom and my booking agent Dennis Arfa arranged to have Billy call me. I still have the photo of me on the phone—in complete disbelief! Little did I know that only a couple of years later I'd be sharing the stage with him twice in one week. First, Elton John invited me up onstage to perform with both he and Billy at Madison Square Garden. A week later, I was seeing Billy's solo show at Nassau Coliseum, where I first saw him at eight years old, and a crew guy came and grabbed me before the encores and told me Billy wanted to invite me onstage. He said, 'You take the grand center stage and I'll take the keyboard in the back. "Keeping the Faith," key of B flat.' I couldn't believe it!"[134]

Gibson's publicist, David Salidor, was there: "This was 1988. It was an Elton John show at Madison Square Garden, and Billy Joel just happened to be there. How that came about was, I had arranged to get the tickets through Tony King, who was working with Elton back then, and he works for Mick Jagger at the moment. Tony also gave us backstage passes. We went backstage to see Elton before the show. Debbie was of course very excited about meeting Elton. However, when we got backstage there was Billy Joel as well. Debbie was thrilled, since these were her two biggest idols. During the concert Billy got up onstage and performed with Elton. Then Elton invited Debbie to join the two of them up onstage while they did 'Lucy in the Sky with Diamonds.' It was really an unforgettable evening."[135]

BILLY JOEL

As it came time for Billy to plan his next studio album, *Storm Front,* he made other decisions to distance himself from several people other than Frank Weber. The first person to go was Phil Ramone. Their last collaboration for a long time was the song "Why Should I Worry" from the 1988 *Oliver & Company* soundtrack album. Instead, he decided upon using Mick Jones from the rock group Foreigner to coproduce the LP with him. According to Billy, this particular professional "divorce" was an amicable one. "Phil and I were fine," he explained. "We were just sort of married for too long. And we just didn't have anything to say anymore. I just thought it was time to jump into bed with someone else, so to speak. It was time to have a wild, flaming sonic love affair. Originally I thought of having Eddie Van Halen produce *Storm Front.* I think he's a fantastic musician. And I like the energy in Van Halen records. Our schedules didn't line up, but we had fun meeting at this Italian restaurant in Manhattan. People would look at us and say, 'Isn't that *him* and *him?* What are they doing? And where's [his wife] Valerie [Bertinelli] while all this is going on? I worked with Mick [Jones] because I wanted somebody who was a musician and a songwriter, somebody who I could have some great arguments with about material. Mick and I hit it off right away. But we didn't hit it off like he was going to be a pushover. He had very strong opinions. But I like that. I respected that."[125]

Billy did all he could to downplay the split: "It was a good working relationship with Phil Ramone. I had no problem with it. I just thought it was time to work with someone with a different spin on things. Mick Jones is a songwriter, so there we had a good relationship. He is a good musician, a good guitar player, and I thought that would give him a little more insight into what I'm trying to do. I still can't be objective about my own production. I don't have as much faith in my abilities as a recording artist or singer or pop star as I should have. I've got to have another set of brains to tell me what they hear."[32]

In spite of what was said in the press, Liberty DeVitto insists that Phil Ramone was deeply hurt and upset that he had not been asked to produce the next Billy Joel studio album. Liberty also claims that this is the usual way in which Billy dismisses people from his life. He simply cuts them off and ceases communication.

It was at this same time that Billy chose to fire half of his band as well—including David Brown and his longtime friends Doug Stegmeyer and Russell Javors. Well, he didn't exactly fire them, he just went into the recording studio and hired new musicians to record with, and to tour with.

BILLY JOEL

Liberty says that he knew what was going to happen long before anyone else. It was during the previous tour he first got wind of what was going on in Billy's mind: "I was backstage with Billy. We went back to Australia. We went to Australia twice on that *Bridge* tour. But, *The Bridge* tour was the Russian tour. We recorded the Russian album, and then we go back to Australia again, 'cause the Russian album sold really well in Australia. We went back for a second time. That's when Billy gets me in his dressing room and says, 'What would you think if we record the next album, just you and me and bunch of new guys?' I had a family. It was my gig or my family."[62] In other words, he was afraid to question what Billy was doing, for fear that he, too, could be on the list for getting fired from the band.

Liberty admitted that he was a bit shocked at this sudden planned change: "He had had it with Doug. People were in his ear: '[Doug's] overweight.' 'He looks terrible onstage.' It was very convenient to get rid of Russell at the same time."[62]

Apparently, Doug Stegmeyer had been on Billy's bad side for a long time. One of the things that singled him out for his sudden expulsion was his negative attitude. "We used to call Doug, 'Dr. No.'" recalls Liberty. "He was Mr. Negatory, he always found the dark side to everything. When the band was at its peak, we were creating music that people were saying, 'Man, this is like the greatest thing.' He felt like he was Billy's left hand on the bass."[63]

Stegmeyer never married and was something of the loner of the group: "Doug loved cars and women. Loved women. He was sensitive, a nice guy. He took my sister out a few times. He wanted to be loved, but he didn't want to be held down by a marriage or something like that. He wanted to be able to play the field."[62]

Then there was Doug's excessive cocaine and liquor use, which intensified the whole situation. He would go into bouts of depression and started drinking alone in his room. What was the root of the problem with Doug? Says Liberty, "His drug thing. He got too involved, and started hooking up with the wrong people on Long Island: club owners, things like that. He was very thin all the time. Then he started to gain weight and that's when Billy started to not use us for videos."[62]

Since the use of cocaine usually blocks one's desire to eat food, most cokeheads are thin. With regard to Stegmeyer's weight gain, Liberty explained, "Coke people, when they stop the habit, they start eating. A rock star I once worked for used to be on her Exercycle with a cheeseburger in her hands and some cocaine."[62]

When Liberty is asked the question "Where did it all start to fall apart with Billy?" he solemnly replies, "People influence him. He listens to the wrong people."[62]

Liberty DeVitto never thought he would see this come to pass. After all, at that point it was Doug Stegmeyer who was in the band the longest time: "A year before I was with Billy, Doug was playing bass guitar with him. He got me the gig. We did *Turnstiles, The Stranger, 52nd Street, Glass Houses, Songs in the Attic, The Nylon Curtain*, then there was the *Greatest Hits* album that came after that, *An Innocent Man*, then *The Bridge*. For *The Bridge* tour, we went to Russia. Then that album came out: *Kohuept*. So, ten albums, Doug was on. Then Billy decided that he wanted to change everything. Doug and Russell, he let go. At the same time, he let Phil Ramone go, who was producing all of the albums. Because he wanted to change. Billy likes change: one album will have horns, one album won't have horns."[63]

Everyone involved with Billy seemed in shock at the "insensitive" way in which his band's lineup transition was handled. As bizarre as it seems, the way that the band members learned of their abrupt dismissal was by hearing it announced on the radio and television! Billy Joel didn't want to confront them, he just wanted them to go away.

In retrospect, Liberty DeVitto says, "The way that Billy handled the band's termination should have been a sign to me of things to come. The band found out they were terminated when the information was broadcast on MTV. I had called Billy and told him he should call the guys and let them know what was going on. I said, 'It would be nice if they heard it from you. I think that would be the right thing to do.' He yelled into my ear through the phone, 'I'm Billy Joel, it's MY career and MY life! I don't owe anyone any explanation. I can do whatever I want.'"[62]

In one clean sweep Billy coldly cut off all ties with everybody in the band but Mark Rivera (sax), David Brown (guitar), and Liberty DeVitto (drums). That left Liberty as the only member of Billy's original 1970s band to remain in the lineup. New members of the band included Schuyler Deale (bass), Jeff Jacobs (synthesizers), and the first woman in his group, Crystal Taliefero (sax and percussion). Deale and Taliefero were also the first black members of the band.

Billy spoke to Long Island newspaper *Newsday* and did the best he could to diffuse the harsh feelings that he knew his newly fired former band members were feeling. Said Billy, "It got to the point, it became such a big business, what we were doing. We did arena tour after arena tour, and

rather than be friends like we used to be, we became business associates. People would kvetch about money, and their deal, and we weren't close. Everybody was looking in everybody else's pocket. On the *Bridge* album, it came to a head. We weren't having fun; it just wasn't fun. And before I came to do this album [*Storm Front*], I realized you not only had to reinvent yourself, but you have to refresh your memory about why you're doing what you're doing. It wasn't a matter that I called people up and fired them. I discussed it with the guys who aren't with me, and they were gonna do other projects anyway. I haven't closed the door on working with anyone again; I just wanted to try something different. As a writer, you have an obligation to explore other means of expression."[32]

Russell Javors was never told in person that he was no longer employed by Billy: "I was driving in my car one day listening to the radio. I was shocked to hear that Billy had a new album with a reconfigured band. That's how I found out. Obviously, I was disappointed. I was hurt that after all the years I spent with Billy, that I didn't even get a phone call. I certainly had to struggle to get my life back on track after that. I wasn't a kid anymore and I had a family to take care of."[64]

According to him, there was no warning whatsoever: "What would happen was, you would finish an album and you finish a tour, and you wait for the next one. After twelve years of playing with Billy, you figure the next one's coming. Nobody told me anything. Then I hear on the radio one day, and I hear that he's got a new album out. I said, 'Holy shit! Nobody called me!' So, even the guys who were still there never called me. He probably told them not to. It was tough."[65]

Discussing the firing of himself, Doug, and David, Russell claims, "In my mind, I don't think that I mattered to the situation enough of—in terms of—it wasn't dollars with me. Doug was making more than I was. So, maybe he justified getting rid of Doug by getting rid of me, and made it a whole new band. I don't know. Maybe that's just my ego talking. If he was unhappy with me, then if so, so be it."[65]

Russell Javors also feels that Billy never really understood him musically. "At the end of the day, it's Billy, and it's his thing. There's a part of it, where you are on the way up, and people are promising you stuff, and doing stuff, it's our livelihood at that point. So the only bitter thing that I have about it is, that I read after I found out that we weren't in the band anymore, and Billy justified it by saying, 'Well, all they cared about was money.' That just . . . ," the tone of Russell's voice sounds as if he is about to lose control of it, then he pauses for a moment composing his thoughts. "First of all, I don't

BILLY JOEL

know what the other guys made. I know we didn't all make the same amount of money. I wasn't getting rich off of Billy. And I wasn't in it for the money. And I really took great offense to that. I always kinda figured maybe he had a problem with Doug, and made it look better if we got rid of everybody else. Plus, to be honest with you, I don't really think Billy understood me in the band. I wasn't flashy like David [Brown]. To me, the best compliments I would get is like: 'Wow! I don't know what you're doing, but it sounds bad when you stop.' 'Whatever it is, keep doin' it!'"[65]

Russell claimed to the press, at the time, "After thirteen years, it would've been nice to have gotten a phone call. I wrote him a letter and said, 'When I met you, I had no hair on my chest; now I do—but it's gray!' But I want to look back on the good stuff we did."[32] That was an optimistic and idealistic way of looking at things.

Bass player Doug Stegmeyer took the news less well. At the time, he said, "I can understand completely wanting to change players. That I can respect 100 percent. I'm still friendly with him—I don't want this to be a sour-grapes-type of vibe. But, I feel, after fourteen years, I couldn't quite get it out of him [that he was being replaced]. But Liberty told him I was this close to hearing it on the street."[32] Had it not been for MTV news and radio broadcasts, Doug and Russell might never have realized they were no longer part of the band. Doug ended up taking a job as the bass player in fellow Long Islander Debbie Gibson's band, and Russell Javors began a series of jobs in and outside of the show business world. Suddenly they had to reinvent themselves, apart from the Billy Joel band.

Billy and Christie also made some changes in their personal lives as well. As planned, Billy sold his Manhattan apartment to fellow rock star Sting, and he and Christie purchased a huge house in the Hamptons, out on Long Island. Once they settled in, Billy discovered a deep fascination with the history of the Long Island fishermen in Gardiners Bay, Block Island Sound, and other surrounding areas. He read the book *Men's Lives* by Peter Matthiesen, which outlined the hard life that the fishermen on the east end of Long Island endured. There had been a fishing industry that had been in place since the seventeenth century. Billy Joel found this book to be a pivotal reference point for his newfound fascination with the subject of the baymen.

When Christie, Alexa, and Billy moved from Manhattan to East Hampton, they became friendly with a woman by the name of Adelaide de Menil. She was a friend of Matthiesen's and she also knew Arnold Leo, who was the secretary of the East Hampton Baymen's Association.

According to Leo, the bay fishermen's two main industries were scallops and striped bass. A brown algae infestation in the Peconic Bay forced out the scallops. And, striped bass was taken off the marketplace that season because excessive levels of PCBs were present in them from pollution.

Arnold Leo was startled to have his phone ring one day, only to find Billy Joel on the other end of the line. "Adelaide is a dear friend of ours and she told Billy about the baymen. He called me up," Leo recalled, "and you could have knocked me over with a feather. Out of the blue, he asked me to lunch, said he wanted to talk about what he could do. In East Hampton, it's not uncommon for me to get called up to meet a celebrity or some very wealthy person. I've learned that some are very genuine people, and some are shallow publicity hounds. So I went with an open mind to meet Billy. He is a very simple, real person. I really do like and respect him. I've asked him to appear here or there for us, sometimes do an interview. He even put in a phone call to the Governor's office on one occasion."[32]

Speaking of the scallops and the striped bass, Arnold Leo pointed out, "We lost both of them the same year, and that's what Billy's song ["The Downeaster 'Alexa'"] is about, because it was a devastating blow. The fishing community just started to cave in." Said Leo, "This song, the baymen love it, because it really does catch the feeling of the plight. Of being confronted by these changes that you don't really have any power over. This little corner of Long Island was an undisturbed part of the world until relatively recently. It's very hard to see very old, beautiful things just altered irrevocably."[32]

On the subject of the baymen's plight, Billy explained, "My feeling is they're being put out of business by politicians, developers, industrial pollution, agricultural insecticide run-off and the sport-fishing lobby. I feel that if these guys disappear we've lost a lot of the identity of what Long Island is. Especially if you go back in the history and culture of Long Island; Herman Melville wrote stories about them. Winslow Homer painted them. Walt Whitman wrote poems about them. . . . A lot of cultural identity of Long Island has a lot to do with these people. If they go, we're just a suburb. We're no longer an island. People forget that—we're an island."[32] Meanwhile, Billy continued to be supportive of his benevolent organization, Charity Begins at Home, every December. The Long Island baymen and their needs became one of the regular beneficiaries of funds from Charity Begins at Home from this point forward.

Living back on Long Island was eye opening for him in many ways. Said Billy, "I met a guy the other day out in Montauk. He's the same age as me

BILLY JOEL

Billy's drinking began to affect his concerts. When he lost his balance and fell on stage, Elton John had to have a talk with him. *[Courtesy of the author]*

On January 26, 2003, Billy Joel had the second of his three highly publicized car accidents, this time hitting this tree in Sag Harbor, Long Island. *[Courtesy of www.DerekStorm.com]*

Billy Joel with the "red cup" at Madison Square Garden, December 5, 1998. Is it full of alcohol or water? *[Courtesy of www.DerekStorm.com]*

Autographed ticket to Billy Joel's Master Class at NYC's Town Hall, May 16, 1996. *[Courtesy of Tom Cuddy of WPLJ Radio]*

NEW YORK

Presents

Billy Joel

An Evening of Questions & Answers...
& A Little Music

Thursday, May 16th, 1996 7:30 pm
Town Hall, 123 West 43rd Street, NY, NY

A special live radio broadcast in celebration of
WPLJ's 25th anniversary and Billy Joel's 25th anniversary as a solo artist.

Proceeds Benefitting A Musical Scholarship
at City College, N.Y., N.Y.

Billy Joel exits NYC's Cooper Union after one of his many college tour Q&As, November 1, 2001. *[Courtesy of www.DerekStorm.com]*

The Piano Man performs at the Hartford Civic Center in Connecticut, February 6, 2002. *[Courtesy of www.DerekStorm.com]*

Billy Joel always stops for the fans. He is seen here signing autographs in Rockefeller Center at *The Today Show*, September 14, 2004. *[Courtesy of www.DerekStorm.com]*

Liberty DeVitto hitting the stage at the Cutting Room in Manhattan, February 23, 2006. *[Courtesy of www.DerekStorm.com]*

Richie Cannata taking a break at his office in Cove City Sound Studio on Long Island. *[Courtesy of www.DerekStorm.com]*

Billy Joel exits the Cutting Room after his daughter Alexa Ray makes her NYC debut, December 11, 2005.
[Courtesy of www.DerekStorm.com]

Alexa Ray Joel under a painting of Ray Charles, her namesake, at the Cutting Room after one of her gigs, January 30, 2006. The portrait artist is Kathrina Miccio. *[Courtesy of www.DerekStorm.com]*

Author Mark Bego rockin' at NYC's Cutting Room with Liberty DeVitto and Richie Cannata. *[Courtesy of www.DerekStorm.com]*

Billy Joel opening night at the record-breaking twelve sold-out shows at Madison Square Garden, NYC, January 23, 2006. *[Courtesy of www.DerekStorm.com]*

Opening night backstage pass, Madison Square Garden, NYC, January 23, 2006. *[Courtesy of www.DerekStorm.com]*

DEREK STORM

DEREK STORM

DEREK STORM

Christie Brinkley and Alexa Ray Joel were on hand opening night at Madison Square Garden, January 23, 2006. *[Courtesy of www.DerekStorm.com]*

Billy Joel's twelve-sold-out-show run at NYC's Madison Square Garden in 2006 yielded a double CD. *[Courtesy of www.DerekStorm.com]*

Bob Buchman of radio station Q104.3 presents Billy Joel with a banner commemorating his twelfth record breaking show at Madison Square Garden, April 24th 2006. *[Courtesy of www.DerekStorm.com]*

Author Mark Bego snags a quick "photo op" with Katie Lee Joel in midtown Manhattan. *[Courtesy of www.DerekStorm.com]*

Billy Joel performs with Tony Bennett at *The Today Show*, September 22, 2006, in support of Bennett's newly released *Duets* CD. *[Courtesy of www.DerekStorm.com]*

The Piano Man celebrates his first year of sobriety with a triumphant world tour in 2006. *[Courtesy of www.DerekStorm.com]*

DEREK STORM

and was a good friend when we were in high school. He was one of the high school heroes. All the girls wanted to go out with him. He went into the Marines; a big strapping guy. I saw him in Montauk. He lives in a camper. He said, 'Billy, the American Dream is dead. There's no way I can afford to buy a house. I can't live on Long Island the way my parents did.' He's got his kid in the camper with him. He was saying, 'I'm waiting for my kid to be old enough to take care of himself, then I'm outta here.' It really chilled me. There's a lot of people like that, who fell through the cracks."[32]

Liberty DeVitto was quoted in *Rolling Stone* magazine as saying: "Some people don't understand that Billy is still a guy from Long Island. That guy who lives in a big house now is the same guy who grew up in that little house in Levittown."[125]

On May 9, 1989, Billy turned forty years old. He said, "Turning 30 was a trauma, but 40 wasn't at all bad. At 40, you may have to take a little more inventory, but you tend to deal with things a little more calmly. And you know that you don't have the corner on wisdom at any age."[136]

With all of the changes he had made in his business relationships, it was clear that this year was a milestone turning point. When it came time to start writing songs for his fourteenth album, Billy recorded several demos for potential album tracks. One of the songs that was not included on the album was called "Money or Love." In the lyrics, Billy asks a friend why he is in his life. Is it for the money? Or, is it for the love of being a friend? According to Liberty, Billy Joel wrote this song specifically about Doug Stegmeyer. It remained "in the can" until 2005, when it was released on the *My Lives* boxed set.

Meanwhile, Billy was out expanding his performing repertoire. On Monday, July 31, 1989, he presented the first in what was to grow to be a series of master classes on his life and his music. This first one was held at the Performing Arts Center of Long Island University's campus in Southhampton. In the evening session, Billy addressed the audience, told stories, and intermittently sang a song or two. The show was part of the Altec Lansing Music Festival. The $20 admission went toward a music scholarship fund.

Said the president of the East End radio station HB-107, Eddie Simon, "This is going to be an exploration of the creative process, dependent on questions and answers, and dialogue."[19] Eddie, also happens to be singer Paul Simon's twin brother. To put an added twist on the event, Paul's sometime song partner Art Garfunkel also happened to be in the audience that night.

Billy was reportedly very engaging in addressing his audience. He was thrilled to be asked by the audience about his songwriting and musicianship, as opposed to being bombarded by questions about his personal life. He proclaimed from the stage that night, "Usually somebody wants to know, 'What does Christie look like in the morning?' She looks good, so let's get that out of the way." Speaking of his songwriting he said, "I always wanted somebody to tell me, 'I love you just the way you are.' It's not a new sentiment: The Four Seasons had 'Rag Doll.'"[19] This master class forum has proven a very satisfying one for Billy. According to him, he is educating aspiring young people about the ins and outs of the music business. It was an education that he, himself, wished had been imparted upon him when he was starting out his career.

On September 24 of that year, while Billy was awaiting the release of his fourteenth album, he had planned a trip to London. It was also one day before the official filing of the Frank Weber lawsuit. However, when Billy arrived at John F. Kennedy Airport, he was reportedly experiencing severely sharp abdominal pains and had to be hospitalized. The cause of the pain was diagnosed as a recurrence of kidney stones. The event made headlines in the next day's newspapers. Billy later explained of the incident, "And of course the papers had me collapsing at JFK Airport. I didn't collapse at JFK. I had kidney stones before this. I just called the doctor, and I said, 'Should I go to Europe?' He said, 'No, come in. Let's take care of it.' So I went into the hospital. When I was in there, I got flowers from everybody, and I also got this bottle of Jack Daniels from Axl Rose, who I met once. 'Get well,' with a bottle of booze. It turns out he used to work in a record store and had all these questions about my old records. I was surprised. So I have the same sort of stupid preconceptions about other people that people have about me. But the lawsuit coming at the same time as the kidney stones was the double whammy. The press couldn't resist it."[125] On September 26, Billy was successfully operated on at New York University Medical Center in Manhattan, for the removal of the offending kidney stones.

In October 1989, the *Storm Front* was released by Columbia Records. With Mick Jones sharing production credits with Billy, the result is an album that has a harder rock edge to it, and musically extends in some new directions. "My game plan for *Storm Front* was simply to make a better record, one that I liked," claimed Billy Joel. "I was unhappy with the way *The Bridge* came out. You can hear the seams on that album—it was a bad stitching job. Christie and I'd just had Alexa, and you can hear on that

BILLY JOEL

record that I would rather have been at home with the baby than with the band in the studio. That's what the song 'Temptation' [from *The Bridge*] was all about—the temptation was a baby—not another woman."[125]

The song "That's Not Her Style" kicks off the proceedings with a strong boogie beat. The band sounds hot and lively on this rocking ode to Billy's wife. Here we find him actively denying all of the press rumors written about the alluring Christie Lee, presumably in the tabloids. Explained Billy at the time, "Yes, there's some rocky stuff on *Storm Front*, but anyone who's been following my career shouldn't be surprised at all. I'm not just this ballad guy—just because 'Piano Man' was my first hit, some people still think of me as 'the piano man.' But that was something I did for nine months. Most of my life I played with rock bands. Sure, I wrote the songs and had the spotlight on me a lot of the time, but I'm still a guy who plays in rock bands. And naturally, there's some meaty stuff on the album for this band to sink its teeth into like 'That's Not Her Style.'"[125]

With regard to the inspiration for this song, Billy said that he was trying to dispel what the tabloids were reporting about his wife: "That's a dilemma for me, because no one knew that other woman I was married to. So I could write 'Just the Way You Are' and other songs and people would identify with it. With Christie, if I write a love song about a woman or if I write *anything* about a woman, people assume I'm writing about her. And I know if it were me listening, I'd be going, 'God, there's that jerk singing about his beautiful supermodel wife again. I'm so sick of reading about the two of them. Screw him.' But I also know that a lot of great artists— Picasso, Chopin, others—used the women they loved as their muse, to represent women in general. So I'm glad I'm in good company."[125]

"We Didn't Start the Fire" is undoubtedly the catchiest, bounciest hit of his entire career. His nonstop travelogue through the four decades that had transpired between 1949 and 1989 was immediately appealing. From Doris Day to Princess Grace to Beatlemania to AIDS, he covered it all to a rocking beat. According to Billy, "I started doing that as a mental exercise. I had turned 40. It was 1989. Okay: Harry Truman was the President. Popular singer of the day: Doris Day. China went Communist. Another pop star: Johnny Ray. Big Broadway show: South Pacific. Journalist: Walter Winchell. Athlete: Joe DiMaggio. Then I went to 1950: Richard Nixon, Joe McCartney, big cars, Studebaker, television, etcetera, etcetera . . . it was kind of a mind game. That's one of the few times I've written the lyrics first, which should make it obvious why I usually prefer to write the music first, because that melody is horrendous. It's like a mosquito droning. It's one of the worst melodies I've ever written. I kind of like the lyric though. I thought it was a clever one."[50]

He explains, "The whole stimulus of writing it came from a conversation I was having with a guy who had just entered his 20s and was feeling a little depressed about the world situation. You gotta understand, this was '89, before the whole Iron Curtain came down. He was worried about AIDS . . . pollution . . . the situation in Red China. I said, 'Wait a minute, didn't you ever hear of Dien Bien Phu . . . the Hungarian freedom fighters . . . the Suez Canal crisis?' He never heard of any this stuff. I started jotting these images down, these flashes of newspaper headlines that occurred to me. I actually tried to write them down in chronological order, like it was a mental exercise. It wasn't meant to be a record at the time. I went home and checked my encyclopedia to see how close I was to the chronology of the events. As it turned out, I was almost dead on the money. I'd say about three or four changes came from reading the encyclopedia."[35]

Musically, Billy recalls that he had a demo for a song that he was going to call "Jolene." He ended up adapting the music he had written for "Jolene" and made it into "We Didn't Start the Fire."

"What I wanted to do lyrically," he explains, "was sum up at the end of these years of names and faces and say, 'Hey, we didn't start this mess, we certainly did our best to make it better. It's not something we started and it's probably not something we're going to be able to finish. For the foreseeable future, this kind of craziness is going to go on and on. That's how life is.' When I finished writing this song, I didn't know it was going to be a hit."[35]

According to him part of the reason of its success was its brilliant rock & roll edge, as influenced by the song's producer, Mick Jones. "It needed a good kick in the ass to get away from the pseudo-intellectual type of recording. It needed to be played like a rock & roll song. After that, we started perceiving that this might end up actually being a single."[35]

The dramatic "The Downeaster 'Alexa'" was a sincerely heartfelt one for Billy for a couple of reasons. First of all, this soulfully sung song is all about the plight of the fishermen and baymen of Long Island Sound. Helping them out had become his own personal project, ever since he moved out to the eastern part of Long Island. The second reason was that he christened the song's fictional ship *Alexa* as a way of working his daughter's name into his lyrics. When the album was released, he received a lot of bad publicity from critics who claimed that he was nothing more than another rich guy pontificating about the way things should be. However, Billy claimed that his was a genuine concern.

"I know what being a commercial fisherman is—I did it," he stated. "Most of my life I was poor. Most of my life I had weird jobs. But there's also a thing called imagination, which is what writers have. We should be able to use pronouns any which way we want to get a narrative across. I don't like getting up on a soap box, being one of those social-political-message guys. I think the best way to do it is to tell a story about a human being, not about an issue. And hey, I know I'm not the guy in the song. I've said, 'I'm living here in Allentown,' and I don't live in Allentown. I said we were sharp as knives in Vietnam, and I wasn't in Vietnam. So I don't buy it."[125]

The rocking "I Go to Extremes" finds Billy trying to explain his personal mood swings. In the album's most straightforward rock number, he sings with passion about the way his life has no middle ground. He is either "too high" or "too low." Presumably addressing Christie here as "darling," he proclaims that whatever his sleepless nights are about, eventually the pendulum will swing back the other way.

Explained Billy, "It's kind of an ode to manic depression. 'Summer, Highland Falls' is kind of like that. I think all artists, to one degree or another, are manic depressive."[113] The background chorus on this song consists of Mick Jones, Joe Lynn Turner, and Ian Lloyd of the group Stories ("Brother Louie," 1973).

According to Liberty DeVitto, "I Go to Extremes" is one song he had a big hand in creating. "I came in with a rhythm, and I said, 'Write a song around this.'" he recalls. "There's all kinds of stuff that I did. He would call me all the time and sing songs over the phone and I would say, 'That sucks,' or 'That's good.'"[63]

"Shameless" is a medium-tempo torch song of love and devotion. At this point, it was the closest Billy had come to adopting a country rock, Eagles-like sound in his music. Although standard rock guitars are used here, they echo Sneaky Pete's pedal steel guitar work from Billy's earlier albums. David Brown's guitar solo in the middle of the song, Liberty DeVitto's driving drumbeat, and the strong background vocals by Patti Darcy, Crystal Taliefero, and Frank Floyd make for a sparkling ensemble. Says Billy, "And yeah, a song like 'Shameless' has plenty of barbecue sauce on it, as they say. But that's only natural. I mean, anyone who thinks of us as mellow should have heard us doing Zeppelin, Cream and Hendrix at sound check!"[125]

His second seafaring song on this album is the title track, "Storm Front." In this rocker he equates navigating through love's perils and pitfalls with being the captain of a ship. Here he claims that he has somehow driven away the object of his affection. Again, it is easy to read between the lines of this autobiographical look at love in the last decade of the twentieth century. The Memphis Horns, Andrew Love and Wayne Jackson, perfectly punctuate the track, giving this storm-size song a brilliant big band kind of sound. Rocker Richard Marx is heard on this track, joining the vocal trio that was featured on the previous cut. This track is one of the best examples of how well the new band members meshed with one another. The arrangement is punchy, and Billy sings with gale-force drive.

In Billy Joel terms: the song "Leningrad" is to the cold war, what "Goodnight Saigon" is to the Vietnam War. This emotion-charged composition parallels his childhood in Levittown, featuring a slightly fictionalized version of a Russian circus clown he had met during his history-making tour of the USSR in 1987.

The inspiration for the song was a man named Viktor, with whom Billy became acquainted in Gorky Park while he was in Moscow. As in the lyrics of the song, Viktor worked as a professional clown, and, on a stroll through the park, he caught the eye of one-and-a-half year-old Alexa and greatly amused her. Viktor and Billy struck up a conversation with each other via an interpreter and found an immediate rapport. Billy was delighted when Viktor came to Leningrad for his concert there. It was at the airport that he and Viktor last spoke, but the clown left a lasting impression on the American songwriter.

Billy said at the time, "Right now we're looking at what could be the beginning of the end of the Cold War. I wanted to make a comment on it because I'm a little surprised at how blasé people seem to be about it. When I was a kid we [Americans] all thought we could all be blown to smithereens at any minute.[136]

"In writing the song, I took a little artistic license. The song says he was born in '44, when he was actually a few years younger than me. But I wanted him to stand for the universal Russian. Since I returned I got a note from him written in Cyrillic, which I had translated. He got a letter from me. But we haven't spoken. I've tried to reach him, but it's hard to contact people there."[136]

In the song Billy sings of both he and Viktor losing their fathers at an early age. While Viktor was taught to serve the state, Billy was taught to hide under his school desk in case the Russians dropped a bomb. He sings here that Viktor made his daughter laugh, which began a friendship that was purely a human connection, and nothing to do with the teachings from two opposing countries that once considered each other their mortal enemy. A slow and effective ballad with a sweeping background, "Leningrad" is made even more poignant with the addition of the choral voices of Chuck Arnold and several members of the Hicksville High School chorus.

In "State of Grace," Billy sings of being frustrated in his relationship with Christie. In this medium-tempo ballad he claims in the lyrics that she slips away from him just as the words he says to her evaporate into the air unheard. According to Liberty DeVitto, "State of Grace" clearly reveals the unraveling of Billy and Christie's relationship. Whenever she was upset with her husband, her escape would come in mentally leaving the room. "Listen to the song on *Storm Front*, the album before *River of Dreams*, called 'State of Grace,'" says Liberty. "The song opens up with him singing about slipping away into a 'state of grace.' It's about him trying to say something to her, as she slips into this 'State of Grace.' It's like she just goes off somewhere else. She is listening, but the words are going right through her. And then he says to her that she is not the same as him, but he begs her not to leave him now. To me, that being said, that was the beginning of the end right there."[62]

Picking up the pace, in "When in Rome," Billy Joel sings about watching his lady put on her makeup and clothes, preparing to go off to work. Here he paints himself as the superstar house-husband waiting for his gorgeous wife to come home from a day in front of the cameras. However, when she comes home, the lyrics continue, she can let her hair down and be herself with him. A contemporary rocker with a great saxophone solo by Lenny Picket, "When in Rome" has an infectious beat, and a nice sassy interplay between Billy Joel and his new band.

While commenting on the song "When in Rome," Billy quickly pointed out that it personifies his present life in the "Billy and Christie" fishbowl: "There's a song on *Storm Front* called 'When in Rome,' about a working couple—working like us. Now, we may not have the same kind of jobs everybody else has. But we *do* work. We probably work harder than the people who comment on us. I've actually had journalists write nasty lies about my kid. She never hurt anybody. She's not even four years old."[125]

Well, yes, both he and Christie work, but he isn't exactly a steelworker in "Allentown." What he is is a multimillionaire singer, with an equally famous and beautiful wife who just happens to be a world-famous top model. This song talks more specifically about their life together than just the daily routine of your average John and Jane Doe.

The album ends with the poignant piano and vocal ballad "And So It Goes," which is arguably among the most beautiful and heartfelt songs Billy Joel has ever written and recorded. In this slow, sad lament, Billy sings about giving his heart to someone who has the power to break it into a million pieces. It is a song of love and extreme vulnerability and is the album's strongest, most sincerely touching performance.

Billy reveals that this particular song actually "was written back in 1983 during the time I was writing songs of *An Innocent Man.* I was a newly unmarried man, I was dating beautiful women at the time, it was a great time in my life."[113] And it so perfectly personified where his marriage to Christie was headed.

Although it remains one of his all-time most popular albums, the critical reviews for *Storm Front* were quite mixed. In *Us* magazine, Sean Plottner snidely wrote, "Looks like stormy weather for the piano man. He charts a smooth course through parts of this LP, including two sea-inspired sagas: the title track and a tragic tale of fishermen aboard 'The Downeaster "Alexa."' . . . And when he sings about life with a model in 'When in Rome' and 'That's Not Her Style,' it's time to head for the lifeboats . . . he's best when he avoids introspection and tells a moving story. He doesn't do that enough on *Storm Front.*"[137]

Acknowledging *Storm Front*'s instant success on the charts, *Time* magazine complained, "A monster hit album, with Joel's crazily catchy buzzword history of the past 40 years, 'We Didn't Start the Fire,' plus nine other effortlessly obnoxious ditties that take on such subjects as glasnost and the plight of Long Island fishermen. The musical equivalent of a sociology lecture by Ralph Kramden."[138]

Some writers even used their reviews as a chance to take potshots at Billy's entire career. According to Julian Dibbell in *Spin,* "Billy Joel just isn't the dick he used to be. Once upon a time his work rested on what a generous critic called 'the most throughly objectionable persona since Bob Hope.' It was smarmy, self-romanticizing and relentlessly condescending to women and just about anyone else unlucky enough to catch Joel's attention. . . . His is a scattershot genius, better suited to the greatest-hits compilation than to first-run albums like *Storm Front,* on which the nonentities outnumber the gems by a typical three to one. It's a miracle he blunders into brilliance as often as he does."[139]

And Chuck Eddy in the *Village Voice* complained, "Like too many white musicians his age and tax bracket, he's been drowning his sorrows in too much old soul music. 'Storm Front' buys 'Get Happy' Elvis C. [Costello] a sinking ship. 'Shameless' wastes a great title on a queasy John Haitt imitation. 'When in Rome' laps up the black coffee Squeeze spilled on their sheets back in '82. . . . 'The Downeaster "Alexa"' is the latest in Joel's string of classy physical-displacement ditties. . . . 'And So It Goes' comes off a little too heart-wrenchingly sincere."[140]

Ironically, it was John McAlley in *Rolling Stone* who gave the LP its most glowing review: "On *Storm Front* . . . Billy Joel throws off pop complacency for an angry, committed—and often moving—exploration of life in modern America. . . . *Storm Front*'s propulsive first single, 'We Didn't Start the Fire,' sounds the alarm on a society that has lost its moral center and is spinning out of control. . . . The lover in 'Shameless' sings with perverse pride about his enslavement to his woman's affections, while his swaggering alter ego in 'Storm Front' disowns domestic bliss and sets sail on a sea of temptation. . . . Musically, *Storm Front* struts with insistent rock & roll authority. . . . The hymnlike 'And So It Goes' takes the record's turbulent emotions and stills them in a moment of quiet revelation. . . . It is a note of startling maturity, at once mournful and bracing. And as the final word on an album that takes a serious look at a troubled world, it reflects the hard-earned wisdom of a no longer innocent man."[141]

Regardless of what the reviews said, the *Storm Front* album was universally appealing from the moment it hit the stores. In America it became his third number 1 album, and it peaked at number 5 in England. It also contained six chart hits, keeping him on the airwaves for more than a year. The biggest smash was the massively successful "We Didn't Start the Fire," which became his third number 1 single in the United States, which peaked in England at number 7. Billy Joel's consecutive hits from *Storm Front* included "Leningrad" (number 53 UK), "I Go to Extremes" (number 6 US/number 70 UK), "The Downeaster 'Alexa'" (number 57 US), "That's Not Her Style" (number 77 US), "And So It Goes" (number 37 US).

Furthermore, in addition to the above successes, the song "We Didn't Start the Fire" went on to become one of the hugest international hits of Billy's entire career. It hit the top 5 in Australia, Canada, Japan, and Germany. And, it was in the top 10 in the Netherlands, Norway, and New Zealand. Now the world truly was his oyster!

In November 1989, while the first bricks of the Berlin Wall were being removed in Germany, Billy and his new band assembled at the Suffolk County Police Academy in West Hampton, Long Island, to rehearse for their first tour together. For the tour, additions to the aforementioned reconfigured band included Mindy Jostyn (rhythm guitar/violin/harp), and Jeff Jacobs (synthesizers).

The band toured from 1989 to 1990 and was quite successful. With regard to that series of concerts, Billy proclaimed, "Listen, I might be an antique, just like The [Rolling] Stones, but antiques are of value. Antiques hold their value. We even get more valuable with age. And people want collectibles. Also, maybe people are finally getting tired of paying hard-earned money to see nothing up there. Maybe folks are tired of video stars who can't deliver live. They want substance, too."[125]

Liberty DeVitto recalls that this was the tour where he realized that his friendship with Billy was becoming more and more a business association than a lifelong friendship as collaborators and working partners. Once Billy began managing himself, Liberty started to make less money than he had earned in the past. He began to feel like a hired hand, and not the man who helped create all those great drum parts on all those million-selling albums.

"I think the drummer gets the short end of the stick, to be honest," he says. "Obviously, we thought we were part of a band, but we weren't part of a band, because he [Billy] was the one who was signed to the label. We got paid from him. In the beginning it's like, 'When we all get rich. . . . ' Wait a minute, what happened? After Frank [Weber], the guy who ripped him off was fired, a group of new accountants came, and they were like, 'Billy, you got the deal. You make the money. The band is to be considered "side guys."' And, that's what happened. We were suddenly the 'side guys.' But, in the studio, it was *like* we were a band. He is writing the songs, just like if you look at what Ringo Starr was to the Beatles. Except each of the Beatles were signed to the record label, not just Paul and John. We always assumed that we were like the Beatles."[63]

Now that Doug and Russell were gone, everything was different, especially the amount of money band members were paid. "Well, in the past we had gotten 'bonuses'—they were called—from Billy," Liberty explains. "Every time a record sold a certain amount, he wanted to encourage us to get out on the road and play harder. The more albums we sold, we would get some more money, too. Those are all of the things that he took away when Frank was taken out of the picture."[63] Now, a deeper resentment began to grow behind the scenes.

Billy claimed in the press that it was his show, and he had the right to hire and fire people as he wanted: "It is too big a business for people not to change. For friendships and relationships not to change. There's too much money to be made. There's too many other corporate entities that enter into the thing. And it's perfectly natural for somebody to want to work with other people. In my case, I was unhappy with the *Bridge* album and tour and wanted to make some changes. It's only natural."[125]

Around this same era came the first rumors that Billy and Christie's marriage had hit some rocky terrain. The advent of these kinds of things showing up in gossip columns only further infuriated Billy and fueled his careerlong feud with the media. He said he was sick of his personal life being used for attention grabbing headlines: "To tell you the truth, the effort to make the music, the work that goes into it, the touring, the writing, the arranging, producing, recording—is all I owe. I don't feel that I have to be very accessible other than that, because that [the music] is the essence of what people liked in the first place. I don't feel I need to keep myself exposed, because the private life being sacrosanct is fodder for the artistic cannon."[32]

It was then that Billy reluctantly submitted to being interviewed on the short-lived broadcast series *People Magazine on TV*. Since the press had been circulating news of a rift between the superstar Joel couple, Brinkley insisted that this was a surefire way of quelling the rumors. Prior to the taping, Billy complained, "I didn't want to do it, didn't want to do it. There were all these rumors around the time: that we were getting a divorce. Christie says, 'You have to show up, be on camera for a minute, just to deny the rumor.' I said, 'I'm not gonna deny every cockamamie rumor that comes down the pike. It lends credence to it. I refuse, I refuse, I refuse.'"[32]

According to him, it was Christie who finally talked him into it. "So she hits me with this: 'Mick [Jagger] would do it for Jerry.' I said, 'Aw, low blow.' So, I said, 'O.K.' As I am going to sleep that night, the last thought I had before my head hit the pillow was, 'Wait a minute! I married you!' But the next day they were in there with cameras in the house, it was very uncomfortable. There are some things that should just remain private."[32]

The week of December 16, 1989, *Storm Front* topped the American album charts in *Billboard* magazine, the same week that "We Didn't Start the Fire" also hit number 1 on the singles chart. With all of the ups and downs that he had experienced in his career, Billy truly appreciated having accomplished this feat. Comparing this return to the top to his other chart toppers, he said, "In the old days I used to think, 'Number One? What does that mean?' I was a real pigheaded little prick back then. Now I realize that Number One does mean a lot to people who have stuck with me and put up with a lot of crap in the last few years."[125]

The 1989–1990 *Storm Front* tour kicked off in Worcester, Massachusetts, on December 6, 1989. In addition to doing the obvious hits, and songs from the new album, Billy and his newly reconfigured band also reportedly performed a loopy seasonal medley juxtaposing the profane and the sacred, which included "Hark the Herald Angels Sing," "Come All Ye Faithful," Guns n' Roses' "Paradise City," and Aerosmith's "Love in an Elevator." The tour ultimately spanned 16 months, 174 shows, in 16 different countries around the globe.

The song "We Didn't Start the Fire" was such a runaway success on the charts that it actually served for an educational springboard for the history of the second half of the twentieth century: A fifth grade class at Banta Elementary School in Menasha, Wisconsin, used the song in the classroom as a learning tool. The students were asked to pick one of the topics, events, or personalities mentioned in the song, as the subject of a history report. In January 1990, CBS Records released a run of forty thousand limited-edition cassettes of the song "We Didn't Start the Fire," complete with a ten-minute talk by Billy Joel about the lyrics. The cassettes were delivered to schools with copies of the educational publications *Junior Scholastic* and *Update* magazines.

As part of his minihistory lesson Billy Joel announced on the tape, "I think the letters I have gotten from teachers and students alike have been really encouraging. . . . A lot of people tend to think history is just this drab series of boring names and dates that you just have to connect to pass the test. Really, history is a living thing. We are where we are today, and we are who we are today, because of our history."[142]

The years 1990 and 1991 turned out to be very high-profile years for Billy, who was touring the world with Christie and Alexa, with his band and entourage in tow. Since he brought along his own wife and daughter, he encouraged the other members of his troupe to do so as well. Recalls Liberty DeVitto, with a great deal of fondness for his boss's wife, "Christie Brinkley treated my children like they were hers. When we were out on the road, they would play with Alexa. If Alexa is dressed up in a ballerina suit, she had ballerina suits for my girls. She even took photographs of them."[62]

While they were on the road, lots of career-shaping events were concurrently taking place. On January 22, 1990, a New York State Supreme

Court judge awarded Billy a partial summary judgment of 2 million dollars in his case against former manager Frank Weber. In February of that year, the RIAA certified the album, *The Stranger,* a seven-million seller. This milestone feat was not wasted on Billy Joel. Contemplating this fact at the time, he said, "If you sell seven or eight million albums, try to grasp seven or eight million people. You can't. It's beyond comprehension. 'Number One' I can understand. '*Platinum*' album I can understand. 'Biggest-selling record, at that time, in Columbia Records' history'—that I can understand. But, 'seven million?'"[32]

Instead of being humiliated by the mess that his finances were in, Billy simply shrugged his shoulders and admitted, "I think I was stupid, to tell you the truth. It wasn't my job, I trusted other people to look after my money. Time and time again I was accused of doing things for money, selling out, being commercial and having hit records—like I planned it, right? And all these years later, I find myself thinking, 'Well, gee, I was accused of being a capitalist fascist pig—maybe I should have looked after my business a little bit more.' But I didn't."[125]

He wasn't about to cry over spilled milk. There was only one way to go in his life and his career, and that was "forward": "What am I gonna do? Artists don't think like accountants. We think like artists. We're supposed to represent the other side. We're knuckleheads when it comes to business. Money isn't why I did what I've done in my life. I did what I did because it made me happy. But I'm tired of letting it be taken away from me by other people who haven't earned it. I do all the work—shouldn't I have the money? And what about my kid's future? There's a lot of sharks out there. She's going to need all the protection she can get. I don't think money solves problems. I think money creates more problems than anything else. And fame is the great neutralizer when it comes to wealth."[125]

During all of this, Billy Joel was still having a careerlong feud with the press. He hated being criticized publicly. "I've had a pissing war with the press going on forever, and that's one war you cannot win. But it sure built a lot of character. Listen, I know I've created most of my own problems, and I really don't care anymore. You'll find a lot of the landed gentry of rock 'critification' are *irked* by me. So I was never really woven into their rock & roll pantheon."[125]

Even after several years of marriage, Billy was amazed at the way that having Christie as his wife magnified every move he made. "Well, she certainly is somebody that people love to write about," he said. "What bothers me is when—because of what she looks like and what she does for a living—people fall back on the stereotype of her as being a dumb blonde, which she definitely is *not*. They say 'supermodel' like that's supposed to mean she's vapid and shallow—which she's *not*. Not that I mind people appreciating how beautiful she is. I know how beautiful she is. I know guys married to beautiful women who are very insecure about it. I'm the opposite. I say, 'Go ahead, check it out. She's pretty, isn't she? Look all you want. And she's married to *me*, you know?'"[125]

He especially hated the fact that the tabloids tended to blow things out of proportion. When asked if this bothered him, he replied, "You bet it does. People talk about 'Billy Joel and his supermodel wife' as if somehow Christie and I don't love and hurt and feel the same things that anybody else does. What do they think we do—walk in the door and fly around on gossamer and glitzy gliders? Don't people realize that the minute the door closes, all of the silly rock star/supermodel stuff goes right out the window? Then it's just me and her and real man-and-wife time."[125]

On March 8, 9, 12, 13, 16, and 17, Billy Joel and his band broke the existing house record at the Miami Arena, in Florida. He sold out six shows, playing in front of a total of 96,044 spectators, for the amount of $2,184,091. On April 11, in Richmond, Virginia, a judge dismissed an attempted countersuit that Frank Weber had filed against Billy. On May 21, while on the European leg of his current concert tour, Billy headlined at Wembley Arena, in England. That spring he announced that part of the proceeds of his concurrent single, "The Downeaster 'Alexa,'" would go to the East Hampton Baymen's Association, and to the Coast Alliance.

On June 22 and 23, Billy Joel became the very first rock act to perform at New York's Yankee Stadium, in the Bronx, selling out the 103,367-seat sports venue for a pair of back-to-back shows. A concert video, *Live at Yankee Stadium,* was filmed and released, chronicling these shows. Billy was treated like a homecoming hero on a triumphant return to the borough of his birth.

One of the most conspicuous things that was missing from Billy's shows during this tour was the song "Just the Way You Are," which he decided to omit from this tour. While the lawsuit against Frank Weber was still in the hands of the lawyers, he didn't want to be reminded of the woman he had written that song about—Elizabeth—his ex-wife and Frank's sister. "I'm just sick of it," Billy explained at the time. "Maybe it will come back sometime, but I'm not ready to do it again. There was one time when I was going through the divorce from my first wife, and I drifted away while singing it. I was so bored I started thinking, 'Well, I'll get back to the hotel about midnight, and they have prime rib on the room-service menu,' and then I lost the words. So I'm looking at Liberty, who sings the words all the time to help me pick it up, and I'm following his lips, and he's singing to me, 'She's got the house, the dog, the car,' and [then] that's what I sang. And the audience 'booed,' and I realized I shouldn't be doing this song. The song became 'Feelings' for a while," he said, referring to that overrecorded 1970s ballad. "And I realized it's a gyp for me to do a song just because people expect it. It's pandering. I've got to have a vested interest in doing a song, for crying out loud."125

Billy Joel was especially incensed about the fact that someone would dare to take away the rights to something he created. He said defiantly, "There are a number of lawsuits where my copyrights are in question. For better or worse, your songs are your kids. Then somebody comes along and tells you that they're not your kids anymore. The bank is going to take your kid. And I don't know how many mortgages there are on my copyrights these days. There's a lot of things involved in this lawsuit. Forget about what happens to the lawsuit. Forget about the lawyers. I'd rather be the same stupid dickhead I was and not have learned the lesson."125

As the concert tour rolled along, Billy continued to break records at different venues across America. On July 3 and 5, he grossed a reported $716,670 selling out two shows at the Omni in Atlanta, Georgia, while "That's Not Her Style," his latest single from the *Storm Front* album climbed the charts. On August 30, Billy was onstage with Paul Simon at a benefit that Simon had organized to raise funds for the preservation of the Montauk Point Lighthouse on the eastern end of Long Island. Together Simon and Joel performed their version of Frankie Ford's 1959 hit, "Sea Cruise." A few days later Billy showed up at a Van Morrison performance in Amagansett, at the Stephen Talkhouse. Together, Morrison and Joel sang duet versions of Ray Charles's "What'd I Say" and Sam Cooke's "Bring It On Home to Me." A week after the lighthouse benefit, the Simon and Joel duo did a reprise of their duet at Billy's own charity concert for the East Hampton Baymen's Association.

In an August 1990 issue of *Rolling Stone* magazine, Billy was asked to list his favorite Beatles songs. According to him, his top ten Beatles tunes were, in order: 1. "Strawberry Fields Forever," 2. "She Loves You," 3. "Yes It Is [Please Don't Wear Red Tonight]," 4. "I Am the Walrus," 5. "Ticket to Ride," 6. "She Said, She Said," 7. Norwegian Wood," 8. "I'm Looking Through You," 9. "A Day in the Life," and 10. "No Reply."

With regard to the number 1 Beatles song on his list, Billy explained, "Of all The Beatles' records, I enjoy 'Strawberry Fields' the most because it contains many of the elements that made The Beatles music so enjoyable and innovative. It is both sardonic and naive, melodic and dissonant. There are a great many liberties taken with the time signature, yet the listener is never left out of the whole musical process. It is almost as if one is being allowed to peek in on the recording session itself. Although 'Strawberry Fields' features one of Ringo's finest performances, you can hear each of The Beatles' individual and distinct contributions come together in a unified musical work. The production of this record contains just about every excess that The Beatles were accused of in their psychedelic era (e.g., tapes played backward, overabundance of chugging strings and multi-tracked drums). And somehow, it worked, probably for the last time ever. I even tried to re-create this type of texture on one of my own records, 'Scandinavian Skies.'"[143]

As his concert tour continued, Billy was very verbal about complaining about life on the road: "Well, I hate hotels. I hate matching furniture. I hate airports. I hate flying. I hate being without my family." Then why did he plan a yearlong tour? "I like to play. It goes back to before I was a recording artist or any of this rock-star crap. I was a player. That's what the fun is. It's as close to sex as you can get. For this tour, we've set up a schedule where we are on for six weeks and we go home for two, which I think is civilized. Which I always asked for in the past, and for some reason or other, with the people who used to be handling my career, that never happened. Because it didn't pay off for them. Fortunately, my kid is in nursery school, so if she joins me on the road somewhere, it's not like she's missing English Lit Five."[125]

Regardless of all of this, the *Storm Front* tour forded ahead. On November 13, 15, 16, and 19, Billy and his entourage broke another house record for selling out four consecutive shows at the Target Center, in Minneapolis, Minnesota. Over the course of those four nights, Billy Joel played in front of 72,332 patrons who shelled out a cumulative $1,677,284 for concert tickets.

On December 5, 1990, along with Johnny Cash, Quincy Jones, and Aretha Franklin, Billy received a lifetime Grammy Award titled a "Grammy Living Legend Award," for his career achievements. Billy viewed the honor with skepticism and criticism. "I'll never forget there was an awards show that was fairly cooked up for TV, which is how most awards shows are," he complained. "They're cooked up so they get celebrity names to come to this thing so they get their *tchotchke* [Yiddish for "worthless trinket"]. Here's the *tchotchke*. And they don't get any money, they just get a *tchotchke*. It's

BILLY JOEL

probably worth about twenty bucks at the trophy store: 'World's Greatest Dad,' you know? You ever take a good look at a Grammy? The horn spins right off. The plaque falls off. It's a piece of junk. Not the Oscar, that's a substantial thing, this big heavy thing. The Grammy's like 'World's Greatest Dad.' So they had this show called *The Grammy's Living Legends Awards,* and it was people who had won a certain amount of Grammys who they decided now are 'Grammy Living Legends.' So they wanted to give me one of these. My first instinct was, 'Do I have a fatal disease I don't know about?' Why force this honor upon me? I'm fairly young. You know, they're not telling me something. Then they tell you, 'We're going to have this celebrity introduce you on the TV show.' I hate doing TV. TV has no concept of rock & roll, or music, or anything. The difference between the music business and TV is this: In the music business they lie to you, but they don't expect you to believe them. In TV they lie to you and actually expect you to believe them, because they're wearing suits. They think you're going to believe them. And they lie to you."[31]

Before the year was up, there was still one more house record to break on the *Storm Front* concert tour. On December 9 and 16–18, Billy and his musical troupe packed the Knickerbocker Arena, in Albany, New York, bringing in a cumulative crowd of 66,733 cheering fans. He was so warmly welcomed there that it was officially declared "Billy Joel Day" in Albany County.

Billy was on such a huge streak of popularity in 1990, it was kind of odd that he was one of the few major celebrities who didn't cash in on his fame by doing product endorsements. It was the era of celebrity promotions, the biggest was the deal that Madonna made with Pepsi-Cola. They paid her millions of dollars to film a series of commercials. However, when her controversial "Like a Prayer" music video enraged the Catholic Church, Pepsi canceled the deal and pulled the commercials off the air, and Madonna got to keep the cash. Why didn't Billy throw his hat into the ring as well? "I'm not going to condemn people for doing endorsements," he said. "I might even do it myself, even though, 'I haven't done it yet.' I'm not going to get up on a big high holy cloud and say, 'I am rock & roller holier than thou.' What's the difference between CBS and Dodge? They're both corporations. There's no difference at all, but it just never felt right to me. But if it didn't compromise my art, and I didn't think I was telling kids to drink something that was going to rot their teeth out or drive something that was going to get them killed on the highway, I might do it. You're damn straight I might. The Catch-22 is, not doing it has increased my value. So, I've

BILLY JOEL

turned them all down. Pepsi offered me Madonna's deal. Coke offered me George Michael's deal. Millions and millions of dollars. Now that don't make me a saint. Part of me is going, 'I should have done it.' And part of me is glad I didn't. I still don't know if I'm gonna do it. But you notice I have been mentioned that often when people write about people who don't do deals. I may be a little bitter about this, but it bugs me. I'm not asking for special consideration. Just don't say I suck this way, and then not mention me at all when I'm supposedly doing the right thing."[125]

Following a sold-out string of shows in Japan, the Australian leg of Billy's *Storm Front* tour began on January 22, 1991, at the Entertainment Centre, in Sydney. The troupe then proceeded on to concerts in Melbourne, Brisbane, Adelaide, and Perth. While in the land down under, his Australian record label, Sony Music, presented Billy Joel with a Crystal Award, thus crowning him as the largest-selling in the entire history of the company.

When the Grammy Award nominations were announced in January 1991, Billy was up for awards in the categories of "Best Pop Vocal Performance, Male" and "Producer of the Year," both specifically for the *Storm Front* album. In March, *Rolling Stone* magazine announced that Billy Joel had been voted "Best Keyboard Player" in the publication's annual "Reader's Picks" awards. While Billy was being heralded as something of a genius as a composer, he tended to brush aside the parallels that the press often made between him and some of his music-writing idols: "I think in terms of [Irving] Berlin, or Shostakovich, these guys who live to be 90 or 100 years old. I feel like I'm in the early part of my composing, my productivity as a musician."[32]

As a musician, he claimed that he was in for a long-running career. "You don't necessarily have to be on the cutting edge, or a celebrity, or a rock star to be a musician," he claimed. "This is just one phase of it. Maybe I'll look back and say, this was the blue period. But I intend to be an artist all my life. I don't intend to stop making music just because I'm not a commercial recording artist."[32]

Already he was projecting a future leg of his career, where he would no longer chase hit records and would just make music to be making music: "My priorities now are family, music, then everything else. I need substance in my life. And the world needs substance. The world doesn't need any more *hip*. Hip is dead. The world doesn't need more *cool*, more *clever*. The world needs substantial things. The world needs greatness. We need more

Picassos, more Mozarts, more John Singer Sargents, not more *Milli Vanilli*. Not more haircuts," he said and laughed.[125]

Finally, on March 19, 20, 23, and 24, 1991, the *Storm Front* tour played its final dates, in Mexico City. Again Billy and his band broke records. The four sell-out concerts that they performed there were viewed by a cumulative audience of 80,832. The following month, the RIAA certified Billy's *52nd Street* album as sextuple platinum, and his *Greatest Hits, Volume I & II* album quadruple platinum, for multimillion sales in the United States.

As another one of his charitable deeds, on May 11, Billy autographed a $12,000 Young Chang grand piano. The instrument was then auctioned, and its sale raised funds for the "Give Kids the World Foundation." And, on the fifteenth of the month, Billy was bestowed an honorary doctorate of humane letters from Fairfield University in Fairfield, Connecticut. Not everyone was impressed with his being honored by the university. Philosophy professor, the Reverend Thomas Regan publicly complained that Billy Joel was "not someone with a lifetime commitment of serving humanity."[144]

Another further honor came when the city of Huntington, Long Island, dedicated the Billy Joel Cold Spring Harbor Park, on July 17, 1991. Billy arrived at the event to find the streets lined with cheering fans. His mother, Rosalind Joel, was also in attendance; along with press, local fans, and political officials. Doing some more of his local fund-raising, Billy was the headliner at a pair of benefits for the South Fork/Shelter Island chapter of the National Conservancy. Held at the Indian Field Ranch, in Montauk, Long Island, Billy was joined on stage by Paul Simon and Don Henley.

In September 1991, Disney Records released an album of new interpretations of several Disney classic songs called *Simply Mad About the Mouse*. On the album and in the video, Billy is heard singing the song "When You Wish upon a Star," which was originally featured in the animated film *Pinocchio*. Also on the album were a mixed bag of performers, including "Zip-A-Dee-Doo-Dah" by L. L. Cool J, "The Bear Necessities" by Harry Connick, Jr., and "Someday My Prince Will Come" by EnVogue.

The week of November 16, 1991, on the Country chart in *Billboard* magazine, Garth Brooks hit number 1 with his version of the Billy Joel composition "Shameless." This is the first time that one of Billy's songs had become a number 1 hit by someone else. It had been a lifelong dream of his. According to Billy, "Now, 36 years later, I finally have a Number One record by another artist doing my song in a completely different genre. This is what I was hoping for a long, long time ago. . . . This is definitely a career highlight. . . . I told Christie the other night, 'There's a Number One Country song about you.' She got a kick out of that."[145]

In January 1992, Billy's performance in the video version of "When You Wish upon a Star" was nominated for a Grammy Award, in the category of "Best Short-Form Video." At the same time, his *Live at Yankee Stadium* concert package was also nominated for a Grammy, in the category of "Best Long-Form Video." On the twenty-second of that month, Billy Joel inducted the legendary soul duo, Sam & Dave, into the Rock & Roll Hall of Fame. The ceremony took place in New York City at the Waldorf-Astoria Hotel. Going from "inductor" to "inductee," on May 27, 1992, it was Paul Simon who inducted Billy into the Songwriters Hall of Fame, at a gala ceremony held in New York City.

That same month, on Memorial Day weekend 1992, Billy and his band went up to Boston to record a song for the soundtrack album for a forthcoming film about a women's baseball team, called *A League of Their Own*. It starred Geena Davis, Madonna, Rosie O'Donnell, and Tom Hanks. The song he recorded with his band was a classic Duke Ellington song. Somewhere during that weekend, Billy's wallet went missing. According to a press report, a postal clerk by the name of Phil Sica found the wallet when he was sorting the mail. Apparently someone had dropped the wallet into a mailbox on the street, and it turned up at the Post Office. According to a press story on the subject, the socially conscious Sica returned the wallet to Billy, fully intact. At the time it made a cute and innocent-sounding little "human interest" press story.

However, Liberty DeVitto specifically recalls some slightly less-innocent circumstances surrounding the disappearance of the billfold. Says Liberty, "Billy went up to Boston the night before the band did to record the song 'In a Sentimental Mood' for the soundtrack to the film *A League of Their Own*. In the hotel, there was a baby grand piano. When we arrived we were told by a member of the entourage that Billy picked up a woman who proceeded to give him a blow job under the piano. After the woman left, Billy discovered that his wallet was gone."[3]

Finally, on Wednesday, June 24, 1992, Billy Joel was given his high school diploma alongside that year's graduating class at Hicksville High School. In the audience that night was his mother, Rosalind Joel, who had waited for decades for this event.

The concurrent school principal, Richard Hogan, pointed out to the Class of 1992 that Billy was denied his high school diploma originally because, "He [Billy] was missing one credit in English." Ironically, Principal Hogan had originally been Joel's fifth grade gym teacher.

However, more than twenty years later, Billy was not just handed his diploma because he was now a singing star. According to Hogan, "He submitted more of his actual works, and we said, 'My gosh, this more than satisfies."[146]

Following speeches by the Class of '92 valedictorian and salutatorian, after a two and a half decade break between his senior year and diploma receipt, Billy Joel took the podium. He proclaimed that evening, "Well, here I am Mom. I'm actually going to get my high school diploma, and it's only twenty-five years after everyone else gets theirs. But Mom, don't worry. I can finally pull myself out of this dead-end job I have and start working on a career with a real future."[146]

With regard to his own high school career, Billy told the graduating class, "We all went a little crazy then. We grew our hair, wore love beads and dropped out for a while. It was almost as if we knew that we had only one more moment to be kids before all hell would break loose in the year to follow, a year that would terrify us with the assassinations of Martin Luther King Jr. and Bobby Kennedy, and the shock of the Tet offensive and the debacle of the Chicago Democratic Convention."[146]

Billy's advice to the Hicksville High Class of 1992 included the thoughts: "Don't rush blindly into some convenient job that you will hate in a few years. Don't make a lot of logical tidy, sensible plans right away. Why not kick back for a few weeks and give yourselves a long, sweet summer of love? Drop out for a while, dye your hair purple, have your head shaved, get a tattoo. Get yourself a big old Harley-Davidson and drive it all the way to San Jose, but *please:* not while you're drinking. Fall in love with someone, but do make sure you bring something to put on while you're at it."[146]

In the summer of 1992, Billy Joel was one of the singing stars who contributed fresh interpretations of some of Elvis Presley's greatest hits to the soundtrack album for the comedy film *Honeymoon in Vegas*, starring Sarah Jessica Parker, Nicolas Cage, and James Caan. Billy was the only performer to contribute two tracks: "Heartbreak Hotel" and "All Shook Up." Also included on the album were country stars and rockers Travis Tritt ("Burning Love"), Bryan Ferry ("Are You Lonesome Tonight"), Tricia Yearwood ("[You're a] Devil in Disguise"), and Bono ("Can't Help Falling In Love"). Billy's rendition of "All Shook Up" was released as a single and became a chart hit on both sides of the Atlantic: number 27/UK and number 92/US.

The soundtrack reminded Billy Joel of the feeling that rock music gave him when he was a teenager. In the 1990s he attested to still be in love with the slightly subversive edge of rock & roll. He claimed, "Rock & roll isn't supposed to be legal. Rock & roll is *supposed* to be rebellious crap. Rock & roll is *supposed* to be about humping and fucking and sneaking around behind the parents and proclaiming your freedom, your independence. And what a lot of very important critics represent is really the authority. And I happen to think that if authority disapproves of you, then you *must* be doing the right thing."[125] Well, he still was a rebellious rocker, but now at least he was finally a high school graduate as well.

BILLY JOEL

15
RIVER
OF DREAMS

DURING THE 1992–1993 era, while his career was in high gear, Billy's legal problems were being sorted out by lawyers, courts, and judges. In his personal life, things weren't going all that swimmingly either. More and more rumors circulated about the impending demise of his marriage. For all of their public denials to the contrary—in retrospect—even the music he was writing for his next album revealed that theirs was a love in danger of heading for the rocks. Financially, the extensive touring that he and his band had done since 1991 had significantly straightened out many of the problems that Frank Weber's mismanagement actions had undermined.

On September 23, 1992, Billy filed another $90 million lawsuit. This time around it was against his former lawyer Allen Grubman, and his law firm, as well as Grubman's legal partners Ian Indursky, and Paul Schinder. The suit, which was filed in New York Supreme Court, claimed that the parties named in it committed malpractice and fraud. Among the allegations was that Billy had been signed to the law firm of Grubman & Indursky in 1980, and that the firm had in turn paid Frank Weber "payoffs, kickbacks and other illegal activities at the expense of Mr. Joel," if Weber assisted in helping the firm to build "a clientele of artists."[147] At the time of this suit, the firm now known as Grubman, Indursky, Schindler & Goldstein had handled such diverse clients as Madonna, Bruce Springsteen, Michael Jackson, MCA Records chairman Al Teller, and Sony Records president Tommy Mottola.

Billy's current lawyer, who was handling the case, was Leonard Marks. His clients included Eddie Murphy, David Bowie, as well as the Joels. At the time Marks stated, "If the case against Allen Grubman, who is the most powerful attorney in the business, is successful, it's certainly going to make others a lot more careful in the way they conduct themselves."[148]

One of Leonard Marks's other clients had been the songwriting duo of Jerry Leiber and Mike Stoller ["Jailhouse Rock"], who had used his services in recouping past song royalties and rights. With regard to the Billy Joel case, Leiber placed bets on the outcome: "I think it's a bitch of a race. Allen Grubman is real smart, but he's not smarter than Len. Marks is like [Alan] Dershowitz—he's in that category. I put my money on Leonard Marks. I like guys who eat up the scenery."[148]

According to Billy, these lawsuits had a numbing effect on him: "The situation had knocked me back so far that I questioned my capacity to write anymore. I mean, if you lose your faith in humanity, what are you gonna write about? How much you hate everyone? How life is a cesspool? I don't want to do that."[149]

On February 25, 1993, Billy won a further summary judgment of $676,670.68 with interest attached, in his ongoing legal battles against Frank Weber. The judgment was handed down by New York Supreme Court Judge Edward Lehner. These cases were to take several more months to be resolved.

There was no question in Billy's mind that he had absolutely had it with ever trusting an outside manager to organize his affairs. "I will never trust on that level again . . . but it doesn't obsess me," he claimed. "I ask a lot more questions, I pay more attention to that aspect of things. I won't allow myself to be managed anymore. I'm a manager."[150]

Billy continued to do his ongoing charity work throughout this time. On November 18, 1992, he performed at a cocktail and dinner party that was staged as a benefit for AIDS Project Los Angeles. It was billed as "Commitment to Life VI," and it was held at Universal Amphitheatre in Universal City, California. The event honored the efforts of Barbra Streisand and David Geffen, both of whom had generously helped raise funds through their humanitarian efforts to assist those infected with the AIDS virus. In March 1993, Billy Joel donated a nine-foot-long grand piano to Long

Island's University of New York at its Stony Brook campus. The grand piano that the university had previously possessed was destroyed in a flood that had occurred in February of that year.

On May 1, 1993, Billy was the recipient of an honorary degree from Berklee College of Music in Boston, Massachusetts. It was there that he delivered the commencement speech to the class of '93. Then, on June 5, he was one of the high-profile guests at the wedding of Tommy Mottola and pop songbird Mariah Carey. It was a lavish no-holds-barred ceremony that was so opulent that it was actually modeled after Prince Charles's wedding to Diana Spencer. It took place at St. Thomas Episcopal Church on Fifth Avenue. Two days later, on June 7, Billy was present at the groundbreaking ceremony for the Rock & Roll Hall of Fame building in Cleveland, Ohio.

As early as 1993, Billy began contemplating doing a Broadway show comprised of his music. There was a whole market for rock-oriented musicals, and it seemed like a natural move for him to make. Elton John became the first rock star in the 1990s to become a writer of songs for Broadway musicals, via the Tony Award–winning *Lion King*, after having composed the music for the original 1994 animated Disney film of the same name.

With regard to Broadway, Billy said at the time, "I get asked about this, and I always say, 'Yeah, I want to do it.' But I don't know if I want to write a musical and then have it go to Broadway, where they charge $65 [a ticket]. But I'd like to give it a shot."[151]

Meanwhile, the music scene continued to evolve in the early nineties. Suddenly country music took several steps closer to paralleling rock & roll. The same way that MTV had changed the rock world, in country now the new wave of singers not only had to sound great but look great, too, to accommodate the need for youthful and appealing videos. Hot young acts Alan Jackson, Lorrie Morgan, Brooks & Dunn, Vince Gill, Patty Loveless, and Billy Ray Cyrus added a new sex appeal to country music. But the biggest seller of all was Billy Joel fan Garth Brooks.

At the same time, the rock world experienced a big, unexpected change as well. The new big thing at the time was the whole "grunge" scene coming out of Seattle, Washington, as spearheaded by the trio Nirvana. They opened the door for the spotlight to be thrown on other self-contained bands coming out of Seattle, such as Pearl Jam, Soundgarden, Alice in Chains, and Hole.

Of these, Billy commented, "I think people have re-discovered bands, and that's all to the good, because I came out of bands. People think I was this piano man all my life, but I only played the piano bar for six months. We still work as a band; I just happen to be the guy who writes songs and sings. I'm not trying to co-opt anything, but I don't feel that far away from grunge."[151]

This was all magnified at the time when the lead singer of Nirvana, Kurt Cobain, committed suicide by a self-inflicted shotgun blast, in April 1994. This suddenly glamorized this form of suicide as a grunge rock & roll way to end it all. There was also a controversy at the time, since Cobain was the magical age of twenty-seven when he took his life. That is exactly the same age that rockers Janis Joplin, Jimi Hendrix, and Jim Morrison all died, instantly magnifying and romanticizing their short lives. Did Cobain plan his untimely death at the age of twenty-seven as a way to guarantee rock immortality, too? If he did, it sure worked well.

Billy didn't buy into it: "There is an elitist position that rock stars should either retire very early or die young. To them I say, 'Fuck you!'"[150]

His own life was changing, evolving. He began to take a good, hard look at his own existence, and even his own mortality. "I used to be a stone-cold atheist, and I'm not sure about my old beliefs anymore. You have to ask yourself these questions as you get older."[150] At the age of forty-four, he was claiming to finally be comfortable in his own skin as well. "Yeah, I dig being middle-aged. I probably look better now than I used to. Men can actually grow into a look," he claimed.[151]

The time had finally come for Billy Joel to start work on his fifteenth solo album. The sessions for the *River of Dreams* album began in the summer of 1992, in a recording studio on Shelter Island, on the far east end of Long Island. Originally the working title of the album was *The Shelter Island Sessions*. As he prepared for the June 1993 release of the album Billy explained, "The last album that I made that took this long was *The Nylon Curtain*. [*River of Dreams*] was a lot of work, but I'm glad I did it."[149]

It was a long process and was to produce a milestone album for so many reasons. *River of Dreams* was to be one of the most successful albums of his career, in terms of sales. It was to be one of his most personal and revealing albums, as far as exposing his emotions. It was to rekindle old relationships. It also represented the end of other relationships. And, no one knew at the time that it was also destined to be known as the last rock & roll album of all-new material that he was ever to record and release.

When it came time to choose a producer for *River of Dreams*, Billy selected someone completely new to the band to interpret his musical vision for the album: Danny Kortchmar. Danny had been on the music scene for quite some time. A contemporary of James Taylor's, Kortchmar had met Taylor on the island of Martha's Vineyard in the early 1960s, and they began playing folk gigs together. Danny was part of James's first band, the Flying Machine. After Taylor signed with the Beatles' Apple Records label in 1969, his original recordings and demos were released on *James Taylor and the Original Flying Machine,* which also featured Danny. Through the musical contacts that he made, Danny started playing guitar on other people's albums, including Carole King's blockbuster LP *Tapestry* and James Taylor's breakthrough disc *Sweet Baby James.*

One thing led to another, and before long Danny was featured as a guitar player on albums by Bonnie Raitt, David Crosby and Graham Nash, Jackson Browne, and Linda Ronstadt. He started working as a producer on the debut album by Louise Goffin, the daughter of Carole King and her ex-husband Gerry Goffin, who together wrote some of the most important music in rock history, including the Monkees' "Pleasant Valley Sunday," the Shirelles' "Will You Love Me Tomorrow?" and Little Eva's "The Locomotion." Danny formed a band called the Attitudes in the late seventies, and they were signed to George Harrison's Dark Horse Records. In the early eighties, Danny cowrote with Jackson Browne the huge smash "Somebody's Baby," which became the biggest hit single of Browne's career. Danny continued to do studio session work and went on to record tracks for Neil Young, Jon Bon Jovi, and the Spin Doctors.

He had the kind of creativity that Billy Joel really liked. Danny Kortchmar was a real hands-on producer, since he was an accomplished guitarist as well. Billy liked Danny's ideas, and so he enlisted him to be the producer on the *River of Dreams* album (he is credited as coproducer on two tracks).

The majority of the album was recorded at Billy's own recording studio, which he called the Boathouse, at the Island Boatyard on Shelter Island. The rest of it was recorded at Richie Cannata's totally state-of-the-art recording studio in Glen Cove, Long Island. This represented a long-overdue professional and personal reunion with Cannata, who was back in the Joel inner circle for the first time since he recorded the 1981 *Songs in the Attic* album and worked on developing horn parts for *The Nylon Curtain* album.

Unlike most of the other players who left the Joel camp, Richie Cannata was the one original band member who remained friendly with Billy. Richie explains how this reunion came about: "There was never ever a disagreement. He called me a 'survivor.' And he liked that about me. He knew that I wasn't going to go after him for royalties, or go after him for this or that. I always survived. There was never a bad feeling. And, I think that people always looked for that."[44]

Now, just like the old days, Richie played the tenor saxophone on the track called "A Minor Variation," recorded in his own studio. He recalls of the session, "He brought in Danny Kortchmar. And he asked me if he could record out there, and do part of it out here. So, I said, 'Sure.' Christie was in the picture then and Christie and Billy were out here, he was on Long Island, and he said, 'Let's do some of the mixing, the vocals, and the horns; let's do it out here.' I said, 'Absolutely. Fine.' So, we did that here. And he was terrific then. He was really good. We had invented all of these mics for him, and he ended up using a $100 microphone. And so we hooked up there."[44]

Although it was a professional reunion, Richie was quick to point out that he had no desire to return to his sax post when Billy next went out on tour. As he explains, "People are always saying to me, 'What did you say to him? What did he say to you?' Well, it's something else, guys. It's just something else. If he had said to me, 'Come back and play with me,' I don't know, I wasn't ready. You can only play so many arenas and so many stadiums, and I wasn't any better. I was getting worse as a player. You are in a Billy Joel 'cover band.' You are always doing Billy Joel material, and the sounds we made were the best part, the fun—even though it *was* my music—and I didn't have to learn someone else's saxophone parts. And, I played the keyboard parts, too, I had my own grand piano onstage, there was my section of the stage. Billy would come up and play it, and I would play it once in a while. So, it was a good position for me to be in, to play all of these instruments, but I was done with it."[44]

Said Billy about his fifteenth album, "I will never run out of musical ideas, but I find sometimes that words, rather than enhancing music, can tend to limit it. I don't set out to write a song about anything; I want to write a piece of music that really moves me, and then I go, 'How do I interpret this lyrically?' Like 'The River of Dreams' was pure stream of consciousness, the moment of pure inspiration. We dream all the time; we have a few dreams every night, and we forget there's no editor up there [gazing heavenward] and so that's my theory: that I've dreamt it, I forgot it, and it just recurred to me. I say, 'Where did I hear this before?' and then I realize, 'Wait a minute, you dreamt this, you idiot! You actually did create this with no censors.' I don't chalk it up to God or anything."[10]

While working on *River of Dreams*, Billy claimed that he did a lot of thinking about his favorite classical composer, Beethoven: "I figured that cats like Beethoven had their own intrigues to deal with, like the royal courts. He had some emotion he was trying to express; there's a human thing in there that we all respond to—that's why his music has been around for so long. So I listened to his symphonies over and over again, and I started to get it. I call it 'breaking the Beethoven codes.'"[149]

This album, more than his most recent releases, was more introspective, more revealing, and more personal. As Billy explained, "At the beginning, I was searching for justice. By the end, I've realized that nobody gets any justice; all we have is faith in something—in ourselves, in love, in humanity. But the record starts off very bitter, angry and pessimistic. I'm aware that people perceive me as this highly successful rock star married to Christie Brinkley, and who am I to get the blues? But I did have the blues. I'm as human as anyone else—just a lot luckier."[149]

Liberty DeVitto points out that a lot of what was then going on in Billy's life is reflected on this, his last full album of new rock & roll material. Billy's crumbling marriage to Christie was one of the most evident themes that punctuated much of the material. Says Liberty, "On *River of Dreams* is his confusion. Staying up in the middle of the night thinking about his life. And "Lullaby," the song to his daughter, is about 'I know I'm getting divorced. I know me and Mommy are breaking up, but I'll always be there for you.'"[62]

The album opens with "No Man's Land," which is about the urban and suburban sprawl that had taken over so much of Billy's beloved Long Island. Here, to a rocking beat, he points out how strip malls and housing developments have eaten up much of the unspoiled countryside. At one point in the song he seems to throw his hands in the air in desperation, and asks for someone to pass him a glass of wine.

According to Jay Pomerantz, a longtime Billy Joel fan and collector who lives on Long Island, this song particularly resonates as a very touching and revealing one. "I have small children, and as we drive around Long Island in the car, I am constantly pointing out areas where shopping centers and business parks now stand. I say to them, 'I used to remember this as a pristine wooded area that no longer exists.' The song 'No Man's Land' is my favorite Billy Joel track because of this. On this song he perfectly points out the spoils of urban waste that much of Long Island now represents."[152]

"The Great Wall of China" is a blatant rant against Billy's former manager, Frank Weber, about how Weber could have had his enviable job forever if he hadn't gotten greedy along the way. A medium-paced rocker, it doesn't have the universality of some of Billy's stronger material, but it

BILLY JOEL

certainly drives the point home on how it feels to be stabbed in the back by somebody who had previously been called a friend.

In "Blonde over Blue" Billy sings of his troubled marriage. Clearly the "blonde" in the lyrics is Christie Brinkley. The lyrics concern his life on the road, being stuck in a prisonlike hotel room, longing for their relationship to reach a healing point. The slower, slinkier "A Minor Variation" finds Billy singing more blues. Complete with Richie Cannata on the tenor sax, here he sings of how inconsolable he has become of late.

The next track, the punchy "Shades of Grey," was produced by Billy Joel, with additional production by Dave Thoener. It is also the only song on the album to feature longtime drummer Libery DeVitto. Here Billy claims that his blues have all turned to a numbing neutral tone. He bays at the moon, and claims that he can no longer see the rainbow of happiness.

The final five songs are this album's most poignant ones. In "All About Soul," Billy suddenly swings into high gear, as he sings again of Christie Brinkley, and this time around he takes a good hard look at their marriage. With the popular nineties vocal group Color Me Badd providing guest vocals, this is one of the most satisfying songs on the album. Billy sings about how "she" has had the opportunity to leave him several times, but somehow she has yet to turn around and walk away.

Although "All About Soul" finds Billy claiming that Brinkley has yet to leave him, in the touching "Lullabye (Goodnight, My Angel)," it's pretty evident that the marital breakup is near. It echos the same sentiment that Cher sang of in the classic sixties hit song "You Better Sit Down Kids." Singing to his sole and soulful piano and additional strings, in this number he tells Alexa that Daddy is about to go away, and how she is not to fret. A truly sad song of good-bye, it is a touching message from soon-to-be-estranged father to his child.

Said Billy at the time, "I wrote it originally as a classical piano piece. It had no lyric. I actually wrote it when I knew that Christie and I were going to split up. My daughter did ask me, 'What happens when you die?' So that was part of it. But the other part of the song was, 'Mommy and I are going to leave each other, but I'm never going to leave you. I'll never leave you, I'll always be there,' which a lot of fathers have to say to their children because most of the time, the mothers get custody. The fathers have to leave the children's lives, which I think is very unfair, but I don't know how else to do it. I had a hard time recording that one, to sing it was like, my throat was starting to close up. We'd have to stop and start it again. But that means it's a good song."[31]

The masterful and musically effective "The River of Dreams," which was coproduced by Joe Nicolo, is truly the album's masterpiece. Harkening back to his doo-wop roots, in this song Billy finds redemption. With a strong gospel chorus behind him, the track represents one of Billy's careerlong high points. Here he sounds renewed, and somehow spiritually realigned. As he explained it, "I still feel very much like an atheist in the religious aspect of things. But there are spiritual planes that I'm aware of that I don't know anything about, that I can't explain. That's why I think musicians are so revered and so important to our culture: We're the wizards, we sort of reveal a little bit of this extra-powerful communicative force. I recently rediscovered that I was enchanted with music and the creative arts as a little child because I thought there was an element of alchemy in them."[10]

As the 1990s marched along, everyone was looking toward the year 2000 as the start of a whole new era. Billy addresses this important passage of time in the effectively slow and building "Two Thousand Years." In the lyrics he looks forward to the new millennium with hope and optimism.

While much of this album revealed his relationships with Christie, Frank Weber, and his daughter, "Famous Last Words" finishes off the album in more ways than one. No one knew at the time that this was going to be the final pop-rock album, and that this was to be the last song on it. Here he reminisces about his life, and how he has put his blood, sweat, and tears into his music for over twenty years; this song represents the end of it all. Although the sentiment is one of sadness, the music that propels it is jaunty and upbeat.

Billy Joel explained of this final track, "On the last album, *River of Dreams*, I'd written what I thought was enough songs and I mentally closed up shop. And then I recorded. And there's another thing, and I would advise people to keep this in mind. It's not an airplane unless it flies. You can draw it like an airplane, you can build it like an airplane, it can be on the runway and look like an airplane, but if it doesn't fly, it's not an airplane. So that's right there with this one song I had towards the end of the *River of Dreams* album. I thought it was going to be the last song, built the airplane, put it on the run way and it wouldn't take off. It laid there like a lox, and it started to smell. I had to take it out back and shoot it. So now here I am, shop's closed, everybody went home. There's 'condemned' on the building. And I can't write. I have got this block, this incredible block."[31]

According to Billy, it was his new producer who prodded this last song out of him. "Danny Korchmar, who was producing the album was just trying to nudge me into writing something: 'C'mon, c'mon, write something else,'" he recalls. "And I think what happens is a lot of writers that he may have been used to working with, always have extra stuff floating around. Or, they just write more. I know a guy like Bruce Springsteen will have way more than enough songs for an album and he'll cull through his material that is best for the album. I don't write like that. I write an album from A to Z. If there's ten songs, I write 'one' through 'ten,' that's it. If I die tomorrow, there's no basement tapes, there's no Billy Joel memorial. You won't find all this Jimi Hendrix stuff flying around. If there ain't an airplane, it doesn't usually get recorded. And I usually know if it's not an airplane before the recording process. However in this case, I didn't know till the recording was made that this thing couldn't fly. So I had to write another song, and it took me weeks and weeks of banging my head against the wall. And the last song I wrote was 'Famous Last Words,' which was very apropos because it's really the last words I have to say. I realized that as I was writing it, I was kind of working this out. . . . It was kind of prophetic because really that's the last complete song with lyrics and words that I wrote. That was 1993."[31]

The cover of the *River of Dreams* album was a painting by Christie Brinkley. It depicts a closed-eye portrait of Billy surrounded by different visions of the subjects addressed in the lyrics of the songs. There is a fishing boat, the Great Wall of China, an angel, an Adam and Eve depiction, rows of cookie-cutter-shaped houses, and urban pollution. It seemed that people either loved this impressionistic illustration or hated it. Stated Billy at the time, "This is her impression of what I look like."[150]

One anonymous Columbia/Sony Records employee reveals of the Brinkley portrait, "She painted that horrendous cover, which—by the way—was a huge source of conflict within the company. Everyone thought it was ugly as hell. He dug his feet in, and certainly he had earned that right."[5] And so, he won this battle.

The single version of "River of Dreams" debuted on the *Billboard* charts the week of July 31, 1993, and the album was officially released on August 10. In the United States the album made Billy Joel history, as it was his first and only album to *enter* the charts at number 1 (the week of August 21, 1993). This was an amazing feat in itself and, record-wise, it doesn't get much better than that. In addition, the "River of Dreams" single also hit number 3 in America. In England, both the album and the single peaked at an impressive number 3. It also contained three more hit singles: "All

About Soul" (number 29 US/number 32 UK), "No Man's Land" (number 50 UK), and "Lullaby (Good Night My Angel)" (number 77 US).

Unlike most of Billy's albums, *River of Dreams* was number 1 before most rock critics could even file their reviews with their publications. However, they were unusually glowing this time around. According to Greg Sandow in *Entertainment Weekly*, "He's shallow, and (a related offense) he's just too slick—a pop machine who will sit down at the piano and bang out a tune, seemingly without stopping to think. . . . He's hardly the writer of empty pop hits that his critical reputation suggests. Even his early albums are full of off-center surprises. . . . But this time it's hard to dismiss him as shallow. The songs rock hard, and his music and singing are too persuasive. . . . *River of Dreams* is a popmeister's epiphany, a pensive record that also manages to be irresistible . . . when he probes this far into himself, it becomes something stronger, almost a state of musical grace."[153]

Richard Corliss in *Time* magazine loved the album and praised Billy: "In a splendid set, the popmeister goes mopin,' hopin and do-woppin' in no-man's land. . . . He surely had the itch to write a song cycle; he is, after all, the last, finest heir to the songwriter tradition of soulful '60s pop. The miracle deal is that *River of Dreams* works not just as a cohesive concept album but also as a bunch of damn fine songs with heart and hooks. . . . He's a hip pontificator—the Boss with a higher I.Q."[154]

Once again it seemed like Billy's business dealings were a virtual minefield of recurring legal problems. The release of this latest album tipped off a new controversy. On August 10, 1993, a $10 million lawsuit was filed in Manhattan Federal Court on behalf of a songwriter by the name of Gary Zimmerman. It seemed that Zimmerman claimed that the songs "River of Dreams," "No Man's Land," and "We Didn't Start the Fire" were all taken from his composition "Nowhere Land." Billy Joel's lawyer, Leonard Marks, went on record as to state, "Billy thinks the suit is utter horse shit."[144] The claims proved unfounded.

Meanwhile, Billy's career continued on a very successful and high-profile vein. On August 30, 1993, he was the first musical guest on the debut of the TV program *Late Show with David Letterman*, when it was first broadcast on CBS-TV, live from the Ed Sullivan Theater on Broadway. Letterman had previously hosted his own nighttime show on NBC-TV, and this was his way of making a ratings splash at his new network home. PBS-TV debuted their documentary *Billy Joel: Shades of Grey* on October 13, which was about the making of the *River of Dreams* album. On the twenty-third of that same month, Billy and his band were the musical guests on *Saturday Night Live.*

During all of this activity, he and the band were on the first leg of their *River of Dreams* tour. They ended 1993 and started 1994 by headlining at Long Island's Nassau Coliseum for five sold-out nights (December 29, 31, and January 2, 6, and 8), grossing $2,874,480.

At the beginning of the year, in *Rolling Stone* magazine, Billy was heralded as the "Best Keyboardist" in the annual Music Awards/Reader's Picks. Conversely, the painting that Christie Brinkley did to grace the cover of *River of Dreams* was chosen as the "Worst Album Cover" in the poll.

Also in January 1994, he was nominated for Grammy Awards in four separate categories for his latest releases: in the categories of Album of the Year (*River of Dreams,*) Best Pop Vocal Performance, Male (the song "River of Dreams"), Record of the Year ("River of Dreams"), and Song of the Year ("River of Dreams"), When the trophies were handed out on March 1, 1994, he lost out to Whitney Houston's *Bodyguard* blockbuster album, the *Aladdin* soundtrack, and to Sting. Amid the international telecast, which was held at the Shrine Auditorium in Los Angeles, Billy was seen performing his hit "River of Dreams."

While on tour in Richfield, Ohio, on March 17, 1994, Billy got a ride to his concert at the Richfield Coliseum in a Richfield Fire Department emergency vehicle. It seems that the van he was riding in was hit by a truck on their way to the venue, so the crew in the emergency vehicle gave him a lift to the show. According to the report, the drivers of the Fire Department vehicle were reprimanded for doing this, as chauffeuring a rock star to a performance was not considered an official "emergency."

It was in April 1994 when the news of Billy and Christie's breakup became public. However, in reality it had been a union that had been slowly dissolving for several years. As early as 1990 the *National Enquirer* had been reporting that the marriage was in trouble. There were published rumors of Billy's picking up a girl in a San Francisco bar and having a hot affair with her, causing a big fight with Christie. Billy denied the story, but Liberty DeVitto states, "It was true."[3]

As things became more and more tense between husband and wife, Billy turned to the bottle. This was especially true on the road, during concert tours. Looking at a Derek Storm photograph of Billy Joel in concert, Liberty DeVitto points to a red plastic drinking cup on the black baby grand piano and says, "If there was a red cup, there was a blue cup also. One had water in it, and the other one was full of Scotch."[3]

In 1991 the *National Enquirer* had been on the case when Billy and Christie got into a huge fight while on vacation in Honolulu. Jerry George, one of the top reporters for the publication, recalls this particular messy altercation: "I went to Hawaii. I was staying at the Kahala Hilton. It was the midnineties, and he was supposedly beating her up—Christie. It was a real scandal at the time. The magazine had me go so far as to go snooping in their garbage at the hotel for any clues."[155]

According to the story, the Joels were staying in room 1132 of that same hotel when an argument ensued. "When Christie shrieked, 'I want a divorce!' Billy went berserk—picking up a lamp and hurling it through a sliding glass door, smashing the door to bits!" When other hotel patrons complained of the sound of yelling and broken glass, security guards were summoned. "Billy was sweating and had a wild look in his eyes. His hands and left leg had been cut by glass and were dripping blood," claimed one source interviewed for the story. Christie took Alexa, and they spent the night elsewhere. According to the article, after refusing medical attention, "Billy ordered a bottle of Scotch and drank himself into oblivion."[156] However, by the next day they had reconciled, and the Joels and their daughter were seen together on the beach.

Their arguments went on through the early nineties with regularity. Said Liberty DeVitto, "When he and Christie used to fight, she used to say, 'If you don't stop this, or if you don't do this, I'm leaving you.' He told me once, he said, 'I finally said to her, "Leave. Because if you do, then you can't threaten me with it anymore."' It was like: 'How can I stop her from telling me to leave?' Leave. 'How can I stop this?' 'Let's get rid of it!' 'What am I gonna do about Doug?' It's your problem. 'I'll get rid of him.'"[62]

Liberty claims that Billy used to unnerve Brinkley so much, he could witness visible signs of the irritated mood her husband would put her in. "Christie was so agitated with him at that point that her face would literally twitch when she was on the phone with Billy. I saw it for myself. As soon as she got on the phone with him, she developed an uncontrollable twitch. That was the effect he had on her."[3]

Yet, they consistently denied their troubles in the press. In 1993 Christie told one interviewer that they were hoping to have more children. And Billy claimed to be happy in July of that year, stating, "I've got a successful career, a beautiful wife."[157] But, Liberty explains, "Christie wanted more kids with Billy, but Billy was always drunk."[3]

While all this was going on, Liberty and Christie always got along well as friends, and very often he found himself in the middle of battles between the couple, not wanting to pick sides. He remembers, "When it was evident that Christie and Billy were going to get a divorce, she would say to me, 'You may have to take the stand in my defense!' She knew that I knew the real story about their marriage falling apart."[3]

By Thanksgiving 1993, the couple had started living separate lives; however, they did their best to maintain their friendship. When Billy had a recurrence of kidney stones in February 1994, Christie was there for him, playing nursemaid. However, by then she was already dating wealthy businessman Rick Taubman. In early April, she accepted an invitation from Taubman to come out to Telluride, Colorado, to go skiing with him. The plan was to go heli-skiing, which entails taking a helicopter to a remote slope and skiing down on the fresh snow. When they took the helicopter to the top of a summit, the spot it landed on was not stable, and a crosswind hit the blades of the aircraft. The helicopter rolled down a forty-degree slope for more than two hundred feet. The tail of the helicopter broke off, and Taubman was thrown from the vehicle's passenger compartment.

Rick Taubman sustained several broken ribs, as well as breaks to his collarbone and scapula. Christie was unharmed for the most part, aside from some bruises and a sore wrist. Billy, who was on a concert tour at the time, came rushing to her side and accompanied her back to their home on Long Island. After she was stable, Billy returned to his scheduled *River of Dreams* concert performances, for the tour was concurrently underway. Christie then returned to Colorado, and to Taubman's side, with Alexa in tow.

Billy admitted that as his marriage to Brinkley came to an end he sought the help of a therapist. "Yeah, yeah, sure—toward the end of the relationship with Christie," he said. "I thought, 'Maybe it's me?' But it didn't teach me anything. The piano was a better therapist. Whenever I've been down or hurt, I can go to the piano, and I feel so much better when I walk away."[11]

Was he upset by the divorce? "Yes," he claimed. "If you want to stay married, do not become a touring musician. But my big, big reason for being upset was that Christie and my daughter were going to be living in Colorado. And [that] my daughter could be taken far away from me was absolutely unbelievable. I think I speak for a lot of divorced fathers when I voice my dissatisfaction with being second-class parents."[11]

At the time, Billy Zampino was serving as the tour's road manager. He recalls, "On April 16, 1994, in Miami, I was on tour with Billy and I knew he was distressed about the breakup of his marriage to Christie, and not being able to see enough of his daughter, Alexa. Suddenly, he cut 'Movin' Out' from his set because a local writer had wrongly said it was a slap at Christie. Instead, he substituted 'Shades of Grey' from *River of Dreams*. But as a prelude, he went into 'Adagio For Strings,' playing it on his synthesizer's string setting. I looked at the pain on his face, and it was a heart-rending moment. But that's one of Billy's greatest: He finds ways to preserve and keep alive the things he loves."[10]

In August 1994 the Billy-Christie divorce was finalized, and Brinkley almost immediately married Rick Taubman. In early 1995 she gave birth to their son, Jack. When Jack was only six weeks old, Christie ended up leaving Taubman and Colorado, and she moved back to New York City. She then divorced Taubman.

Liberty DeVitto remembers that Billy's split from Christie put him in an uncomfortably awkward position. Speaking of his friendship with Billy, Liberty explained, "Well, the relationship went downhill when he and Christie broke up. I had a hard time, because of the relationship that my family had with Billy and Christie and Alexa. My ex-wife was continuing to be friends with Christie. So I was caught in the middle. He's the boss, he's going *that* way. He doesn't want to have anything to do with Christie, and I am going to visit with her, because I'm bringing my kids to see Alexa. He would tell me, 'I like that Alexa and your daughters are friends. It's good.' But then he'd say, 'Now, watch what you say.' You know, sometimes I would just be talking."[62]

Meanwhile, after Billy announced his split from Christie, the *River of Dreams* tour continued into the spring. It ended with two dates at the Forum in Los Angeles on April 29 and 30. It then went across the Atlantic Ocean to play several dates in Europe. May 7, 9, and 11 found Billy and his band headlining at Earls Court Exhibition Centre in London, England. With just a few short weeks between them, the *River of Dreams* tour came to an end, and an exciting new concept tour was to begin.

It was truly an inspired idea to put Billy Joel and Elton John together to create an entire concert event from their pairing. In terms of creating a box-office smash, this virtually guaranteed sellout crowds wherever the tour was booked. In fact, it was such a hit that the concert tour with these two piano men continued to be mounted for several years to come.

The tour concept was a hit the minute that they launched it. One of their first joint bookings was at Giants Stadium in East Rutherford, New Jersey, on July 22, 24, 26, 28, and 29, 1994. All five shows sold out at a reported box office gross of $14,889,127. As Liberty DeVitto explained to the press during one of the Joel/John tours, "Elton's having a gas with Billy. Where we couldn't sell out in certain markets, Elton carries us. And where Elton couldn't sell out, we carry him. So it's great, we're lovin' it."[158]

Elton is openly gay, British, very flamboyant in his mode of dress, and has based much of his career on being as outrageous as possible. Also, in the past he had his own substance abuse demons that he confronted, and he was at this point in time "clean and sober." Billy is heterosexual, has a tough scrappy attitude, almost exclusively dresses in black, and at the time was a heavy Scotch drinker. Although Elton John and Billy Joel were—and are—totally different people in their personal lives, their mutual love and respect of music put them on a complete parallel.

One of the things that Billy liked the most about Elton was their mutual love of music, and of performing live. Said Billy in 1994, "I recently talked with Elton, and he asked me who I felt kinship to musically. I said, 'I actually feel a kinship with [George Gershwin], because Gershwin always started with the music and then he had somebody else write the lyrics.' The old, traditional way of writing a song in America, going back to Stephen Foster was taking poetry and setting it to music. Very few songwriters actually wrote the music first and then wrote lyrics."[10]

One former Columbia Records employee remembers how successful the Elton/Billy tours were from the very start. Claims the source, "At that time, 1993, he was still getting played on top 40 radio. This was before all the 'rap' stuff happened, and kids who can't sing. This was back when it was okay to be a singer-songwriter, and it was still popular. So, there was a big push to force him to put out more music. So then they put out the Russian concert, and they started putting together compilation after compilation, *Greatest Hits Volume I, Greatest Hits Volume II,* as a means of keeping him in the public eye. When the Billy Joel/Elton John collaboration was presented, the story that was told to us was that they were both sick of playing their old songs, so they would get together, play their songs, but also play each other's songs. And they did have an extraordinarily good time on that tour. And that was also one of the first times Billy stopped drinking, because Elton wasn't drinking or doing any drugs anymore. That was one of his most sober periods, supposedly because Elton had some strict rule. They say that that was a very cogent period of his life. And, I know that they loved doing the tour together, because I had them doing that tour all over the country. I was in New York by then. That was true fun. They were having fun, the audience was having fun. It was a good thing."[5]

On September 7, 1994, after his first tour with Elton was completed, Billy appeared with James Taylor at a benefit at David's Island House on Martha's Vineyard in Massachusetts. And, October 3 found him doing his master class sessions at the Ivy League Harvard University. The event was billed as "An Evening of Questions and Answers and Perhaps a Few Songs" and held at Harvard's Sanders Theater, in Cambridge, Massachusetts. Later that month, on October 17, Billy Joel's solo *River of Dreams* tour continued, with a sold-out night at the Gateway Arena in Cleveland, Ohio. That evening the place was packed to the rafters with a crowd of 19,687 screaming fans.

While Billy continued to tour, his entire catalog of albums continued to sell. In 1994, the RIAA certified several of his releases multiple platinum for sales into the millions. They included *Songs in the Attic* and *The Nylon Curtain* (double platinum), *Storm Front* (quadruple platinum), and *52nd Street*, *Glass Houses*, and *An Innocent Man* (septuple platinum). Topping them all at 9 million copies was *The Stranger*.

His marriage to Christie was all over, Alexa was now in Colorado with his mother, and Billy began to feel very alone. He began drinking heavily. Liberty DeVitto claims of one such alcoholic-infused incident, "We got drunk on the airplane, and we were walking through the Dallas airport and he's like, 'Get the fuck out of my way, I'm Billy Joel! Get out of my way!'"[62]

An anonymous source who worked at Columbia Records at the time was responsible for bringing local radio personalities backstage to meet Joel in the cities in which he was performing. The former Columbia employee claims that Billy was often drunk and rude after the shows were over. A plan had to be devised to keep the press from seeing this side of him.

"He was always polite," the person recalls. "He was more cognizant than most artists are, of the role that people in the rest of the country play. There was never an issue in particular that way. What would happen though, was that when we would take people for a 'meet and greet,' after the show, when he was drinking, he could get mean. What I ended up doing with him— since you are in charge of your own area—I started asking, 'Could we please do it during the [preshow] soundcheck, before the drinking starts?' It wasn't so much a 'nasty drunk,' but it was like he couldn't give a shit. And the people who were coming back to meet him usually are adoring fans or programmers. You know, stand for a photo, sign some stupid things, and get it over with. So, I found I had to—that I made that request—and it ended up that the whole country fell in line with that."[5]

BILLY JOEL

By November 14, 1994, Billy and his band were in Australia, on the international leg of his *River of Dreams* tour. Just as Frank Sinatra had done so many times in the past, Billy Joel announced that this present tour was going to be the last one of his entire career. While still in Australia, he was seen on international television on December 7, accepting *Billboard* magazine's "Century Award," which was given to him in commemoration of his entire lifetime of career accomplishments. The presentation was made by singer Tori Amos, and seen on Fox-TV via satellite from Sydney.

For an essay in *Billboard* magazine, Timothy White included statements from both of Billy's parents. According to his mother, Rosalind, "Billy should love himself half as much as others love him and then he'd be in good shape." And, stated his father, Howard, "It's fantastic what's he's done. He works very hard, and he's got a certain measure of luck, but he's a very talented fellow."[10]

January 1995 found Billy and his band in Japan, still amid the *River of Dreams* world tour. The final dates were played on January 23 and 24, 1995, at the Budokan venue in Tokyo.

The beginning of 1995 found Billy back on the road with Elton John, breaking attendance records wherever they went. On April 13 and 14 they set new records at Joe Robbie Stadium in Miami, Florida. The box office gross was $4,385,725 for their two dates at that venue, where they performed in front of a cumulative total of 103,694 concert fans. On July 30 Billy made an appearance at the Newport Rhythm and Blues Festival in Newport, Rhode Island, at the Fort Adams State Park.

Only a year after Kurt Cobain of the rock group Nirvana took his life by shooting himself in the head with a shotgun, former Billy Joel bass player Doug Stegmeyer did the same thing. Prior to his August 24, 1995, suicide, Doug was quite verbal to friends and associates about how it was his unceremonious firing by Billy that had begun the downward spiral that drove him to take his own life.

At this point in time it had been more than twenty years since all of these Long Island friends had first met, played together, and defined the hit-making sound of the Billy Joel band. An awful lot of water had flowed under the bridge since then. There were differences of opinion, bad feelings, separations, and—in the case of Richie Cannata—reconciliations. For the most part, when Billy Joel is finished with his relationships, it was final. This was certainly the case with Doug Stegmeyer, Russell Javors, and eventually even Liberty DeVitto. Once the friendship and working relationship with Billy Joel was over, Doug was never able to get beyond the disappointment.

Liberty recalls the events that led to Doug's banishment from the Joel camp: "We went to Russia in 1987. On the tour for the Russian album, we went on tour to Australia twice. After that, Doug was cut off. He had been with Billy from 1973 to 1987. That was the peak. The album *Storm Front* peaked again, because of 'We Didn't Start the Fire'; Doug wasn't on that. Here he was in on creating the monster that became 'Billy Joel,' yet he was reduced to listening to the constant reminders that the band was still on top, but without him. He would still get people calling him on the phone and saying, 'Hey, I see you and Billy are coming here on tour . . . can you get me tickets?' Then it becomes, 'Well, why are you out of the group?' And poor Doug would have to honestly say, 'I don't know why.'"[63]

What were Doug's feelings about this banishment? Says Liberty, "He was very bitter about it. You don't get fired, you just don't get asked back for the next tour. Like I didn't get officially fired. I was just not asked to go back again. So, when you're not asked back to do something, it's always this feeling of, 'Well, maybe next time I'll be asked again.' And that always lingers in your head, and then people look at you and go, 'Get it through your skull, you're done.' And you either accept it, or you go, 'No, no, I think that there's still hope here.' Or, you just can't believe, 'How can I be "done?" I've given this person everything! What did I do wrong?' Doug could never get over that. Never get over that. Never could imagine what he did wrong. And he didn't do anything wrong. He had a problem. So, instead of us trying to fix it, Billy said, 'Get somebody else.'"[62]

Liberty remembers seeing Doug from time to time, following his firing: "After he was cut off, he would come to some of the shows. I don't know how he did it, but he would come to Nassau Coliseum, and he would watch somebody else playing his stuff—the music that he created. It is hard to go from Billy Joel's fame, to like, nothing. Nothing."[63]

Frank Sagarese, who used to play with Doug and Liberty at the Long Island catering hall all those years ago, distinctly recalls, "Doug was a good bass player, a nice guy, easygoing. No head trips, no ego. Nothing. Just a nice guy. We had this thing that we were rehearsing and then he and Liberty just took off, and the next thing I knew they just took off and they were on TV and doing it all. I really lost contact with them when they took off to play with Billy."[61]

Sagarese did his best to stay in touch with his old friends. "At one point I invited Liberty and Doug out to my in-laws' home in the Hamptons, and we had spent a weekend out there. We were pretty good friends. Then just as a coincidence, I was teaching elementary school in Massapequah and

I ended up teaching Liberty's daughter, Devon. She was playing saxophone at the time, and she started taking piano lessons. I taught her for about a year, a year and a half. And Russell Javors, his son was at the same school. They must have all moved to that one area in Massapequah. So the kids all ended up at the same elementary school, and I was the band director there. This was Birch Lane Elementary School. And that was in the Bar Harbor section of Massapequah. That was the more upscale section of that town."[61]

Frank also remembers, "I guess that when they went for their tour of Japan, or whereever they went for a long time, Liberty's daughter traveled with them. And her homework assignment was to keep a journal and a photo album of her experience on the trip. And when she came back, I got to see some of that. And when they stopped over in Hawaii on the way back, the whole band was there—Christie Brinkley and the whole crew. So I got to see some of that, and what my old musician buddies were up to, through her pictures."[61]

Richie Cannata recalls that after he left the Billy Joel band in the early eighties, for a long time he lost touch with Billy, Liberty, and Doug: "I love Liberty to death, but he was busy doing the Billy gig. I didn't hear from those guys, Doug, either. I think that they thought they were in a better position than I was, and that they were always gonna be taken care of, which was not always the case. I took care of myself. And, I think financially—I don't know if I did better—but I think I did. I am not boasting about that, but I socked enough away to be able to do my own projects." He appeared on the albums of several high-profile artists: "Brian Wilson's record, I played on. I produced Tommy Shaw [of Styx], and Lita Ford [of the Runaways]."[44] Richie's successful Long Island studio became the site of several mainstream recording projects, including LPs by Celine Dion, Taylor Dayne, and the soundtrack album for the film *Chicago*. It was an investment that has accrued in value and kept him involved in the music business.

Not everyone from the Joel camp was so fortunate. Richie Cannata explains, "I look at what the other musicians who have played with Billy had done since their gigs with Billy. Mark Rivera is a car salesman. They all do these other things. I am able to do what I want. I think at that time, when I left the band, I think that Doug and Lib thought they had one up on me."[44]

He always felt odd whenever a Billy Joel tour was announced, and family and friends assumed that he would have full access to concert tickets.

Richie says, "I think my family had a tougher time of it than I had, because they didn't have anywhere to go when Billy came to town and he played Madison Square Garden. I didn't care. I found my 'jam' nights, I found my own gigs, I found that I was just really happy playing. I became a ten-times-better player. And I am a better player now than I was back then."[44]

Once he left Billy Joel's band, Richie felt somewhat deserted by his friends, "I lost contact with those guys. One thing that bothered me, that happened," he recalls with sadness, "I think that people don't have to change when they become successful or famous, they don't really have to. You really don't have to. If you really got to a place because of people who helped you get where you are, then you should reconnect with them. My father had passed away, and not one of them called. And, they knew my dad, and someone should have called me. Someone should have said, 'I'm sorry your dad died.' They knew my dad, and I was very, very close to my father. That was another confirmation that maybe I made the right decision. Not one of them showed up at the funeral. And they live out here. I thought that was a little bit on the bad side. But you know what? I let it go. My family was irate about it. They said, 'How could your friends do that?' I said, 'Hey, maybe they're not my friends.'"[44]

While Richie took his money and invested it well, the other guys were welded to the gig with Billy, subject to his whims and his schedule. That was their main source of income. "They were totally strapped and dependant to that," Richie says. "Unfortunately, it became less and less. Billy toured less, and then Doug was gone."[44]

Says Richie, "Doug was the keeper of the band. He basically got all of us in the band. His brother found me. I think he put the thing together with Liberty. He never let us forgot that, and he was very emotional about that. When we would be interviewed or introduced in front of twenty thousand people, 'On guitar, Doug Stegmeyer,' he would draw modest applause. He was the bass player, he never got the huge applause. He was a little bitter about it. I wasn't there when he got fired. He got fired—unlike myself. And David Brown got fired. Everyone else got fired, and these guys heard about it on the radio. Billy had hired a new band, and they didn't even know that something had happened. Doug couldn't get used to life after Billy Joel."[44]

His longtime friend Bruce Gentile recalls that Doug's depression was fueled by his habitual drug dependency. "Doug Stegmeyer went through a lot of money because his nose got very big. You know that Al Stewart song, 'Time Passages?' With Doug, I used to parody that song as 'Nasal Passages.'

Whenever I would run into Doug, he would come in and ask me, 'Who's got drugs here?'"[36]

When Doug Stegmeyer opened his own recording studio, one of the aspiring Long Island musicians who sought out his services was a singer-songwriter by the name of Steve Ericson. Along the five-year span of their working together in the studio they became quite good friends. "I had met Doug in 1990," recalls Ericson. "This was around the time that I had just broken up with my band. I tried a couple of other attempts at putting a band together. I thought, 'I want to go and find another studio where I feel comfortable again.' I had worked in one studio, but they had closed down. But it was great. It was in this guy's house, and his name was Donny Williamson, and he was just a really great guy. It was just a very relaxed atmosphere. After my band broke up and Donny went out of business, I thought, 'I want to record my songs again. I want to go into the studio just to prove that I could do it without a band.' Be my own little Billy Joel, I guess."[159]

He decided to book some studio time, and record some of his own compositions. "I tried checking out some of the places on Long Island. I was flipping through the *Good Times* magazine, and there was a little ad there that said, 'Stegmeyer Studios. Let my experience of working in the industry, with Bill Joel for over fifteen years, help you succeed in the business.' This was 1990. I called him up, and said, 'Yeah, I'd love to meet with you. Come on over, and I will show you my studio and tell you what I am all about. If you want to come by, why don't you come by tomorrow?' And, I said, 'Sure.' He said, 'Well how about seven thirty, have to leave at eight, but why don't you come by at about seven thirty, and I will try and give you as much time as I have?'"[159] Steve agreed to that plan.

The next evening Ericson went to see Doug's at-home studio setup, at the appointed time. He recalls how proudly the bass player talked of his time as part of the Billy Joel band. "He was a really nice guy with short spiky hair on top, with a mullet-type deal going on. And, he said, 'Hey come on in.' I knew that he said that he was with Billy Joel, but he didn't say to what capacity. I was walking around with him, and he's got gold records everywhere. And he was like, 'Oh yeah, I played bass with Billy for like fifteen years, and these were all of the albums I was on."[159]

Ericson and Stegmeyer struck up a nice rapport and talked and listened to music from seven thirty until nine in the evening. Doug encouraged Steve to forget the material that he had written with his former group, and to write some new songs that expressed his thoughts at the present time.

Both men were actively trying to move forward in their lives and found that they shared a lot in common.

Steve recalls that Doug was looking for an artist whom he could manage and produce, as he saw his future as being in the production end of the business. When it came time for Steve to return and record his new songs, Doug assumed the role of recording producer. He even played bass on several tracks that Steve recorded.

According to Steve there were other disappointments in Doug's life, "At this same time, Debbie Gibson had asked him to work on her album. He told me he was going to do it, and then the next time I came in, he had done it, and he said, 'They want me to go on tour with them.'" However, things did not work out the way that Doug had expected. Says Steve, "At the last minute, when he was all set to go, they pulled the plug on him, and decided to go with a more ethnic-based band—Debbie. And Doug was confounded: like, 'How could she have done this to me?'"[159]

Time passed, and Steve suddenly got the urge to move to Florida. After two years in the Sunshine State, he was disenchanted with it. Having gotten that out of his system, he returned to Long Island, revived his dreams of writing and recording his own songs. He tracked down Doug Stegmeyer, and they revived their friendship and working relationship. Doug was setting up a new studio in a different location, and Steve would check in with him every couple of weeks. Finally Stegmeyer was ready for Ericson to resume recording with him as the producer.

Steve recalls, "He always spoke about Billy with a lot of respect. Billy was still his friend, but he was very hurt by what happened. Very hurt. I don't think that he completely blamed Billy for what was happening, I think he blamed Christie Brinkley for changing Billy into what he was becoming. . . . When Christie Brinkley came into the picture, suddenly Billy wasn't hanging out with the guys after the show. He was pretty distant from everybody. She was trying to mold him and the band into being more 'user friendly' to the public."[159]

Steve would have long conversations with Doug, who "had said that he couldn't believe that all of the musicians who were with Billy: suddenly one guy was homeless, another guy was having to work in a grocery store, and he was totally dumbfounded. These people poured their hearts and their souls into making great music, and now they were penniless and having to fight for their money. And, I guess that Doug had also reached that point. He had some money, but not nearly like where he could rest on his laurels."[159]

BILLY JOEL

According to Steve, Doug claimed that Billy Joel turned down his requests for financial help. "I heard this from Liberty in our e-mails, that Doug had actually asked Billy for help, and that's when Billy cut him off, and told him through the manager that it's not working out."[159]

He also reveals that Doug lived with the hope that eventually he would be invited back into the band he helped to form. "As musicians, we always believe that one day, they're gonna call you back and say, 'You know what? It was a mistake. You should come back.' I think that he hoped that Billy would say, 'Hey you know, I'm really sorry.' He never did. As a matter of fact, from what I heard . . . was that he was excommunicated, and nobody was allowed to speak to him."[159]

Another thing that Steve Ericson observed, was the way wannabe musicians would look at Doug Stegmeyer as a mere stepping stone to get to the Piano Man. "People would come to the studio for interviews, and it was all about Billy Joel," says Steve. "Nobody wanted to know who Doug Stegmeyer was. They didn't want to know about Doug Stegmeyer, they wanted to know, 'Is there dirt on Billy Joel?' 'Can you introduce me to Billy Joel?' And the poor guy was just kicked in the ass by Billy Joel, the last thing that he wanted to do was have people walking around going, 'Hey, what can you do for us?' . . . It seemed to wear on him."[159]

Steve spoke to Doug near the end of his life. At the time Doug was complaining of a nagging toothache, then the last straw came when his beloved pet dog was terminally ill. Then there were a couple of business deals that went sour as well. Steve also remembers a set of audio tapes that Doug was not properly paid for, which the bass player subsequently refused to release. This unleashed a series of harassing calls from lawyers. "They were really wanting these tapes," Steve claims. "They were like, 'We're gonna sue you,' and Doug said, 'Over my dead body.' And they said, 'All right, if that's what it takes.'"[159]

Another topic that they had openly discussed was the recent suicide of Kurt Cobain by self-inflicted rifle wound. Around this same time, Steve noticed that Doug started going out with some buddies who liked to go to a rifle-firing range. Doug Stegmeyer enjoyed firing the rifles and became something of a gun enthusiast.

Looking back at the week prior to Doug's suicide, Steve observes, "I would say that there was a downward spiral. I spoke to Doug the Monday before he went. You could see everything chipping away at Doug. And I could tell towards the end—hindsight being 20/20—then you can see it.

. . . All these little things, and he was doing the best he could to let it all roll off of his back, and try and keep going, and try and keep focus. I think that one thing led to another, and then he just snapped. I think it was part the 'Billy Joel wannabes,' part this deal that was going south with the tape he had made, and then there was some fighting with his brother-in-law. . . . I think he just reached a break point where it was like: 'This isn't my life anymore, this is Billy's shadow's life. I don't want to be Billy's shadow anymore."[159]

Steve Ericson details the great lengths to which Stegmeyer went to tie up all of the loose ends in his life: "The scary thing was, that he put Post-It notes on everything that he wanted people to have: all his gold records, his guitars. He put Post-It notes everywhere. And then he took the people's stuff [recordings] that he was working on, and he put Post-It notes on them, and lined them up on the recording console before he killed himself."[159]

Steve, of course, only heard Doug's side of the story and says with bitterness, "If Billy needed help, these guys would give their shirts, their blood, their organs—whatever—to help Billy. But when Billy was in a position to help them, just a little bit, he told them to 'Go fuck themselves.' And that's the bottom line. And I think that it is so sad that these guys gave up their lives. They could have gone on and done other things with their lives, but they dedicated their lives to this man who obviously didn't have any regard for them. In the end, they were just the help.[159]

"Also, Billy apparently had a lot of resentment towards him, that he wrote a song about him called 'Money or Love.' I thought that was kinda cheesy, 'cause Doug was all about the love of the music. It wasn't money to him, but when he couldn't pay his bills, and he asked Billy for help, and Billy kicked him in the ass.[159]

"When Doug finally did what he did, I had to step back and think about this. Was this really worth all that? He was a fantastic guy, and I wish to God that there was something I could have done to help him."[159]

The news of Doug's suicide was very haunting to his old friend Frank Sagarese. "I have no idea what that was about," he claims. "I thought to myself, 'This poor guy must have gone through a lot of crap to get to this point in his life.' When we were all playing at that catering hall we were all about twenty years old or so. I was a little older than that, because I was in college and teaching school at the same time, and these guys were playing their music and trying to make it as musicians. And, they did. The shame of it is that Doug isn't around to talk about it. I don't know what transpired there for that to have happened. He was just one of those nice guys you meet along the way. I was happy for his success. And then when I heard that he took his own life, that was devastating."[61]

Said Russell Javors, "Doug had his problems. And, I didn't always agree with everything he did. But we were brothers. You know, I loved the guy like a brother. And he just couldn't . . ." he said, and then he suddenly stopped midsentence. Then he took a deep breath and continued. "You know, once Billy happened, and we had a certain measure of fame, and that's the kind of lifestyle that really draws you in. And after a while his identity got wrapped up in it. He was an important part of that band, and it was what it was. I used to tell him, 'You forget that you were part of something, man. You have nothing to be ashamed of. You know, things happen in life.' I would try to pump him up."[65]

What did Russell think or feel about Doug's suicide? When asked that question he answers, "This is a tough one. Doug was my best friend. We had an apartment together for a while. He was the best man at my wedding. We had a great chemistry together as musicians. After it ended with Billy, I knew he was depressed. I would tell him to move on. That what he did was important and that he should be proud of it, but that he had to turn the page. When I look back now, I can see the clues. Right before he died, I had the sketch of a song. I called him up and said that we should make some time to lay it down. That we both needed to remind ourselves who we were. I had a complete melody, but only a couple of lyrics. I was hoping it would come together for me when I got together with him. We made plans to get together sometime in the next week. I called his studio to confirm the date. I spoke to his friend Kato (John Mongiardo), who worked with him in the studio. John said that Doug would call me back. He never did. The next day I got a call from my friend Dean. He and a guitarist, Neil Posner, had a session with Doug that day. They saw Doug's car outside, but the door to the studio was locked. They broke in and found Doug. I'm the one who called everyone to tell them what happened. It was like losing a brother."[64]

Richie Cannata says of Doug Stegmeyer, "He had a tough time. He had issues. He had his demons. We all do. He was sorting them out. And, I think his demons took control. He did 'the death dance,' so to speak. Where he prepared for his suicide, where he wrote letters. He said good-bye to people. He gave 'Blondie,' which was his bass, to Billy. He gave checks and deposits back. He had a little studio that failed. It was failing, and wasn't doing great at all. He had one before that. His dog has passed away. It was a great dog. We all loved his dog, which he had for years. It was a downward spiral. He had clients at the studio, and he made sure that all of the tapes went to the right person. And, then he wrapped himself up in a blanket and shot himself. To do that—I don't know if it's 'courage.' What it takes to do that, I can't imagine. Why not just concentrate those efforts in putting it back together as opposed to pulling it apart. In one of his letters he said, 'Let me just do this. When I get my feet back on the ground, and when I do I'll be back.' I thought it was just a temporary thing. And, he put a shotgun to his head, in his studio."[44]

Richie remembers how he learned about the tragedy: "Billy called me first. I was on the road with the Beach Boys, and he called me: 'Rico.' 'Hey Billy, what's up man?' 'Doug's dead.' 'Wow!' So, it was a tough one for us. I think we all took a little guilt. I know Billy must have. I did, and Liberty definitely did. Then we all got mad. We went through an angry period. 'Fuck you, man! How could you do that? How could you do that to us? You make us live with this for the rest of our lives. Taking the weak way out to save yours? That's not fair, man. You should have come to us, let us help you.' 'I'm on the verge of suicide, man, I need help. I'm thinking about it.' He definitely just didn't do it on a whim. No, he planned this thing. He did 'the death dance'—I call it. He could have called me up and said, 'This is really weird, I am thinking about killing myself, and I am planning this whole thing. Can someone come over here? Can somebody help me? I'm really not well. Can somebody get me into a hospital?' That's what I wish I would have done. I think that Billy says that. I know I did, and that Liberty did. I was disconnected. Doug would come here a bunch of times looking for work. Looking for help. I had put him on this record: [Beach Boy] Al Jardine's son, Matt Jardine. I produced a record for him, and I used Liberty and Doug on it. I tried to help. Again, I was that same person. I had left the band, and they were all out there on the road. I was open armed to him. That's the music business. And Doug and Liberty were great on that session. Shortly after that, Doug took his life. It was really hard for me. I didn't know how to approach it.[44]

"And then his family did something very cool. Where 'Scenes from an Italian Restaurant' was written about, was this Italian restaurant in Syosset, Long Island, called Christiano's. And they had like a cool little reception there. We all came there, and Liberty did not show up. I wonder why. I never knew. And that's how we said good-bye to Doug. I still have his name in my Rolodex. I look at it every day. I remember what he looked like when he was healthy. He had put on a lot of weight, and he was troubled. He was definitely troubled."[44]

In an e-mail Russell Javors wrote, "I have attached a copy of the Doug song demo. It's just me playing acoustic guitar and singing. David Brown did the drum loop. I never went into the studio to record it for real. Anyway, it turned out that the lyrics were about Doug all along."[64] When downloaded, the attached MP3 sound file revealed a sensitively sung and performed composition that Javors entitled, "Best of Me." It remains a rare but fitting tribute to Stegmeyer.

Says Russell, "For years we couldn't even watch the videos because Doug was in them. To this day, I still have Doug's guitar pick with me, that I usually carry so that I don't forget him."[65]

Liberty DeVitto recalls that Doug was often in a negative frame of mind, so that it was difficult to discern just how depressed Doug really was. "The last couple of messages that I had on my answering machine, I am listening to him talking to me: 'Please call me back.' He sounds bad, but not *that* bad."[62]

Liberty DeVitto reveals, "There is a note somewhere that the lawyer had—I don't know if he still has it; he's not a lawyer anymore, but he was representing Doug—that Doug wrote to Billy. The lawyer told me, 'I'm not showing this to Billy.' He out and out blames Billy for why Doug shot himself.[62]

"Doug took this note to a lawyer. Doug shot himself. Doug directly said [in the note], 'It's Billy for being so fucking cheap.'"[62]

To this day, Liberty DeVitto speaks of Doug Stegmeyer with a deep sadness: "Nobody really killed him, but we coulda done a hell of a lot more to keep him alive."[62]

16
TWO THOUSAND YEARS

NOW IN HIS midforties, Billy Joel completely turned his back on the idea of ever recording another new album of rock & roll music. Instead he filled his time with concert touring, recording an occasional single song or two for a soundtrack or a compilation album, and listening to and writing classical music. In his love life, during the rest of the decade, Billy found himself dating a series of different women. Although his career was at such a high pinnacle that he could afford to creatively coast through on his laurels for the next couple of years, in his personal life he was undeniably in a steady downward spiral. During this period he was drinking Scotch and wine very heavily, and by the beginning of the new century he had noticeably begun to lose control of his life.

According to Liberty DeVitto, the latter part of the nineties saw some of Billy's heaviest onstage drinking problems: "There is a photograph that a fan took during one of the Elton John/Billy Joel concerts which captures Billy drunk onstage, tripping over a monitor, and falling to the stage floor in the middle of the show. This took place at Giants Stadium in 1995. Elton took Billy out to talk to him after that photo was taken."[37]

An anonymous VH1 employee recalls attending one of Billy's master class sessions, and she got a startling surprise. "I was there to watch the show and was seated in the front row. Throughout the duration of the performance, Billy had a big bottle of Evian water and a plastic cup with him onstage, which he continually drank from. At the end of the show I went to take his cup and bottle offstage and got a good wiff of the liquid in the cup, and realized the bottle of Evian was just a front. It was pure liquor!"[160]

In October 1995 Billy was one of the featured performers included on the album *Tower of Song: The Songs of Leonard Cohen*. Cohen was one of his all-time favorite singer-songwriters, and for this album Billy gladly recorded his interpretation of one of Cohen's compositions. The LP also featured Cohen songs recorded by Elton John, Don Henley, Bono, Willie Nelson, Suzanne Vega, Sting, Peter Gabriel, and Trisha Yearwood. Billy's contribution was his recording of "Light as a Breeze." The song was recorded in Nashville, produced by Tony Brown, and featured the harmonica of Clint Black, with background vocals by Yearwood.

Throughout the 1990s the double-star billing of Billy Joel and Elton John in concert continued to be a recurring draw. They even compared notes on songwriting. In 1996 Billy told *The Performing Songwriter* magazine, "It's interesting. I'm staying here with my daughter and I talked to her about this project I'm doing with Elton. Now Elton gets lyrics from Bernie Taupin and says to me, 'See what you think.' I'm looking at these lyrics and I can't make head or tail of how to do this, because what it means to me is that the music is secondary to the lyric. In other words, the music isn't the motivational beginning of the song getting written. That's how Elton does it. And that's actually—that's the—traditional way to write a song, is to take a poem and set it to music. That's how a lot of songs got written. A lot of writers write like that. I'm the opposite."[31]

Liberty DeVitto claims that the collaborative tours with Elton John were among the most enjoyable experiences he had in his three decades on the road with Billy Joel. "That was probably some of the best stuff we ever did," he says with a smile. "I got to talk to Elton John, like, for two minutes, every night. Billy and Elton would go up and just do the pianos. Then Elton's band would go up and do an hour. We would go up and do an hour. And then both bands do the encores. So, before we go up for the encores, I would come back down offstage after our hour, stand by the side of the stage. Then Elton would come out, and we'd both have a foot on the stairs, going on up to the stage. He would ask me about Billy, how he is tonight. And 'How are things going?' It was nice just chatting. I wore a hat, every show, and I would ask him if this hat made me look 'gay.' He would say, 'You always look gay to me!'" Liberty laughs. "He was just a wonderful, wonderful human being."[63]

Liberty believes Elton is one of the most down-to-earth stars he has ever worked with; Elton knows he is a star, knows he is eccentric, and plays it to the hilt. "He's one of those people who have come to the fact of knowing who he is: 'This is what I am, and this is what I do. I am a pop star, musician, creative writer. I can't live without doing this.'" says Liberty. "Stevie Nicks is like that. Paul McCartney is like that. But there are some people who just go, 'I want to be a normal human being.' Well, you're not. Sorry. It's not gonna work."[63]

On February 28, 1996, Billy Joel was one of the guest stars on the telecast of the annual Grammy Awards. They were broadcast live, and Billy was to perform a salute to a pair of deceased musical legends. That same year, Frank Sinatra was nominated in the category of "Best Traditional Pop Album" for *Duets II*, which was produced by Phil Ramone. Sinatra won the award. However, when he took center stage to give his acceptance speech, he was unceremoniously cut off for a commercial break. This is how TV treats a show business legend like Frank Sinatra? Well, Billy was quite verbal when he saw that happen.

Said Billy at the time, "They treat music like a bastard child. It's just for their purpose, they don't care how they cut it. They cut Frank Sinatra off at the Grammys, they had to do a commercial. So the guy was rambling, so what? He's Frank Sinatra, let him ramble. But they've got to get in their commercial. So they did this show. James Woods introduces me, and I'm a fan of James Woods, so I was impressed by that. And I do this acceptance speech. It wasn't a long speech. But part of this speech is that I nod my head to the fact that that year, two of the greatest American composers who ever lived [had] died—Leonard Bernstein and Aaron Copland. And I was actually choked up to say their names. I owe a great debt to these two great composers, and then I watched the re-broadcast of the show and they cut that whole part of the speech out. I said, 'Why did you cut that out? It was only about five seconds, ten seconds tops.' 'We had to cut it for air time, commercial time.' Why would you cut out Aaron Copland and Leonard Bernstein? People need to hear that. Kids need to hear those names. They decided that they didn't need to be heard. Editing. Always try to have control of the editing. If it's got to be done, you might as well do it."[31]

That spring, Billy was kept busy, making several of his visits to college campuses, delivering his question-and-answer formatted master classes.

As one former Columbia Records executive explains, "Billy decided to go on the road and do these kind of master classes. . . . So, I went on the road to do these classes and he was doing them at colleges for music students, and it was billed as 'Some Stories, A Cautionary Tale, and a Little Bit of Music.' So what he would do, he would get up and he had a piano, and he would fiddle around, but he would talk mostly. And he would talk a lot about watching your money, how to do it. So he was only doing colleges and things, and he didn't want industry people there. So, he would come back through the markets, and everybody wanted to see him and say hello, but he wouldn't. And, that became an issue. Apparently he was spoken to, that 'You're kinda alienating all the radio stations that have been playing all your music for such a long time.'[5]

"What happened was he was doing it in New York at Town Hall, and the whole Columbia Records field staff was in town for national meetings. The whole company was in New York. So, apparently it was a huge battle; he didn't want the record company people there. But, we were all there and he was doing this thing at Town Hall. . . . From what I gather, it took an enormous amount of beating his management and himself over the head, to say, 'We need a couple of rows in the balcony.' And, that's basically all we got. We were all the way in the back."[5]

The former Columbia Records employee recalls that the president of Billy's record label, Donny Ienner, was in the audience at Town Hall that night as well. "Donny Ienner is a large man, and very aggressive, and very, very intimidating in every way. And he is very clear, if you're going to work for him, it's survival of the fittest. . . . Ienner was sitting down front—not totally down front—but maybe ten rows back, and in the middle, and, he wrote a question. Billy was answering other questions from the students that were all music students, and he wrote it again. It was his PR person who was bringing them back and forth. And, I had noticed, because you watched Donny all the time to see what you should be doing, he wrote the same question again, and Billy put it aside. Then Ienner screams out in the middle of the thing, 'When you gonna give us another new record?' And Billy takes the note and says, 'Ladies and gentlemen, we are honored to have a special guest here tonight. This is Don Ienner, president of Columbia Records. And the answer is: "When I'm ready."' And, I'll tell, you, if Donny could have gone up there and strangled him, he would have."[5]

The May 16, 1996, appearance at Town Hall also commemorated the twenty-fifth anniversary of New York City radio station WPLJ. It was presented as a special live broadcast on that radio station, and it also celebrated

Billy Joel's twenty-fifth year as a solo artist. He said that evening that choosing a career in the music business is quite a challenge: "You will find it discouraging. It's not the easiest life to live. There's a lot of difficulties. There's a lot of obstacles out there. If you think in your heart that that's what you should do, then don't let anybody talk you out of it. You should follow your heart and do what your heart tells you to do. I truly believe that people who do what they love are committed through their work. And what we need is people who really love their work and are committed to their work, and do really quality work. Because I think that a lot of the problems in the world are caused by a lot of unhappy people who don't like their lives."[161]

Billy has admitted that songwriting, at times, frightens him, "The factor that has changed is the fear factor, because whenever I start a writing project, there's a great deal of trepidation. Where I used to approach it with absolute white knuckle terror, now I just have the everyday ordinary jitters. So I must be extremely compelled to write because I find it to be a difficult process, excruciating sometimes. That's the difficulty factor. I'm not terrified because I've proven to myself that I can do it if I set myself to do it and I have a proper amount of input and motivation and all the emotional necessities.[31]

"Musically, when I'm not writing, I'm not necessarily doing anything actively but passively, all kinds of things are going on. I dream music almost every night I know, because when I wake up in the morning I'm either humming or whistling something that was programmed in my dream. Either someone else's song or a song I wrote in my head. That's how I feel the writing process begins to work itself out for me, it starts to get written while I'm sleeping. I think there's a great deal of input that comes in. Emotional input, visual input, technological input—whether I'm aware of it or not. There's just noise that goes into my head. I don't know about you, but when I'm on the subway or even in the car and there's highway strips, I start hearing a rhythm and making a musical thing out of it. It's just a game I play, but it's become ingrained. There will be times I'll walk over to the piano and I'll noodle a little bit, but I'll keep reminding myself, 'You're not writing. Don't write.' I'll even hold back: 'Don't you dare sit down and try to write right now, you're not motivated.' 'You're not in harness,' I call it."[31]

Meanwhile, his love life, and his career continued to evolve and grow. Romantically, Billy spent a lot of time with artist Carolyn Beegan in the mid-1990s. Although he was not actively recording, his catalog of rock albums continued to sell, having been publicized by his global touring. In

August 1996, the RIAA certified the Russian concert album, *Kohuept,* as million-selling platinum.

On March 18, 1997, Billy was honored by the song publishing organization ASCAP (America Society of Composers and Performers) for his body of work. The fete took place in Washington, D.C., and featured several performers including Nickolas Ashford and Valerie Simpson, Broadway composer Cy Coleman, Jimmy Webb, Marvin Hamlisch, and country star Garth Brooks.

The following week, on March 25, Billy was one of the guests at Elton John's fiftieth birthday party, which was held in London. The event was quite the extravagant gala, in the form of a costume ball. The birthday boy dressed as a member of the eighteenth-century French royal court, complete with a three-and-a-half-foot-tall silver wig. His ostrich feather–lined train was so long that it required attendants to carry the end of it. The event was attended by Andrew Lloyd Webber, designer Jean-Paul Gaultier, and of course Elton's boyfriend, David Furnish. Billy Joel and Charlie Watts of the Rolling Stones both chose to wear World War II U.S. military uniforms. Billy and Charlie were photographed for the "Startracks" section of *People* magazine, looking like they were having a great time. A smiling Billy Joel is shown holding a full martini glass in his left hand.

Billy did his best to portray himself as being just a regular guy. He especially had a camaraderie with Manhattan-area audiences. New York City radio personality Ken Dashow recalls an especially memorable Billy Joel performance from this time. "You know, one of the best things that I've ever seen happen at Madison Square Garden, was [what] I refer to as 'the pizza story.' I was backstage at a concert at the Garden . . . and he ordered twenty pizzas. They brought them in, and his manager at the time brought the kid who delivered the pizzas up onstage—it was just the local pizza place by the Garden—and just walked him to the side of the stage, where he waited for the song to finish. He was just a young kid, and he walked up on the stage, and delivered the pizzas to Billy, onstage in the middle of the show! And Billy just stopped and looked, and the whole crowd is going nuts! And, Billy pats his back pockets, pats his side pockets: 'Liberty, you have any money? Mark, do you have any money? Anybody? Does anybody have anything? I want to give the kid a couple of bucks. Like, somebody in the crowd gave Billy ten dollars, so he gave the kid ten bucks. And everybody in the band took a slice, and he passed the pizzas out into the Garden. In terms of showmanship—lighting effects, smoke, mirrors, some of the most gorgeous lighting—I don't think there's anything that's as cool or as casual as this one: 'Does anyone have any cash for the pizza guy?'" Ken laughs. "He just shared it, and everybody just had some pizza in the middle of the show. And, he bullshitted with the crowd: 'How you doin'?' He took a bite of pizza, and then he went back and played the next song."[111]

Still, there were visible signs that Billy Joel was not always the happy-go-lucky guy he liked to personify. He was feeling pressure from many sides and sometimes behaved obnoxiously. In 1997 he said, "I write the music first. Then I write lyrics. So I'm translating the music so people can understand what I did. Then I've got to translate it into a video so the *dumbos* can get an idea of what's all about. I'm a pissed off musician. I'm fuckin' sick of being a Goddamn clown. 'I am the Entertainer?' Well, 'Fuck you! I don't want to be 'The Entertainer.' Not anymore."[162]

He claimed that he was losing his enchantment with the music business. "I don't even listen to songs so much anymore. I only hear pop music accidentally or incidentally. What I listen to now almost exclusively is classical music, and it's been like that for the last three to five years, maybe longer. I've rediscovered my love of classical music and I've learned to pick out a good amount of the symphonies on the piano by ear. I'm learning a lot by doing that, learning a lot about theory, learning a lot about playing, learning a lot about composition. What it's made me realize also is that I was always writing classical music, even the popular songs I wrote. I recognize a lot of them as being as classical piano pieces and that's how I started composing when I was a little kid."[31]

He was especially angry about the way radio stations program their music. According to Billy, "It has nothing to do with quality. It has to do with radio formats, which are narrow-casted now and only separate us from each other. You either like heavy metal or soft rock, and suddenly I'm one of those 'soft rock' guys, which to me sounds like 'soft cock.' Well, sorry, I'm not a 'soft cock' guy. Half the music I make is raucous, but it's difficult for them to program. The hard rock stations don't want to program Billy Joel, because it's difficult for their audiences to accept him. Well, 'Fuck you!' I'm pissed off at radio. They're a bunch of Goddamn wimps. If they never play my records again, I don't give a rat's ass!"[162]

Like Prince and George Michael before him, Billy started to rip apart the record business in his comments to the press—essentially biting the hand that was feeding him. "It's the record companies, too. It's like, 'Why should we push Billy Joel's good stuff? Why don't we push Billy Joel's *soft* stuff?' Everybody's expecting 'the new Billy Joel ballad.' I don't write 'ballads!' I write an album's worth of material at a time. I don't want it all to be 'bang, bang, bang, bang!' When you think of Beethoven, what do you think of: soft or hard? . . . If The Beatles had been typecast by radio after 'Yesterday,' would we have ever been able to hear 'Helter Skelter?' I'm sick of these fuckin' rabbis and priests. 'Fuck 'em. Fuck 'em all.'"[162]

And then he was still—perpetually—mad at the press itself. He was especially tired of being asked the same questions over and over again. He complained in *Musician* magazine, "People just don't hear music without words. It's like 'Did you write that for Christie when you were breaking up?' 'Fuck you! I don't want to tell you!'"[162]

It had been four years since the release of his number 1 multimillion-selling *River of Dreams*. His record company wanted more "product" from him. Columbia was consistently bugging Billy for him to produce another rock & roll album.

In desperation, the company reached into Billy's back catalog and created a single disc album called *Billy Joel: Greatest Hits, Volume Three*. Billy even agreed to go into the studio and record two new songs: his version of Carole King and Gerry Goffin's "Hey Girl," and Bob Dylan's "To Make You Feel My Love." The song "Hey Girl" was originally a hit for Freddie Scott in 1963. According to Billy, "When it came out, I was 13. It had a big impact on me because it coincided with my first break-up with my first girlfriend."[163]

The song "To Make You Feel My Love" was one that Dylan had written and recorded, but had never released. It was treated like a top secret project. According to Billy, "[Dylan] sent a guy to my house with this demo tape of Bob singing 'To Make You Feel My Love.' They wouldn't send the tape by mail. . . . I guess he's paranoid about tapes getting out. . . . Anyway, as soon as I heard the song, I said, 'This song is fantastic. I want to do this song!' And Bob actually wanted me to do it. So, who am I to disagree with Bob Dylan?" With regard to his singing of the song, Billy claimed, "A Bob Dylan song is not supposed to be all sweet and sugary. . . . It couldn't be polished, it couldn't be too smooth, it couldn't be too rich. It has to be a little lean and salty."[164] Billy performed the number with the same slightly raspy-voiced approach that has become Dylan's trademark.

The *Billy Joel: Greatest Hits, Volume Three* album was a huge success. It hit number 9 in the United States, and number 23 in England. The song "To Make You Feel My Love" was released as a single, peaking at number 50 on the *Billboard* charts in America. Furthermore, that same year the RIAA certified *Billy Joel: Greatest Hits, Volumes One & Two* as being eighteen times platinum in the United States. In addition, the *Streetlife Serenade* album was finally certified million-selling platinum as well.

To pull of these projects together, Columbia Records packaged all three of the *Greatest Hits* albums together into a boxed set of CDs called *1973–1997: The Complete Hits*. It included a new deluxe booklet, and a fourth disc containing some live rarities, plus some of the material recorded during Billy's lecture series. The master class material culled together on this disc includes recordings from the prestigious Columbia, Princeton, Harvard, and Hofstra universities.

His most visible performance during this time was as a guest star at Garth Brooks's incredibly successful free concert in New York City's Central Park. Billy Joel joined the million-selling country sensation on Garth's hit "Ain't Goin' Down till the Sun Comes Up," Billy's "You May Be Right," as well as a performance of "New York State of Mind." The concert was broadcast on HBO as a TV special, and it was subsequently released commercially as a videocassette.

Speaking of this evening, one unidentified ex-Columbia Records executive says, "I am very close to his PR person, who is Claire Mercuri. She's head of PR at Columbia now. She was always very close to him, and told about the wild parties at his house in the Hamptons, but I wasn't at any of them. He was sort of like a kid who never grew up. And, apparently he was fairly difficult to work with, unless he was told 'You have to be good today.' I did catch a glimpse of it backstage. When Garth Brooks played Central Park, he was the guest, and that project was given to me, so I was sort of babysitting him that night. That was the night I saw the petulant little child kind of thing, and I remember I kept thinking to myself, 'What's he doing here if he didn't have to?' At one point I said to him, 'Are you close to Garth?' And he was like, 'Well, ehhhhh.' He is not particularly communicative, and never really gave me a straight answer. He got on stage, did his thing, and then he took off. He got on his bus and was gone. He did 'New York State of Mind' with Garth and that was it. I had expected him to come back on for the encore or whatever, and his piece was about the length of one song or two. I didn't know what he was getting paid for it, but it certainly didn't seem like it was out of friendship. It may have been: 'Look, there's going to be however many hundreds of thousands of people, maybe make an appearance.' But there didn't seem to be any sort of chemistry between them. I didn't get a sense of warmth between Garth and Billy, like I did with the Elton John tour that he was doing it out of friendship."[5]

In January 1998 Billy and his band embarked on a series of tour dates, commencing with an appearance at the Cumberland County Civic Center, located in Portland, Maine. The concert kicked off the tour with a full sell-out crowd. In March of that year, the album *Billy Joel: Greatest Hits, Volume Three,* was certified platinum. Based upon figures compiled by the RIAA, it was announced that year that at that point in his career Billy Joel had sold over 60 million records—in the United States alone. The touring and the record sales continued throughout the year.

Liberty DeVitto remembers that the once-tight camaraderie that had existed in the old days between Billy and the band was long gone. He tells the story of "David Santos, who is the bass player for a while." According to Liberty, "David is the sweetest, sweetest man that you would ever want to meet. He's almost, like, naive, he's so sweet. But he had just finished playing with Crosby, Stills & Nash, then he played with John Fogerty for a while. He was so abused on our tour, that people—like sound guys and light guys on our tour—were telling him what to do, and how to play. He said, 'I've never been called out at a gig. You're hired because of the way you play.' The guys in Billy's organization treat the musicians like they are in second place—the bottom of the barrel. Last."[62]

It was becoming very competitive backstage, and not everyone got along well. Recalls Liberty, "Crystal Taliefero: we called her 'Cookie X.' We discovered whatever she was wearing first thing in the morning was who she was that day. If she came down dressed in a dress like a lady, she was going to be nice to us. If she came down in her beret and her dark glasses, she was 'Cookie X,' and she didn't want anything to do with us."[37]

Liberty claims that finances became an ongoing issue as well. At that time, Billy was being paid approximately $1 million per performance. As part of his band, the players were each paid less than $2,000 per performance. "The most money I have ever made with Billy Joel is $13,000 a week," says Liberty. "We never got paid when we were off the road. Only on the road. So each tour, it lasted ten weeks, that's what you make for the year? Being in a top band. And he's making a million bucks a night! Everybody thinks we're rich, but we're not. No one has ever become rich playing with Billy Joel. Not one of the band members."[62]

He also complains that a lot of bonuses that were promised to the band never materialized: "He promised us a lot of stuff from the tours. Stuff that never happened." Another point of contention became a concert that they performed in Frankfurt, Germany. Liberty alleges that Billy knew he had already sold the videotape of the show to a television network, but intended not to pay the band one cent more for their film rights: "It ran on the Disney Channel, and it came out on a DVD. And all we were paid was a thousand bucks."[62]

On one hand, Liberty acknowledges that there are outside influences telling their star performer what to do. But on the other, he believes that Billy has to have full knowledge as to what everyone else's financial arrangements are. Had Billy gotten screwed over so many times, that he became greedy? Liberty's describes Billy's attitude as, "It became *me*. 'All about *me*.'"[62]

In addition to the touring as the sole star whenever it could be arranged, Billy Joel and his band would reunite for another leg of Elton John duet concerts as well. In March 1998 they began a three-week concert tour across the continent of Australia. It kicked off on the tenth of the month at the Entertainment Centre in Brisbane. The tour then continued on to Europe. When they appeared together in Vienna, Austria, it was broadcast as an HBO special on June 20.

During all of this activity, on April 27, 1998, Billy Joel came to New York to be one of the celebrity performers at Carnegie Hall for the Ninth Annual Rainforest Foundation concert. The bill that night included Elton John, Sting, James Taylor, and Martha Reeves. According to Martha, "The only time I was in Billy's presence was at Sting's Rainforest Foundation concert in Carnegie Hall. I have admired his music for years. After the show that night, Billy had us all come over to his apartment for an impromptu party. Everyone from Sting to Elton to James, to Katie Couric, all came along with us. Billy is just so talented, and he was really relaxed and looked like he was having a good time. He sat at the piano, and really let go, playing and singing all of these great songs for us in a private concert. It was really a wonderful night."[165]

The following year, on March 15, 1999, Billy Joel was inducted into the Rock & Roll Hall of Fame. The ceremony, the Fourteenth Annual Induction Dinner, took place at the prestigious Waldorf-Astoria Hotel in New York City. It was fittingly Billy's idol, Ray Charles, who was chosen to be the celebrity to induct Billy at the all-star gala ceremony. The Hall of Fame's "Class of '99" included Joel, Paul McCartney, Bruce Springsteen, Curtis Mayfield, Del Shannon, Dusty Springfield, the Staple Singers, Charles Brown, Bob Wills and His Texas Playboys, and record producer George Martin. Billy took part in the famed postawards jam session. Among the highlights for Billy was singing a duet version of "Let It Be" with Paul McCartney.

April 17, 1999, again found him at Carnegie Hall for Sting's annual Rainforest Foundation benefit concert. On hand that evening were headliners Elton John, Don Henley, and James Taylor. Also that year, Billy was featured on the soundtrack album for the Julia Roberts/Richard Gere film *The Runaway Bride*. On the soundtrack album Billy is heard singing "Where Were You (On Our Wedding Day)." The song had originally been a top 40 hit for Lloyd Price in 1959.

Meanwhile, every December, Billy Joel continued to be supportive of the benevolent association that he had helped to found, Charity Begins at Home. During the year 1999, his disc jockey friend from WBAB on Long Island, Bob Buchman, landed a top job at Manhattan radio station WAXQ. Recalls Buchman, "When I got this job in '99, Billy called me just to congratulate me. And I said to him, 'Hey, look I want to take the Charity Begins at Home concept, and take it with me. I was the only fund-raiser for Charity Begins at Home. He donates privately and quietly every year. But he doesn't fund-raise for them anymore. He stopped fund-raising for them when I got started in [19]80. So, by '80, '81, he was done fund-raising for them, and it became my job. He launched it and said, 'Bob, you be the fund-raiser.' I was all too happy to do it. And since that time, nothing has changed. He still continues to quietly donate, and he always joins me on the radio during our big radiothon, and helps raise funds. But he is just thrilled that it was able to stay this long."[99]

Bob recalls, "1999 was the year that I went to a tristate area radio station instead of just WBAB. And, this station that we're at right now, Q104.3, WAXQ, transmits from the Empire State Building, and reaches a much larger universe: twenty-two counties instead of two [in] New Jersey and Connecticut. So I said to Billy, 'Hey, can we broaden the scope? It can still be, "Put your money where your house is," but now we just have a larger number of houses—it covers more geography.' And, he said, 'Yes!' So Charity Begins at Home changed the charter in '99 to include the tristate area. But it never funds outside of the tristate area."[99]

As the dawn of the new century approached, Billy Joel took time to reflect on his past achievements. "I think one of the reasons I've been able to be successful in this business is [that] I never had an idea of who this Billy Joel guy was," he claimed. "I was whoever the song wanted me to be. If I wrote a song that was like a Ray Charles song, I was kind of like a Ray Charles guy. If I wrote a song that was like a Stones thing, I was kind of like a Stones guy. That's the beauty of rock & roll, that's American popular music. You can be whoever you think you can be. You can be whoever you want to be."[29]

Billy Joel and an enhanced version of his band headlined a sold-out New Year's Eve concert in New York on Millennium Eve, December 31, 1999. The show was audiotaped and released as an album in May 2000, titled: *2000 Years—The Millennium Concert*. Produced by Don DeVito, the two-CD set contains all the requisite Billy hits, with the addition of unique live versions of the songs "Auld Lang Syne," the Rolling Stones' "Honky Tonk Woman," and Sly and the Family Stone's "Dance to the Music."

In addition to his regular touring band, including Liberty DeVitto, Crystal Taliefero, Mark Rivera, David Santos, and Tommy Byrnes, original saxophone player Richie Cannata was invited back into the band for a special one-night-only appearance.

Recalls Richie, "I didn't want to do anything more than that. He said, 'Let's bring you back for that.' And, I said okay. But it was more like I was coming back because I was an original band member. It was kinda cool, and my son got to be part of that—he just was there [in the audience]. It was important for him to see me doing that, and my mom. It was emotional, it was very emotional. And it was intense that night, they were predicting that the world was gonna end that night."[44]

Liberty DeVitto openly complains about the small amount of money that the band was paid for gigs like this, which became "live" album releases for Billy. "Now, this is the stuff that I heard; this is what you hear when you are on tour," he says. "On the Elton John/Billy Joel tour, after all the expenses were done, Billy and Elton were walking away with 750,000 to a million dollars each, in their pockets—*each* show. On New Year's Eve [1999], when we played the millennium, how much were the tickets? Probably $1,000 apiece or something ridiculous. In reality, the monies that he paid us to play New Year's Eve, the front row paid for the band. Just the front row. . . . He paid the band, like, $2,500 apiece for the main guys. . . . I know people who have played weddings and corporate gigs, that got more money than that. That's the way he thinks.[62]

"I have a deposition at home. I threw drumsticks once; well, I used to throw them into the audience [as a souvenir]. Well, it turns out that this one girl said that I threw multiple sticks at her, and hit her, and she had to go for an operation on her nose, broke her nose, and all this kind of stuff like that. Total bullshit. She probably got beat up in the parking lot, and needed something to blame it on to get insurance. Anyway, they take us to court, sue for five million dollars, and Billy had to go for a deposition, and we all had depositions done. I finally read some of these depositions, and one of the questions [to Billy] is 'Do you ever think about getting rid of Liberty?' And he says, 'Only if he starts to ask for too much money.'"[62]

Other people think of Billy and his generosity and grace with his time. New York City disc jockey Race Taylor recalls, "The millennium show . . . when that CD was just coming out, because it was springtime, and we were at Tower Records, and he looked phenomenal. You had heard and you had seen the shows with Elton John and he had the beard, and his face was red and he looked like he was putting on muscle—so to speak. And this was his first appearance since the first of the year, and he was in an electric blue shirt and his hair looked great, and the line in front of Tower Records went down Broadway, around Sixty-sixth Street. It was just amazing. He was only going to be there for, like, two hours, just to sign everything."[166] Taylor claims that he was very impressed by Billy's patience with the crowds and keeping all the fans happy.

When the *2000 Years: Millennium Concert* album was released, it drew strong reviews. David Wild wrote in *Rolling Stone*, "The concert documented here is a lively reminder of Joel's massively crowd-pleasing way with an arena. . . . *The Millennium Concert* set list is surprisingly imaginative, including early gems like 'Summer, Highland Falls'. . . . There are also rollicking covers of 'Honky Tonk Woman' and 'Dance to the Music' that prove Billy and the band know how to kick out the party jams."[167] On the charts *2000 Years: The Millennium Concert* album made it to number 40 in the United States.

Billy found himself in the news again in 2000, for financial reasons. This time around, it was for selling his Long Island beach house to TV star Jerry Seinfeld for a reported $34 million. He explained at the time, "That was a big oceanfront house I built when I was married to Christie. I found myself living there alone, and I'm not really an ocean guy. The ocean is where you lie down on the beach and get skin cancer. After Christie and I split up, she had to get her share of what the house was appraised at. Did I need the money? I thought I needed to make up for what had been taken away from me [in legal problems]. I got my clock cleaned for $30 million. I had to be on the road a lot. I didn't want to do that anymore, and this was a way to fill that hole. I knew Jerry was looking for a place. I keep reading these stories where we were like *hondling* each other [a Yiddish term meaning "haggling for price"]. He came in. He walked around. I named a number and he said, 'O.K.' And I said, 'O.K.' We went out to dinner, and that was it."[16]

In the new century Billy resumed his touring with Elton John. When he was asked about their camaraderie backstage, Billy confessed, "Well, we don't really hang out. I'll go to his dressing room, which is done like the last great days of the Roman Empire: He's got layer after layer of drapery hung, plus guys hanging around wearing olive branches on their heads and little charioteer outfits. He's got 55 pairs of shoes and 1,000 pairs of sunglasses. It's like going shopping—at Versace. We're like *The Odd Couple*. He'll come to my dressing room sometimes, which he says is like the 'delivery entrance' to some deli. We've got a bottle of Dewers, a couple of beers, some soda, and that's it. And Elton looks through my wardrobe before the show, and he goes, 'Let's see, what colors will we wear tonight? Oh: black, black, black, black, black, charcoal. Ooh, navy blue. How outrageous! And, then he leaves."[16]

In January 2000 Billy broke up with Carolyn Beegan, and he began dating Trish Bergin, a TV reporter. He and Carolyn had been dating on and off for two years.

By 2001 Billy had a new love in his life, whom he identified in the press: "Her name is Dina Meyer. She's an actress."[11] During this same period, the *New York Post* ran a cover story about Billy's being involved in a "love triangle" with former girlfriend Bergin and Dr. Sean Kenniff, of the TV show *Survivor*. He was reportedly a bit embarrassed to have his personal life smeared on the cover of Manhattan's most tabloidlike major daily newspaper.

He was getting quite the reputation for being a womanizer. What is his role in these relationships? Was he the aggressor? "The pursuer! Always," he claims. "No hesitation at all. It's hormonal, it's chemical, it's a woman thing, and it drives me completely out of my skull. And I'll trip, and I'll fumble, and all my wisdom and logic goes out the window. I just like romance. People have pointed out that I am short, but when I talk to someone, I am looking into their eyes, so I am not aware of physical limitations until I see photos of me with other people. I suppose what I've got is a certain amount of confidence because of what I've accomplished. I wouldn't know if I come on strong; I'm not aware of any game plan. And thought, 'I've been with models and actresses, I'm not that interested in having a trophy on my arm.' When I'm interested in someone, it's not for a momentary distraction or to get them into bed. If I have a crush, it's major. And maybe women like that. Nothing appeals more to a woman than knowing she is loved."[11]

In recent years Billy had put on weight. He was rounder in the face than he had been as a young man, and his hairline was receding quite dramatically. Speaking of his own changing hairstyle, he claimed in the year 2000, "It was always problematic. I used to look like I had an Afro. Hendrix made the Afro cool for a while—that lasted about 15 minutes. I always hated my hair, so now it's going away. Why am I surprised?"[16]

In 2001, when Billy was asked how he saw himself, he confidently answered, "I'm a musician, a pianist, a guy from Long Island. A father, most importantly of all. And right up there with father, a composer."[11]

In 2001, he was very content to let *River of Dreams* stand as his last album of all-new rock & roll material. "At the end of every album of songs, I always feel burnt-out. That's kind of a given because the writing process is very draining and emotionally exhausting. So whenever I get to the end of an album, I go, 'Oh thank God,' and then there's all this anxiety that I'll have to do it all again. It's sort of like eviscerating yourself, in a way. You tear open your abdomen, you put your guts on the table, and you sift through them and you stuff them back in and you sew yourself back up. Then you've got to do it again on the next album. This time it wasn't just burnout from writing an album's worth of songs. It was a real sense of 'I have done this and done this, and now I want to do something else.' I really feel that now would be a time to try my hand at a different kind of writing. I want to be able to expand on a theme. I want to be able to do expositions. I want to be able to do variations. I don't want to have to repeat a motif over and over. I don't want to work in song form. I don't want to have to create within that box."[50]

As far as creating new rock & roll tunes, his creativity was on hold. As Billy explained, "What I'm doing is coasting. I'm irrelevant musically right now. I'm 52, jumping around on stage like I'm 21 and thinking, 'This is not right.' I'm dreading the point where I start to feel I'm becoming a nostalgia act. And when people pay $100 for a ticket, it's like there's an unwritten agreement that they are not obligated to get crazy. Or even worse. I'm on the road. I have no home. I have no wife. There's really nothing tethering me to this earth except my daughter. She's the most interesting person I've ever met in my life."[11]

He might be in the new century, but he claimed that his sensibilities were welded in the former one. "I'm hopelessly 20th Century. I collect old watches. I have a boat building business. I got a Honda Valkyrie Interstate

BILLY JOEL

motorcycle that's about the size of half a station wagon. I have a black pug named Finola that I got for my daughter, even though Daddy does all the cleaning up. What else? Good friendship, good food, good wine, a good cigar—although if I smoke one halfway down, I'll think, 'Jesus Christ, I need a shower!'"[11]

Billy had also come to an understanding with his ex-wife, Christie Brinkley: "We're good friends. We stay in constant contact. Christie has a whole other life, a different husband, two other children. But we go to Alexa's school functions together. It's always good for the children of divorced parents to see that their parents can act like adults."[11]

During the year 2001, Phil Ramone went into the studio to produce a duets album for jazz-pop superstar Tony Bennett. Since Ramone had done two very successful duets albums with Bennett contemporary Frank Sinatra, in the 1990s, it seemed like a perfect package to put Bennett in the studio with a glittering roster of pop, blues, jazz, and rock luminaries.

Called *Playin' with My Friends: Bennett Sings the Blues*, the album features the classic crooner singing a slowed-down, decidedly jazzy version of "New York State of Mind" with its composer, Billy. The resulting recording was a great vocal showcase for both Joel and Bennett.

The entire album was done with a small ensemble called the Ralph Sharon Quartet (Ron Sharon, piano; Clayton Cameron, drums; Paul Langosch, bass; Gray Sargent, piano), so the whole album has a smoky blues/jazz club feel to it. Among the other memorable tracks on the disc are Bennett singing with Natalie Cole in "Stormy Weather," with Bonnie Raitt in "I Gotta Right to Sing the Blues," with B. B. King in "Let the Good Times Roll," with Sheryl Crow in "Good Morning Heartache," with Ray Charles in "Evenin,'" and with Kay Starr in Duke Ellington's "Blue and Sentimental."

The album ends up with a track that brings together Tony Bennett and several of the guest stars who appear with him on individual duet tracks. It is Robert Cray's composition "Playin' with My Friends," where everyone chimes in for a couple of lines of lyrics. Tony sets up the song, claiming that he is going to rent a hall with a kitchen and throw a bash for him and his buddies so they can all party and sing. Natalie Cole is the first guest up on the track, and here she sings about cooking up a pot of pasta with marinara sauce. Next comes Sheryl Crow who sings that she is going to pass around the microphone for everyone to vocalize. Then k.d. lang chimes in for the chorus. When it comes time for Billy Joel to join the proceedings, he amusingly sings about bringing red wine, which he plans to drink out of a paper cup. Eventually B. B. King, Kay Starr, Bonnie Raitt, and Stevie Wonder also join the mix as well. It is ironic—knowing what was going on in his life at the time—that Billy was given the lyric line about being responsible for bringing the wine. Obviously, it was a subject about which he was quite knowledgeable.

On September 11, 2001, the World Trade Center was brought down at the hand of terrorists, an event to live in history as a day of infamy. Thousands of people were killed in a matter of hours, and where the once-grand twin towers had stood, now a twisted pit of rubble and carrion remained. Over the next weeks, a slow parade of notable people came by to officially pay their respects to the deceased, including President George W. Bush, Senator Hillary Clinton, and New York mayor Rudolph Giuliani.

Kevin McCarthy, who has since retired from the police force to become a professional actor, was an NYPD detective assigned to the site of the former World Trade Center during those days after September 11. The area, then dubbed "Ground Zero," was off limits to the public. As the police force and other rescue personnel sifted through the ruins of the former tallest buildings in the world, it was a tragic and mournful site. In those sad days in mid-September, only those with official business were allowed in the immediate area and Lower Manhattan was officially deemed to be in a state of emergency, patrolled by the National Guard.

Kevin recalls meeting Billy there. "Several celebrities and politicians were allowed to be escorted to the site to witness the aftermath of the disaster, and to offer moral support to the police, fire department, and other rescue and law enforcement officers. Among those who came down to the area was Billy Joel. Obviously it was a very somber setting, and we were still sifting through the debris looking for survivors of the World Trade Center, and/or identifying victims and their remains. None of us had ever seen anything like it. Billy was very respectful and subdued. He shook hands with several of us officers and was genuinely touched by the tragic site that he witnessed. I was very impressed with his friendliness and his sincere concern for those of us working down there in these crucial days following the tragedy."[168]

When it came time for the entertainment world to step up to the plate to help raise consciousness, Billy Joel was present to lend a hand and a voice at the two biggest staged events. On September 21, 2001, Billy was seen by 89 million viewers on the telethon *America: A Tribute to Heroes*. The event included Bruce Springsteen, Stevie Wonder, U2, Faith Hill, Neil

Young, Alicia Keys, Dave Matthews, Mariah Carey, Sting, Sheryl Crow, Bon Jovi, Paul Simon, Celine Dion, Willie Nelson, and the Dixie Chicks. Billy Joel was heard singing his signature song, "New York State of Mind." Funds were raised for the "September 11 Telethon Fund." The event also yielded a two-CD release, a DVD, and a videocassette.

Just less than a month later, on October 20, another televised all-star musical event, *The Concert for New York City*, took place at Madison Square Garden. It was simulcast on VH1-TV, the VH1 radio network, and broadcast on Westwood One radio network as well. In addition to Billy Joel, also on the bill that night were Paul McCartney, the Who, Eric Clapton, David Bowie, the Goo Goo Dolls, Melissa Etheridge, James Taylor, James Mellencamp, India.Arie, Bon Jovi, Keith Richards, Mick Jagger, and Elton John. The one nod to newer, circa 1990s performers was the inclusion of Destiny's Child.

Among the songs that Billy Joel sang that night were "Miami 2017 (Seen the Lights Go Out on Broadway)," and "New York State of Mind." He also sang a duet version of "Your Song" with Elton John. As he sang "New York State of Mind" that historic night, Billy had a NYFD fireman's helmet on top of the grand piano that he was playing. Billy explained of the helmet's origin, "It was from the Station Two guys—that's a particular fire department in New York that took a pretty bad hit. A lot of their people didn't make it. When I saw that helmet, I said, 'That's got to go on the piano,' because that's really who the real heroes were. When we were backstage at the telethon, seeing the other people who were performing, there really wasn't any of that usual music business banter or award show self-congratulatory emotion going on. There was almost a sense of inadequacy among a lot of the performers, as if what we're doing really isn't enough. Everybody wanted to be able to do more, but that was what we could do, so that's what we did.[50]

"I think artists are going to be reflecting on the anxieties of the time. It's very important that art communicate to people who have no voice right now. I've been actually trying to get my hands around the emotional impact it's had on me. I went down to Ground Zero after that telethon and tried to get a handle on the scope of this thing. It was like being kicked in the stomach. I don't ever recall having a feeling like that in my life. I think it's going to take a while for it to translate into music. I don't even think words are adequate. Somebody had asked me recently, 'If you were going to write lyrics addressing this, how would you go about it?' And, I said, 'Well, first I'd have a collaborator like Winston Churchill to lend some eloquence to whatever lyric I'd try to write.' Unfortunately, we don't have lyricists like him around anymore."[50]

Billy also pointed out that he was obviously one of the "classic" rockers to be on the bill, and that the new wave of the concurrent twenty-something performers were conspicuously missing: "Well, I noticed that for the telethon they turned to the chestnuts. They got Paul Simon, they got Bruce Springsteen, they got me. They didn't really go to the Backstreet Boys or Britney Spears. The people who've been doing it a long time would know how to do this, I think they have authority. But there's a whole crop of new people who really don't know how to do much of anything, unfortunately. And that was painfully obvious by their not being included."[50]

Billy's presence that evening was especially significant, as he is viewed in the rock world as the most important of all the New York rockers. It was so ironic to have Billy Joel sing his classic song "Miami 2017 (Seen the Lights Go Out on Broadway)" that night at Madison Square Garden. Since it was about seeing Manhattan in ruins, it became even more tragic a reminder of what a brutal place the world can be. And "New York State of Mind" was now, not only a song about longing for the Empire State, but a true song to herald the resilience of it, even in the face of terrorism and tragedy.

17
FANTASIES
AND DELUSIONS

IN ADDITION TO all of the changes that the world was going through, in 2001 Billy Joel suddenly found himself redefining his image as a pop star. A new documentary about Billy's paternal grandfather, which was made in Germany, was suddenly making the rounds of film festivals. Columbia Records was actively marketing another new compilation album. And, in the middle of it all, Billy finally released his years-in-the-making classical album of hits. The idea of doing a full-length Broadway show using the music of Billy Joel had been bantered around for a long time. Suddenly that opportunity was about to present itself as well. Through it all, some very old and important relationships were eroding, and some important new relationships were beginning.

His record company was still after him to record and release a new rock album. It had been eight years since *River of Dreams* entered the album charts at number 1, and Columbia Records longed for him to hit another "home run" like that. One particular Columbia Records employee recalls asking Billy point-blank when he was going to do his next rock album. According to this source, "He went on to say, 'I'm not feeling very motivated now, I'm seriously thinking about doing a classical album and a Broadway show.'"5 That wasn't exactly what Columbia had in mind, however; in reality, at this point they were eager to release any sort of album that Billy Joel wished to create.

The documentary film, *Die Akte Joel*, written and directed by Beate Thalberg, was first exhibited in Europe. It was the winner of the Golden Rose Award in Montreux, Switzerland, in 2001 and was broadcast in Germany and France in December of that same year. Although Billy took part in the documentary, as did his father and half brother, the film is not about his life or career at all, it is the story of the Joel Company in 1930s Germany.

Since that time, the American version of the documentary, *The Joel File: A Story of Two Families,* has been broadcast on cable TV and PBS-owned stations. It features an all new English-language narration by actor John Hurt.

The evolution of this documentary came about in a roundabout way. Beate Thalberg had first done a film about Billy's half brother, Viennese musician Alexander Joel. That's when she discovered the story of Billy's grandfather, Karl Joel, and how Josef Neckermann came to own his company. Her fascination with the story led her to conceive of this particular film idea.

Billy was interviewed on camera, as was Alexander Joel, their father Howard, and three of the grandchildren of Josef Neckermann. Through the making of this documentary, a lot of new information was unearthed. According to Billy, "My first reaction was, 'So that's what happened.' Because I didn't really know my father well when I was growing up, and by the time I met him again, he really didn't want to talk about it. . . . It did give me some understanding of the mystery of the man who is my father. I know my father has a dark area in his life that he doesn't discuss."[169]

Whatever business dealings that Josef Neckermann and Karl Joel had was nearly seventy years in the past. And, by now, both of these men were long since deceased. The segment of the film where both men's grandchildren meet for the first time was a bit anticlimactic but was telling of the natural passage of time. Should Billy and Alexander have been upset that the Neckermann descendants reaped the majority of the financial rewards for the Joel Company? Could they legitimately blame these people for something that their grandfather was involved in? Should the Neckermann grandchildren have offered some sort of olive branch of peace to the Joels?

Said Alexander Joel, "The important thing is always to not be bitter about what happened, because, my generation wasn't there. Thank God.

BILLY JOEL

We didn't have to live through it. But we have to be more than ever aware of what happened."[7]

Upon meeting the Neckermann descendents, Billy Joel said, "You can never really right something that was terribly, terribly wrong. But you can try to understand it in its historical place. I'm not going to blame the children for the sins of their parents. Because I don't want to be blamed for whatever my parents did in their time."[7]

However, he felt a little disappointed that the Neckermann grandchildren seemed very blasé and matter-of-fact like about the whole encounter. It wasn't as if he expected the Neckermann descendants to say, "Here is a check for that extra 10 million deutsche marks our grandfather should have paid your grandfather for his company." Still, he didn't get the emotional sense of closure he had expected. Said Billy, "I came away with the sense that they didn't really try in any way. I sense that a lot of this was new to them and they didn't know how to deal with it."[169]

He also stated philosophically about people who hold long-standing grudges, "You have to learn how to remember something, but not let it turn you into something bitter or something hateful, because then 'they' won. If 'they' destroy your soul, 'the bad guys' win."[7]

Meanwhile, Billy's musical taste was transitioning out of rock & roll, and into classical music. In the year 2000 he announced in the *New York Times* that he had composed a suite of orchestral music that he titled "The Scrimshaw Pieces." It is over forty minutes long. He explained, "I wanted to write music about where I came from. We start with the early Long Island and the landing of the first settlers who were refugees from the Massachusetts Bay Colony. The sound movement evokes the building of the place, and third is an elegy I call 'The Great Peconic.'"[163]

The suite ended up being included on an album called *Music of Hope,* which was produced to raise funds for the American Cancer Society, released on February 13, 2001. The album features classical recordings composed by Paul McCartney, Ray Charles, and Billy Joel. There are also performances by Andre Previn, and by classical pianist Emanuel Ax. Billy's contribution was the recording of "Elegy: The Great Peconic" performed not by him, but by the London Symphony Orchestra, under the direction of David Snell. It was later included in Billy's 2005 boxed set, *My Lives.*

For a long time Billy had dreamed of composing his own complete album of classical music. In 2001, with his *Fantasies and Delusions* disc, it was a dream come true. Billy fashioned a dozen well-crafted classical

pieces. However, he chose not to play the piano for this album, for fear that his own piano-playing limitations would render a less than perfect product.

"Obviously, I'm not doing this for the money," said Billy at the time. "This is purely a labor of love, I'm not expecting it to be a huge commercial success. What I wanted to do was open people's ears and maybe open their minds to listening to music that they might not have listened to before. A lot of people are intimidated by what's called classical music. I don't even refer to it as instrumental piano music. But if they're in any way interested because of the work I've done before, maybe they'll give this a listen. Perhaps they might be motivated to go to the classical section in a music shop and pick up some of the works of Chopin or maybe give Beethoven a listen. I think that it will open up an amazing world that they've kind of shut themselves off from. I think we've lost the whole Baby Boomer generation in terms of classical music. The classical world is kind of running out of an audience now. They're dying off. They didn't reach out enough to the Boomers. The powers that be were pretty much promoting late 20th Century dissonant, atonal, modern 12-tone compositions. They were scoffing at melodic composition."[50]

He explains that the first piece he wrote for the album was "Soliloquy (On a Separation)." This was written for Alexa: "Divorced fathers usually don't get to spend much time with their children. I had this terrible feeling every time my daughter would leave, and I started to write a four-note motif based on the words, 'We say goodbye.' The music was so evocative and expressive that I decided I didn't need words, and so I kept on writing, and it turned into a Rachmaninoffesque piano piece I called 'Soliloquy.'"[163]

Slowly he felt himself falling into the spell of creating classical music. Explains Billy, "So, I'm just writing what I'm feeling, and the melody is becoming more and more extended, and I haven't written lyrics yet. And I get to a point where I just said, 'Why do I have to write words? Lyrics seem redundant. This music is saying everything.' In trying to write lyrics, I was painting a mustache on my own picture. So I didn't write any words, and it became the piano piece 'Soliloquy (On a Separation).' And I kept writing music like that."[29]

He found, with the *Fantasies and Delusions* album, that his old formula of having one song unfolding into the next one also came into play. "That's true," he insists. "It's the same process here, where each piece kicked off another piece. I think once I wrote the 'Soliloquy,' that's when I wrote 'Waltz #1.' 'Fantasy' was kind of an ambitious work. It's subtitled 'Film Noir.' I was actually thinking of these old movie scores, of these black & white movies from the '40s, these private eye movies. I was thinking in terms of a film score, almost orchestral in scope. That was another new kind of writing for me. A little more modern. I didn't get too deeply into the 20th century, but I tried to touch on it there. I'm assuming that the next group of compositions I attempt will be closer to 20th century tonalities. I'll probably have a little more dissonance, but I don't think I'm ever going to be completely non-melodic. I don't think what I write is ever going to be not singable in some way. I spent so much of my life as a songwriter—to throw that away would be stupid, a terrible waste of a great deal of knowledge. I think the fact that a lot of these pieces are infused with a certain 'songness' is good."[50]

It was through his half brother that he met pianist Richard Joo. Says Billy, "My brother is a classical conductor who lives in Vienna. Richard is one of the guys my brother knows, and my brother is tied in with the classical community there. He's very good friends with one of the top violinists in the world right now—a guy named Julian Rachlin—and a lot of other wild and crazy Eastern European classical musicians who end up in Vienna. They have their own kind of bohemian community. They don't make a lot of money. The work is hard to come by, but they're very, very dedicated to being musicians. They remind me of how musicians were when I was starting out in rock & roll back in the '60s. We were all kind of bohemian guys. Nobody had any money, nobody had any prospects for making a living, but we were very dedicated to the music. We ate, breathed, slept, dreamt, and made love, and it was all we talked about. These guys are like that. It was very inspiring and very spiritually nourishing to hang out with all these guys. Richard was one of them. I met him about seven years ago [1994] and we had done a concert and my brother introduced us. It was a well-advised relationship. I'm glad I met him."[50]

For creative help, he turned as well to his half brother, Alexander Joel: "I took advice from my brother. There was a lot I had to learn, and I had to ask a lot of questions. I wanted to ask the right people. I needed some instruction and guidance. Not that anyone wrote the notes for me, but a lot of times it was pointed out to me, 'You can't do that, you're quoting Chopin.' Or Richard would say, 'You shouldn't play that, because that's Ravel.' And I don't even know if I unconsciously knew it was Ravel. Part of me was saying to myself, 'Hey, I must be pretty good if I'm writing Ravel. But they did help me to avoid making too many quotes. There are references to other classical composers. I think that's normal. But the notes are mine, the themes are mine, the melodies are mine."[50]

Richard Joo says of the Piano Man, "I just want to say that Billy Joel has always been a classical composer to me. Schubert and Mozart and Beethoven and Chopin are definitely his grandfathers and Lennon & McCartney his distant cousins."[170]

Although one might expect a rock star to be trounced by the critics for trying his hand at classical music, the resulting press reviews were quite strong. According to James Hunter in *Rolling Stone*, "This collection of pieces for solo piano written by Joel and performed with highly extroverted skill by Richard Joo represents, in essence, Joel's roots album. As a restless rock & roller, and now as a composer, he restages the scarlet-hued 19th century thrusts and taxing engagements of legendary Russian and German composers . . . but for the most part, Joel doesn't let his delusions get the best of him."[171]

Although it only made it to number 83 on the standard *Billboard* album chart, *Fantasies and Delusions* hit number 1 on the Classical Albums chart, and stayed there for a consecutive eighteen weeks. It was an exciting and flattering ride for Billy. Said Billy, "I knocked Yo-Yo Ma out of Number One, which I actually feel bad about. But now I've been blown away by Pavarotti, so it's poetic justice."[29]

Just to hedge their bets on the success of Billy's classical album, at the same time Columbia Records released the two-disc set *The Essential Billy Joel*. Compiling together thirty-six Billy Joel performances, the album ends with two of his classical compositions. In this way it wasn't just a rock & roll hits package, it was something that was truly career spanning. *The Essential Billy Joel* made it to number 29 on the album chart in America. In Europe and Australia, a two-disc "greatest hits" package, *The Ultimate Collection*, was released in 2001.

Naturally, it made everyone want to know if "popular" music still meant rock & roll to Billy Joel. He responded at the time, "Yes, but now I'm too old to hear it with open ears. I was very arrogant in my youth: Rock & roll was a religion to me. Now it's a genre. It's just part of the big musical picture. Rock & roll was a temptress, a seductress who came along, wearing torn fishnet stockings and smoking cigarettes when I was about 13 years old, and she dragged me away and seduced me. We had a wild affair for 35 years, and now it's cooled down."[16]

By the year 2000, Sony Music owned Columbia Records. With regard to *The Essential Billy Joel* being released at the same time as *Fantasies and Delusions*, Billy claimed, "That's all Sony and their marketing. I don't really have any control over that. I assume that what they're doing is piggy backing on the fact that I'm going to be high profile promoting *Fantasies & Delusions*, doing TV, radio, and interviews, so they think, 'Oh this is a good opportunity for us to sell some old used cars.' I'm not going to disown the songs. I'm proud of them. I wrote them and recorded them and I'm not going to distance myself from them. However, it wasn't my idea to have these things come out simultaneously. Or to put out another compilation at all. I think there's plenty enough of them to go around. But to be fair to Sony, I haven't given them a new recording in eight years, so they've got to sell something."[50]

Addressing the audience of one of his master class sessions at Cooper Union in New York City, Billy commented jokingly, "I've just written a classical record. Look at what I called the album, *Fantasies and Delusions*. I wanted it to be just *Delusions*. You know? Like, who the hell do I think I am? But people said, 'Oh, it's too negative, it's too self-deprecating.' Real Joel. I don't even want to call it classical. It's more like romantically influenced, instrumental pre-20th century music. I'm writing this because this music is my first love."[170]

However, he claimed, "I'm not saying that I won't write songs anymore ever. It's just for the foreseeable future. Right now my heart is in classical music. Actually it always has been."[163]

Throughout this period of time, Billy continued to tour, and he was genuinely interested in doing his master class sessions: "I like speaking to college audiences because they ask great questions. And what you say is relevant to their lives. You really can't just give an answer that is good for your recording career or that's self-serving. You can be totally unselfconscious and self-effacing, completely giving in a teaching way. I've got all this information up in my head that I can share. I've made every mistake you can make in this business a couple of times over and survived to tell the tale. Why not help some young girl or guy who's starting out to avoid the same mistakes I made? I just want to help. I want to help because I sure could have used the advice when I started."[29]

What was it that made him want to do these entertaining seminars? "When I was getting started, I wrote to The Beatles to ask what they were thinking when they wrote certain songs, and then I get this brochure back. But I wish that I had been able to ask them how to navigate the music business. There's a lot of job to the gig. I can help you kids, because I got all this stuff."[170]

In *The New Yorker*, writer Eric Konigsberg wrote, "Joel's stage routine turned out to be less 'Master Class' than a standup-heavy lounge act, somewhere between Victor Borge and Andrew Dice Clay. There were deft impressions of The Rolling Stones, Procol Harum, Gordon Lightfoot, and The Beatles."[170]

In early 2002, Billy and Elton John resumed their "Face to Face" concert touring. However, it didn't all go as planned. Following his March 15, 2002, concert appearance with Elton at Madison Square Garden, Billy abruptly canceled the rest of their concert tour together. According to a reviewer from the *New York Times* who witnessed the show that evening, Billy "seemed to have ingested something quite a bit stronger than cough syrup." Apparently, midshow Billy began yelling out the names of famous American military battles—"Midway!" . . . "Guadalcanal!"—and rambling onstage. Billy himself dismissed the accusations, stating at the time, "I did take medication—under my doctor's supervision. The media speculate that I was on something stronger, and this is just not true. I had difficulty breathing and felt light-headed and disoriented, close to passing out."[172] It was suspected that he was actually drunk onstage that night. And, the press was not quiet about their suspicions.

As he canceled the tour, he lamented, "[That] made me very depressed. I've been touring for 30 years and have only had to cancel a handful of shows in my life, so I took this really hard. I then began what I ultimately realized was a prolonged period of overindulgence. I don't want to get more specific. There wasn't any specific incident that triggered my decision. It was more of a gradual realization during the last couple of months. I became concerned enough to want to voluntarily seek help. My main concern right now is with my own well-being."[172]

People magazine reported that on the Friday beginning Memorial Day weekend, a fan ran into Billy at a Manhattan restaurant. He was drinking alone, and looking despondent. The fan was quoted as saying, "You'd think someone like Billy Joel would have someone to have a drink with. He did not appear to be drunk, but he looked sad and lonely. When he left, we all heard him whistling 'New York State of Mind' as he was walking down the street. It looked as if he was wandering."[172]

Then, on Wednesday, June 12, 2002, something occurred that was a major "reality check" for Billy Joel. While driving his 1999 Mercedes-Benz sedan on a winding section of road in East Hampton, New York, he somehow lost control of his car, which struck a post. Although Billy sustained cuts on his face from the accident, he declined medical attention. Although there was speculation that Billy had possibly been drinking and driving, according to the East Hampton police chief Todd Sarris, "There was no evidence of alcohol."[172]

There was some speculation that Billy was depressed at the time, knowing that his most recent girlfriend, reporter for TV's *Inside Edition*—Trish Bergin—was married to a lawyer named Randi Weichbrodt on June 4. Only four days previous, Billy appeared on TV's *Today Show* and complained regrettably that the accomplishment that was most conspicuously missing from his accomplished life was that he had yet to "have a long-term successful relationship with a woman."[172]

New York Daily News columnists Rush & Molloy reported in an item headlined "Hitting a Sour Note," that the automobile accident stopped Billy Joel from making a scheduled appearance at the annual Songwriters Hall of Fame dinner on Thursday, June 13. According to Billy's spokeswoman, in a statement to Rush & Molloy, with regard to the dinner, "He was driving in the rain down a slippery road in Sag Harbor and his car swerved and hit a pole. Nobody else was hurt but his face was bruised and swollen on one side, so he decided not to go. He was extremely disappointed to miss it."[173]

Five days after his car accident, on June 17, Billy Joel sought professional help for his "substance abuse" problem. Although it was not disclosed at the time, the suspected substance was alcohol. He checked himself in the famed Silver Hill Hospital. Located in New Canaan, Connecticut, it is a facility that has hosted several other celebrities with similar problems, including Liza Minnelli, Mariah Carey, and Joan Kennedy.

He claimed at the time, "I told my daughter that I recognized I was having a problem. And my gift to her for Father's Day was going to be cleaning up my act."[172]

Meanwhile, in Liberty DeVitto's life, things had been changing as well. After eighteen years, his marriage to second wife, Mary, came to an end. "She just decided at the end that she didn't want to do this anymore," he says. "She didn't want to be second fiddle to Billy Joel's drummer all of her life. There's one thing being Billy Joel's drummer, and there's another thing with being the wife of Billy Joel's drummer."[62]

Not long afterward, Liberty met a new love while participating in "fantasy camp." It was a camp where middle-aged rock & roll wannabes could have a weekend of lessons and jamming, with several of the top-flight rock musicians they had grown up listening to on the radio, like Mick Fleetwood, Steven Van Zandt, and Liberty DeVitto. "I met my girlfriend Anna at a rock & roll fantasy camp," DeVitto recalls. "She worked for [concert promoter] David Fishoff. She was his assistant. The camp was in L.A., in 2002, and we just hit it off as buddies. I was going through my separation with my second wife. It's nice when you think you love somebody. That's a great feeling. But when you have somebody that loves you, that's even a better feeling. And this is the first time, I think, that somebody loves me. Sometimes she'll do something, and I think, 'Oh my God, this person *loves* me!' I've never felt that from anyone but my mother. She's fantastic."[62]

At this point in time, Liberty felt that his three-decade friendship with Billy was really falling apart. According to Liberty, no one ever gets into a big blowout fight with Billy, it starts with diminishing access to him, then one day the door is slammed shut and there is no further communication.

"It had nothing to do with the two of us sitting down," recounts Liberty. "We would have been able to have talked then. We always used to hang out in the tour manager's room, Max [Loubiere]. That's how we found out information. Max would be on the phone. He'd be talking to Cincinnati. I said, 'I guess we're going to Cincinnati.' That would mean that if you saw the whole first leg of the tour schedule, and Cincinnati isn't on it, suddenly: 'So, I guess they're gonna add another leg.' Max hated me for doing that, because sometimes the information I would leave with wasn't true. He would say, 'You're building up stories, and making people think weird things.' So he didn't like that at all. But, we used to go and hang out in Max's room anyway because there was nothing else to do at the hotel we were staying at."[62]

Then, on one particular occasion while hanging out in Max Loubiere's room, Liberty remembers making one of his humorously snide comments to Billy. It was something that he had done several times before, it had always been the way they had communicated. Later they would laugh it off. In this instance, Billy wasn't laughing. Say Liberty, "One day Billy was in there, and Max says to Billy, 'Well, when we're in San Francisco, after the show your plane will be ready, and we'll take you to New York.' I just looked at Billy and thinking how it was when we first started. And I looked at Billy and go [in a condescending tone], 'Oh, *your* plane will be ready!' He got so pissed off, he threw his paper on the floor and said, 'I want everybody out of this fucking room! . . . I don't want everyone knowing my business, *just get out!*' We all got out of the room. And I did what any crazy American male would do: I went shopping!" He laughs.[62]

After his exploration of the local mall, Liberty returned to the hotel, wanting to make amends with Billy. "I went shopping, and I came back and I had the bags with me and I knocked on his door. And he opens the door, and I said, 'I want to talk to you.' And I explained to him why we would go into Max's room. I said to him, 'I was just teasing. You took it so personally.' Then he kinda calmed down and he said, 'I just don't want everybody to know my business any more. I just don't want it.' And that's how the separation was, it was slowly. It was a slow separation: 'I don't want everyone to know my business.' Then the next thing I know it's: 'I'm gonna come late for the gigs.'"[62]

Liberty thought back to the old days with Billy Joel and his close relationship with his band. They were like a band of musketeers, doing everything together like a team of friends. Those days were long gone. Liberty found himself hanging out with the roadies and the tech crew. He was suddenly no longer on the "A" list of Billy's friends. "It was a separation between the band and Billy. He would only travel with Max, his security guy—Noel, Brian [Ruggles] the sound guy, and Steve the light guy. That was his posse. So he would get a six-seater Lear Jet, instead of like Stevie [Nicks, who] would get a plane that everybody could go on. So they would fly in and out for the gigs. They would actually be based in Chicago when we were playing the Midwest. And we'd be on buses going to the next show, while they were going back to Chicago. And they'd go out, they'd go out to dinner, and they'd hang out and they would talk about the show. We were never able to tell Billy what *we* thought about the show. Because he was gone. Usually we'd come back the next day and say, 'You're playing too fast. Out front you sound like shit.'"[62]

Instead of making the band feel they were an important part of the whole operation, Billy chose to hold them off to the side as if they were just the hired help. He now expected to be given the star treatment even by his immediate colleagues.

Says Liberty, "The separation got to the point where we would do a sound check. The band would do a sound check at a gig. We'd be done, and then Billy would go up and play piano by himself. And then the sound guy and the light guy would fly in with Billy. We'd be done fooling around at a sound check at five o'clock. They wouldn't come flying in until, like, six thirty. So we would have our meal backstage, and they would come and Brian [Ruggles] would say, 'Come on, you gotta go do the drums.' You know, not like, 'The musicians are here, Brian, you've got to be ready for us.' It was the other way around. So at night, after the shows, instead of driving with the band, I would go with the crew. I loved the crew. Loved them. Hate everybody now, but I loved them," he says laughingly. "They were fun. They were real people; the crew members. . . . I would hear from the lighting guy: 'Hey, you don't have to hang out with them.' 'I want to.' It was my choice to go that way instead of Billy's way. There was a 'thing' there. If I had decided to go with Billy, then I would be a part of that, instead of part of the band."[62]

It was Liberty who had been with the band the longest. As he saw everything deteriorating right before his very eyes, he felt that it was his duty to do something to patch up the increasing bad feelings between the band and their leader. "I thought I was gonna become the middle man between the band and Billy," he explains. "But Tommy Byrnes took over. The biggest mistake that Max Loubiere made is, when we started out with Elton John, when we toured together, they put the musicians together: all the musicians in Elton's band, and all the musicians in our band. We never had a musical director. There was nothing like that. No one's had that title. Max saw in Elton's [souvenir tour] book that Davey Johnstone has the title of musical director. So, Max went, 'Well, okay, we need one. I'm gonna make Tommy Byrnes the musical director.' That caused so much stress in the band. Max later said, 'I didn't do it on purpose, I just thought it would be a good idea at the time.' Then in the next tour book it was taken out."[62] However, it caused a lot of irreparable damage to the morale of the rest of the group.

One of Billy Joel's biggest artistic triumphs of the new century came with his long-anticipated debut in the Broadway realm. The show *Movin' Out* brought his music to another level, and it reached another whole new audience. So many writers and critics had likened his classy story-songs to mini-musicals, that it seemed like a natural move for Billy's music to be heard on the Great White Way.

In 1989, right after he was "let go" from the Joel band, former guitar player Russell Javors said of Billy, "Billy could turn Broadway upside down. He could be the kingpin. He's got influences from Gershwin to Lerner and Loewe. . . . He wrote a theme for something like that, and the theme is gorgeous. And it's a great way to get old. He wouldn't have to look over his shoulder at Bruce [Springsteen] or anybody else. He writes songs that stand the test of time, and nobody else can touch him. He can wipe the floor with guys like Andrew Lloyd Webber."[32]

Originally, the concept of Billy entering the Broadway market would have most likely cast him as the composer of totally fresh material, in much the same way that Elton John has done with *Aida*, *The Lion King*, and the short-lived *Lestat*. Or, he would write a rock opera in much the same way that the Who did with *Tommy*, which ended up with a successful run on

Broadway as well. However, *Movin' Out* had a totally different gestation process. It was award-winning choreographer Twyla Tharp who conceived of this whole project.

Tharp, who has a long and illustrious career as an innovative choreographer, fell in love with the idea of bringing the music of Billy Joel to the world of dance, and more importantly, to Broadway. She had choreographed films before—*Hair, Amadeus,* and *Ragtime*—and she even directed a Broadway show: 1985's *Singin' in the Rain.* However, she was longing to take her choreographing talents and her dancers to the Broadway stage.

So many of Billy Joel's best-loved songs cast vivid visual images in the mind of the listener. "Scenes from an Italian Restaurant," "Goodnight Saigon," "Captain Jack" and "Uptown Girl"—each conjures up such strong pictures in the mind's eye, that it became easy for Twyla to string together a worthy decade-spanning story about a group of teenagers from Hicksville, Long Island, and what happens to them in the passage of time.

Twyla came to Billy with her ideas for a show and presented it to him. According to her, "There was a bigger context in Billy's music that could support a more epic construct."[174]

At first he was skeptical about what he was going to see and hear. "I expected a cringefest, but I was really moved—these songs that I kind of dismissed sounded new again."[174]

He especially had a strange vision in his mind as to the kind of singing he expected to hear as his music morphed with musical theater. He confessed, "I was worried, God, what if they're singing my stuff like Ethel Merman?"[175]

He was pleasantly surprised at what Twyla had conceived of mounting. And, since Billy was now a classical composer, the show could even be interspersed with classically inspired ballet moves set to Billy's new *Fantasies & Delusions* classical pieces. The show did follow the story of Brenda and Eddie—and their envisioned social gang from "Scenes from an Italian Restaurant" and "Tony" of "Movin' Out (Anthony's Song,)" and traced their lives through the the Vietnam War ("Goodnight Saigon,") their downward spiral into drug use ("Captain Jack,") their redemption ("River of Dreams,") and their reminiscences ("I've Loved These Days.")

A Columbia Records executive recalls discussing the *Movin' Out* project with Billy before it opened: "[He said,] 'I have been approached about doing a Broadway show so many times, but I wouldn't be in it, so I don't know who would do it.' Then he found that kid [pianist-singer Michael Cavanaugh]—he discovered him in Vegas, and he was so impressed. But he found him, and he was so impressed that he said he would do it. He was shocked by its success. He never dreamed. He just didn't know if it was going to translate. But the dancers were fabulous, and it was much more interesting than I expected it to be. I thought that it would be more revue-like, and wasn't."[5]

There was an out-of-town dry run of the play in Chicago. The critics unanimously had problems following the loosely strung plot in the first act. "I pretty much agreed with them. So did Twyla," Billy revealed.[175] But after a few adjustments, they were ready for Broadway. Twyla had put together an incredible cast of innovative dancers. The band was led by Michael Cavanaugh, a talented young man who essentially sang and played the character of singing narrator who is essentially Billy Joel.

With the exception of a couple of shouted words from the drill sergeant in the "Goodnight Saigon" segment, there was no spoken dialogue. It was all dance, music, the songs, the band, the dramatic lights, and very minimalist, suggested sets. Were the tough Broadway critics ready for Billy Joel of Hicksville? Apparently so.

Some critics loved it. "A shimmering portrait of an American generation! *Movin' Out* is brilliant—and it's even better the second time around" said Ben Brantley in the *New York Times*. "The most dazzling Broadway dancing ever!" claimed Charles Isherwood in *Variety*. And Michael Sommers in the *Newark Star-Ledger* wrote "Take nearly 30 of Billy Joel's best songs, flesh them out as an exciting chain of kinetic Twyla Tharp dance dramas, dazzlingly performed by an athletic company, and a kick-butt band. That's *Movin' Out*. The powerhouse combo of Tharp's staging and Joel's songs offer an electric experience unlike any other."[176] WOR radio's David Richardson called *Movin' Out* "a spectacular must-see."[180]

Other critics loathed it. Lisa Schwarzbaum penned a review in *Entertainment Weekly* titled "Billy Clubbed." She wrote, "One way to make sense of *Movin' Out* is to imagine it on skates. A couple of triple lutzes cleanly landed would go a long way toward defining the carney sensibilities of the show, in which familiar old songs by Billy Joel, performed by an onstage band, are dramatized . . . a hectic, second-rate plot . . . songs so redolent with memory that what's on stage is a distraction from what's in the head. . . . *Movin' Out* as a hybrid experiment in dancing-singing, or even as a fine old-fashioned pageant of nostalgia, is overridden: what we've got here is Joelscapades."[177]

Reviewing the stage presentation from a dance standpoint, Joan Acocella in *The New Yorker*, made some very good points when she wrote,

"Twenty-seven songs by Billy Joel . . . has no dialogue, even though it has a fairly bulky plot to carry. . . . All of this unfolds in song and dance alone . . . the things that Tharp is counting on, the music and the dance, do indeed keep the show afloat much of the time. If you like Billy Joel, you will probably like *Movin' Out*. . . . Tharp needs no arguing for as a choreographer. She is the most inventive dance-maker of her generation, and her crossing of classical ballet with popular forms . . . [in] this imperfect but bold and serious show."[178]

The show opened on October 24, 2002, and was a huge box office success, running until December 2005. When the 2003 Tony Award nominations were announced, *Movin' Out* was competing for trophies in ten different categories. Ultimately, the show won two of them: Twyla Tharp, for Best Choreography, and Billy Joel, for Best Orchestration.

On opening night, Billy was quoted in *Playbill* magazine as having announced his idea for his next musical show: "I'm talking to numerous people about writing a book and I have sketches of music. The working title is *Good Career Move*. It's about the music business. I'm going to take it apart. What Mel Brooks did to Broadway in *The Producers*, I'll do to the music business."[179] Suddenly Billy was hooked on Broadway.

Naturally, Columbia Records released the original cast album for *Movin' Out*, right after the play opened. Since the turn of the new century, the company has released five new Billy Joel albums: a live album, a European and a totally different American "greatest hits" package, a classical album, and a Broadway cast album comprised of his old songs. The latter two discs didn't even contain a vocal or instrumental appearance by Billy Joel, they were merely others' interpretations of musical compositions.

The advent of the *Movin' Out* show on Broadway drove a huge wedge between Liberty DeVitto and Billy. Liberty remembers when Billy first told him about the theatrical project. At first he described it to his longtime drummer as a "dance recital" set to his music: "He suggested this to me, when he was with Twyla Tharp, and she was saying, 'What other uptempo songs that you've got that we can put in at the end of the show?' And, he was concerned about the show. I remember telling the other guys in the band, when they were excited about the show, I said, 'If he does this show, that's it. We're done. We're *done*. Because its gonna be other people who are gonna play the music. He is breeding all our replacements.' The guy who's going on the road [2006 concert tour] to play the drums, he's the guy from the show! I told them, 'This is the worst thing that can happen to us.'"[62]

Liberty claims that he wanted nothing to do with *Movin' Out*. He didn't want to hear the music that he helped to create turned into a soundtrack for a dance piece. In fact he refused to go and see a performance of it: "Billy told me, 'You gotta go see my show.' I said, 'I don't want to see it.' I know what the songs were like when we recorded them in the studio, and the feeling I had. I just can't see people prancing on 'Goodnight Saigon.' I don't want to see that. I want to see people putting the studio music to 'Goodnight Saigon' on, people who maybe had brothers or whatever that died in Vietnam, or whatever. And, Billy cried when we originally played just the basic track to it in the studio. And then to see people dancing to it? I don't wanna see it. I want to remember the way it was. I think that video destroys the song for me. When I have an idea in my head, and I sit and listen to the lyric; then watching the video, I go, 'That's not what I imagined it would be like.'"[62] He felt the same would be true for *Movin' Out*.

When Billy made his former guitarist the Broadway show's musical director, it really made Liberty mad and hurt his feelings. Again he had been snubbed by Billy. "And then Tommy Byrnes became the musical director of the show," says Liberty. "He was the guitar player in the band. . . . I called him 'a prick,' in that letter that I wrote to Billy. You read that. He's the guy. He told the musicians [who played in *Movin' Out*], 'Do not contact any of the guys who originally were on the songs.' We had nothing to do with that show at all. That pissed me off when they won the Tony for best musical arrangements. And I wrote in that letter to Billy, 'Anything that you won the Tony for was created in the studio years before.' That probably really pissed him off."[62]

In January 2003, Billy had his second in a series of three potentially life-threatening car accidents on Long Island. This time, he had to be pulled from the crumpled wreckage of another of his Mercedes-Benzes, after he had swerved off the road and hit a tree. Again there were rumors that he was under the influence while he was driving, yet no DUI charges were formally filed. Rumors of him being an intoxicated motorist ran rampant, like wildfire. The tabloids had a field day with this news. One writer referred to him as a "garage-rocking punk, superstar slinger of gooey ballads, classical gasser, angry young man, innocent man, falling down drunk."[1]

Billy at least kept his sense of humor about his recent mishaps. Says Russell Javors, "I saw Billy when he played a concert in Detroit. He was funny. He saw me and my wife, Suzanne. He came over to us and said, "In honor of Earth Day, I'm going to drive an electric car into a tree."[64]

When *Movin' Out* opened on Broadway, Billy was asked in the press what new pop songs he was writing, and he replied, "I write my best stuff to a particular person, but right now, I'm between relationships."[175] Well, that was all about to change, in a most surprising way. Billy Joel was fifty-three years old when he met twenty-one-year-old Katie Lee. His own daughter, Alexa, who was seventeen at the time, was almost close enough in age to Katie to be one of her college classmates.

They met while vacationing on the island of St. Bart's in the Caribbean in 2003. Billy was just a single multimillionaire rock star, and Katie was a restaurant correspondent on the PBS TV series *Living It Up*. In January 2004 they announced their engagement and began to make wedding plans.

Fashion consultant Sindi Kaplan recalls that in 2003, not long after Billy met Katie, she encountered him at Tiffany's Fifth Avenue store in Manhattan. "I was where the really impressive diamond, emerald, sapphire, and ruby rings are sold, and there standing next to me was Billy Joel. He was all alone, and dressed in a casual shirt and suit jacket, looking very 'Piano Man.' I hung out near him for a while, and I eavesdropped on his conversation with the salesperson. What he was looking at were the really big engagement rings. He was clearly a man who was deeply in love."[181]

In April 2004, Billy was back in the news for still another automobile accident. This time around, he claimed to have lost control of his vintage Citroën, veered off the road, and in doing so slammed the vehicle into a house inhabited by a ninety-three-year-old woman. This was beginning to become something of a troublesome pattern for Billy. Again, although substance abuse was hinted at, no formal charges were filed against him.

That summer he signed a contract with Scholastic Books to produce his own line of children's books. The first one that was released was an illustrated storybook version of his song "Lullabye (Goodnight My Angel)."

In September, Billy Joel had his name immortalized on the Hollywood Walk of Fame. It is located right in front of L.A.'s Pantages Theater, where his Tony Award–winning musical was concurrently playing. At the dedication ceremony, Billy was accompanied by his fiancée, Katie Lee.

The big date was set, and Billy made plans to marry Katie Lee on October 2, 2004, at his massive new estate on Centre Island, off the shore of his beloved Long Island. It was to be an elaborate wedding of fitting rock & roll excess. The wedding invitations were already sent out, and plans were underway for the event to be a gala occasion. Conspicuously *not* on the wedding invitation list was Liberty DeVitto.

Between the car accidents, and the Broadway show, and Katie Lee now in his life, Billy hadn't been touring for over a year. One of Liberty's last conversations with him was to let him know that he was in bad financial shape; and the drummer asked if he could get an advance on future work. Billy told him to talk to his managers, as he didn't handle the money. Liberty did so and was promptly turned down. When Billy didn't get back in touch with him, Liberty knew that something was up.

Consider Liberty's awkward position at this time. He had been with Billy for three decades and was minimally paid for his vast contributions to the performer's recordings and to his career. Billy didn't pay him a cent in royalties, stopped paying him bonuses, and now rarely toured. Liberty wasn't asking for a handout. For the first time in thirty years he was respectfully asking for an advance on future touring, even though a timely gift of cash would not have been inappropriate. Billy is a multimillionaire, and Liberty had helped him to make that money without arguing, suing, drama, or bullshit. Liberty just wanted to cover his bills until the next tour. This certainly didn't sound like an unreasonable request.

Was that why Billy chose not to invite him to his wedding? "Exactly," says Liberty. According to him, Billy must have thought: "'Liberty's in trouble now, he needs money. His ex-wives divorced him and took everything. What am I gonna do? I'll get rid of him.'"[62]

The wedding invitation snub was the last straw. Liberty had to stand up and speak his mind. "Now I had to know that I was finished, because I wasn't invited to the wedding," he says. "That's what I was writing this letter about: 'Why wasn't I invited to this wedding? Something's up here.' So I decided to find out. So I wrote the letter, and I said, 'You know what? Fuck it. I'm just laying it all on the line. Because I've been quiet for too long, and I'm getting screwed because I've been quiet.' I feel like instead of being punched in the face, I'm gonna throw the punch. I'm going for it. My opinion was, 'You've been playing long enough. You're not invited to the wedding. Somebody is screwing you here.' So, I wrote this letter."[62]

The letter that Liberty sent to Billy Joel is absolutely explosive. In it, the drummer told the Piano Man just what he thought of him, and what he thought about several key people in his organization. He exposed one member of the entourage for scalping concert tickets behind Billy's back, referred to Tommy Byrnes as "a prick," and blamed others for maliciously misrepresenting his statements. Most of all he told Billy how hurt he was at the loss of their friendship.

Liberty claims that the tone of the letter was intended to say, "'I want to talk about this.' 'Why are we breaking up?'" He then explains, "In it I said, 'I love you Billy. If you ever want to talk about anything, call me. My number's there, everything. Call me up.'" But instead, "He let *everybody* read this letter. Everybody. I called Max Loubiere to find out what happened. So when I called Max, I said, 'Max, what happened?' Max didn't call me back for about three or four days. He said, 'I'm sorry I didn't call you back right away, the reason being, is I really had to think about you personally, and what happened. And, I've got to tell you, "I don't know." You don't deserve any of this. He feels whatever he feels—like getting rid of somebody, he'll get rid of somebody for whatever reason he wants. If he finds out I'm talking to you right now, he might want to get rid of me. That's the way Billy is. I don't know why he does what he does, but he did it.' Then he said, 'It might have been your relationship with Christie.' I was told that it was because I called him 'a drunk' in an interview. Which I didn't. Then I was told by Mark Rivera that that letter was the thing that killed everything. But the letter was sent out there when I was already not invited to the wedding."[62]

When Liberty wrote the letter did he really think that Billy would answer it? "I definitely thought he would respond," says the disappointed drummer.[62]

It is sad to read, and it is the type of letter that can only be written from one friend to another when all communication has failed. Liberty put down in black and white all of the thoughts and feelings that he had for so long held deep inside. It was composed in a way that would either repair their friendship with sincerity, or destroy it with frankness. Apparently it was the latter option that prevailed.

The closest thing to a reply came in Billy's fan letter that he sends out to his mailing list. Explains Liberty, "Then Billy Zampino writes in his column, in the fan mail newsletter that Billy sends out, he read the letter, because I could see it in his writing. This one person wrote to the newsletter, 'Liberty wrote a brother-to-brother letter to Billy.' And Billy Zampino writes back, 'It wasn't a brother-to-brother letter. It was a self-serving letter that Lib wrote.'"[62]

Although Liberty was not asked to attend Billy's wedding to Katie Lee, Billy's original saxophone player, Richie Cannata, was an invited guest. Says Richie, "I went to Billy's fiftieth birthday party, and I was at the recent wedding. I am always in there."[44]

How ironic that Richie ended up back in the inner circle, just as Liberty was let go. It left Liberty mystified: "He went from 'Love me, love my band' to what *really* happened. We always have that question. That burning question, 'Like, *what* happened to that?' [62]

"The funny thing is that Billy loves that song, 'Honesty,' which is a fantastic song. It's very insightful about how very difficult you find people to be honest with you all of the time. And he's probably the most dishonest person—with himself. If the reason why is because I called him 'an alcoholic,' I didn't say he was. Well, he proved me right when he went to rehab. He gets upset because somebody says something because they love him. He thinks everybody's out to get him. He thinks *everybody* is out to get him. Not because you love him. If I were to say to him, 'Billy, you drink too much,' it's because I love you. It's not that 'I hate your guts and want to embarrass you in front of people.' No! But he takes it like that. And you can't tell him, 'Don't do something.' I learned that from Christie. If you tell him not to drink, he'll drink more. If you tell him not to eat that, he'll eat more. That's the kind of person that Billy is."[62]

Would Liberty say that Billy removes people from his life to protect himself? "I think so," he replies. "You have to go back to Billy just being the man of the house when his father left. Maybe he never trusted his father in leaving. Maybe that's why he never trusted anyone else. And having all that power and money makes you paranoid. It's like Stalin: the more powerful he got, the more paranoid he got. Because there's more to take away now."[62]

There is a classic episode of the TV show *The Twilight Zone,* which was later remade as part of the 1983 film of the same name. In the original, child actor Billy Mumy played a spoiled child who had extreme psychic and telekinetic powers. If anyone displeased him, he simply banished them into a television screen or off to other faraway places where they would meet their demise. Behind the scenes in the Billy Joel camp, it obviously became much the same as this *Twilight Zone* episode. Everyone became afraid of displeasing Billy, for fear of the consequences. Apparently the universal cure within the Joel camp was banishment. If he had any sort of conflict or problem with his band members, he would simply make certain that they disappeared from his sight. Now it was his longtime friend Liberty DeVitto who found himself banished from what he refers to as: "Billy World."

18
EVERYBODY HAS A DREAM

WHAT'S IT LIKE to be Billy Joel today? What would it feel like to live his lifestyle in the twenty-first century? It is an opulent world, to say the least. In addition to owning several residences, he also possesses his own armada of boats. His mansion on Centre Island, off the shore of Long Island, is situated in Oyster Bay on a spot that makes it ecologically unsound to install a dock, so Billy has purchased a twenty-eight-foot aluminum catamaran to take him from the shore to any of his larger yachts. When you are so rich that you have to buy a twenty-eight-foot boat just to take you to your other vessels, and you personally employ a full-time captain as does the Piano Man, you are undeniably living one pretty rich existence.

Just how many boats does he own? Several. He buys them, fixes them up, sells them, designs them, has them built, and takes friends out for a ride in them. One of the latest he has added to his collection is a fifty-seven-foot commuter yacht he designed himself, which he has christened the *Vendetta*, "Because living well is the best revenge. I live in a Gatsby-type house, now I have a Gatsby-type boat. I enjoy that lifestyle."[182] *Vendetta* is living proof of this. It cost Billy over $2 million, and it was custom built to his own specifications.

Since he was a boy, his entire life can be told through his fascination with boats. That passion dates back to the 1960s; as a child he would see them sailing in Oyster Bay and Cold Spring Harbor, when he went on family excursions accompanied by his mother and sister. As a teenager he would go to the water and take other people's boats out for a spin when no one was looking. He recalls, "I used to 'borrow' boats. I would just unclip them from the moorings, motor them around, bring them back and clean them up. It's a good way to learn how to be a good boater because you don't mess up with somebody else's boat."[183]

Not long after the release of his *Cold Spring Harbor* album in 1971, he bought his first boat. It reflected his wealth at the time. "My first boat was a rowboat," Billy says. "I bought it in Hampton Bays. It was an 18-foot wood lapstrake whaling dory. It was a heart attack rowing this thing, so I got a little money and bought myself a kicker, a 10 horsepower Evinrude outboard."[183]

In 1975, when he and Elizabeth rented a place on Oyster Bay, he purchased a seventeen-foot Boston whaler. As time marched on, he divorced and remarried, and his wealth increased, in the 1980s he and Christie Brinkley bought a house by the water at Lloyd Harbor. By now he had moved up to a twenty-foot Shamrock skiff.

Next came the *Sea Minor,* which was a thirty-three-foot cruiser he used for offshore fishing. Then he had a larger, thirty-eight-foot boat, custom built for taking people out sport fishing. He named that one the *Sea Major.* In the early 1990s, around the time he penned the song "The Downeaster 'Alexa,'" he met with Peter Needham, who is the vice president of Coecles Harbor, and was able to personally supervise the construction of a boat that both of them designed. It was a thirty-six-foot version of a swordfishing boat that Billy describes as "a lobster boat with no frills." It was the first in a series of boats he had a hand in designing, and he proudly named it after his daughter, Alexa. For that reason, it is still the pride of his fleet. This is one boat he has no intention of parting with. "*Alexa* I'll probably never sell, because that's my good all-around, all-purpose boat. I mostly use *Alexa* now for taking people out for cruises."[183]

Since that time, his bank account and his personal fleet have continued to grow. Next he bought a twenty-eight-foot Ellis brand cruiser named the *Half Shell.* While at the vacation home Billy owns in Menemsha on the island of Martha's Vineyard, in Massachusetts, he met a lobster fisherman named Dave Neilsen. When Dave died suddenly in a storm, Billy Joel purchased the boat he owned, from the family. He kept it for four years and then sold it.

Then, while in Florida he discovered a sixty-five-foot minicargo ship called the *Red Head*, which, over the next six years he renovated, and then sold. As he explains, "I didn't use *Red Head* enough. I would use the boat maybe half a dozen times a year."[183]

By far, Billy's most famous boat-building adventure manifested itself in 1996, when he came up with the specifications for a boat he wanted built, called the *Shelter Island Roundabout*. It is a thirty-eight-foot model he refers to as a "picnic boat."[183] It was such a hit that several more identical Billy Joel–designed boats have been ordered constructed. The asking price for them starts at $356,800, and, as of 2005, thirty-nine of them had been sold.

Now in the new century, as the American economy went into a slump, his boatbuilders faced possible job layoffs. The design and ordering of the *Vendetta* served a dual purpose. It yielded Billy's dream boat and kept the boatbuilding crew busy. For that reason, he ordered the construction of *Vendetta* from Coecles Harbor. "I've seen too many boat businesses disappear," he claims.[183]

Utilizing designer Doug Zurn, Billy ended up with the seacraft he desired. Ultimately the *Vendetta* became a stunning black vessel with white cabins, teakwood accents, and a classy gold pinstripe along the top of the hull. Equipped with 1,300-horsepower twin engines, it can be taken up to a speed of sixty-five miles per hour. The whole idea behind the *Vendetta* was to have his own private yacht to take him from his Long Island mansion into Manhattan. According to Billy Joel, "I always thought that it was a great tradition during the '20s and '30s that these guys would go into Wall Street via Long Island Sound and the East River."[183]

As he was getting ready to go on the first test drive he claimed, "I think I'll be able to get to Manhattan within a half an hour at cruising speed. I go into the city more and more these days because I live closer to the city, my daughter goes to school in the city. I'm going to have an apartment in the city and I'm newly married and my wife has her interests in the city, too."[183] Whenever he goes into the city nowadays, he always takes his boat.

Although he has his own full-time captain for the *Vendetta*, Billy likes to take the wheel as well: "I like to go about 45 miles per hour. I don't care about the wind blowing in my hair. Hell, I don't have any hair left anyway."[182]

Since Billy's home on Centre Island is the gem among his real estate holdings, what is it like to live there? The estate includes three buildings:

a large brick Georgian mansion, an ample garage, and a substantial additional house in between. It is on the second floor of the middle house where Billy keeps his drafting table, upon which he designs his boats. He refers to this as the "chart room." The walls of it are clad in photos of Billy's beloved Long Island baymen, and various nautical prints.

Billy Joel's sea of gold and platinum records and awards are relegated to the basement area of the main house, leaving the rest of the decor of it unsurprisingly in a nautical motif. The library has several ship models, including a replica of the luxury cruise ship the *Queen Mary*, and an ivory scrimshaw sailboat. There are also several nautical paintings on the walls.

In Billy's office hangs a portrait of daughter Alexa, and a pair of paintings of the boat *Alexa* as well. An Edward Hopper watercolor painting of a sailboat is also framed and displayed there amid the sea of other nautical items. One hallway contains a replica model of the "tall ship" known as the *Pride of Baltimore*.

Billy has occupied the house since 2002 and has made several modifications. Where there once was a full-size sunken swimming pool, the Piano Man has removed the water, covered the area with wooden flooring, and there sits his grand piano. The basement also contains an after-dinner smoking room, where the art is all classic nautical posters. Then there is also a downstairs pub and wine cellar where the seafaring theme is all *Titanic* memorabilia and posters.

The one room in the house that is devoid of a nautical motif is the huge kitchen. Since the third Mrs. Joel is a well-known culinary expert, this is her realm, and it is decorated to her own taste. "It's Katie's command post," explains the seasoned rock star. She, too, shares his fascination with the sea. "She loves it. She's from West Virginia, so it's a new thrill for her," Billy explains.[183]

Inspired by his surroundings and the decor, much of the music that Billy has been composing matches this fascination with the sea. He says, "There's a lot of nautical themes. They're reminiscent of the 19th century chanteys that sailors would sing on whaling expeditions."[183] In other words, one should not expect to hear him compose the next "Movin' Out" or "It's Still Rock & Roll to Me" anytime soon.

Although he grew up in Levittown with next to nothing, he now lives an incredible jet-setting millionaire's life. Apparently living the lifestyle of the rich and famous suits him. He claims, "When I was a kid, I used to ride my bike up here with my friends and just look through the gates at the end of these drives and go, 'Wow! These rich bastards living behind these wrought-iron gates. . . . ' I didn't like rich people. And now I am one!"[1]

This is an existence that should make anyone happy, yet Billy has continued to display signs that he is anything but content or bathed in happiness. His actions—particularly his alcohol consumption—have suggested something very different.

Billy had only been married for a few months, when Katie was already concerned about her husband's drinking habits. A week before he checked himself into rehab, Katie and Billy had gone out to dinner with radio personality Howard Stern and his girlfriend Beth Ostrosky, at the chic Tribeca eatery, Nobu. Billy reportedly drank water that night and bragged about doing so. However, according to one report, when the Joels returned to their Long Island home, Billy went downstairs and proceeded to drink alone.

According to the *National Enquirer* account of the story, a source identified as "a friend" claimed that "Kate found Billy asleep in the wine cellar of their home. She told him she could no longer watch the brilliant man she loves, drink himself into an early grave and Billy had to choose—her or the grave." Apparently he liked to go down there and drink in solitude, and he was also taken to passing out while down in the liquor-stocked room. The same source also claimed, "Kate kept telling Billy he had to stop drinking for himself, for their marriage and for his reputation. But nothing she said sunk in—until she made Billy understand that this time, the marriage itself was on the line."[184]

It was reported the next week in the *National Enquirer* that "Billy's new wife and a few others got together and staged an intervention. They saw that he was slipping back into heavy-duty drinking." The article went on to say, "When he first went, he was so severely depressed that he was put on suicide watch. His family and doctors were seriously concerned that he would take his own life."[185]

On March 10, 2005, Billy Joel admitted himself to the Betty Ford Clinic in Rancho Mirage, California. He checked out of the clinic after the full thirty days required for the total regimen. It was his longest stretch in rehab yet, and, according to several sources, this time it was going to do the trick.

Everything was kept under wraps until March 15, when Billy's publicist, Claire Mercuri, publicly admitted that he was indeed going through the Betty Ford Clinic regimen to detox from alcohol abuse.

As reported in the *New York Daily News,* Katie Lee flew out to California with the couple's two pug dogs, Fionnula and Sabrina, to meet Billy as he checked out of the clinic at 6:30 A.M. on April 10, 2005. They then flew back to Long Island together. The article's anonymously quoted source claimed they encountered Billy Joel and found, "He looks really fit. He's dedicated to a healthy and sober lifestyle. Billy has completely sworn off all alcohol."[186]

When he was released, Billy claimed that he was feeling better than ever and began talking openly about his problem drinking. Was he embarrassed that he had gone through this process? "Look, in this business, [rehabilitation] is like going to get your teeth cleaned," he announced. "I haven't gone this long without anything to drink in my whole life. 'Just don't drink?' I never thought of that!"[1]

One thing that he did want to do was to set the record straight about some details concerning his life: "I've seen references to my drinking Jack Daniels. I only drank Scotch. Dewar's White Label."[1]

All of his fans hoped that this time it would stick. He had gone into rehab once before, right after his 2002 car accident, but apparently his old habits died hard; it wasn't long before he was drinking heavily again. Then came the next two car accidents. Maybe this time it would work. His friends and fans certainly hoped so, too.

Radio personality Ken Dashow points out, "When he was drinking heavily, it was sad. It just seems that he is loved so much, you want him—we all root for him so much—to find a happier place to be in to live. You don't want to keep reading about car accidents on Long Island. He's been so nice to everyone locally on Long Island. People love him. It's not that he think's he's a big shot. He is a guy that everybody roots for."[111]

Once out of rehab, Billy began to repair his public image. In September 2005 he was in the news for inaugurating what he called the Billy Joel Endowment Fund. It was a new initiative started to provide money, scholarships, and endowments to several East Coast colleges, universities, and music schools.

In 2005 two more compilations were issued of Billy's music. In Europe and other international markets, the single disc, nineteen-track *Piano Man: The Very Best of Billy Joel* was released. But the big splashy album was *My Lives,* a five-disc boxed set of rarities, outtakes, "B" sides, soundtrack cuts, and even a couple of Billy classics in rough form. Four of the discs are of rare music, and the fifth disc is a DVD of concert footage taken on the *River Dreams Tour.*

Billy had a hand in compiling all of the music that is contained on this boxed set. It traces his career from the Lost Souls, to the Hassles, to Attila, to his first solo demo recordings. This package was very different from the "greatest hits" packages that have been done of his highest-charting songs. Says Billy, "I owe a great deal of whatever success I've had in my career to [the] album tracks, as much as the hit singles. People who just know Billy Joel from Top 40 singles may not like Billy Joel, and I can't say I necessarily blame them. I don't think that really represents the sum and substance of my work."[29]

One of the cleverest aspects of *My Lives* is the fact that some songs are recognizable through their embryonic versions. For instance, "These Rhinestone Days," which is on this album, eventually evolved into the song "I've Loved These Days," which is on *Turnstiles*. As Billy explained it, "That's an example of how I would write songs. I would primarily just write music, and I would use a lyric to carry the melodic phrasing along, so I could fix in my head how the phrasing, the imprint of the lyric, the cadence, should be. There are examples of that sprinkled throughout this set. Another one is 'Prime of Your Life,' which ended up becoming 'The Longest Time.'"[29]

The package features a black-and-white cartoon portrait of Billy, drawn by his daughter, Alexa Ray Joel. He also personally chose the title of the album. "*My Lives* is the right title for this thing, 'cause I feel like I've had a series of lives," he claims.[1]

The album included the song from the Disney film he recorded, the Leonard Cohen tribute song, and even some attempts at doing country-style songs "I wanted some more obscure things to be represented on this set, I said, 'Let's dig into the tapes, the B-sides, the recording sessions and movie songs that had never been released officially.'"[29]

There was even a remixed dance version of "Keeping the Faith," from 1984: "This was from when 'house music' was really big in the mid-'80s. These crazy guys from Philly did the remix, and they were in the studio just going nuts. I kind of dug it, 'cause they took it a direction I hadn't even considered. I liked all the syncopation going on, the percussion and different sounds. A good piece of music should be malleable."[1]

One of the most interesting previously unreleased tracks is his version of Bob Dylan's "Highway 61 Revisited," a demo from 1999. Proclaims Billy, "Bob Dylan was a real inspiration to me. The imagery he came up with for this song was so fantastic. Whether you know what it means or not, it doesn't really frickin' matter. What matters is how it hits you. It's a fun song to play on the piano, too. It's got a real boogie-woogie thing going on."[1]

He also included his recording of Dylan's "To Make You Feel My Love," which was on the *Greatest Hits, Volume Three* album. Billy describes the song as "a jewel that nobody had ever heard."[163]

In November 2005, Billy released the second in his series of children's books. This time around he took another of his songs to create the book *New York State of Mind*. It was illustrated by Izak Zenou. The book was presented in a way that could be read by children aged four to eight.

On November 29, 2005, Billy presented another one of his master class sessions in New York City, at the 92nd Street Y. It followed the format of his previous presentations: several stories and a song or two as well. This one was sponsored by NARAS (National Academy of Recording Arts and Sciences). Billy Joel posed for photos with the president of the Grammy Awards organization, Carlos Allomar, and appeared to be in good spirits.

After the show, the backstage door was deluged by Billy fans who wanted a close-up glimpse of him, an autograph, or a handshake. In spite of heavy rain, fans were undeterred. Wearing a hooded green parka that covered much of his face, Billy suddenly appeared in the stage doorway, and he was whisked to his waiting car by an unfriendly bunch of hired bodyguards. However, he was in a great mood and stopped to shake a few hands. Once he got to the black SUV that he and Katie Lee were being driven in, he laughingly admonished the assembled crowd by yelling out to them, "It's raining, get out of here!" He clearly looked pleased that his faithful followers felt compelled to wait in the pouring rain for him.[187]

In December 2005, Billy Joel and Christie Brinkley's daughter, Alexa, made her professional singing debut at the rock & roll nightclub, the Cutting Room. It is a club owned by Chris Noth of *Law & Order* and *Sex and the City* fame, and his business partner, Steve Walter. The night of her debut, both of Alexa's parents were in the audience, at separate tables. Christie was surrounded by several of her friends, and Billy appeared to be surrounded by bodyguards. Alexa is musically talented and entertaining, and she presents her self-penned material like a young Carole King, or a contemporary of Sarah McLachlan's. She apparently has a big future ahead of her in the music business.

That same month New York radio station Q104.3 (WAXQ) again hosted its annual 104.3-hour Rock Marathon to raise funds for Charity Begins at Home, which was founded by Billy Joel. In 2005 it was announced that more than $250,000 was raised by December 15. With regard to the way in which the raised funds are doled out, Bob Buchman, who is the main fund-raiser, explains, "Everything goes through Louise Friedman. Now she's eighty-three. I am not even a board member of the charity, and neither is Billy. And I think we prefer it that way. We prefer the distance. We work for the charity, but we are not actually a board member, which is fine by us. It leaves the distribution of the funds for the professionals in a not-for-profit way, and Louise and her board definitely is great. This woman's going straight to heaven. She certainly is. She is just an amazing woman, and Billy loves her. He was with me on the air, just a couple of months ago and said on the air, 'Having Louise Friedman in your corner is something everybody would want if they knew her as we do.' So, she's great. So, she really fulfills his mission. I fundraise, she makes it happen, and he continues to be in the loop."99

In the fall of 2005, the big news was that Billy Joel was finally going to return to concert touring. Originally there had been talk of a tour in the spring of 2005, but that was not to be. Recalls Richie Cannata, "He booked a small tour last Easter, and that's when he went into rehab, March 10 [2005]. We were going to go out and do a handful of dates back then, and they didn't happen. So then everything was on the back burner, and waiting. And then he called me up again, and he said he had booked a bunch of dates."44

There was also plenty of gossip surrounding the musicians with whom Billy chose to tour this time around. Fans were thrilled that Richie Cannata, the original sax player in the Joel band, was rejoining the ensemble. However, they were shocked to find out that, for the first time in three decades, Liberty DeVitto was specifically *not* asked to join the tour.

Furthermore, as the band members signed on for this tour, they were each required to sign a document stating that they were not to talk to the press, and also they were not to talk to Liberty DeVitto. This ignited something of a behind-the-scenes battle. When Liberty found out that the drummer who was asked to fill in his place in the show was the drummer from the just-closed Broadway show *Movin' Out,* he was furious. It was exactly as he had predicted when the Broadway show opened: Billy would be using *Movin' Out* as a recruiting ground for band replacements. His premonition was coming true before his very eyes, which Liberty found both insulting and infuriating.

During the fall of 2005, before contracts and the infamous "nondisclosure agreement" were signed, when it was still in the developmental states, Richie Cannata was very optimistic about the tour. Had he and Billy remained friends all this time? According to Richie, "We kept in contact. He is my neighbor, he was out on Long Island here. I saw him on the Fourth of July. He had this beautiful boat, and he gave me the boat for the Fourth of July, and I brought my family out on it. We stayed at the house, and we stayed on the boat. It was great. The women he would be dating at the time, we'd go out to dinner. He would call up, and say, 'Hey let's go out to dinner.' It was always friendly. I loved it. I loved the opportunities that he gave me, and in reverse—the ideas that I gave him: the holes that were missing in some of these songs. They got us to this point. Like I said, 'Twenty-five or thirty years later, the songs still sound great.' Look at 'Scenes From an Italian Restaurant.'"[44]

Prior to signing any contracts, Richie freely spoke of his professional reunion with Joel. "Billy's asked me to rejoin the band. And, I said, 'Yes.' Have we come to terms yet? 'Not as of the moment.' This is for a four month tour starting in January. They are booking dates now." Would this grow to become a "world tour?" Claimed Richie, "It's up to Billy. If Billy feels healthy enough that he wants to do this tour, then he'll do it."[44]

Richie claimed that he had no interest in seeing Billy's Broadway show, *Movin' Out,* even though it was about to close that December. "I didn't see it. I know all of the guys in it, and they are all great players. But, think about it, they are reading the notes. It has to be the same every night. It has to be exactly the same. It is not a rock & roll show. If the sax player doesn't play that part that night, there are three subs right behind him."[44]

In December 2005, when he found out that Richie was returning to the band but that he was not invited back, Liberty DeVitto was not only insulted he also expressed concern for his old friend Richie. Said Liberty: "I can't believe that he's gonna do it again!"[62]

When Billy Joel started announcing concert dates for Madison Square Garden, beginning on January 23, 2006, it was undetermined how many concerts would ultimately be scheduled as part of the run. The subsequent dates were added one at a time, and the tickets were snapped up the minute they went on sale. The previous record holder at the Garden had been Bruce Springsteen, who had sold out a series of ten shows. The demand for tickets for Billy's concerts was so great, that shows continued to be added and to sell out: nine, ten, eleven, and finally record-setting show number twelve—to be held April 24, 2006.

As he was about to do the first show in January, Billy told the *New York Post,* "Honestly, I thought I was better live 20 years ago. I looked the part then. I had a lot more hair, I was skinnier, and I was able to hang upside down from speaker cables. I was able to do a lot of crazy stuff I can't do now. I was more of a fireball eater."[188] Indeed, circa 2006, Billy looks less like a rock star than he does a middle-aged accountant. He has short, cropped hair and a decidedly chunky physique. He can still strut around the stage with aplomb, but he performs with a lot less acrobatic agility than he used to display midshow. The most winning and appealing aspect of seeing Billy nowadays is that he is sounding better than ever. His voice is a bit lower than it used to be, but he still knows how to command a rock & roll stage brilliantly, and with flair and attitude.

During the twelfth 2006 Madison Square Garden show, his radio buddy Bob Buchman came out onstage after the show began and announced that Billy had broken a house record with this historic show number twelve. With that, a "player's" sports banner was descended from the rafters, with the words "Joel 12" in huge letters, at which time hundreds, if not thousands, of colored balloons were released from the rafters. That night the crowd went crazy with enthusiastic cheering. Billy is now the only nonathlete to have a number "retired" and displayed at Madison Square Garden.

Based on her culinary skills, and no doubt partially due to the fact that she was Mrs. Billy Joel, in 2006, twenty-four-year-old Katie Lee Joel became the star of a competitive cooking show on the Bravo cable TV network, called *Top Chef.* The format of the program pitted the innovative cooking skills of a dozen chefs who vied for the title of "top chef," thousands of dollars' worth of prizes, and $100,000. Each week, one of the twelve contestants was thrown off the show, until one prevailing survivor remained. It was kind of like *American Idol,* but transposed to the kitchen.

Katie, who is very sophisticated in her manner of dressing, speaking, and presenting herself, played her role as a cool-as-a-cucumber hostess. She was seen on camera impeccably clad and carrying herself like a young Ali McGraw or Jacqueline Kennedy. She comes across as being very centered and highly "no nonsense" on camera. The first season of the show debuted on March 15, 2006, and ran for ten episodes. In June 2006, it was announced that Katie would not be returning for the second season.

The couple was also in the news for mega-million-dollar real estate shopping in both Miami and Brooklyn. Billy had learned years ago that real estate was a sound investment, and he continued to buy and sell property. In May 2006 it was announced that Billy Joel's young life and early career were due to become a television series on the Showtime cable network.

On June 13, 2006, Billy released his twenty-fourth album, *12 Gardens Live.* It was a two-disc in-concert album recorded during the sold-out dates at Madison Square Garden earlier that year. The album highlighted several of Billy's rarely performed songs, such as "The Entertainer" and

"The Ballad of Billy the Kid." The rarest of all is "The Night Is Still Young," which was originally on his *Greatest Hits, Volumes One and Two* set. There are also hidden "bonus" tracks on the album: the song "A Room of Our Own" is unlisted on the label but serves as the end track to Disc One, and "It's Still Rock & Roll to Me" is the uncredited sixteenth track on Disc Two. The sound quality on *12 Gardens Live* is great, and it is a highly successful musical chronicle of these historic concert performances.

The album was also a critical success. Andrew Marton in the *Fort Worth Star–Telegram* claimed, "Billy Joel, classic rock's quintessential Piano Man, has never issued a career-encompassing live recording. . . . The melodic bard of Bayside is back—and firing on all cylinders with *12 Gardens Live* . . . *12 Gardens'* two disks act as a musical biography, delivering Joel hits that span three decades. . . . Backed by a stellar group of musicians, Joel reproduces live the same shimmering sound, gorgeously hand-tooled melodies and taut arrangements from the song's studio versions. . . . Billy Joel, the prescient pianist, is back."[189] The album peaked at number 14 on the *Billboard* chart in America.

It is admirable how Billy has managed to remain a force in the record business, even though he turned his back on recording new rock material after 1993. According to Andy Skurow, a record producer for Universal and Motown Records, "I have never seen someone who is able to keep his fan base without giving them any new material in over twelve years. The live albums, the compilations, the new classical album, have only made his fans want more rock & roll from him. Yet he resists the temptation to give them what they want. I have never seen anything like it. The fact that he was able to place his *12 Gardens Live* album in the top 20, with not one new song on it, is amazing to me. He has recycling down to a science!"[190]

In June and July 2006, Billy took his successful new stage act and superband on the road for a world tour. Ironically, although he is prominently featured on the *12 Gardens Live* album, when it came time to mount the European leg of the tour, Richie Cannata was not asked to be part of it. The concerts in Europe began in Vienna, Austria, and went on to several cities in Germany, England, the Netherlands, and Ireland and ended up with a free show at the Colosseum in Rome, Italy, on July 31.

Internationally acclaimed painter Mark Kostabi was one of the celebrities who was present at that particular concert in Italy. The following day he reported via e-mail, "I went to the Billy Joel concert last night here in

Rome. The press reported that there were at least 200,000 to 300,000 in attendance and reported that the city officials said there were 500,000 but implied that 500,000 may have been an exaggeration. I was in the Telecom guest section for 3,000 Telecom guests near the front. Telecomitalia, a phone company, was the sponsor for the concert. I was not able to go backstage. At the concert I was recognized by a journalist and was interviewed for the national newspaper: *La Repubblica*. I was asked who I preferred: Bryan Adams (the opening act) or Billy Joel? My quote published in today's *La Repubblica* is: 'Adoro Billy Joel, sono qui apposto per lui e la sua fantastica musica,' which translates to: 'I adore Billy Joel. I'm here for him and his fantastic music.'"[191]

According to Kostabi, "On another note I found it very inspiring when Billy Joel once said, to *Billboard* magazine: 'It's hard to know when to stop quivering with a certain feeling and just let it become a song.' As an artist whose inspiration often comes from personal life experience I can really relate to that reflection. Sometimes when I'm battling inner demons or suffering in the woes of some relationship disaster I think about that Billy Joel quote and just drop the misery on the floor and then mop it up with my paint brushes and put it on the canvas where it belongs and where everyone can relate to it better—rather than listening to me whine on the phone. I find that the more personal I get in my art, the more universal it becomes, and I imagine that Billy Joel discovered a similar dynamic when he wrote songs like 'Uptown Girl' and 'Piano Man.'"[191]

Meanwhile, ever since he left Billy Joel's band in the late 1980s, Russell Javors has worked very hard to reinvent himself. "I came out of Billy['s band] with nothing," he claims. "I was broke when I was done with Billy. So, I struggled, and I had to pick myself and 'do what I gotta do.' My résumé's like *The Three Faces of Eve*. 'How do you get from there to there?' 'What the hell is that about?' I would just try stuff, and see, and whatever. If something sticks, 'Go with it.' I guess if I had it to do over again, and I was a little smarter, or had a little bit more business savvy in the beginning, I probably wouldn't have made the choices I made. Now, at the end of the day, if you get a little bit of respect for what you do, and a little bit of security or whatever, it isn't such a bad thing."[65]

He tried his hand at being a show business manager. "I produced and managed a reggae singer. We had a deal on Columbia, a guy named Tony Rebel. And I did some really good stuff with him." But, according to Russell, after Doug Stegmeyer's suicide he lost his interest in the music business all together: "I guess I just kinda blocked it off. After Doug died, I just walked away from it. I just didn't care anymore."[65]

He admits that he didn't have a strong game plan at the time. "I was not money driven. I got into the business world after Billy. And frankly, I had so many opportunities and situations that I was always doing what I thought were creative projects and things that would move me, but I don't know if my business sense was all that great. I tried doing a million things."[65]

Among other projects, Russell tried launching a show on ballroom dancing. It nearly went into production but then never quite got off of the ground. There were budgeting problems, and conflicting creative visions. It was finished before it began. "I had a lot of things in development," he says. "I wrote a sitcom for Ringo [Starr], and he passed because he didn't want to play a musician. But it was a very cool idea, and King World went into 'development' on that. I rewrote it for [Sam] Kinisen, then once for Alice Cooper. I worked forever on these projects, and I wrote a bunch of stuff."[65]

He even tried his hand at a career in finance. "I passed my Series Seven, and became an investment banker. I hated it!" He laughs.[65] Then he suddenly found an ideal job, quite by accident.

"In the midst of all of this, my brother-in-law was in the toy business, and he asked me to do some projects for him. It started out with a sound chip. He was over at my place, and he played it, and he was freaking out because he was going to miss a shipment. It was a sound chip that had to be all cut up and edited, and I heard it, and I went to this guy on Long Island who had a studio." Russell Javors solved the problem, and suddenly he found himself in the toy business. He explains, "It became the state-of-the-art sound chip for toys, and I started to get all this consulting work in the toy business. It was starting to get a little more steady than the work I was getting in the music business, and I had a pretty good take on it, just instinctively."[65]

The next thing he knew, he and his wife, Suzanne, moved to the Detroit suburb of Milford, where the toy manufacturer had offices. While there he invented a toy that did well on the market place. "Today I work for a big toy company in Hong Kong, and it is what it is." He laughs again.[65]

"All the negative stuff aside, I can say, 'Billy gave me an opportunity to see and do things I never would have done in my life. So, with all the other nonsense aside, still when I look back, people will say, 'That's the guy who used to play with Billy Joel.'"[65]

"When I look back and remember those times, that's what I kinda draw out of it. And, my wife doesn't always agree with me," says Russell. "She's entitled to her opinion. She lived through it just like we did. Her life got affected. I look at it more pragmatic. I figure, 'If it's my band, and I want to change guys, or do whatever, for whatever reason, then that's my right to do it.' But it's all a question of 'Why?' There were still outstanding issues. The money thing kills me."[65]

While he is happy to just chalk it up to "experience," he admits, "my wife doesn't agree with me, I will be honest with you. I don't want to tie my stomach in a knot when I think about it."[65]

Russell today claims that he has it all in perspective. "I used to say to Lib, 'It's like we went to war together' or something, or you won a World Series together. And whether you liked all the guys you were with, or you had good times or bad times or whatever, only you guys can share that. There is still a part of our lives that we all shared, and we will always be brothers that way. So, no matter what happens, with all the guys and all the nonsense, and all the crap, we always have that bond."[65]

Says Russell Javors of his Billy Joel adventure, "I am not bitter. I have my own opinions on what kinda guy the guy is, but whatever. But I certainly think I have a pretty clear picture of what happened and how it happened, and whatever. And it is what it is. I am not going there. I have a family to support, I got stuff to do. I know Liberty is very upset. It's funny. Playing in a band is like playing on a baseball team or something else. You've got all these people, that you love them to death, and they're your brothers, and you care about them on a lot of levels. And sometimes you can't even have dinner with them because everybody pisses you off so bad. It's like that type of thing where there's a lot of things about all these guys that I love. Liberty's my brother and I have been with him since I was fifteen. He went to elementary school with my wife. Liberty's sister introduced me to my wife when we were nineteen, and we've been together ever since. We have been through the thick and thin of it."[65]

These days much of the focus of the key players in the Billy Joel story is set on their sons and daughters. In the same way that Billy is supportive of Alexa's musical aspirations, Richie Cannata, Liberty DeVitto, and Russell Javors are encouraging their own children's show business careers.

Richie says, "Billy and Christie's daughter and my son were both at NYU together. She is not there any longer. But when I was at the wedding [of Billy and Katie], Christie was at the wedding, and we talked about Eren and

Alexa being at NYU, and they saw each other at some NYU function. And Alexa came here [Cove City Sound] and recorded something Billy wanted her to record when she first started out."[44]

Richie has put a lot of his energy and industry know-how in getting behind his son, Eren, and his budding career. Eren Cannata has headlined such New York City clubs as the Bitter End and the Cutting Room. Naturally, his horn-playing dad usually ends up on stage doing a guest saxophone solo in the middle of the sets. Says Richie, "Number one in my life is my son, and his music. I would give up all of this for his success, to be comfortable, and letting the world know his talent and his music. He just turned twenty. For me, he is 'it.' He is my hero, he is everything. That's really number one. I don't care about the fame or the fortune. We're comfortable. But his music is that good. It should be heard."[44]

When Liberty DeVitto is asked if he is happy with the choices he has made in life, he replies, "I wouldn't change a thing. I would only change one thing in my life. I would have been in the Beatles, instead of with Billy Joel! I can't say that I wouldn't have married my ex-wives, because I have beautiful children."[63]

One of his daughters, Torrey DeVitto, is a budding actress. Says Liberty, "She is making a movie now, *I'll Always Know What You Did Last Summer*. She sent me pictures of her dead on the floor. A guy put a hook in her stomach, but in the photo she is smiling." He laughs.[63]

Russell Javor's son Jesse is a talented blues guitarist. "I always wanted him to be the best that he could be," says Russell. "Jesse plays like [a] Robert Johnson type of blues. He's awesome. He is in television programming. He is at AMC [American Movie Classics]. But, he's awesome. So, he also goes out and does some gigs and stuff. I think he *saw* the music business. He grew up in it."[65]

After Billy Joel had his highly publicized car accidents, there were several press accounts about Christie Brinkley not wanting Alexa riding in the car while Billy was behind the wheel. Explains Richie Cannata, "Christie is very concerned about Alexa's safety. You can follow that in the press, with the accidents and stuff. And, I am that way with Eren, too. So, Christie and I, and surely my wife are in agreement in the protection of our kids, whether it be NYU or just being in an automobile."[44]

From the perspective of 2006, Billy dismissed any responsibility for the automotive mishaps. According to him, "I'm not the only person in the world who's had accidents. They were just bad luck. The first one I was avoiding hitting a deer, the second one was an icy road, and the third one happened on a rainy road—I skidded and tapped a guy's house. Before that I never had accidents."[188]

These days, Christie's contact with Billy comes mainly where their daughter Alexa is concerned. When Billy headlined the first of his sold-out 2006 dates at Madison Square Garden, both Christie and Alexa were in the audience.

On July 12, 2006, it was announced that Brinkley was divorcing her fourth husband, Peter Cook. The following week the story erupted into a juicy scandal when it was revealed that Cook had been having an affair with an eighteen-year-old girl. Suddenly Christie Brinkley's name and face were all over the Internet, and featured on the covers of the tabloid newspapers. Every story seemed to mention that she was formerly married to Billy Joel. At the time he made no public comment about Christie's divorce, or his relationship with her.

Several people close to Billy Joel claim that he has built quite an emotional wall around himself. The man who was around him the most was Liberty, who says, "Bill Zampino may be Billy's oldest best friend, but he is on the payroll. Billy has no friends who are just friends. Even [former tour manager] Jeff Schock claims, 'Billy wouldn't let anyone near him.'"[3]

Entertainment journalist Marcy MacDonald has observed, "He is very contradictory. Billy clearly prefers live performances more than anything, but in a close-up social setting he completely distances himself from people. I have seen him sitting alone in a corner at a party. I can only think that he just prefers it that way."[192]

With regard to having made his 1993 *River of Dreams* album his last new rock & roll creation, Billy claims, "I've always admired guys who walked away at the top of their game. DiMaggio did it. I've had my time in the sun. You can't squeeze blood from a stone."[1] If retiring "at the top" from the world of new rock & roll recordings was his goal, he certainly accomplished it. But his fans and peers would still like to see and hear more new music from him.

Dana Bove of VH1 wrote,"Growing up on Long Island, everyone loved Billy Joel. And once MTV started up 25 years ago, he was an even bigger household name, if that was possible! His videos for 'Pressure' and 'For the Longest Time' are still two of my favorites from my childhood. Considering the impact he had on music over the years, it's no wonder VH1 Classic has so much of his work in rotation."[193]

The keyboard player from the group Three Dog Night, Jimmy Greenspoon, has long been an admirer of Billy's: "You are great Billy, a wonderful

BILLY JOEL

talent. Wish you would go back and record some more of your beautiful, classy pop songs."[39]

On the other side of the coin, Randy Jones, the original cowboy from the group Village People, writes, "I can totally see Billy Joel's logic for not wanting to record another studio rock & roll album. With hits like 'Just the Way You Are,' 'New York State of Mind,' and 'Uptown Girl' to his credit, what more does he need? He can make a fortune performing those songs live in concert for years to come. His last rock album was in 1993 and it hit Number One. With the kind of wealth that he has amassed, why would he want to compete with himself? He walked away from recording rock music while he was at the top of his game. This way his star status will always be intact. I think that—along with Elton John, and Freddie Mercury—that Billy Joel's voice rates as one of the Top Three greatest pop/rock voices of all times. And, of course they all have had great producers too!"[194]

Mary Wilson of the Supremes is a big fan of Billy's: "I love how he weaves the jazz in with his pop music. I sing his 'New York State of Mind' in my jazz shows. I think he is an excellent pianist and writer. I listen to him all the time."[195]

From the very beginning of his career, Billy Joel has had a very spotty track record with the press. Some people love him, others not at all. According to Jed Ryan of Long Island's *PM* magazine, "Billy Joel seems to distance himself from much of the industry. What is up with that? There's a whole world out there that he could lend a compassionate hand to. I'm not saying that he has to be Bono of U2, but he doesn't have to act so reclusive. Look at someone like Cher. She is always doing something for her fans. What's with Billy Joel's big disappearing act? Someone like Madonna—crazy bitch that she is—she is always out there commenting on some way to make the world a better place to live in. Why can't Billy Joel use his celebrity clout for more worthy causes more often? He is an icon, so what he says will be listened to, because he has the power, and he has the voice to make his opinion heard."[196]

Radio personality Ken Dashow foresees the possibility of Billy going back into the recording studio in the near future. "I think that's what he's trying to figure out right now, 'What's the idiom that I want to be in?' I think he's too brilliant a songwriter not to write another rock album. People like Billy were born with a gift of being able to express something musically and simply. Sometimes the gift slows down, or things get in the way, or you don't have the passion for it. . . . Billy, who's sort of been opening up his limitations, and doing whatever he wants, I think it's easy for him to come up with another great album. It might be an album of original jazz standards that he writes."[111]

The head of Sony Music, Don Ienner, kept calling Billy to see if he could squeeze another album out of him. Ienner revealed that the answer was always the same: "He says he's not ready; I get disappointed." Billy just shrugs and says, "I've done pretty well for Columbia Records."[1]

Bob Buchman of Manhattan radio station Q104.3 says of Billy, "He's just a very engaging guy, and it goes way beyond songwriting and music. He can hold an audience spellbound, and not even play a note, and not even be on a stage. If he was at a comedy club, he could honestly do stand-up. That's because he's just a funny guy, and he's a real guy, and there's humor in just the way he speaks with people, converses with people."[99]

Said Deborah Gibson in 2006, "About a week ago I was in a Starbucks in L.A. and I said something about 'Piano Man' and the kid behind the counter said, 'What's that?' I said, 'A song by Billy Joel,' and he said, 'Who?' I said, 'You should be ashamed of yourself.' This generation is missing out. There is no *next* Billy Joel.' There is and will always be *only* one."[134]

When asked the question "How do you feel about Billy today?" Russell Javors replies, "I'm sure I think about Billy as much as he thinks about me. I don't live in the past. I'm proud of what we did together, but I've built a new life for myself."[64]

If Billy Joel phoned him today, would he go to work for him again? Russell answers, "Well, I doubt that will ever happen. When I played with Billy, we were a band. Playing in that band meant more to me than playing with Billy. In those days, Billy had Phil and he had us. That was a pretty good support group. A lot has happened since then. Billy has guys around him now that he feels comfortable with. So be it. I guess the only thing I wonder about is, if he's so comfortable with these guys, why isn't he making records?"[64]

Russell believes that Billy Joel still has several new albums' worth of music in him. "There is probably the best album of his life in there, how do you pull it out?" He is amazed that he has heard no new rock music from Billy in over a dozen years. "If Doug were alive today, me, Lib and Doug could go into a room and we could kick everybody's ass! I still believe that," Russell insists. "My ego tells me, if Doug were still here, and we cleared everybody out of the room, and we sat him down, that we could probably make the best album he ever made in his life. . . . There's nothing in my mind that says he's not capable of making a great record."[65]

When Elton John was asked in 2005 if he would tour with Billy Joel again, he enthusiastically replied, "Yeah, I would, because I love him dearly. My greatest wish is for Billy Joel to have a Number One album and get his confidence back. That would make me so happy. You know, we've never been rivals, we've always been friends. Part of my Captain Fantastic's next 30 years include Billy Joel. And it would be great to do a duet."[197]

With regard to this, Billy claims, "I know Elton John has said in a couple of interviews, 'I hope Billy gets his confidence back and has a Number One album.' But I think Elton might be mistaking confidence for desire. You have to have the *desire* to be competitive in the rock & roll world. I don't have it."[1]

Billy claims that he likes to tour with Elton, because they have a friendly competitiveness between the two of them. "If I'd been a band do you know how long ago I would have broken up," says Joel, "But a solo artist can't break up. All I can do is join something. It was fun working with Elton because we shared the work, and he kicked my ass. You're sitting backstage and hearing hit after hit, and you're going, 'How am I going to follow that?' And he's a great piano player. We do this dueling piano bit, and I'm thinking, 'Where did he come up with that?' And I've got to dig way down in my chops to answer him. And that's a really good thing—somebody's kicking my ass, and I've got to kick his ass. It's like a friendly rivalry, but it's a rivalry nonetheless, and it makes it fun to work. I respect him a lot."[29]

In February 2006, Liberty DeVitto was quoted in the *New York Post*, complaining about the way Billy had treated him. According to inside sources in the Joel camp, the next concert date that Billy played on his concurrent tour, he snidely dedicated his performance of the song "Big Shot" to Liberty for going to the press.

These days, there are nothing but bad feelings between Liberty and Billy. While the latter is in the news every several months for having either bought or sold a new multimillion dollar piece of real estate in Miami, or Long Island, or Manhattan, or for buying a new boat, Liberty's life is quite different. Billy Joel is megawealthy at this point. Liberty DeVitto had kept hoping that he would be asked on the 2006 tour. When Billy didn't call, he knew that was the end of their friendship. When Liberty is asked if he has any nice stories that he wants to recall, he proclaims, "I'd rather tell you the bad stuff about Billy. Like how we had to kick in the door to get him up."[62]

If Liberty was to describe Billy Joel from this perspective of today, what would he say? How would he describe him? After pausing for a moment, Liberty replies, "I would say that Billy is the kinda guy that, if he has a dent

BILLY JOEL

in his car. . . . Let's just say, he loves his car. He has a beautiful car. He opens it up in a parking lot and dents the door. He will drive the whole car into a wall. That one dent ruins it for him. It's ruined forever. He will be so pissed off that it happened, he will ruin the whole thing."[62]

According to Liberty, "Billy's self-destructive. He's a great talent. He writes what everyone wants to say in three minutes. He is a great piano player. He is a wonderful dad, you know, when we were with the kids. He is a terrible husband." He laughs. "I think we're all terrible husbands! I don't think anybody can get close to him, like to be a friend, like somebody who can say something. If you had a friend who can say something to you, that will make you cry, and you will think, 'I never thought anybody ever felt like that about me.' He doesn't let anybody get close to him. You can't get close to him, for some strange reason. Billy has you at arm's distance. I mean, I've gone places with him that no one's gone with him, playing his music. Wives haven't gone there, nobody. But we had that brother/friend-ship kind of thing. To be able to argue: 'Fuck you!' 'No, *fuck you!*'"[62]

Musically, Liberty brought a unique and driving sound to the drums that he played. He was very rock & roll in his approach. "That's why it worked so well," he explains, "is that [Billy] was classical, with some R&B in him. And I think that I am the guy who brought the music to the street. He is the guy who wrote the pretty melodies, and made the girls swoon. A lot of people tell me that I am a big part of Billy Joel's sound. I am the sound. It's him and me, and then you go with the band. The best band was me, Russell Javors, David Brown, Richie Cannata, and Doug Stegmeyer, and me—evidenced on *Glass Houses*. There are no overdubs, it's just that band."[63]

Does Liberty think that Billy's ego got in the way, and that things just sort of went to his head? "At first he tried not to let it go to his head. But I think that people were feeding him. He always said—and this *is* what he said, 'A star is a ball of mass that will eventually burn itself out. I will never be a star, until the drummer tells me I am.' It was the last thing I expected him to say, but 'Billy, after what you've done to me: You really *are* a star!'"[62]

Musically, how does Billy see himself? "I don't think of myself as a singer really. I think of myself as a writer and I'm able to write all over the place, so I'll change my voice depending on the mood of the music. I'm not a stylist, I never have been, as a singer. I always wanted to sound like a black man from Georgia. I always wanted to sing like Ray Charles or Wilson Pickett. Or when I was singing a ballad I thought of [Paul] McCartney, or I thought of [Harry] Nilsson, or John Lennon. A lot of different voices. So I'm not really sure what my voice is, but it doesn't bother me, I don't really care. I

BILLY JOEL

think with certain journalists, they have a problem with that though, because they think that I live in a stylistic no man's land, that I'm some kind of a Zelig. But I'm not doing it consciously, I'm just doing it as an extension of the writer. It's like when you hear a conductor singing along with what he's conducting, the audience doesn't want to hear it, but the conductor's doing it anyway. That's his way of conducting, he sings along with what he's doing. Some jazz guys sing with what they play. I'm actually just singing with what I'm writing, that's how I think of my voice."[31]

Some performers hate to hear themselves on record. How does Billy Joel feel listening to his own singing? In the 1990s he proclaimed, "I'm probably happy with more than half of the recordings. The writer, I'm happy with; the singer, I'm never happy with. He always lets me down, because my heroes were always black singers and I'm not black. I'm just a little Jewish kid from Levittown who's trying to sound black, but I'm not kidding me."[10]

Nowadays he does whatever kind of music he likes, without regard for its commerciality. "When people ask me what I've been doing for the last few years, I say, 'If you want to know about my life, listen to *Fantasies & Delusions.*' And they say, 'But there's no lyrics.' And I answer, 'Yes, but it's all there.' Every instrumental piece has an inherent lyric in it. This is what I've wanted to do all along.'"[29]

In the 1980s, when he was at the height of his success, Billy had a clearcut way that he wanted his creative legacy to be observed. "I would like the music to have meant something during the time in which I lived. It doesn't necessarily have to represent what was going on, but I would like to be thought of as of that time. And to be able to transcend that time. I think that piece of music that is written well enough can continue. I don't even know if the lyric has to. I think if a jazz musician thirty years from now could play 'Baby Grand,' 'Just the Way You Are" or 'New York State of Mind' as a standard, then the music still will have a life."[40]

One thing that he has vowed never to do is to sell his songs for use in TV commercials. As he explains it, "I haven't done it—not because I'm a snob and not because I think my music is somehow sacrosanct—but just because I thought it was kind of cheesy and I didn't like the whole idea. I didn't want my music to be perceived as a huckster for somebody's product. If I believed in something and I thought that it was a compatible campaign, and they paid me gazillions of dollars, I'd consider it, absolutely. But if they come to me with deodorant for 'Matter of Trust' and 'She's Always a Woman' for feminine hygiene spray, I got a problem with that. Now I'm fortunate—let me be clear about this—I'm fortunate that I can afford my conscience. A lot of people can't. I can afford to sit and judge: 'I don't want to do this. I don't want to do that.' Most people can't. So I don't want to appear like I think I'm so great because I haven't done that. And I'm also, again in the press, somewhat typed as somebody who's commercial. There's this whole image of me as well: 'He's had so many hits, he's sold out.' Look, I don't make 'em hits, I just wrote the songs and recorded them. You made them hits, not me. So why shouldn't I sell my songs, if I'm going to be perceived as a sell-out anyway, what the hell do I care? Frankly, I really don't care what somebody thinks of me. All I care is what I think of me."[31]

"I like different kinds of music. It always shocks me that there are people who only like rock & roll, or people who only like classical, or people who only like authentic American blues, who can't listen to Cream or John Hammond, Jr. There are people who only like jazz from a particular era—only swing and only be-bop. My view is, 'There's all kinds of food. Are you only going to eat one kind?'"[29]

Musically, what does the future hold for him? "I want to continue composing instrumental music, as least for the foreseeable future," he says. "If I get ideas to write songs, I'm not going to stop myself. I'll certainly sit down and write songs. I haven't closed the door on that altogether. I just don't feel compelled to write lyrics these days. I'm actually very comfortable writing in the abstract. I was always a literal lyricist anyway, and it used to bother me, how literal I was. I always admired lyricists like Paul Simon or Bob Dylan who were comfortable in an abstract vernacular. That's what writing instrumental music is doing for me. It's allowing me to express myself in an abstract way. But if I come up with some song ideas, I'll write them. I'm not going to censor myself. With my instrumental music, I'll probably be expanding from solo piano to piano with a solo instrument, like piano with violin, piano with cello, piano with clarinet, and from there moving into ensemble arrangements, possibly quartets, and them maybe on to chamber-size, and then maybe on to full orchestral-size works. It's going to take a while, and I'm going to do this slowly, so I feel like I'm comfortable with the idiom. I'm still learning."[50]

In January 2007 Billy was in the news again, and in the public eye again as well. It was announced on "Page Six" in the New York Post that Billy had gone into Legacy Recording Studio in New York City and recorded a new song called "All My Life." Fans were optimistic that this was finally a sign of some more new music to come. On February 4, 2007, Billy was seen by countless millions of television viewers as he performed the National Anthem on the telecast of Super Bowl XLI game. This appearance at Dolphin Stadium in South Florida made him the first performer to have ever sung the National Anthem at a Super Bowl game twice.

What is his life like at the moment? "I'm content. Content to the point where I'm not feeling like it's necessary for me to prove anything." And how is his marriage to Katie? "It's going great. Having your personal life not be in turmoil is nice.[1]

"I don't think about critics. I don't think about radio. I don't think about the record company. I don't think about you. I just think about me. What do I want to hear? I'm just going to do what I want to hear. The original thing that got me mesmerized and enchanted about music was sound. I just wanted to reproduce that for my own high, for lack of a better word. I wanted to tap into that alchemy, to be one of those wizards, to learn that language. And I did. There are days I just sit and play, and I'm not thinking about posterity or immortality. I'm not thinking about anybody or anything. I'm just playing music, and I'm so carried away."[29]

The challenge of effectively describing Billy Joel is a daunting task. Everyone who knows him seems to have a strikingly different opinion of who this man is, and what he represents to them. To Richie Cannata, Billy is someone who has always been a recurring friend in his life. To Liberty DeVitto, he is cold, cheap, and disloyal to his friends. To Bob Buchman and Ken Dashow, Billy is benevolent and caring. To friends of the late Doug Stegmeyer, he is a heel. To the Long Island Baymen, he is a hero. To Russell Javors, he is someone he used to work with two decades ago but never felt extremely close to as a friend. To rock critics, he is still something of an arrogant punk. To his daughter Alexa, he is an inspiration. To his millions of fans, he is an unfaltering idol who writes songs that reach their souls. Among all of these people, who is correct? Like different pieces of the same puzzle, from everyone's perspective, they are all correct in their assessment.

It's been years since Brenda and Eddie first went steady in Billy Joel's fabled story song. By now they would be chasing their grandchildren around a Long Island shopping mall. It also has been decades since anyone described him as "an innocent man." He no longer composes the kind of rock & roll music that made him a superstar. He now dabbles in classical compositions, designs boats, and occasionally goes out on tour. Billy Joel is by now many incarnations away from being the same young keyboard-playing piano man he once personified, and then glorified.

He is truly a complex person. He is classically trained, yet he took his musical knowledge and turned himself into a rock & roll legend. Some people admire him greatly and appreciate his creativity, and others criticize him for his shortcomings and his mistakes. Through it all, he has remained true to himself. The body of musical work that he has created throughout his five decades as a recording artist continues to sell, and his concert performances still draw millions to arenas around the world. He is a dreamer, a troubadour, a poet, a father, a lover, a classical pianist, and a nautical draftsman. Yet, in everyone's mind he will always be thought of as being "the piano man." He is Billy Joel.

BILLY JOEL

QUOTE SOURCES

1 Tom Sinclair, "The Many Lives of Billy Joel," *Entertainment Weekly*, November 25, 2005.

2 George Rush and Joanna Rush Malloy, "Drummer Says Joel Moved Him Out," *New York Post*, February 23, 2006.

3 Author's interview with Liberty DeVitto, the Cedar Tavern, New York City, February 17, 2006.

4 Author's e-mail from Russell Javors, July 7, 2006.

5 Author's interview with an unnamed former Columbia Records employee, New York City, September 30, 2005.

6 Author's e-mail from an unnamed source, July 18, 2006.

7 *The Joel File: A Story of Two Families*, a documentary, 2000.

8 Julius Streicher, a cover story article on Karl Joel, *Der Strümer*, Nuremberg, Germany, 1934.

9 Josef Neckermann, with Carl Fredrich Mossdorf, *Josef Neckermann* (Germany: CoPress-Verl., 1969).

10 Timothy White, "Billy Joel," *Billboard*, December 3, 1994.

11 David A. Keeps, "Keeping the Faith," *US Weekly*, May 28, 2001.

12 David and Victoria Sheff, "Playboy Interview: Billy Joel," *Playboy*, May 1982.

13 Timothy White, "A Portrait of the Artist: Billy Joel," *Billboard*, December 4, 1994.

14 Timothy White, "Billy Joel Is Angry," *Rolling Stone*, September 4, 1980.

15 Tony Schwartz, "Billy the Kid," *Newsweek*, December 11, 1978.

16 "Billy Joel," *Blender*, 2000.

17 Christopher Connelly, "Billy Joel: Not as Bad as You Think," *Rolling Stone*, October 28, 1982.

18 Dave Marsh, "Billy Joel: The Miracle of 52nd Street," *Rolling Stone*, December 14, 1978.

19 Wayne Robins, "Just the Way He Is," *Newsday*, August 2, 1989.

20 Paramount Records press biography, 1971.

21 "Billy Joel: The Street Kid Drives Home in His Mercedes," *New York Sunday News,* January 17, 1982.

22 Columbia Records press biography, March 1984.

23 Fred Schruers, "Cool Hand Billy," *Sunday News Magazine,* January 17, 1982.

24 Author's interview with Micky Dolenz, March 13, 2006.

25 Author's interview with Isiah James, May 13, 2006.

26 Jay Cocks, "The Brash Ballad of Billy Joel," *Time,* February 13, 1978.

27 Roman Kozak, "Billy Joel: Superstar with His Own Entertainment Complex," *Billboard,* August 9, 1980.

28 Author's e-mail from Lou Christie, New York City, December 23, 2006.

29 *My Lives,* album liner notes by Anthony DeCurtis, Columbia/Legacy Records, 2005.

30 Author's conversation with LaLa Brooks, New York City, March 7, 2006.

31 Bill DeMain, "Billy Joel: Scenes from a Musical Life," *Performing Songwriter,* January–February 1996.

32 Wayne Robins, "Billy Joel Charting a New Course," *Newsday,* October 29, 1989.

33 Idea associations paper, filled out by Billy Joel, then a student at Hicksville High School, Hicksville, New York, January 21, 1966. From school records made public.

34 Letter from Rosalind Joel to Dr. Leon Green, Hicksville High School psychologist, June 15, 1966. From school records made public.

35 Fred Bronson, *The Billboard Book of Number One Hits,* (New York: Billboard Books, 2003).

36 Hank Bordowitz, *Billy Joel: The Life and Times of an Angry Man,* (New York: Billboard Books, 2005).

37 Author's conversation with Liberty DeVitto, New York City, March 9, 2006.

38 Author's interview with Roger DiMaio, at Hudson Place Restaurant, New York City, February 7, 2006.

39 Author's interview with Jimmy Greenspoon, Don Schula's Steakhouse, New York City, September 1, 2005.

40 Anthony DeCurtis, "The Rolling Stone Interview: Billy Joel," *Rolling Stone,* November 6, 1986.

41 Author's telephone interview with David Salidor, February 28, 2006.

42 Author's telephone conversation with Peter Schekeryk, July 5, 2006.

43 Andy Childs, "Billy Joel: Piano Man," *ZigZag,* July 1975.

44 Author's interview with Richie Cannata, Cove City Sound, Long Island, October 18, 2005.

45 Don Heckman, "Pop Festival Excitement Grows as Night and the Stars Appear," *The New York Times,* April 3, 1972.

46 Author's interview with Melanie, The Cutting Room, New York City, June 16, 2006.

47 Jim Kippenberg, "Billy Joel: One of the Brightest of the New Stars," *Cincinnati Enquirer,* January 20, 1974.

48 David Crosby and Carl Gottlieb, *Long Time Gone: The Autobiography of David Crosby,* (New York: Doubleday, 1988).

49 Author's e-mail from Derek Storm, August 24, 2005.

50 Bill DeMain, "In a New Romantic State of Mind," *Performing Songwriter,* November 2001.

[51] John Rockwell, performance review of Henry Gross and Billy Joel, *New York Times,* February 23, 1974.

[52] "Love's Lyrics Lost," a performance review, *Village Voice,* May 30, 1974.

[53] Author's interview with May Pang, the Tribeca Grand Hotel, New York City, May 16, 2006.

[54] Jack Breschar, review of the *Piano Man* album, *Rolling Stone,* March 14, 1974.

[55] Author's interview with Susan Mittelkauf, New York City, March 4, 2006.

[56] Author's telephone interview with Don Kirshner, February 21, 2006.

[57] Carl Arrington, "Billy Joel Makes It After 10 Years of Trying," *Us,* April 4, 1978.

[58] Stephen Holden, review of the *Streetlife Serenade* album, *Rolling Stone,* December 5, 1974.

[59] Barry Millman, "Billy Joel Talks Back," *Spin,* June 1985.

[60] Dennis Freeland, "Billy Joel," *Music/Sound Output,* August 1985.

[61] Author's telephone interview with Frank Sagarese, January 22, 2006.

[62] Author's interview with Liberty DeVitto, at the Euro Diner and at Hudson Place, both at Third Avenue and Thirty-sixth Street, New York City.

[63] Author's interview with Liberty DeVitto, in a conference room at the offices of Clear Channel Radio, New York City, October 1, 2005.

[64] Author's e-mail from Russell Javors, July 10, 2006.

[65] Author's telephone conversation with Russell Javors, July 11, 2006 (Javors in Hong Kong, Bego in Detroit).

[66] Author's conversation with Steve Van Zandt, at the Hammerstein Ballroom, New York City, during the charity dinner and awards ceremony "We Are Family," April 25, 2006.

[67] Author's e-mail from Liberty DeVitto, September 30, 2005.

[68] Parke Puterbaugh, review of *An Innocent Man, Rolling Stone,* August 18, 1983

[69] Author's interview with Derek Storm, New York City, March 2, 2006.

[70] Vladimir Bogdanov, Chris Woodstra, and Stephen Thomas Erlewine, eds., *All Music Guide,* (New York: Hal Leonard Publishing, 2001).

[71] *Songs in the Attic,* liner notes, Columbia Records, 1981.

[72] Billy Amendola, "Phil Ramone: Trusting the Drummer," *Modern Drummer,* March 2002.

[73] Julie Fanselow, "Phil Ramone," *Music/Sound Output,* August 1985.

[74] Bob Bank, "Phil Ramone: Engineer/Producer," *Recording Engineer/Producer,* October 1977.

[75] Author's telephone interview with Liberty DeVitto, March 28, 2006.

[76] Phil Ramone and Charles L. Granata, *Makin' Records* (New York: Hyperion Books, 2006).

[77] Author and Derek Storm's conversation with Phoebe Snow, at May Pang's barbecue, Pamona, New York, September 3, 2005.

[78] Ira Mayer, review of *The Stranger, Rolling Stone,* December 15, 1977.

[79] Author's interview with Cheryl Khaner, New York City, September 25, 2005.

[80] Jim Jerome, "For a Song: If Billy Joel Doesn't Love You 'Just The Way You Are' Don't Argue," *People,* March 6, 1978.

[81] Author's interview with Liberty DeVitto, New York City, September 28, 2005.

[82] Stephen Holden, review of *52nd Street, Rolling Stone,* December 14, 1978.

[83] Richard Riegel, review of *52nd Street, Creem,* February 1979.

BILLY JOEL

84 John Rockwell, "Billy Joel Sings the Praises of New York," *New York Times*, December 10, 1978.

85 John Rockwell, "Rock Tour by Billy Joel," *New York Times*, December 16, 1978.

86 Geoffrey Stokes, "Billy Joel: Local Boy Makes Nice," *Village Voice*, December 25, 1978.

87 Author's e-mail from Liberty DeVitto, April 12, 2006.

88 Jim Jerome, "Billy Joel Rocks Cuba: Cubans Would Never Again Say 'Yanquis, Go Home! After the 1979 'Bay of Gigs,'" *People*, March 19, 1979.

89 John Rockwell, "Billy Joel Brings Cuban Crowd to Its Feet," *New York Times*, March 6, 1979.

90 Author's e-mail from Randy Jones, July 7, 2006.

91 Bob Doerschuk, "The Piano Man Rocks On," *Keyboard*, December 1981.

92 Author's e-mail from Liberty DeVitto, April 18, 2006.

93 "Billy Joel: 2000 Years: The Millennium Concert," *MSN Live*, May 1, 2000.

94 Peter Reilly, "Billy Joel's *Glass Houses:* Beyond Category," *Stereo Review,* June 1980.

95 Paul Nelson, "Billy Joel's Songs for Swingin' Lovers," *Rolling Stone*, May 1, 1980.

96 Timothy White, "Billy Joel," *Rolling Stone*, October 15, 1992.

97 Robert Palmer, "Pop: Five Nights for Billy Joel at the Garden," *New York Times*, June 25, 1980.

98 "Dakota Blocks Billy Joel's Bid to Buy Apartment," *New York Times*, June 28, 1980.

99 Author's interview with Bob Buchman, at his office in Manhattan, February 1, 2006.

100 Merry Aronson, "Interview with Billy Joel," *Root Beer Rag* (Billy Joel fan magazine), Fall 1981.

101 "Backstage Visit with Brian Ruggles," *Root Beer Rag,* Fall 1981.

102 Timothy White, "Billy Joel Retraces His Halting Early Steps," *Rolling Stone,* November 12, 2006.

103 Marc Kirkeby, "Record Chain Guilty in Counterfeiting Case," *Rolling Stone,* May 28, 1981.

104 Stephen Holden, "Billy Joel on the Dark Side," *New York Times*, December 29, 1982.

105 "Billy Joel Recovering," *New York Times,* April 17, 1982.

106 "Joel Pulls Back *Nylon Curtain,*" *Rolling Stone,* September 2, 1982.

107 Stephen Holden, review of *The Nylon Curtain, Rolling Stone,* October 14, 1982.

108 "Billy Joel: Nylon Curtain," review of *The Nylon Curtain, Billboard,* quoted in *Columbia Record & Tape Club Magazine,* February 1983.

109 Richard Riegel, "Revenge of the Suburbs," a review of *The Nylon Curtain, Creem,* January 1983.

110 Stephen Holden, "Billy Joel Reaches Out to Embrace Pop," by *New York Times,* August 3, 1986.

111 Author's interview with Ken Dashow, the Sunflower Diner, Third Avenue, New York City, December 12, 2005.

112 Jock Baird, "Phil Ramone," *Musician,* November 1984.

[113] Melinda Newman, "Joel Sees Pop Exit with *Greatest Hits 3*," *Billboard*, July 26, 1997.

[114] Author's conversation with Bobby Funaro, the Palm Restaurant, West Fiftieth Street, April 27, 2006.

[115] Author's conversation with Marcy MacDonald, May 1, 2006.

[116] Zach Dunkin, "Billy Joel Still Has the Touch," *Indianapolis News*, February 6, 1984.

[117] "A Dreamboat Wedding," *People*, April 8, 1985.

[118] "Billy Joel: Choose Life," *The Record*, October 1985.

[119] Gary L. Brock, "AOL Chat with Billy Joel," America Online, Winter 1994.

[120] Wayne Robins, "Billy Joel," *Newsday*, October 29, 1999.

[121] Author's telephone conversation with and e-mail from Joe Salvatto, July 17, 2006.

[122] Martin Torgoff, "Special *Bridge* Tour Edition," *Root Beer Rag*, Winter 1986.

[123] Columbia Records press release, to publicize *The Bridge* album, 1986.

[124] Anthony DeCurtis, review of *The Bridge*, *Rolling Stone*, September 11, 1986.

[125] David Wall, "On Fire Again: Billy Joel," *Rolling Stone*, January 25, 1990.

[126] "Billy Joel Has a Tantrum," *New York Times*, July 28, 1987.

[127] Walter Yetnikoff with David Ritz, *Howling at the Moon* (New York: Broadway Books, 2004).

[128] John O'Connor, "Billy Joel's Soviet Tour," *New York Times*, June 15, 1988.

[129] Guy D. Garcia, "People" page, *Time*, August, 10, 1987.

[130] Felicity Barringer, "Rocking Billy Joel Breaks Through Soviet Reserve,"*The New York Times*, July 27, 1987.

[131] Review of *Billy Joel from Leningrad, USSR*, *TV Guide*, October 24, 1987.

[132] Jeff Jarvis, "Tube" review of *Billy Joel from Leningrad, USSR*, *People*, October 26, 1987.

[133] Steve Dougherty, "A $90 Million Matter of Distrust Pits Billy Joel against His Ex-Manager," *People*, October 9, 1989.

[134] Author's e-mail from Deborah Gibson, July 11, 2006.

[135] Author's conversation with David Salidor, July 14, 2006.

[136] Stephen Holden, "Pop Life/Billy Joel at 40," *New York Times*, October 18, 1989.

[137] Sean Plottner, review of the *Storm Front* album, *Us*, November 13, 1989.

[138] Andrea Sachs, compiler, "Critic's Voices," review of the *Storm Front* album, *Time*, January 8, 1990.

[139] Julian Dibbell, review of the *Storm Front* album, *Spin*, January 1990.

[140] Chuck Eddy, "It's Not His Fault!" *Village Voice*, November 21, 1989.

[141] John McAlley, a review of *Storm Front*, *Rolling Stone*, November 30, 1989.

[142] Associated Press, "Joel Lights a Fire in a Classroom," *Newsday*, January 19, 1990.

[143] "Classic Songs," song choices by Roger McGuinn, Billy Joel, Steven Tyler, Steve Vai, Keith Richards, and Paul McCartney, *Rolling Stone*, August 23, 1990.

[144] Dafydd Rees and Luke Crampton, *VH1 Rock Stars Encyclopedia* (New York: DK Publishing, 1999).

[145] Debbie Holly and Ed Morris, "Joel 'Shamelessly' Endorses Brooks Hit," *Billboard*, November 3, 1991.

[146] Nadine Brozan, "Chronicle," *New York Times*, June 26, 1992.

147 Geraldine Fabrikant, "Billy Joel Takes His Lawyers to Court," *New York Times*, September 24, 1992.

148 Fred Goodman, "It's Music Crusader vs. Ultimate Insider in $90 Million Billy Joel Legal Brawl," *New York Observer*.

149 Elysa Gardner, "After the Storm/Billy Joel Turns to Beethoven for 'Dreams,'" *Rolling Stone,* June 10, 1994.

150 Christine Sparta, "For Billy Joel, Revised 'Dreams,'" *USA Today,* August 12, 1993.

151 Jancee Dunn, "Billy Joel," *Rolling Stone,* December 23, 1993–January 6, 1994.

152 Author's e-mail from Jay Pomerantz, March 23, 2006.

153 Greg Sandow, "Ode to Billy Joel," *Entertainment Weekly,* August 13, 1993.

154 Richard Corliss, "The Last Songwriter," *Time,* August 30, 1993.

155 Author's telephone interview with Jerome George, March 22, 2006.

156 Jerome George, "Billy Joel Trashes Posh Hotel Room in Bloody Rampage," *National Enquirer,* April 2, 1991.

157 Tom Gliatto, "Split Decisions," *People,* April 25, 1994.

158 Don Zalaica, "Interview: Liberty DeVitto, Drummer for Billy Joel," LiveDaily (Internet news service), March 14, 2001.

159 Author's telephone interview with Steve Ericson, March 28, 2006.

160 Author's conversation with an unnamed VH1 employee, at Elaine's restaurant, New York City, June 19, 2006.

161 *Billy Joel Live at Town Hall,* New York City, May 16, 1996, presented on WPLJ 95.9 radio, courtesy of Tom Cuddy of WPLJ.

162 Robert Doerschuk, "Front Man: Billy Joel," *Musician,* December 1997.

163 Stephen Holden, "Adrift From Pop, Billy Joel Takes a Classical Turn," *New York Times,* September 14, 1997.

164 Gary Graff, "Piano Man Offers His Final Notes for the Pop World," Reuters News Service, August 14, 1997.

165 Author's telephone interview with Martha Reeves, March 19, 2006.

166 Author's interview with WPLJ radio disc jockey, Race Taylor, the China Club, New York City, September 26, 2005.

167 David Wild, review of *2000 Years: The Millennium Concert, Rolling Stone,* May 11, 2000.

168 Author's conversation with Kevin McCarthy, July 6, 2006.

169 Karin Lipson, "Riches to Ruins" *Newsday,* January 7, 2003.

170 Eric Konigsberg, "Lessons: Piano Man, Part Two," *The New Yorker,* December 3, 2001.

171 James Hunter, review of *Fantasies & Delusions, Rolling Stone,* November 8, 2001.

172 Jim Jerome, with Rebecca Paley, Rachel Felder, and Debbie Seaman, "Self Admission," *People,* July 8, 2002.

173 Rush & Molloy, "Hitting a Sour Note," *New York Daily News,* June 15, 2002.

174 John Istel, "Dance Music: Billy Joel and Twyla Tharp," *Elle,* 2002.

175 Rob Tannenbaum, "It Takes Two," *New York Metro.com* magazine, 2002.

176 Brochure to advertise *Movin' Out,* quoting various reviews, 2002.

177 Lisa Schwarzbaum, "Billy Clubbed," *Entertainment Weekly,* November 8, 2002.

178 Joan Acocella, review of "Twyla Tharp's *Movin' Out,*" *The New Yorker,* November 4, 2002.

179 *Playbill,* Billy Joel item, 2002.

180 David Richardson, WOR Radio, New York City.

181 Author's conversation with Sindi Kaplan, July 13, 2006.

182 Peter A. Janssen, "Rush Hour: Billy Joel Builds a Gorgeous New 57-Foot Commuter to Bring Back the Golden Age of Yachting," *Yachting,* October 2005.

183 Bill Bleyer, "Piano Man as Boat-Builder," *Newsday,* January 14, 2005.

184 Jeff Samuels, "Billy Joel Gets Ultimatum from His New Wife Kate: It's Me or the Booze," *National Enquirer,* April 4, 2005.

185 Robin Mizrahi, "Billy Joel Suicide Watch," *National Enquirer,* April 11, 2005.

186 Ben Widdicombe, Jo Piazza, and Chris Rovzar, "Billy's in a Rehabbed State of Mind," *New York Daily News,* April 12, 2005.

187 Author's observations, 92nd Street Y, New York City, November 29, 2005.

188 Dan Aquilante, "Billy's Big Record," *New York Post,* January 22, 2006.

189 Andrew Marton, "*12 Gardens* Blooms with Billy's Best," *Fort Worth Star–Telegram,* June 11, 2006.

190 Author's telephone conversation with Andy Skurow, July 6, 2006.

191 Author's e-mail from Mark Kostabi, August 1, 2006.

192 Author's telephone conversation with Marcy MacDonald, June 22, 2006.

193 Author's e-mail from Dana Bove, July 5, 2006.

194 Author's e-mail correspondence with Randy Jones, June 22, 2006.

195 Author's e-mail from Mary Wilson, June 22, 2006.

196 Author's telephone interview with Jed Ryan, March 19, 2006.

197 Melinda Newman, "Elton Talks," *Billboard,* September 10, 2005.

BILLY JOEL

DISCOGRAPHY

ALBUMS

1. **COLD SPRING HARBOR**
   (1971/Original Vinyl release ABC/Paramount Records)
   (Remastered and rereleased with corrected speed 1983 Columbia Records)
   Produced by Artie Ripp
   Executive producer Irwin Mazur
   1. "She's Got a Way"   (Billy Joel)
   2. "You Can Make Me Free"   (Billy Joel)
   3. "Everybody Loves You Now"   (Billy Joel)
   4. "Why Judy Why"   (Billy Joel)
   5. "Falling of the Rain"   (Billy Joel)
   6. "Turn Around"   (Billy Joel)
   7. "You Look So Good to Me"   (Billy Joel)
   8. "Tomorrow Is Today"   (Billy Joel)
   9. "Nocturne"   (Billy Joel)
   10. "Got to Begin Again"   (Billy Joel)

2. **PIANO MAN**
   (1973/Columbia Records)
   Produced by Michael Stewart
   1. "Travelin' Prayer"   (Billy Joel)
   2. "Piano Man"   (Billy Joel)
   3. "Ain't No Crime"   (Billy Joel)
   4. "You're My Home"   (Billy Joel)
   5. "The Ballad of Billy the Kid"   (Billy Joel)
   6. "Worse Comes to Worst"   (Billy Joel)
   7. "Stop in Nevada"   (Billy Joel)

8. "If I Only Had the Words (To Tell You)"   (Billy Joel)
9. "Somewhere Along the Line"   (Billy Joel)
10. "Captain Jack"   (Billy Joel)

3. STREETLIFE SERENADE
(1974/Columbia Records)
Produced by Michael Stewart
1. "Streetlife Serenader"   (Billy Joel)
2. "Los Angelenos"   (Billy Joel)
3. "The Great Suburban Showdown"   (Billy Joel)
4. "Root Beer Rag"   (Billy Joel)
5. "Roberta"   (Billy Joel)
6. "The Entertainer"   (Billy Joel)
7. "Last of the Big Time Spenders"   (Billy Joel)
8. "Weekend Song"   (Billy Joel)
9. "Souvenir"   (Billy Joel)
10. "The Mexican Connection"   (Billy Joel)

4. TURNSTILES
(1976/Columbia Records)
Produced by Billy Joel
1. "Say Goodbye to Hollywood"   (Billy Joel)
2. "Summer, Highland Falls"   (Billy Joel)
3. "All You Wanna Do Is Dance"   (Billy Joel)
4. "New York State of Mind"   (Billy Joel)
5. "James"   (Billy Joel)
6. "Prelude/Angry Young Man"   (Billy Joel)
7. "I've Loved These Days"   (Billy Joel)
8. "Miami 2017 (Seen the Lights Go Out on Broadway)"   (Billy Joel)

5. THE STRANGER
(1977/Columbia Records)
Produced by Phil Ramone
1. "Movin' Out (Anthony's Song)"   (Billy Joel)
2. "The Stranger"   (Billy Joel)
3. "Just the Way You Are"   (Billy Joel)
4. "Scenes from an Italian Restaurant"   (Billy Joel)
5. "Vienna"   (Billy Joel)
6. "Only the Good Die Young"   (Billy Joel)
7. "She's Always a Woman"   (Billy Joel)
8. "Get It Right the First Time"   (Billy Joel)
9. "Everybody Has a Dream"   (Billy Joel)

6. 52ND STREET
(1978/Columbia Records)
Produced by Phil Ramone
1. "Big Shot"   (Billy Joel)
2. "Honesty"   (Billy Joel)
3. "My Life"   (Billy Joel)

4. "Zanzibar"   (Billy Joel)
5. "Stiletto"   (Billy Joel)
6. "Rosalinda's Eyes"   (Billy Joel)
7. "Half a Mile Away"   (Billy Joel)
8. "Until the Night"   (Billy Joel)
9. "52nd Street"   (Billy Joel)

7. GLASS HOUSES
(1980/Columbia Records)
Produced by Phil Ramone
1. "You May Be Right"   (Billy Joel)
2. "Sometimes a Fantasy"   (Billy Joel)
3. "Don't Ask Me Why"   (Billy Joel)
4. "It's Still Rock & Roll to Me"   (Billy Joel)
5. "All For Leyna"   (Billy Joel)
6. "I Don't Want to Be Alone"   (Billy Joel)
7. "Sleeping with the Television On"   (Billy Joel)
8. "C'etait Toi (You Were the One)"   (Billy Joel)
9. "Close to the Borderline"   (Billy Joel)
10. "Through the Long Night"   (Billy Joel)

8. SONGS IN THE ATTIC
(1981/Columbia Records)
Produced by Phil Ramone
1. "Miami 2017 (Seen the Lights Go Out on Broadway)"
    (Billy Joel)
2. "Summer, Highland Falls"   (Billy Joel)
3. "Streetlife Serenader"   (Billy Joel)
4. "Los Angelenos"   (Billy Joel)
5. "She's Got a Way"   (Billy Joel)
6. "Everybody Loves You Now"   (Billy Joel)
7. "Say Goodbye to Hollywood"   (Billy Joel)
8. "Captain Jack"   (Billy Joel)
9. "You're My Home"   (Billy Joel)
10. "The Ballad of Billy the Kid"   (Billy Joel)
11. "I've Loved These Days"   (Billy Joel)

9. THE NYLON CURTAIN
(1982/Columbia Records)
Produced by Phil Ramone
1. "Allentown"   (Billy Joel)
2. "Laura"   (Billy Joel)
3. "Pressure"   (Billy Joel)
4. "Goodnight Saigon"   (Billy Joel)
5. "She's Right on Time"   (Billy Joel)
6. "A Room of Our Own"   (Billy Joel)
7. "Surprises"   (Billy Joel)
8. "Scandinavian Skies"   (Billy Joel)
9. "Where's the Orchestra?"   (Billy Joel)

BILLY JOEL

10. **AN INNOCENT MAN**
    (1983/Columbia Records)
    Produced by Phil Ramone
    1. "Easy Money"   (Billy Joel)
    2. "An Innocent Man"   (Billy Joel)
    3. "The Longest Time"   (Billy Joel)
    4. "This Night"   (Billy Joel)
    5. "Tell Her About It"   (Billy Joel)
    6. "Uptown Girl"   (Billy Joel)
    7. "Careless Talk"   (Billy Joel)
    8. "Christie Lee"   (Billy Joel)
    9. "Leave a Tender Moment Alone"   (Billy Joel)
    10. "Keeping the Faith"   (Billy Joel)

11. **GREATEST HITS VOLUMES ONE AND TWO**
    (1985/Columbia Records)
    Various producers as per individual tracks
    Disc One
    1. "Piano Man"   (Billy Joel)
    2. "Captain Jack"   (Billy Joel)
    3. "The Entertainer"   (Billy Joel)
    4. "Say Goodbye to Hollywood"   (Billy Joel)
    5. "New York State of Mind"   (Billy Joel)
    6. "The Stranger"   (Billy Joel)
    7. "Scenes from an Italian Restaurant"   (Billy Joel)
    8. "Just the Way You Are"   (Billy Joel)
    9. "Movin' Out (Anthony's Song)"   (Billy Joel)
    10. "Only the Good Die Young"   (Billy Joel)
    11. "She's Always a Woman"   (Billy Joel)
    Disc Two
    1. "My Life"   (Billy Joel)
    2. "Big Shot"   (Billy Joel)
    3. "You May Be Right"   (Billy Joel)
    4. "It's Still Rock & Roll to Me"   (Billy Joel)
    5. "Don't Ask Me Why"   (Billy Joel)
    6. "She's Got a Way"   (Billy Joel)
    7. "Pressure"   (Billy Joel)
    8. "Allentown"   (Billy Joel)
    9. "Goodnight Saigon"   (Billy Joel)
    10. "Tell Her About It"   (Billy Joel)
    11. "Uptown Girl"   (Billy Joel)
    12. "The Longest Time"   (Billy Joel)
    13. "You're Only Human (Second Wind)"   (Billy Joel)
    14. "The Night Is Still Young"   (Billy Joel)

12. **THE BRIDGE**
    (1986/Columbia Records)
    Produced by Phil Ramone
    1. "Running on Ice"   (Billy Joel)

BILLY JOEL

2. "This Is the Time"   (Billy Joel)
3. "A Matter of Trust"   (Billy Joel)
4. "Modern Woman"   (Billy Joel)
5. "Baby Grand" duet with Ray Charles   (Billy Joel)
6. "Big Man on Mulberry Street"   (Billy Joel)
7. "Temptation"   (Billy Joel)
8. "Code of Silence" duet with Cyndi Lauper
   (Billy Joel and Cyndi Lauper)
9. "Getting Closer"   (Billy Joel)

13. KOHUEPT

(1987/Columbia Records)
Produced by Jim Boyer and Brian Ruggles
Executive producers: Frank Weber and Rick London
1. "Odoya"   (Traditional Georgian)
2. "Angry Young Man"   (Billy Joel)
3. "Honesty"   (Billy Joel)
4. "Goodnight Saigon"   (Billy Joel)
5. "Stiletto"   (Billy Joel)
6. "Big Man on Mulberry Street"   (Billy Joel)
7. "Baby Grand"   (Billy Joel)
8. "An Innocent Man"   (Billy Joel)
9. "Allentown"   (Billy Joel)
10. "A Matter of Trust"   (Billy Joel)
11. "Only the Good Die Young"   (Billy Joel)
12. "Sometimes a Fantasy"   (Billy Joel)
13. "Uptown Girl"   (Billy Joel)
14. "Big Shot"   (Billy Joel)
15. "Back in the USSR"   (John Lennon and Paul McCartney)
16. "The Times They Are A-Changin'"   (Bob Dylan)

14. STORM FRONT

(1989/Columbia Records)
Produced by Mick Jones and Billy Joel
1. "That's Not Her Style"   (Billy Joel)
2. "We Didn't Start the Fire"   (Billy Joel)
3. "The Downeaster 'Alexa'"   (Billy Joel)
4. "I Go to Extremes"   (Billy Joel)
5. "Shameless"   (Billy Joel)
6. "Storm Front"   (Billy Joel)
7. "Leningrad"   (Billy Joel)
8. "State of Grace"   (Billy Joel)
9. "When in Rome"   (Billy Joel)
10. "And So It Goes"   (Billy Joel)

15. RIVER OF DREAMS

(1993/Columbia Records)
Produced by Danny Kortchmar
* Produced by Billy Joel, additional production by Dave Thoener

** Coproduced by Joe Nicolo
1. "No Man's Land"   (Billy Joel)
2. "The Great Wall of China"   (Billy Joel)
3. "Blonde over Blue"   (Billy Joel)
4. "A Minor Variation"   (Billy Joel)
5. "Shades of Grey" *   (Billy Joel)
6. "All About Soul"   (Billy Joel)
7. "Lullabye (Goodnight, My Angel)"   (Billy Joel)
8. "The River of Dreams" **   (Billy Joel)
9. "Two Thousand Years"   (Billy Joel)
10. "Famous Last Words"   (Billy Joel)

16. **GREATEST HITS, VOLUME THREE**
(1997/Columbia Records)
Various producers per individual tracks
1. "Keeping the Faith"   (Billy Joel)
2. "An Innocent Man"   (Billy Joel)
3. "A Matter of Time"   (Billy Joel)
4. "Baby Grand" duet with Ray Charles
   (Billy Joel)
5. "This is the Time"   (Billy Joel)
6. "Leningrad"   (Billy Joel)
7. "We Didn't Start the Fire"   (Billy Joel)
8. "I Go to Extremes"   (Billy Joel)
9. "And So it Goes"   (Billy Joel)
10. "The Downeaster 'Alexa'"   (Billy Joel)
11. "Shameless"   (Billy Joel)
12. "All About Soul" (Remix)   (Billy Joel)
13. "Lullabye (Goodnight, My Angel)"   (Billy Joel)
14. "The River of Dreams"   (Billy Joel)
15. "To Make You Feel My Love"   (Bob Dylan)
16. "Hey Girl"   (Carole King and Gerry Goffin)
17. "Light as a Breeze"   (Leonard Cohen)

17. **1973–1997: THE COMPLETE HITS (Boxed Set)**
(1997/Columbia Records)
Various producers as per individual tracks
Disc One
1. "Piano Man"   (Billy Joel)
2. "Captain Jack"   (Billy Joel)
3. "The Entertainer"   (Billy Joel)
4. "Say Goodbye to Hollywood"   (Billy Joel)
5. "New York State of Mind"   (Billy Joel)
6. "The Stranger"   (Billy Joel)
7. "Scenes from an Italian Restaurant"   (Billy Joel)
8. "Just the Way You Are"   (Billy Joel)
9. "Movin' Out (Anthony's Song)"   (Billy Joel)
10. "Only the Good Die Young"   (Billy Joel)
11. "She's Always a Woman"   (Billy Joel)

BILLY JOEL

Disc Two

1. "My Life"   (Billy Joel)
2. "Big Shot"   (Billy Joel)
3. "You May Be Right"   (Billy Joel)
4. "It's Still Rock & Roll to Me"   (Billy Joel)
5. "Don't Ask Me Why"   (Billy Joel)
6. "She's Got a Way"   (Billy Joel)
7. "Pressure"   (Billy Joel)
8. "Allentown"   (Billy Joel)
9. "Goodnight Saigon"   (Billy Joel)
10. "Tell Her About It"   (Billy Joel)
11. "Uptown Girl"   (Billy Joel)
12. "The Longest Time"   (Billy Joel)
13. "You're Only Human (Second Wind)"   (Billy Joel)
14. "The Night Is Still Young"   (Billy Joel)

Disc Three

1. "Keeping the Faith"   (Billy Joel)
2. "An Innocent Man"   (Billy Joel)
3. "A Matter of Time"   (Billy Joel)
4. "Baby Grand" duet with Ray Charles   (Billy Joel)
5. "This Is the Time"   (Billy Joel)
6. "Leningrad"   (Billy Joel)
7. "We Didn't Start the Fire"   (Billy Joel)
8. "I Go to Extremes"   (Billy Joel)
9. "And So It Goes"   (Billy Joel)
10. "The Downeaster 'Alexa'"   (Billy Joel)
11. "Shameless"   (Billy Joel)
12. "All About Soul" (Remix)   (Billy Joel)
13. "Lullabye (Goodnight, My Angel)"   (Billy Joel)
14. "The River of Dreams"   (Billy Joel)
15. "To Make You Feel My Love"   (Bob Dylan)
16. "Hey Girl"   (Carole King & Gerry Goffin)
17. "Light as a Breeze"   (Leonard Cohen)

Disc Four

1. "Billy Joel Spoken Intro/Music Concepts" [Spoken]   (Billy Joel)
2. "Scenes from an Italian Restaurant" (Live Unreleased Version)   (Billy Joel)
3. "Beatles Influence" [Spoken]   (Billy Joel)
4. "Hard Day's Night" (Live Unreleased Version)   (John Lennon & Paul McCartney)
5. "Why Vienna?" [Spoken]   (Billy Joel)
6. "Vienna" (Live Unreleased Version)   (Billy Joel)
7. "History Through Music" [Spoken]   (Billy Joel)
8. "We Didn't Start the Fire" (Live Unreleased Version)   (Billy Joel)
9. "Music Source" [Spoken]   (Billy Joel)
10. "The River of Dreams" (Unreleased Original Studio Version)   (Billy Joel)
11. "Piano Bar" [Spoken]   (Billy Joel)
12. "Piano Man" (Live Unreleased Version)   (Billy Joel)

18. **2000 YEARS: THE MILLENNIUM CONCERT (2000)**
    Produced by Don DeVito
    Disc One
     1. "Beethoven's Ninth Symphony"
        (Ludwig van Beethoven)
     2. "Big Shot"   (Billy Joel)
     3. "Movin' Out (Anthony's Song)"   (Billy Joel)
     4. "Summer Highland Falls"   (Billy Joel)
     5. "The Ballad of Billy the Kid"   (Billy Joel)
     6. "Don't Ask Me Why"   (Billy Joel)
     7. "New York State of Mind"   (Billy Joel)
     8. "I've Loved These Days"   (Billy Joel)
     9. "My Life"   (Billy Joel)
    10. "Allentown"   (Billy Joel)
    11. "Prelude/Angry Young Man"   (Billy Joel)
    12. "Only the Good Die Young"   (Billy Joel)
    Disc Two
     1. "I Go to Extremes"   (Billy Joel)
     2. "Goodnight Saigon"   (Billy Joel)
     3. "We Didn't Start the Fire"   (Billy Joel)
     4. "Big Man on Mulberry Street"   (Billy Joel)
     5. "2000 Years"   (Billy Joel)
     6. "Auld Lang Syne"   (Traditional)
     7. "River of Dreams"   (Billy Joel)
     8. "Scenes from an Italian Restaurant"   (Billy Joel)
     9. "Dance to the Music"   (Sylvester Stewart)
    10. "Honky Tonk Woman"   (Mick Jagger and Keith Richards)
    11. "It's Still Rock & Roll to Me"   (Billy Joel)
    12. "You May Be Right"   (Billy Joel)
    13. "This Night"   (Billy Joel)

19. **FANTASIES AND DELUSIONS**
    (2001/Columbia Records)
    Produced by Don DeVito
    [Billy Joel as classical composer, Richard Joo as solo pianist]
     1. "Opus 3. Reverie (Villa D'Este)"   (Billy Joel)
     2. "Opus 2. Waltz #1 (Nunley's Carousel)"   (Billy Joel)
     3. "Opus 7. Aria (Grand Canal)"   (Billy Joel)
     4. "Opus 6. Invention in C Minor"   (Billy Joel)
     5. "Opus 1. Soliloquy (On a Separation)"   (Billy Joel)
     6. "Opus 8. Suite for Piano (Star Crossed) I. Innamorato"   (Billy Joel)
     7. "II. Sorbetto"   (Billy Joel)
     8. "III. Delusion"   (Billy Joel)
     9. "Opus 5. Waltz #2 (Steinway Hall)"   (Billy Joel)
    10. "Opus 9. Waltz #3 (For Lola)"   (Billy Joel)
    11. "Opus 4. Fantasy (Film Noir)"   (Billy Joel)
    12. "Opus 10. Air (Dublinesque)"   (Billy Joel)

BILLY JOEL

20. **THE ESSENTIAL BILLY JOEL**
   (2001/Columbia Records)
   Various producers as per individual tracks
   Disc One
   1. "Piano Man"   (Billy Joel)
   2. "You're My Home"   (Billy Joel)
   3. "Captain Jack"   (Billy Joel)
   4. "The Entertainer"   (Billy Joel)
   5. "Say Goodbye to Hollywood"   (Billy Joel)
   6. "Miami 2017 (Seen the Lights Go Out on Broadway)"   (Billy Joel)
   7. "New York State of Mind"   (Billy Joel)
   8. "She's Always a Woman"   (Billy Joel)
   9. "Movin' Out (Anthony's Song)"   (Billy Joel)
   10. "Only the Good Die Young"   (Billy Joel)
   11. "Just the Way You Are"   (Billy Joel)
   12. "Honesty"   (Billy Joel)
   13. "My Life"   (Billy Joel)
   14. "It's Still Rock & Roll to Me"   (Billy Joel)
   15. "You May Be Right"   (Billy Joel)
   16. "Don't Ask Me Why"   (Billy Joel)
   17. "She's Got a Way"   (Billy Joel)
   18. "Allentown"   (Billy Joel)
   Disc Two
   1. "Goodnight Saigon"   (Billy Joel)
   2. "An Innocent Man"   (Billy Joel)
   3. "Uptown Girl"   (Billy Joel)
   4. "The Longest Mile"   (Billy Joel)
   5. "Tell Her About It"   (Billy Joel)
   6. "Leave a Tender Moment Alone"   (Billy Joel)
   7. "A Matter of Trust"   (Billy Joel)
   8. "Baby Grand" (Duet with Ray Charles)   (Billy Joel)
   9. "I Go to Extremes"   (Billy Joel)
   10. "We Didn't Start the Fire"   (Billy Joel)
   11. "Leningrad"   (Billy Joel)
   12. "The Downeaster 'Alexa'"   (Billy Joel)
   13. "And So It Goes"   (Billy Joel)
   14. "The River of Dreams"   (Billy Joel)
   15. "All About Soul" (Remix)   (Billy Joel)
   16. "Lullabye (Goodnight My Angel)"   (Billy Joel)
   17. "Opus 2. Waltz #1 (Nunley's Carousel)"   (Billy Joel)
   18. "Opus 6. Invention in C Minor"   (Billy Joel)

21. **THE ULTIMATE COLLECTION [import]**
   (2001/ Sony International Records)
   Various producers per individual tracks
   Disc One
   1. "Just the Way You Are"   (Billy Joel)
   2. "My Life"   (Billy Joel)

3. "It's Still Rock & Roll to Me"   (Billy Joel)
4. "Innocent Man"   (Billy Joel)
5. "Piano Man"   (Billy Joel)
6. "You're My Home"   (Billy Joel)
7. "Everybody Loves You Now"   (Billy Joel)
8. "The Entertainer"   (Billy Joel)
9. "Streetlife Serenader"   (Billy Joel)
10. "New York State of Mind"   (Billy Joel)
11. "Say Goodbye to Hollywood"   (Billy Joel)
12. "She's Got a Way"   (Billy Joel)
13. "Movin' Out"   (Billy Joel)
14. "She's Always a Woman"   (Billy Joel)
15. "Honesty"   (Billy Joel)
16. "You May Be Right"   (Billy Joel)
17. "Don't Ask Me Why"   (Billy Joel)
18. "Miami 2017 (Seen the Lights Go Out on Broadway)"   (Billy Joel)

Disc Two

1. "Uptown Girl"   (Billy Joel)
2. "Tell Her About It"   (Billy Joel)
3. "River of Dreams"   (Billy Joel)
4. "Longest Time"   (Billy Joel)
5. "We Didn't Stop the Fire"   (Billy Joel)
6. "Goodnight Saigon"   (Billy Joel)
7. "Allentown"   (Billy Joel)
8. "All for Leyna"   (Billy Joel)
9. "This Is the Time"   (Billy Joel)
10. "Leave a Tender Moment Alone"   (Billy Joel)
11. "Matter of Trust"   (Billy Joel)
12. "Modern Woman"   (Billy Joel)
13. "Baby Grand" (duet with Ray Charles)   (Billy Joel)
14. "I Go to Extremes"   (Billy Joel)
15. "Leningrad"   (Billy Joel)
16. "Downeaster 'Alexa'"   (Billy Joel)
17. "You're Only Human (Second Wind)"   (Billy Joel)
18. "All About Soul (Second Wind)"   (Billy Joel)

22. **PIANO MAN: THE BEST OF BILLY JOEL [import]**
(2005/Sony International Records)
Various producers per individual tracks
1. "Tell Her About It"   (Billy Joel)
2. "Uptown Girl"   (Billy Joel)
3. "Don't Ask Me Why"   (Billy Joel)
4. "Piano Man"   (Billy Joel)
5. "New York State of Mind"   (Billy Joel)
6. "River of Dreams"   (Billy Joel)
7. "It's Still Rock & Roll to Me"   (Billy Joel)
8. "We Didn't Start the Fire"   (Billy Joel)
9. "Goodnight Saigon"   (Billy Joel)
10. "My Life"   (Billy Joel)

11. "She's Always a Woman"   (Billy Joel)
12. "She's Got a Way"   (Billy Joel)
13. "Scandinavian Skies"   (Billy Joel)
14. "Innocent Man"   (Billy Joel)
15. "Movin' Out (Anthony's Song)"   (Billy Joel)
16. "Only the Good Die Young"   (Billy Joel)
17. "All About Soul"   (Billy Joel)
18. "Honesty"   (Billy Joel)
19. "Just the Way You Are"   (Billy Joel)

23. MY LIVES

(2005/Columbia Legacy Records)
Various producers per individual tracks
Disc One
1. "My Journey's End" The Lost Souls   (Billy Joel)
2. "Time And Time Again" The Lost Souls   (Billy Joel)
3. "Every Step I Take (Every Move I Make)" The Hassles   (Billy Joel)
4. "You've Got Me Hummin'" The Hassles   (Vinnie Gormann, William Joel, and Tony Michaels)
5. "Amplifier Fire" Attila   (William Joel, Jonathan Small)
6. "Only a Man" (Demo, Never Released)   (Billy Joel)
7. "She's Got a Way" (Album Version)   (Billy Joel)
8. "Oyster Bay" (Demo, Never Released)   (Billy Joel)
9. "Piano Man" (Demo, Never Released)   (Billy Joel)
10. "The Siegfried Line" (Demo, Never Released)   (Billy Joel)
11. "New Mexico" (Demo, Never Released—became "Worse Comes to Worst")   (Billy Joel)
12. "Cross to Bear" (Demo, Never Released)   (Billy Joel)
13. "Miami 2017" (Demo, Never Released)   (Billy Joel)
14. "These Rhinestone Days" (Demo, Never Released—became "I Loved These Days")   (Billy Joel)
15. "Everybody Has a Dream"   (Billy Joel)
16. "Only the Good Die Young" (Alternate Version, Never Released) (Billy Joel)
17. "Until the Night" (Album Version)   (Billy Joel)
18. "Zanzibar" (Album Version, Unfaded)   (Billy Joel)
19. "It's Still Rock & Roll to Me" (Album Version)   (Billy Joel)
Disc Two
1. "Captain Jack " (Live Version, Never Released)   (Billy Joel)
2. "The End of the World" (Demo, Never Released—became "Elvis Presley Blvd.")   (Billy Joel)
3. "The Prime of Your Life" (Demo, Never Released—became "For the Longest Time")   (Billy Joel)
4. "She's Right on Time" (Album Version)   (Billy Joel)
5. "Elvis Presley Blvd."   (Billy Joel)
6. "Nobody Knows but Me"   (Billy Joel)
7. "An Innocent Man" (Album Version)   (Billy Joel)
8. "Christie Lee" (Demo, Never Released)   (Billy Joel)
9. "Easy Money" (Album Version)   (Billy Joel)

10. "And So It Goes" (Demo, Never Released)   (Billy Joel)
11. "I'll Cry Instead" (live)   (John Lennon & Paul McCartney)
12. "Keeping the Faith" (12″ Dance Remix Version)   (Billy Joel)
13. "Modern Woman" (Album Version)   (Billy Joel)
14. "Baby Grand" with Ray Charles (Album Version)   (Billy Joel)
15. "Getting Closer" with Steve Winwood (Alternate Version, Never Released)   (Billy Joel)
16. "House of Blue Light" (B-Side Single)   (Billy Joel)
17. "Money or Love" (Demo, Never Released)   (Billy Joel)
18. "The Times They Are A-Changin'" (Live Album Version)   (Bob Dylan)

Disc Three
1. "The Downeaster 'Alexa'" (Album Version)   (Billy Joel)
2. "I Go To Extremes" (Live, Never Released)   (Billy Joel)
3. "Shout"   (O'Kelley Isley, Ronald Isley, and Rudolph Isley)
4. "All Shook Up"   (Otis Blackwell and Elvis Presley)
5. "Heartbreak Hotel"   (May Boren Axton, Tommy Durden, and Elvis Presley)
6. "When You Wish upon a Star"   (Leigh Harline and Ned Washington)
7. "In a Sentimental Mood"   (Duke Ellington, E. Kurtz, and L. Mills)
8. "Motorcycle Song" (Demo, Never Released—became "All About Soul") (Billy Joel)
9. "You Picked a Real Bad Time" (B-Side Single)   (Billy Joel)
10. "The River of Dreams" (Alternate Version, Never Released)   (Billy Joel)
11. "A Hard Day's Night"   (John Lennon and Paul McCartney)
12. "Light as the Breeze"   (Leonard Cohen)
13. "To Make You Feel My Love"   (Bob Dylan)
14. "Hey Girl"   (Carole King and Gerry Goffin)
15. "Why Should I Worry"   (Dan Hartman and Charlie Midnight)
16. "Where Were You (On Our Wedding Day)" (Album Version)   (Lloyd Price, John Patton, and Harold Logan)
17. "Highway 61 Revisited" (Demo, Never Released)   (Bob Dylan)

Disc Four
1. "Movin' Out"   (Billy Joel)
2. "You May Be Right" duet with Elton John * (Live, Never Released) (Billy Joel)
3. "Big Shot"   (Billy Joel)
4. "Don't Worry Baby"   (Roger Christian and Brian Wilson)
5. "Goodnight Saigon" (Vietnam Veterans' Version)   (Billy Joel)
6. "Los Angelenos"   (Billy Joel)
7. "New York State of Mind"   (Billy Joel)
8. "Opus 1. Soliloquy (On a Separation)"   (Billy Joel)
9. "Opus 8. Suite for Piano (Star Crossed)"   (Billy Joel)
10. "Elegy: The Great Peconic"   (Billy Joel)

Disc Five—DVD
1. "No Man's Land"   (Billy Joel)
2. "Pressure"   (Billy Joel)
3. "Ballad of Billy the Kid"   (Billy Joel)
4. "Leningrad"   (Billy Joel)

BILLY JOEL

5. "Allentown"   (Billy Joel)
6. "My Life"   (Billy Joel)
7. "I Go to Extremes"   (Billy Joel)
8. "Shades of Grey"   (Billy Joel)
9. "The River of Dreams"   (Billy Joel)
10. "Goodnight Saigon"   (Billy Joel)
11. "We Didn't Start the Fire"   (Billy Joel)
12. "A Hard Day's Night"   (John Lennon and Paul McCartney)
13. "Big Shot"   (Billy Joel)
14. "Piano Man"   (Billy Joel)

24. 12 GARDENS: LIVE
(2006/Columbia Records)
Produced by: Billy Joel and Steve Lillywhite
Disc One
1. "Angry Young Man"   (Billy Joel)
2. "My Life"   (Billy Joel)
3. "Everybody Loves You Now"   (Billy Joel)
4. "The Ballad of Billy the Kid"   (Billy Joel)
5. "The Entertainer"   (Billy Joel)
6. "Vienna"   (Billy Joel)
7. "New York State of Mind"   (Billy Joel)
8. "The Night Is Still Young"   (Billy Joel)
9. "Zanzibar"   (Billy Joel)
10. "Miami 2017 (I've Seen the Lights Go Out on Broadway)"
     (Billy Joel)
11. "The Great Wall of China"   (Billy Joel)
12. "Allentown"   (Billy Joel)
13. "She's Right on Time"   (Billy Joel)
14. "Don't Ask Me Why"   (Billy Joel)
15. "Laura"   (Billy Joel)
16. "A Room of Our Own " ["hidden" bonus track]   (Billy Joel)
Disc Two
1. "Goodnight Saigon"   (Billy Joel)
2. "Movin' Out (Anthony's Song)"   (Billy Joel)
3. "An Innocent Man"   (Billy Joel)
4. "The Downeaster 'Alexa'"   (Billy Joel)
5. "She's Always a Woman"   (Billy Joel)
6. "Keeping the Faith"   (Billy Joel)
7. "The River of Dreams"   (Billy Joel)
8. "A Matter of Trust"   (Billy Joel)
9. "We Didn't Start the Fire"   (Billy Joel)
10. "Big Shot"   (Billy Joel)
11. "You May Be Right"   (Billy Joel)
12. "Only the Good Die Young"   (Billy Joel)
13. "Scene from an Italian Restaurant"   (Billy Joel)
14. "Piano Man"   (Billy Joel)
15. "And So It Goes"   (Billy Joel)
16. "It's Still Rock & Roll to Me" ["hidden" bonus track]   (Billy Joel)

EASY MONEY
Original Film Soundtrack (1983/Epic Records)
by various artists
> "Easy Money" by Billy Joel

RUTHLESS PEOPLE
Original Film Soundtrack (1985/Epic Records)
by various artists, including Mick Jagger, Luther Vandross, Bruce Springsteen, Paul Young, Dan Hartman, Kool and the Gang
> "Modern Woman" by Billy Joel

SIMPLY MAD ABOUT THE MOUSE
(1991/Disney Records)
by various artists, including L. L. Cool J, Harry Connick, Jr., and EnVogue
> "When You Wish upon a Star" by Billy Joel

A LEAGUE OF THEIR OWN
(1992/Arista Records)
by various artists
> "In a Sentimental Mood" by Billy Joel

TOWER OF SONG: THE SONGS OF LEONARD COHEN
(1995/A&M Records)
by various artists, including Elton John, Don Henley, Bono, Willie Nelson, Clint Black, Suzanne Vega, Sting, Peter Gabriel, and Trisha Yearwood
> "Light as a Breeze" by Billy Joel

RUNAWAY BRIDE
Original Film Soundtrack (1999/Columbia Records)
by various artists, including the Dixie Chicks, U2, Miles Davis, Eric Clapton, Hall & Oates, and Martina McBride
> "Where Were You (On Our Wedding Day)" by Billy Joel

OLIVER & COMPANY
Original Film Soundtrack (2001/Disney Records)
by various artists, including Bette Midler, Ruth Pointer, Huey Lewis, and Rubén Blades
> "Why Should I Worry?" by Billy Joel

PLAYIN' WITH MY FRIENDS: BENNETT SINGS THE BLUES
by Tony Bennett and various artists (2001/Columbia Records)
> "New York State of Mind" by Tony Bennett and Billy Joel
> "Playin' with My Friends" by Tony Bennett, with Billy Joel, Bonnie Raitt, Natalie Cole, Kay Starr, k. d. lang, Sheryl Crow, Diana Krall, B. B. King, and Stevie Wonder

MUSIC OF HOPE
(2001/American Cancer Society Records)
by various artists, including Paul McCartney, Ray Charles, Billy Joel, Andre Previn, and Emanuel Ax

"Elegy: The Great Peconic" performed by the London Symphony Orchestra   (Billy Joel)

TONY BENNETT: DUETS
by Tony Bennett and Various Artists (2006/Columbia Records)

"The Good Life" by Tony Bennett and Billy Joel

BILLY JOEL–RELATED ALBUMS

MOVIN' OUT
Original Broadway Cast Recording (2002/Columbia Records)
1. "Scenes from an Italian Restaurant"   (Billy Joel)
2. "Movin' Out (Anthony's Song)"   (Billy Joel)
3. "Reverie (Villa D'Este)"   (Billy Joel)
4. "Just the Way You Are"   (Billy Joel)
5. "The Longest Time"   (Billy Joel)
6. "Uptown Girl"   (Billy Joel)
7. "This Night"   (Billy Joel)
8. "Summer, Highland Falls"   (Billy Joel)
9. "Waltz #1 (Nunley's Carousel)"   (Billy Joel)
10. "We Didn't Start the Fire"   (Billy Joel)
11. "She's Got a Way"   (Billy Joel)
12. "The Stranger"   (Billy Joel)
13. "Elegy for the Fisherman"   (Billy Joel)
14. "Invention in C Minor"   (Billy Joel)
15. "Angry Young Man"   (Billy Joel)
16. "Big Shot"   (Billy Joel)
17. "Big Man on Mulberry Street"   (Billy Joel)
18. "Captain Jack"   (Billy Joel)
19. "An Innocent Man"   (Billy Joel)
20. "Pressure"   (Billy Joel)
21. "Goodnight Saigon"   (Billy Joel)
22. "Air (Dublinesque)"   (Billy Joel)
23. "Shameless"   (Billy Joel)
24. "James"   (Billy Joel)
25. "The River of Dreams"/"Keeping the Faith"/
    "Only the Good Die Young"   (Billy Joel)
26. "The River of Dreams" (Live)   (Billy Joel)
27. "Keeping the Faith" (Live)   (Billy Joel)
28. "Only the Good Die Young" (Live)   (Billy Joel)
29. "I've Loved These Days"   (Billy Joel)
30. "Scenes from an Italian Restaurant" (Reprise)   (Billy Joel)

GRAMMYS

Billy Joel, songwriter. Song of the Year 1978
—21st Annual Grammy Awards "Just The Way You Are" by Billy Joel
Billy Joel, artist, Phil Ramone, producer. Record of the Year 1978
—21st Annual Grammy Awards "Just The Way You Are"
Billy Joel, artist, Phil Ramone, producer. Album of the Year 1979
—22nd Annual Grammy Awards, the album *52nd Street*
Billy Joel, artist. Pop Best Pop Vocal Performance, Male 1979
—22nd Annual Grammy Awards, the album *52nd Street*
Billy Joel, artist. Best Rock Vocal Performance, Male 1980
—23rd Annual Grammy Awards, the album *Glass Houses*
Billy Joel, Grammy Legend Award, 1991
—34th Annual Grammy Awards

AMERICAN MUSIC AWARDS

1981 American Music Award for "Favorite Album, Pop/Rock" for *52nd Street*

TONY AWARDS

2003 Best Orchestration, *Movin' Out*

INDEX

BILLY JOEL

BILLY JOEL

BILLY JOEL

BILLY JOEL

BILLY JOEL

BILLY JOEL

BILLY JOEL

ABOUT THE AUTHOR

MARK BEGO IS the author of fifty books on rock & roll and show business, including two *New York Times* bestsellers (*Michael!* in 1984 and *Leonardo DiCaprio* in 1998). With more than 10 million books in print, he is acknowledged as the best-selling biographer in the rock and pop music field. Bego's books have included *Madonna: Blonde Ambition*, *Cher: If You Believe*, and *George Strait*. He collaborated with Micky Dolenz on the book *I'm a Believer* in 1993, and Martha Reeves in 1994 on the *Chicago Tribune* best-seller, *Dancing in the Street: Confessions of a Motown Diva*. His biography *I Fall to Pieces: The Music and the Life of Patsy Cline* was named by E! Entertainment Television as one of the top ten pop music biographies of all time. He has recently written his first memoir, *Paperback Writer*. Bego divides his time between New York City, and Tucson, Arizona.